READER'S
DIGEST

IDEAS
FOR YOUR
GARDEN

READER'S DIGEST

IDEAS
FOR YOUR
GARDEN

THE READER'S DIGEST ASSOCIATION, INC., PLEASANTVILLE, NEW YORK/MONTREAL

This 1997 U.S. edition has been thoroughly revised and updated.

Copyright © 1995 The Reader's Digest Association Limited, London.
Copyright © 1995 Reader's Digest Association Far East Limited.
Philippines Copyright © 1995 Reader's Digest Association Far East Limited.

The original edition of this book was published by The Reader's Digest Association Limited, London, in 1995 as GOOD IDEAS FOR YOUR GARDEN.

Library of Congress Cataloging in Publication Data

Reader's digest ideas for your garden.— Rev. and updated ed.
   p.   cm.
   Rev. ed. of: Good ideas for your garden. London : Reader's Digest Association, 1995.
   Includes index.
   ISBN 0-89577-919-6
   1. Landscape gardening. 2. Gardens. 3. Gardening. I. Reader's Digest Association. II. Good ideas for your garden.
SB473.R37   1997   96-34354
712'.6—dc20

Printed in the United States of America

A READER'S DIGEST BOOK

EDITOR
Judith Taylor

ART EDITOR
Judy White

US PROJECT MANAGER
Lynn Yost

US CONSULTANT EDITOR
Rosemary Rennicke

US CONSULTANT
Ruth Clausen

UK CONSULTANT EDITOR
Allen Paterson, M HORT (RHS), MED, FLS

UK CONSULTANT
Kenneth A. Beckett. VMM

MAJOR CONTRIBUTORS
John Brookes, FSGD
Susanna Brown
Nigel Colborn
Sue Fisher
Angela Kirby
Allen Paterson
Geoff Stebbings

ARTISTS
Julia Bickham
Leonora Box
Wendy Bramall
Kevin Dean
Nick Hardcastle
Royston Knipe
Gill Tomblin
Barbara Walker
Anne Winterbotham
John Woodcock

CALLIGRAPHER
Gabrielle Izen

PHOTOGRAPHERS
Jonathan Buckley
Stephen Robson

The publishers would also like to thank the following for their help in the preparation of this book:
Peter Barnes
Helen Baz
Jean and Francine Raymond
Martin and Jenny Thompson,
Ryton Organic Gardens, West Midlands

The credits and acknowledgments that appear on page 336 are hereby made a part of this copyright page.

CONTENTS

A Source of Inspiration

ONE OF THE JOYS of gardening is that there is always more to learn. It is rare to find a gardener who is not entranced by fresh ideas. They are not easy to come by and, indeed, are more often discovered by chance—seen from a car window, for example—than by diligent research.

The original approach of this gardening book, to be inspirational as well as factual, stems from understanding this difficulty. The book shows not only how to choose and care for the right plant in the right environment but also how to combine the plants and create a garden to match your dreams.

Throughout the 14 chapters, an array of designs and plantings is shown, not only in photographs but in original watercolors that bring to life schemes planned by our contributors. There are ideas, vividly described and illustrated, for transforming gardens of all shapes and sizes, no matter how unpromising they may seem at first. Many ideas give delight using color and scent, but others address particular needs—creating an appealing place to sit, adding drama to the garden, growing plants for flower arrangements, and running a garden that is friendly to the environment.

For anyone about to make a new garden, much has to be thought out before planting begins. What shape and size is the plot? What is its soil type? How much time will you have to give to the garden? This book shows how to take stock of your plot as you find it—to evaluate its qualities and come to terms with any of its disadvantages—in order to transform it into the garden you have always wanted.

To help you through the changes, there is plenty of practical advice on making challenging tasks easier, saving money, choosing tools and accessories, rescuing plants in trouble, and making the garden safe.

But while inspiration is important, it is the plants that finally make a garden. These are suggested in abundance throughout the book, and the conditions that suit them best are summarized in tables at the end, where there is also a general index.

The many strands in *Reader's Digest Ideas for Your Garden* will help you to develop your garden to its full potential, treating it both as a blank canvas for your imagination and, ultimately, as a place that will provide many hours of enjoyment and relaxation.

FIRST
IMPRESSIONS

THE FRONT GARDEN can gladden the heart or give a chilly greeting, for this most public part of your domain often receives little thought; it is the more private back garden that claims all the attention. But an attractive, easily maintained design creates a flattering frame for the house and welcomes you, and your guests, all year-round. Whether you have only a pair of tubs at the front door, hanging baskets, and window boxes above a tiny strip of ground, or a more spacious area to develop, make the most of its potential and enjoy the result every time you come home.

Bergenias, Japanese anemones, and a fuchsia make a sympathetic color blend with a pink climbing rose, and their spreading, eager growth covers its leggy stems, to give a pretty finish to a stone cottage.

THE FRONT GARDEN'S ROLES

TOO OFTEN the front garden is dominated by the car and a gathering of trash cans, while horticultural wonders flourish in the back. Yet the front garden has several roles to play. It is a buffer against the world, affording privacy for the house. It gives access to the main door and usually to the rear of the house; it is the service area for trash removal and paper, mail, and other deliveries — and it may be a parking space as well.

The back garden is for relaxation, play, and entertaining. It belongs mainly to the weekends and summer evenings, whereas the front one is used every day.

When it is successful, the front garden enhances the house and gives a lift to the spirits as well as performing its utilitarian functions. It also exposes the owner's personality and taste to public gaze and judgment, and perhaps gardeners feel inhibited by this. But diffidence should be overcome, for there is no right or wrong design; many different plans can work equally well in one plot.

There are, however, three broad guidelines that help to bring about a successful garden. Give it some unity with the lines and materials of the building, choose plants and features of suitable scale for the site, and stick to a style in keeping with the house's character. A rustic wheelbarrow full of pansies does little for a Georgian-style facade; classical urns are much more its style. And an Italianate fountain never looks at home in front of a country cottage, which is suited to perfection by roses around the door.

WHAT GARDENERS WANT NOW

Front gardens have yet to be rethought to suit today's style of living, and Victorian habits of a century ago are still evident in shaved lawns, sharply trimmed at the edges and framed by perfect rows of bedding plants. But the work and expense demanded by such a formal display make it a burden for most homeowners.

Although there is no consensus on a front-garden style for today, there are certain common needs shared by many gardeners — low-maintenance planting, some privacy from passersby, security from intruders, and a space for off-street car parking.

Much enjoyment is to be had in creating the front garden that suits your needs and furnishing it, as you do the rooms indoors, to suit your taste — but with an eye to practical matters as well as appearance. Give the garden robust plants and tough structural materials that will stand up to daily traffic, and be sure to devise a plan that is easily kept in good order with a minimum of work. Then as you or your visitors approach the house, the front garden gives a satisfying first impression.

SYMPATHETIC STYLE This welcoming front garden has a well-marked path leading to the front porch, where there is a generous paved area for visitors. Each spring, bulbs such as *Narcissus* 'Thalia' and *Tulipa* 'Purissima' bloom under a canopy of the ornamental cherry, *Prunus* 'Tai Haku.'

HOUSE FRONT AND DOORWAY

A N ENCOURAGING ASPECT of any front garden is that its size is not everything. Shortage of space can be offset by ingenuity even where all you possess is a foot or two of soil beside the front door. Indeed, in urban settings and in many condominiums, there is not even a strip of soil in front of a house, and the building itself presents the only area where plants can grow.

A Garden on a Wall

In such a situation, compose your garden from annuals, bulbs, and dwarf shrubs in window boxes; vivid annuals in hanging baskets; and evergreens or colorful performers in tubs. Use inexpensive containers as much as you can, since they are vulnerable to knocks, dogs, and vandals.

If you do use an expensive pot, chain it to the railings or to a ring set in the wall, or you can cement the base to the spot — but do not block the drainage holes. A chain can be hidden by plants trailing over the rim of the container, but a cheap container can be hidden in the same way and will cause you far less anxiety.

Fiberglass or plastic urns and planting boxes, in dark green or white, keep down the cost. Galvanized buckets, plastic pots, and even old paint cans make perfectly adequate containers provided they have drainage holes at the bottom.

Fix window boxes firmly on wall brackets, setting them with the rim a little below sill height. You do not want to see the back of a box through the window or have boxes blocking the light. Fill window boxes mainly with low-growing plants to look down on from indoors; flowers turn to face the daylight, so you see only their outline if they are too tall.

When the front of your house has only one ground-floor window, create a greater effect by fixing a window box and standing a deeper and wider trough on the ground under it. Use the same planting scheme in box and trough, putting trailers at the sides to link the two.

Colors to Enhance a Wall

Mutual flattery between the plants and the building is more crucial than usual when they merge as one vertical surface. Put dark red or blue flowers against a strident red brick wall, and they tend to

HANGING GARDENS Lack of soil need not be an obstacle to creating a colorful entrance display. Traditional summer bedding plants — geraniums, lobelias, and petunias — fill hanging baskets and a window box.

MADE FOR EACH OTHER A coppery pink climbing rose, *Rosa* 'Meg,' draws attention to the pretty brick detailing without obscuring it, and the paler color of the rose is a perfect complement to the warm pink brickwork.

vanish, with neither party gaining. But put pale flowers against it and they leap out with extra clarity, while the wall serves as a strong foil.

Mellow old bricks usually mingle several colors. Emphasize their beauty with plants in slightly bolder versions of these shades in your tubs and baskets. For example, grow purple pansies and pink geraniums against rosy old bricks.

Rich, stained-glass colors look good against white walls in an informal setting,

PLANT A WINDOW BOX FOR LONG–LASTING BEAUTY

IN MILDER CLIMATES, try this combination to dress up your windows. Begin planting the box in early fall. Use a fiberglass box to reduce weight and eliminate the need for a waterproof liner. Mount it firmly on the wall with brackets. Instead of putting gravel in the bottom for drainage, use broken-up foam packing.

1. Spread the base with the foam packing and cover it with 2 in (5 cm) of compost. Put in place three sets of three *Tulipa* 'Red Riding Hood'; mark them with stakes and then fill with potting soil.

2. Plant three *Daphne cneorum* 'Alba' along the front, one in the center and one at each corner. Push two groups of five or six snowdrop bulbs in at the back, setting their bases 3 in (7.5 cm) deep.

3. Tuck three perennial forget-me-nots (*Myosotis alpestris*) in each of the two gaps for early summer flowering. Remove the stakes and plant a pansy over each tulip group for fall color.

4. At the end of winter carefully clear out any remaining pansies to avoid a color clash with the spring-flowering tulips. Nip the seed heads off the snowdrops after they finish flowering.

5. In early summer, when the tulip leaves are yellowing, cut off the top growth and plant a *Convolvulus tricolor* 'Blue Flash' in each gap to flower through summer and into fall.

6. In early fall, trim off any remaining forget-me-not foliage and carefully take out the convolvulus plants. In their place plant pansies again to provide continuing color.

whereas the greater formality of stuccoed city walls requires restraint — perhaps the architectural shapeliness of a fatsia or trimly clipped conifers.

DOUBLING THE IMPACT

Twin plantings create a stronger image at the house front than a random assortment of single features. Have matched tubs of plants on either side of the door, matched hanging baskets on the walls, and matched window-box plantings.

Double the size of your hanging baskets as well as match them. There are elongated baskets that make long flowery panels. Some models have built-in water reservoirs to help keep the soil moist. Fill them lavishly with petunias, geraniums, and trailing lobelia, all eager bloomers that put on a long and brilliant display.

SOME GROUND TO PLANT IN

The merest strip of soil along the front of the house gives a welcome opportunity to get some roots in the ground. Separate your plot from the public sidewalk by a row of edging stones or slates, or by raising the bed — just a couple of inches is enough to keep people from stepping on the plants.

Make the little strip a launching pad for flowering climbers or shrubs to train on the wall. Give the plants freedom to smother an ugly wall but always keep the house number plainly in view. If you have a wall of mellow stone, lovely old bricks, or decorative detail, it would be a shame to obscure it completely.

Pick plants to flatter the walls; harmony or contrast give equal satisfaction.

🌷 Against a white masonry wall, the flowering quince (*Chaenomeles speciosa*) can show off its late winter blooms. If the bright red 'Rowallane' is too vivid for your taste, grow 'Pink Lady.'

🌷 For a sandy-buff modern brick wall, plant an apricot-colored quince: 'Geisha Girl.' The fragrant yellow fruits, like small apples, look good too.

🌷 Harsh red brick is cooled by the white stars and dark leaves of *Clematis armandii* or the creamy clusters and fresh foliage of *Hydrangea anomala petiolaris*.

🌷 The hint of purple in a sandstone wall is picked up by a velvety purple *Clematis × jackmannii* 'Superba.'

🌷 Cool gray limestone is warmed by rosy-mauve wisteria or a crimson rose. On an unpretentious cottage grow violet everlasting sweet pea (*Lathyrus latifolius*).

BLUE SYMMETRY Double planting heightens the impact of glorious hydrangea specimens in elegant stone containers, particularly with this restrained color scheme set against white walls.

ROSE WITHOUT THORNS

ROSES NODDING around the front door make even the plainest house pretty, but the thorns on stray shoots can scratch people as they go in and out. Combine beauty with safety by choosing *Rosa* 'Zéphirine Drouhin'; it is a rich pink, perpetual flowering, heavily scented rose — with thornless stems.

PAIRED OFF IN PINK Window boxes are linked by a hanging basket with a unified planting theme — trailing geraniums, fuchsias, and lobelias. The window boxes are placed low enough to avoid obscuring the windows.

❧ Honey-colored stone is a perfect backdrop for a deep yellow rose such as 'Golden Showers.'

In general, deciduous climbers are best confined to stone or brick walls. Painted or stuccoed walls can look shabby when a plant is bare in winter, so grow an evergreen climber there to give year-round cover. Alternatively, you can grow annual climbers such as mauve morning glory (*Ipomoea*), orange black-eyed Susan vine (*Thunbergia alata*), or even scarlet runner beans; these all leave the walls bare in winter for repainting.

COMPANIONS FOR CLIMBERS

The bottom of a climbing plant is rarely worth seeing. Conceal its ungainly feet with shrubs and perennials that complete a harmonious picture along the front of the building. Put together a fresh-looking scheme for a sunny setting with some yellow-centered white *Cistus* × *corbariensis* and lime-green flowered *Euphorbia characias* in front of a yellow-splashed ivy or a yellow-and-white-flowered Japanese honeysuckle.

Make a warmer scheme with white lavender, pink Londonpride saxifrage (*Saxifraga* × *urbium*), and the pink-and-

WINDOW BOXES AND TROUGHS

Hugging the wall of the house, window boxes and many troughs are frequently sheltered from the rain. With only a small amount of soil where roots can seek water, the plants that thrive are those that like dry conditions.

• Basket-of-gold (*Aurinia saxatilis*): broad yellow flower heads cover the low grayish shrub through spring.

• Wallflower (*Erysimum cheiri* 'Tom Thumb Mixed'): scented, early summer flowers in golds and russets.

• *Convolvulus cneorum*: pink buds and white flowers adorn the silvery leaved shrub from spring to autumn.

• Pinks (*Dianthus* × *allwoodii* 'Doris'): clove-scented pink flowers in early summer and again in early fall; 'Show Pearl' is white.

• Ivy (*Hedera helix* 'Tricolor'): trailing evergreen growth has pale green leaves with a white rim that flushes to red during winter.

• Dwarf iris (*Iris pumila*): short-stemmed large spring flowers in white, yellow, or mauve.

• *Mesembryanthemum criniflorum*: pink, mauve, yellow, and orange daisy flowers open when summer sun shines.

• Lavender cotton (*Santolina chamaecyparissus* 'Nana'): dwarf evergreen shrub with feathery silver leaves and yellow July flowers.

• *Sedum* 'Ruby Glow': perennial with blue-gray leaves and large crimson flower heads in high summer.

CITY SOPHISTICATION A smart frontage is made more welcoming by careful planting. An evergreen bay laurel in a dark green planting box adds height, while discreet touches of color enliven a subdued scheme in keeping with the formal style of the house.

white-tipped greenery of the climber *Actinidia kolomikta*. For stronger impact put mauve lavender between a purple clematis and the purple tradescantia 'Isis.'

Create a cool effect on a sheltered sunny wall with white jasmine, in bloom summer through fall, and around its feet set *Ceanothus thyrsiflorus* 'Repens' for its abundant blue flowers in spring and a sprinkling that continues into fall.

Cotoneaster and bergenia give you strong greens with red fall and winter tints, while a fringe of evergreen ferns and silver-edged little boxwood bushes (*Buxus sempervirens* 'Elegantissima') is fresh and neat at the base of a fiery Virginia creeper or a fragrant, lemon-colored rose.

PLAY SAFE NEAR THE ROAD

Pick your plants carefully for a little strip of garden alongside a street. While you may want to ward off passersby, you do not want to hurt them. Thorny berberis and roses — and the poisonous laburnum and yew — are best kept within the garden. On the margin put plants that do not mind being picked at and will not harm passersby. Lavender and *Brachyglottis* 'Sunshine' have tough but attractive gray foliage, and lavender releases its invigorating scent when you touch it.

Where traffic is heavy, choose hearty evergreens. Build a raised bed like a brick box for them in front of the house — leave drainage slits at the base and a little space between the box and the house wall to keep moisture away from the house. Make the bed about knee high to prevent

SAVING PLANTS BY THE ROAD

DUST AND GRIME from traffic exhaust fumes build up on roadside plants until they fail from clogged pores and lack of light. On a roadside grow evergreens with leathery, glossy leaves (which are most tolerant of pollution) and wash them frequently with a gentle jet of water to free them of all traces of dirt.

RAISED GROWTH A walled bed in front of the house gives room for a planting of variegated shrubs. For an area exposed to the street use tough evergreens that are easy to maintain.

litter from blowing in and keep people from walking on the plants.

Filled with a humus-rich soil, the bed will grow anything, regardless of the local soil type; but devote it to skimmias and cotoneasters, laurels and dwarf conifers, evergreen viburnum and holly, all of which are tough, low-maintenance plants tolerant of air pollution. Add pansies or fuchsias for extra color.

BRIDGES AND STEPS

In city streets, many doors are reached by a "bridge" over the basement area. This is the spot for a capacious trough painted the same dark color as a box at the window. Clipped standard bay laurels or hollies in the trough with dark periwinkles and white-edged ivies between look smart. Echo the shape of the scheme with little balls of bay laurel in the window box — again with periwinkles and ivies between. A few yellow spring hyacinths and golden summer marigolds add just enough splashes of bright color.

Seize the opportunity offered by a flight of steps up to the door. It is a ready-made stage for a tumble of color. Put pots on both sides of the steps if there is room, but do not be tempted to narrow the way too much. A flight of five or six steps with a pot at each side adds up to a generous display. Simple planting with a harmonious color theme looks best.

HIGHLIGHTS AT THE DOORWAY

No matter how tiny or large your front garden, design it to focus attention on the house entrance — the centerpiece of your (*continued on p. 18*)

ON THE WAY UP On a sunny flight of steps vibrant mesembryanthemums give the main color, with extra zest from plantings in wall boxes. This planting needs full sun; use bulbs and foliage plants for shadier spots.

MAKING AN ENTRANCE

*As well as securing your privacy and safety, the front door advertises
your tastes, skills, and attitudes. You can translate and vary
the ideas shown here to suit you and your garden.*

THE FRONT DOOR is far too important to treat casually. Keep a generous open space in front of the door where possible. It is where visitors wait to be greeted and where you step out to wish them farewell. A broad, level area allows this. By raising it a little as a wide step, you can emphasize it even more.

A porch always adds importance to a doorway. Just a mere shelf over the door increases its status, and a wide masonry or glass structure is an attractive addition to the facade. Callers have a sheltered place to stand, and, better still from a gardener's point of view, the overhang is a support for climbing plants. Even where there is no room for a real overhang, a similar effect is easy to create with a trellis and a few stout posts. It suits many kinds of house front and gives stronger definition to any door.

You can adapt the plant choices in these examples. Skimmia, for instance, could be substituted for azaleas where the soil is not acid, and the plantings for the Georgian-style door could be replaced in fall by others based on golden mums, hebe, and ivy. None of the schemes, in fact, is intended for posterity. If the plants grow too big, or you want a change, simply put them into a flower bed and start all over again.

Victorian decorum

Diamond tiling is typical of a Victorian townhouse. It is well suited to the autumnal berries of pyracantha and to the spring cascade of wisteria. A variegated giant dracena (*Cordyline*) unites the design.

Winter welcome

Pyramidal bays surrounded by aucuba and trailing ivy are the year-round basis for this display, which in late winter is warmed by hanging baskets of pansies and periwinkle.

Peak perfection

Gray stone backs the white spring flowers of the climber *Clematis armandii* with *Rosa* 'Albertine' to follow. Spreading alchemilla is backed on the left by irises and soaring hollyhocks and on the other side by *Caryopteris*.

Rustic charm

Lack of a front plot is overcome by two half-barrels of begonias and lobelias and matching baskets above them. Canary creepers grow on a trellis; as these are annuals, the choice of climbers can be varied each year.

Cool shade

This shady door has a climbing *Hydrangea anomala petiolaris* in summer, fatsia flowers in fall, and jasmine in winter. Spring adds hellebore then polygonatum, and vinca and boxwood give more evergreen color.

Leafy estate

A hint of woodland is brought to a modern doorway by a tall *Amelanchier*. Ground cover is *Viburnum davidii*, vinca, and juniper. A gray *Chamaecyparis lawsoniana* 'Gimbornii' fronts a screen of ivy.

Georgian grace

A neo-Georgian door lends a colonial flavor to this summer display of a marguerite standard rising from a bowl of ivy and impatiens. It is balanced by a basket of white geraniums in similar company.

Porch promotion

Tiles and brickwork are set off by terra-cotta pots of *Choisya ternata*, whose evergreen leaves are a foil for forsythia in spring; later their white flowers will flatter a yellow scramble of 'Maigold' roses.

Fragrant greeting

In summer honeysuckle, nicotianas, and regal lilies in pots waft a scented welcome, while viburnum adds extra depth. The containers can be moved and replaced with spring bulbs.

Eastern approach

An oriental flavor is conjured out of rock, cobblestones, and gravel. It is enhanced by a shrubby bamboo (*Shibataea kumasasa*), wisteria, and azalea, and in summer by the spires on the *Yucca flaccida*.

ROOM ENOUGH Even a small strip of soil has room for some plants to enhance the front of the house. Spring wallflowers spill over the path in a rich mixture of warm colors with the sweet bonus of unsurpassed fragrance.

home. Dress up the door with color; not just with immaculate paint or gleaming woodwork but with bright flowers climbing around it, frothing out of tubs or tumbling from hanging baskets on either side.

On a decorous formal front, flank the door with elegant topiary. Dark green foliage in a matching green planting box looks sumptuous against stucco walls. Where there is no traffic grime and the walls are stone or brick, white boxes draw attention to the doorway, but dark plants still give the smartest effect.

Boxwood or conifer pyramids and bay laurel standards are conventional, but holly is cheaper for both shapes — and it defends itself against vandals. Cut costs further and reduce maintenance by using a fiberglass planter. It keeps its pristine looks with an occasional wiping and needs no waterproof liner, as wooden boxes do if they are not to deteriorate.

For a more light-hearted version at a country-cottage entrance, grow topiary birds, teddy bears, or cottage shapes in terra-cotta pots.

FOCUS ON THE FRONT DOOR Creamy-flowered honeysuckle draped around the doorway is the epitome of the country idyll. Hanging baskets at the height of their summer display focus attention on the entrance.

THE GARDEN PATH

THE LAYOUT of the front garden must make it quite clear where callers are to go. The solidity and width of a path give unmistakable clues to which is the right way. Be sure to make the main path smooth and broad enough to walk along with ease — no wobbly or uneven paving stones, and no plants, however pretty, that lean so far over the path that they snatch at people's clothes or legs. It may be a joy to brush against sun-baked lavender and release its fresh scent, but touching rain-drenched lavender is a nuisance.

The path to the back door can be noticeably narrower, but should still be wide enough to walk along easily, even when carrying a bag or parcel. A narrower entrance to the path also indicates its subsidiary role. At the point where it reaches the house front, set a pair of shrubs, a trellis panel, or a climber twining around a pillar to make casual visitors feel they cannot go farther without invading private territory.

PROS AND CONS FOR GATEWAYS

Highlight the main path at its beginning with a tall plant on each side or with an intricate gate. A gate finishes off the garden perfectly, completing the sense of privacy when you are within and, from the outside, framing the garden, focusing attention on the path, and so leading the eye to the doorway.

For some households a gate is simply necessary to keep toddlers in and dogs in or out. But gates also tell tales if they are not properly chosen and fitted. A gate left open for days when it is normally shut is a signal that you are away. Hang it on rising buttress hinges, which have a spiral joint so that they always swivel back to the closed position. And have a self-closing catch so that no positive effort is needed to operate it.

Unless you have a foolproof security system, do not have a gate so high and solid that it screens the garden totally and gives cover to intruders. You can avoid such risks by doing without a gate but having substantial gateposts.

Gateposts are especially satisfying as a frame for the house when linked by an arch or beam. Elegant wrought iron looks good over formal pillars; a wisteria-swathed beam is pretty over tall timber

PRECISION PLANTING A strongly rectangular framework is softened by conifers, shrubs, perennials, and container plants. The clear brick path is separated from a gravel area by symmetrical edgings of clipped boxwood that are used to create separate planting areas within the garden.

posts; a smothering of honeysuckle suits trelliswork or rustic poles; and you can, with patience, train conifers or privet to meet in a clipped green arch.

MAKE A GREEN DRY WELL

When a pathway runs along the front of the house, keep it an arm's length away from the wall. You never walk right up against the building, and a hard surface there has a disadvantage: rainwater cannot run off unless the whole path tilts slightly from the house.

Run a narrow bed along between the wall and the path, and rainwater simply soaks into it, but make sure that the soil finishes at least two rows of bricks below the damp-proof course. Green permanent plants in the bed improve an unprepossessing building with a soft fringe at the meeting of two hard surfaces. Keep the growth mainly below windowsill level and do not let it spread forward so far that window-cleaning implements cannot reach the panes. Ferns such as hart's-tongue (*Asplenium scolopendrium*) and soft shield fern (*Polystichum setiferum*) will love the bed if it is on the side of the house that gets the most rain.

WAYS TO DETER INTRUDERS

Gain double value from your bed against the house by filling it mainly with evergreens for year-round interest — and put prickly plants under the windows to ward off would-be thieves. Clipped holly, ferociously armed berberis, and mahonia are hard to improve on. Add rose bushes to give color while still repelling intruders.

Keep plants low near the door, or certainly not high enough to give cover to a burglar. Put any tall plants well to the side of the door. At night, a light over the door or on the porch emphasizes the main entry's status as well as welcoming visitors and illuminating the path. Fit a sensor high on the wall to switch on the light when anyone approaches the front door. A well-lit door is also an effective way of making an intruder pass by. Nor are thieves keen to negotiate a path of crunchy gravel, which declares every footfall and defies a silent approach.

SAFE AND STYLISH PATHS

Gravel scores well on a quite different measure of safety: it gives a nonslip surface, a vital feature for a garden path. There is a range of colors so you can choose one to harmonize with the building.

Concrete is a cheap, hard-wearing, and trouble-free material for paths, and its surface does not have to be corrugated

to make it nonslip, although this unattractive finish is often given to it. Sections of poured concrete imprinted with a small overall design give grip and are far more attractive. Subtle color tints to harmonize with the house also improve it, but these refinements increase the cost.

Concrete slabs are available with a nonslip surface of exposed pebbles. In a pattern inset with bands and blocks of bricks or cobblestones, they make a pleasing surface — as do nonslip slabs of artificial cast "stone" used in similar ways.

Look for combinations that pick up the colors of the building to give the unity a satisfying design demands. For example, use slabs whose color matches the house and inset red bricks if the roof is red-tiled, purple-gray if it is slate.

When their color is close to the local natural stone of an area, cast-stone pavers look good on their own and improve with weathering to make an agreeable foil for plants.

Brick or tile paths are trickier. There are many more cracks for moss to grow in than large slabs offer. Moss creeping onto the surface of bricks or tiles makes them slippery, so use a stiff brush on them frequently. This keeps the surface clean without banishing entirely the soft green tracery in the cracks, which adds charm in an informal or rural garden.

Whatever the path is made of, it must have a very slight pitch or crown to throw off water and no hollows where pools collect. Water that does not run off forms an icy film on cold days, and a path is a bruising surface to fall on. A hard-core

TOPIARY THAT COSTS LESS

READY-SHAPED TOPIARY, attractive in a pot beside the door, is expensive to buy because it takes several years to train a plant. Slash the cost by growing your own pieces, and doing it quickly.

Use a ready-made frame — cone, double-sphere, spiral, lollipop — and grow two or three small-leaved ivies over it. They quickly cover the frame, and clipping them to keep the shape distinct is not hard work.

SEVERELY STYLISH A successfully designed front garden is in keeping with the style of the house. Here the door arch is repeated in the path arch, and clipped shrubs add formality to a planting theme of restrained color.

PRETTY AND PRACTICAL A small bed between the driveway and the house lets rainwater soak away and conceals the hard line where the wall meets the ground. Here nicotianas flower robustly and scent the air around the door.

base packed down by a power tamper and topped with sand makes a stable platform for bricks and slabs. Without a sound foundation they can shift, making dents and dips to stumble on.

A path leading callers unerringly to the principal door need not be a straight central strip. Give it a diagonal route or build in a slight curve or angle. The variation provides more interesting shapes in the garden, but keep any bend slight so that callers can take virtually a straight line from gate to door without cutting across the lawn or a border.

CASUALLY CURVED In this mature garden a curved path softened by aubrietia leads to a door flanked by pots and canopied by an old pear tree. The massed informal planting suits the countrified style of the house.

DESIGNS FOR DEVELOPMENTS

NEWLY CONSTRUCTED developments pose a special challenge. Lawn merges with lawn in a nearly featureless sweep — the homeowner wants to distinguish his yard from those of his neighbors, yet if the garden is to be pleasing it must also harmonize.

The solution, generally, is to pay close attention to the principles that underlie all successful garden design. Link the garden to the house in materials or shapes, keep the planting in scale with the site, and match the character of the garden to its setting.

SPOT THE SHAPE TO DEVELOP

The ground plan works best when it has details that echo those of the house itself, so that the two clearly belong together. For example, a pointed gable breaking the roofline or a pointed porch over the front door suggest a diamond or lozenge shape for a lawn and for decorative motifs in a path. If the house has a curve in a front door panel or at the top of the window or door frame, shape the lawn with curved ends — and insert arcs of brick into a concrete path.

CUTTING DOWN LAWN CARE

Quality turf is the best buy for a small lawn in a show position. The finest grass is the type best adapted to your soil and climate. Healthy turf is naturally disease-, weed-, and insect-proof and will require only minimal care.

If drought is a recurrent problem, keep the lawn small so that watering will be cheap and easy. Even at tabletop size, a lawn gives that smooth green foil for the garden plantings and furnishes the desired air of lush, cool green.

If you garden in an arid climate, however, you should consider substituting a more drought-tolerant ground cover — the local cooperative extension office can advise you on what to plant. Planting a native ground cover often eliminates the chore of mowing. Gravel or paving slabs of different sizes laid in a random pattern are other labor-saving alternatives to plant cover.

Choose hard materials that harmonize with, rather than match, the building. Too much of the same material and color can be overwhelming. Just a few

TROUBLE-FREE GROUND COVER

Varied leaf shape and color, neat weed-smothering growth, and some flowers and berries are provided by these plants, all of them evergreen.

• *Arabis ferdinandi-coburgi* 'Variegata': small, ground-hugging mats of silver-splashed leaves.

• *Daphne retusa*: purple buds among dark leaves open to fragrant white flowers in spring with red berries following in autumn.

• *Euonymus fortunei* 'Silver Queen': wide spreading with firm, shrubby growth of dark cream-trimmed leaves.

• *Hebe buxifolia* 'Nana': a spread of little upright spires of neat leaves stacked horizontally on the shoots.

• Juniper (*Juniperus sabina* 'Tamariscifolia'): the low, wide-spreading growths are densely clothed with bright green needles.

• *Sarcococca confusa*: very fragrant cream flowers in winter hide among evergreen leaves and are followed by red berries that ripen to black.

• *Viburnum davidii*: grooved evergreen leaves; white summer flower heads, and turquoise berries, if plants from different parents are mixed.

• Greater periwinkle (*Vinca major* 'Variegata'): bright green, cream-edged leaves have a scattering of mauve late-spring flowers.

PATHSIDE PLANTING For easy care, plant shrubs — *Juniperus × media* 'Pfitzeriana,' low-growing *J. sabina* 'Tamariscifolia,' red-leaved *Berberis*, and boxwood — and brighten with the flowers of *Osteospermum*.

SMALL AND EASY GARDENS

NO MOWING OR WEEDING Hummocks of low-growing, spreading conifers define the boundary of this garden. A change of scale is given by more upright conifers, and color is added by flowering heathers. The close planting leaves no room for weeds to grow, and there is no lawn to tend.

PAVING OR MULCHING over most of the garden is the biggest labor saver. Tiny patches of grass in an urban or formal setting need to be meticulously cared for. They are not enhanced by the casual scattering of daisies that looks so pretty on country lawns.

But immaculate grass is not achieved without the persistent maintenance most gardeners prefer to reserve for the flower garden. Nor is it easy to maneuver a mower in a small area. It can soon seem too much trouble.

EFFECTS WITH HARD MATERIALS

Hard surfacing — covering the earth with pavement or mulch — may sound unlikely to give the delight that plants do, yet an imaginative use of materials can create a satisfying pattern and color harmony, two chief pleasures of any garden.

Apart from the many sizes and shades of paving slabs (in real stone, cast stone, and concrete), there are stone pavers and a wide choice of bricks. Strong red, soft red, browns, buffs, grays, and purples are available. Tiles offer an unusual and visually distinctive option, but be sure to get a weatherproof type such as quarry tile.

To fill in around formal paving, use less geometric materials that are much easier to manipulate.

- Fine gravel comes in shades from cool off-white and gray to warm rosy hues.
- Marble and flint chippings cover the same range and add greens and mauves.
- Coarser gravels offer oval shapes and subtle colors. Cobblestones — larger, rounded stones, set in mortar of matching or contrasting color — give a softer look.
- To negotiate curves or fill in angles, use brick or pavers set on edge and pushed edge-down into mortar until flush with the surface and fanning out like daisy petals; blues, grays, greens, browns, and reds make up a varied palette.

Tiles are appropriate in a town garden, laid in straightforward checkerboard fashion or in a more decorative pattern focusing on one spot where a single plant commands attention. The plant may be in a pot or a bed; a standard rose or artemisia does well in either.

With a pot you can put different plants such as fuchsias, hydrangeas, palms, and conifers on show at different

insets of matching brick are enough for a visual link. Merge this hard surface with the path to give an impression of greater breadth, a less rigid form to the path, and sharper definition to the planted areas.

HOW TO VARY THE FLATNESS

Give your garden some contours with the plantings, concentrating on foliage plants, which give a longer lasting display than flowers. Put hummocks of knee-high plants at the edge to create the illusion of a boundary. Within, grow large swaths of a few ground-cover species rather than a mosaic of single plants.

Fill any gaps with clumps of spring bulbs and, when you give the garden its major cleanup as the spring blooms fade, buy a couple of trays of yellow and orange nemesia or red and white snapdragons to plant in two or three pools of

color. For an eye-catching focus, grow one tall item. A variegated holly clips into a handsome column, while the slow-growing conifer *Chamaecyparis obtusa* 'Nana Gracilis' makes a head-high globe composed of dark fans of foliage held upright. The cider gum (*Eucalyptus gunnii*) makes a blue-gray bush if you cut it back hard each spring. The leaves have a lovely rosy tinge when new, and if you pinch back the shoots during the summer more new leaves keep coming.

Instead of an evergreen, try *Cornus alba* 'Spaethii'; its cream-splashed leaves fall in autumn, but the bold red upright stems make a brilliant winter display. Finely cut golden foliage is the chief delight of the elder (*Sambucus racemosa* 'Plumosa Aurea'); before the leaves fall in autumn they glow even more than usual around clusters of little red fruits.

PLANS FOR A SMALL TOWN GARDEN

Lack of space does not mean lack of options. An astonishing number of variations can develop from a handful of basic designs. In this square plot an imaginative combination of materials is used to make bold designs. Choose the pattern that pleases you and put your own signature on the garden with the plantings.

COLOR WITHOUT PLANTS

The straight herringbone path is set with terra-cotta bricks that, as a link, are also used to edge the decorative diamond. An attractive ground pattern is made by combining hard surface materials — of blue slate set on edge, cobblestones, and bluestone chips — set into mortar as a mosaic. Four matching plants balance the diamond; these could be either bay laurel or rose standards.

HOT SPOTS IN COOL BLUE

The emphasis on marking the path clearly is cleverly achieved by using a basket-weave pattern of brick paving among gray flagstones. The planting is minimal, and it is the decorative pattern of surfacing that is the strongest design element. The two parallel areas of planting soften the straight lines of the path, and the slightly raised brick planter adds variation in height.

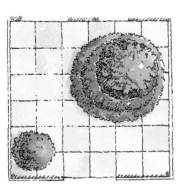

SIMPLE RINGS

The virtues of easy maintenance deriving from hard surfacing are apparent in this design of just two planted areas set within softly colored stone. The area of clear surface and the circular sweep of the greenery create a spacious air. Under the small tree are plants that create distinct tiers for vertical interest.

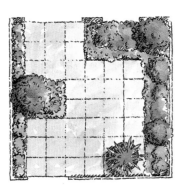

GREEN AND GOLD

Honey-colored paving is used to make the warm-toned floor in a neatly squared plan, given interest by a promontory jutting into it. The large pot next to the side plantings provides a focal point from the window and door and breaks up rigid geometric lines.

GROWING IN KNOTS

An angled path is defined by low hedges of boxwood. A simple adaptation of the intricate formal knot garden makes a perfectly balanced triangular composition. Silvery-leaved santolina and a crimson-leaved berberis are the plants used within the hedging.

23

LIGHT AND SHADE A dramatic idea is based on the contrast of sharp lines and circles. Pots of coppery-leaved giant dracenas (*Cordyline australis* 'Purpurea') stand on rippling circles of buff-colored bricks, showing up the movement of spiky shadows under the summer sun.

seasons. If you decide to have a small bed, you need a plant such as an evergreen berberis or cotoneaster, with more than one period of interest, or a plant with the year-round sculptural quality of holly or the lobed-leaf × *Fatshedera lizei*.

STRONG PATTERNS
FOR LONG-TERM PLEASURE

Lay two or three colors of tiles as a simple knot garden, and its precision will give almost as much pleasure as a knot of plants, without the work of clipping and feeding. Interlaced squares or diamonds are easier to achieve than circles. Put a pot plant or a small bed with an evergreen where the motifs overlap to soften the effect. Neat gray hebes or santolinas look good with terra-cotta and blue tiles; sarcococca or boxwood provide strong green to balance black and white tiles.

You can give variety of texture by using gravels, of two or three different colors, to fill in a pattern laid out in tiles or bricks that echo the color of the building. If you are prepared to take on some hedge clipping, you can make a pattern with low boxwood hedging — perhaps a diamond set in a square — and fill in the enclosed sections with gravel. A rose, bay laurel, or holly standard in each section completes the formal design.

Start making such a garden by covering the ground with landscape fabric that suppresses weeds but lets water drain through. Make slits through which to plant the standards. Then cover the fabric with the colored gravels, which are not to be walked on except for clipping the plants; this is a garden for looking at rather than wandering in.

Simple parterres, in which an outline pattern of low hedging is filled with plants, require sprucing up a couple of times a year but give value with their permanence and satisfying geometry.

An easy plan to lay out and plant is a square outline of boxwood hedging divided into four by more boxwoods. Fill the sections with gray santolina for a cool design. For a warmer look use purple sage or variegated periwinkle with the boxwood.

MODERN STYLE OUT OF TOWN

Even outside urban areas, low-care small gardens are still easiest to create with a hard surface. A modern house allows a striking, simple design of bricks in concentric circles or rectangles, whichever suits the building's detail. A curved bay window or porch top, for example, suggests circles, while a square-cornered bay or porch calls for rectangles.

At the center, plant a dramatic yucca, a fatsia, a New Zealand flax (*Phormium tenax*) with gold or orange stripes on its soaring sword-shaped leaves, or an evergreen *Mahonia japonica*, whose holly-like leaflets are paired on either side of long stalks and whose yellow, scented flowers bloom in winter. Take care that the planting does not block the way to the front door. Push the pattern to one side of the garden area if the front door is at the center of the house front.

Mortar the joints in the brickwork or fill them with fine gravel, matching the color to the bricks. You could also lay porous plastic sheeting under the bricks to suppress weeds. An evergreen fringe of ferns and red-hot pokers (*Kniphofia caulescens*) softens the edges.

When the house walls are of brick that is too insistent in color to repeat over the whole garden, space out the bands of brick with wide strips of gravel between. Around a stone house, make the pattern of stone pavers and encourage moss to fill the gaps. To lower the cost, space out the bands of pavers with strips of gravel.

ADDING BEAUTY TO GRAVEL

Gravel as the main surface cuts down care, but it looks dull on its own. In an informal country garden, inset it with stepping-stones meandering to pools of interest, where groups of two or three boulders are fringed with cobblestones. Amid the main group of boulders, make a bed that is just big enough for a dark cypress, with a steel-blue prostrate juniper and pink and white heathers below it.

You can use cut stone in place of groups of boulders, setting the regular shapes down slightly or raising them up to give variation in contour. Alpines make a pretty green fringe; to increase the relaxed air, let alchemillas, pansies, and helianthemums grow in the gravel.

LARGER GARDENS

THE CHIEF BOON of a larger front garden is that its plants do not have to work as hard as those in a small plot. The point of interest can shift from one part of the garden to another in a way that is not possible in a tiny space. Wallflowers need not follow bulbs, nor penstemons and phlox follow roses, all in the same bed — with the problems of color coordination that such sequences raise. The garden still needs its strong framework of evergreen and other foliage plants, but these can provide the quiet, constant backdrop; they do not have to be the star performers as well.

Even on properties at the edge of a city, it is often possible to create a substantial

RELAXED STYLE On this sloping site, shrubs and conifers in a range of shapes, and a subtle blend of gray, green, and purple, ensure long-term interest. Angled steps and bountiful roses complete a well-composed garden.

front garden by eliminating the front lawn. In a setting of this kind, the lawn serves little practical purpose anyway.

COTTAGE CHARMS UPDATED

The early tenants of country cottages were farm laborers and other rural workers who needed the garden for raising vegetables along with herbs for the pot. An artless miscellany of onions and leeks, edgings of strawberries and peas, a few cabbages tucked here and there, and pyramids of runner beans, all flourishing among roses and hollyhocks (*Althaea rosea*), makes a charming picture still but may not be the dream garden of anyone whose country cottage is the base for daily commuting and all-too-short weekends for relaxing. Romantic rural images can be achieved with minimum effort, however, if you choose the right plan.

Put your main effort into dressing up the door and keep the rest simple. Daisy-spangled grass flanking a stone path is charming in such a setting. Fringe it with purple, mauve, pink, and white lavenders; plant a self-fertilizing

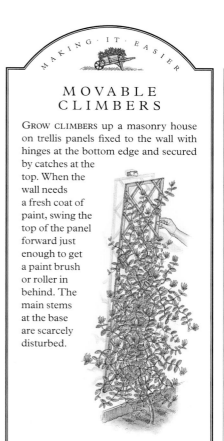

MAKING IT EASIER

MOVABLE CLIMBERS

GROW CLIMBERS up a masonry house on trellis panels fixed to the wall with hinges at the bottom edge and secured by catches at the top. When the wall needs a fresh coat of paint, swing the top of the panel forward just enough to get a paint brush or roller in behind. The main stems at the base are scarcely disturbed.

OLD FAVORITES In a larger garden an expanse of lawn with clipped hedges and shrubs makes a restful background for flowering plants. The roses and lupines, traditional cottage-garden plants, flower year after year, maintaining the colorful show when the rhododendrons begin to fade.

ROOTING OUT WEEDS

LAWN ON PUBLIC VIEW in a front garden needs to be carefully tended, with weeds removed before they can spread. Push a weeder straight down over a weed, and as you pull the tool out, it tightens around the weed and removes it without disturbing the lawn.

apple tree for blossom and scent in late spring, fresh foliage and developing fruits to watch in summer, a crop in fall, and a shape full of character in winter; underplant a mature tree with bulbs. Plant a wooden wheelbarrow with geraniums for summer color.

If you want large areas of flowers, grow old favorites that reseed to return every year — forget-me-nots, yellow doronicums, masses of peonies and poppies, spires of delphiniums, red valerian, blue cranesbill geraniums, spurred columbines, bell-flowered campanulas, honesty, and love-in-a-mist. Contain them all with an edging of pinks and lady's-mantle and thread the fence with a rose and a honeysuckle. Cut back the stems as blooms fade

and pull out seedlings or pop them in beside their fellows to build up sizable masses of each plant.

COUNTRY STYLE IN TOWN

This romantic, flowery image works in the gardens of old country towns and in leafy suburbs, too. Mix the perennials with evergreens for winter interest, since there is no green countryside within view. Suitable candidates are dwarf conifers or the feathery green *Santolina rosmarinifolia*, and *Viburnum × burkwoodii* or a rhododendron, both of which carry their promising fat flower buds through the winter ready for generous displays in late spring. A lawn contributes a welcome stretch of green during winter, too.

ON THE EDGE OF TOWN

Pleasing shapes and materials can be combined with tough but attractive plants in a variety of designs to suit suburbanites — and their cars.

AT THE FRONT of a standard edge-of-town house the challenge is to make a low-maintenance garden where the driveway is integrated into the design rather than dominant. Two principal objectives are to break up the dull square of grass and make a wide, welcoming space for alighting from the car and approaching the front door. The design can be given more interest with just a small change of level and a clear, bold shape.

Screening plants at the roadside give some privacy without masking the view of the door. In each design the planting focus is diagonally opposite the door so that it can be enjoyed from the house.

Balanced setting

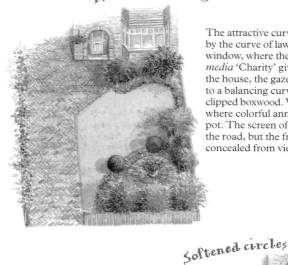

The attractive curve over the door is echoed by the curve of lawn sweeping under the window, where the evergreen *Mahonia × media* 'Charity' gives constant interest. From the house, the gaze is drawn over the lawn to a balancing curve between two pots of clipped boxwood. Within, there is a brick circle where colorful annuals spill out of a large pot. The screen of dark evergreens shuts out the road, but the front of the house is not concealed from view.

Softened circles

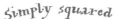

Circles are the theme of a sunken lawn and the raised area of solid brickwork that surrounds it. This is the platform for the garden's focal point — an urn holding a dramatic, spiky phormium. A small tree at the edge of the driveway adds height to the dense plantings of shrubs, which make a softening fringe along the front fence and, for a good succession of color, include camellias, weigela, and a mock orange.

Simply squared

This, the simplest of the options, draws its inspiration from the angular shapes of the window frames. The overlapped rectangles of the lawn, the square paving blocks, and the straight clipped hedge add up to a unified linear design. This is softened by hummocks of hebe fronting the stretch of arching, leafy bamboos and spreading fatsias.

Clear angles

The shape of the bay window is repeated in the angled entrance to the lawn, which gains immensely in impact simply from being raised by the height of two courses of bricks. This raised edge is clear of planting. The plant interest focuses on a golden-leaved tree, a robinia, set off by darker-leaved rhododendrons, laurels, and Mexican orange blossom.

WELL MATCHED Weathered paving is a good choice in front of this mellow stone house and as a background for foliage plants and pockets of flowers, with containers and flagstones making sympathetic decoration. The random pattern of the paving merges gradually with the driveway.

FORM AND FUNCTION A driveway has to be solid and wide enough for cars, but it does not mar the garden when it has an attractive surface — as with these warm beige bricks set in fishscale panels with contrasting outlines.

A lawn comes into its own in a larger garden, where a green foreground flatters the house and is often regarded as the essential background on which to work the embroidery of plantings. A large lawn means much work though, and hard surfacing saves time and effort.

LARGE BUT LABOR-SAVING

Labor-saving is not the same as bare and dull — far from it. Put together two or three principal features, plants that care for themselves and hard materials of lasting beauty, and your garden will give constant pleasure. Since space is ample, you are free from the hunt for miniatures that tests the ingenuity of many gardeners.

Think on a large scale, such as full-size trees, spacious planters, big and bold paved areas. Use mainly large paving slabs, in a random pattern, and make an imperceptible rise from the sides to

the center so that water does not all drain to the same point. A narrow rim of soil at the edge soaks up the water and fosters a luxuriant fringe of plants to soften the scheme.

Grow one or two trees well away from the house and put a very low wall, only two or three courses high, around each tree to avoid the difficulty of paving over thick root ridges near the trunk. Within the wall grow ferns, white-flowered lesser periwinkle, and white-striped *Lamium maculatum* 'Album,' but take care not to heap soil against the trunks.

To further the harmonious scheme the trees could be European birches, magnolias, white lilacs, or *Sorbus hupehensis*, the white-berried mountain ash. To fringe the paving, grow low-care plants, such as lily-of-the-valley, Solomon's seal, variegated white honesty, Corsican hellebore, and *Tiarella cordifolia* for its foam of white flowers. Tulips, *Achillea* 'Moonshine,' and potentilla will add lemon highlights.

PLANS FOR SUBURBAN GARDENS

Older suburban houses frequently have a long, narrow strip of front garden whose shape is a challenging one to make attractive. Some of the best solutions take a lead from grander, formal gardens and divide the strip into "rooms."

Buttresses of hedging, running in pairs from the side boundary toward the path, give a strong structure and create distinct areas for different color schemes. If you keep the hedges low, you can see all the rooms; raise them and some rooms are hidden, providing a chance to use uncoordinated, even clashing, colors.

Low clipped hedges grown in perfect squares among paving are another way of breaking up a long, narrow strip. Fill the squares with flowery perennials and low evergreens for a soft and pretty finish.

ABSORBING THE CAR

A larger garden usually has to provide space for a car, or often two, without looking like a parking lot. You cannot make the driveway less intrusive by shrinking it. It must be wide enough for you to open car doors on both sides without hitting a boundary wall or fence or encountering a scratchy plant.

To reduce a driveway's dominance, give it an attractive surface, make the straight edges less noticeable from the house, and try to merge driveway and garden in a satisfying overall design. As a surface, large areas of asphalt or concrete have no visual appeal, and gravel tends to move. Paving offers better prospects, whether real or reconstituted stone, bricks, or agreeably tinted clay or concrete blocks.

The way the surface is laid makes a big difference. Swirls of pavers, or blocks shaped for laying in a fish-scale pattern, are discreetly attractive. Combinations of materials work well: bands of brick set into paving, gravel, or concrete break up the expanse and can echo a curve, angle, or other detail from the house front.

You can make a gradual transition from driveway to garden with pockets of low plants tucked up to the paving. Planting is the best way to dress up the driveway. Even if it has to be straight-edged, you can blur the line with little promontories of hebe, aubrietia, *Stachys byzantina*, and cistus spilling over the edge to help absorb the driveway into the garden.

ALONG THE SIDE Generous room is needed for car access, but planting a raised bed along the driveway is one way to mask its long straight edge without using too much of the ground space.

MERGING WITH GRAVEL Plants of gently sprawling habit beside the driveway quickly spill out and dissolve rigid lines. These warm shades harmonize well with beige gravel and color-washed bricks.

SIDE SHRUBS Flourishing cistus, a Japanese maple, and *Euphorbia characias* add color and texture to what would otherwise be a flat and stark area between the house and the driveway.

Decorative Boundaries

ANY BOUNDARY, be it a manicured hedge of rich green, a wall clothed with climbers, or a fence softened with trailing plants, has a major role to play in your garden. It screens you from the outside world, creates welcome shade or a sheltered sun trap within, and should be a perfect backdrop for the plants that grow near it. Whatever your practical needs — keeping children in or animals out, hiding ugly buildings nearby, or making a frame for a view — there is no shortage of materials and means to choose from. Turn your back on the mundane and make your boundary work.

The autumn foliage of a clinging Virginia creeper mingles with cream-rimmed ivy to weave a colorful network on a brick-and-trellis boundary.

THE DIVIDING LINE

◆

GARDEN BOUNDARIES can do much more than simply mark the property line. Privacy and security are a priority for everyone: to shut unwanted visitors out, keep children and pets in, and enjoy the garden without the eyes of the world looking in. But a boundary can also shelter plants and act as a windbreak or wind filter, it can screen an ugly view or direct the eye toward an attractive one, and it can be a feature in itself.

The boundary can be living or man-made — a hedge, fence, or wall — or a combination. You can also tailor the boundary to suit particular needs in various parts of the garden: erect a high, solid fence at the side to shut out the neighbors, plant a slow-growing hedge at the far end as a backdrop, or grow a low edging to mark a terrace.

Homes with a view would gain more from a sunken boundary than from a raised one — as owners of estate gardens understood in the past. The view from stately homes was contrived so that it looked as if the owner's property extended as far as the eye could see. The "ha-ha," a ditch with one steep side, kept strangers and animals out, without interrupting the view. Now such devices are used more in zoos than in gardens because people tend to want to enclose their homes. But privacy does not have to mean solid fences.

An informal screen of mixed shrubs or climbers on a trellis creates an airy impression but gives a surprising degree of seclusion. You can combine a glimpse of the view and privacy with a formal boundary, too, perhaps by cutting circles like portholes out of a hedge or fence.

If you are lucky enough to have an old stone or mellow brick wall, enjoy it in all its glory, perhaps with just one or two espaliered or fan-trained fruit trees against it. But if you wish to disguise an ugly wall or fence, or use it as a backdrop for flower displays, there are a host of suitable plants available to boost the design.

CLASSIC CHOICE One traditional boundary, still unbeatable, is a high wall made from local brick or stone with a border in front. Climbing roses and foliage make a pretty tracery on the mellow wall, while mauve irises and the bold, lime-green flower heads of *Euphorbia characias* enliven its base.

FENCES AND WALLS

❖

A MAN-MADE BOUNDARY offers many advantages. It needs far less maintenance than a hedge. You have the option of growing plants up it if you wish and, if you do, it provides them with a firm support. A masonry wall or a fence also gives warmth and shelter and is reassuringly solid — it turns the garden into your own private haven.

Walls may give such a strong character to the garden that you want to reveal them rather than cover them with plants. Walls of local stone and old weathered bricks sometimes match the building materials of the house, linking indoors with outdoors. Stone walls may have crevices in which tough little plants will grow.

CONSIDER THE EFFECTS ON NEARBY PLANTS

Bear in mind that every solid boundary interacts with the wind. A semisolid wall or fence that filters the wind is the kindest to your plants, as well as being the most stable. A solid wall or board fence creates shelter close by the leeward side, but it increases wind turbulence otherwise.

Typically, the turbulence is worse some distance downwind from the barrier. Turbulence caused by a solid barrier 6 ft, 6 in (2 m) high persists for at least ten times the height — a distance of about 65 ft (20 m) — on the leeward side with a strong swirl of wind a few feet from the barrier. A smaller eddy of wind occurs on the windward side. Delicate plants on either side of the barrier may be flattened or damaged.

The traditional practice of surrounding a walled garden with trees combines the filtering effects of a hedge with the heat-storing capacity of the stones or bricks, which on cold nights protect plants growing against them.

USING TRELLISES FOR FENCES AND PLANTINGS

Fencing and trelliswork are now made in many variations on standard designs, permitting numerous opportunities to make something more creative of the boundary.

One very useful variation is a solid panel with a section of trellis on top, usually in a 12 in (30 cm) strip. This lets you grow shrubs along the base and a climber such as jasmine, honeysuckle, or

TRELLIS MADE TO ORDER You can commission a fence to specifications that fit your garden style, or even make one yourself. Dips or "windows" prevent monotony and could frame a view. Decorative post tops add the finishing touch to a trellis that is solidly constructed but airy.

clematis to make a swag of foliage and flowers at the top of the fence.

It is easier, though, and preferable for avoiding turbulence, to use a wind-filtering full-height trellis in the first place, even as an external boundary. And sometimes a flimsy screen that might topple over is more of a deterrent to thieves than a sturdy barrier that gives a foothold. A host of climbers can be planted on a trellis, including ivies, the delicate but vigorous *Clematis tangutica*, annual or everlasting sweet peas, and canary creeper (*Tropaeolum peregrinum*).

A combination of fence and substantial plants is also useful. It may be a mix of an economical fence such as wooden pickets with privet or beech, or it may be

TAKE CUTTINGS

MANY ROSES and shrubs can be easily increased by stem cuttings in autumn. As soon as the leaves fall, take stem cuttings 9 in (23 cm) long of new shoots that have just flowered. Retain two leaves at the top and dip the bottom in hormone rooting powder. Plant the cuttings outdoors in 6 in (15 cm) of coarse sand and soil. Plant out the rooted new plantlets the following year in late fall.

a thrifty curtain of ivy hiding metal stakes with horizontal wires running between them; another alternative is to use mesh netting tied or stapled to wooden poles. Ideally, such a barrier combines light, pretty fencing with beautiful plants, such as tall and climbing roses or wall shrubs.

THE PERFECT PARTNER FOR A TRELLIS

All climbing roses thrive on a trellis. There is better air circulation here than against a house wall, and usually the soil is better in the garden than against the house.

The pink-flowered 'Queen Elizabeth' and yellow 'Chinatown' are good choices because of their great vigor, but prune carefully as they have a tendency to flower at such a height that the blooms are out of sight. The hybrid musk roses 'Penelope' and 'Felicia' are less upright and are perfect in most respects.

A top variety for flower power combined with elegance and attractive foliage is *Rosa × odorata* 'Mutabilis.' The trellis provides a support for the plant to get a larger, more two-dimensional spread than is possible with a bush. The rose makes a large thicket. It needs severe cutting back through the season to encourage the strong new purple shoots — which are naturally growing along the trellis — to produce more flowers. This is a multicolored rose, with flowers that change color as they age. Single blooms open peachy yellow and are deep crimson as they fade. It is healthy and its only fault is a lack of scent.

CHOOSING THE MOST SUITABLE ROSE

As with all climbers, you should check a rose's ultimate height before buying. Where space is limited, choose moderate varieties such as 'Golden Showers,' whose strong upright growth can almost be fan trained. Very strong growers like 'Seagull' and 'Rambling Rector,' both white, are capable of growing arching stems of 30 ft (9 m) or more. They are suitable only for long expanses of trellis where you want a climber on the upper half to make a huge swag of flowers over shrubs or herbaceous plants below.

Look for the exciting new roses that have been bred to suit smaller gardens. Charmingly delicate adornments for an airy trellis are the miniature climbers — leafy, compact plants with masses of

BRINGING A BOARD FENCE TO LIFE

Where your garden flanks that of a neighbor, you usually want a solid fence. Lighten it with a trellis at the top and soften it with plants.

A BOARD FENCE 5 ft (1.5 m) high is tall enough for privacy, especially with 1 ft (30 cm) of trellis above it. Fasten netting to each post for climbers to reach the trellis; the mesh will not show once the plants have grown. A border 2–3 ft (60–90 cm) deep gives you room to plant shrubs and ground cover.

Start by choosing the climbers. Even for this north-facing fence, there are plenty of choices in the shape and color of the blossoms and foliage. The coral plant bears dainty oval leaves and bright orange-red, globular flowers, while the clematis 'Nelly Moser' boasts long elliptical leaves and large open "stars" of pale pink striped in rose.

SCENT AND COLOR ALL YEAR

A honeysuckle is on the post nearest the house so that its flowers scent the paved seating area nearby all summer long. In the mild climate the viburnum in front flowers from November to March — there is always something to see and smell near the house. In the summer months, the pot-grown aspidistra marks the transition from paved area to lawn.

In front of the clematis are several shrubs that offer foliage interest. The Portugal laurel readily fills out whatever clipped shape you desire. The kerria provides apricot flowers in early summer and a sprinkling of blooms until its leaves fall in autumn. In June its leaves drape the fence behind the fatsia.

A mahonia bush fills in the corner. All mahonias have boldly shaped evergreen foliage; the cultivar 'Lionel Fortescue' has finer leaves than others and more leaflets to each leaf. In late autumn it sends out yellow flower racemes, making a splendid show at the end of the garden.

The carpeting cranesbill rapidly covers any bare soil, crowding out weeds. Its prettily veined flowers are in bloom throughout the summer.

Open trellis gives extra height without gloom

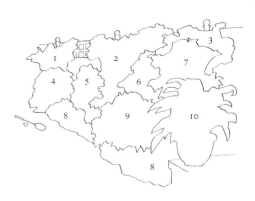

Clematis and honeysuckle clothe
the fence posts

Leafy
evergreens
break the
stretch of
bare
wood.

Cranesbills
add a summer-long
ruff of ground cover

1. Coral plant (*Berberidopsis corallina*)
2. *Clematis* 'Nelly Moser'
3. Japanese honeysuckle (*Lonicera japonica* 'Aureoreticulata')
4. *Mahonia × media* 'Lionel Fortescue'
5. Portugal laurel (*Prunus lusitanica*)
6. *Kerria japonica* 'Variegata'
7. *Viburnum × bodnantense* 'Dawn'
8. Cranesbill (*Geranium × oxonianum* 'Claridge Druce')
9. *Fatsia japonica*
10. *Aspidistra elatior* (in pot)

A FEELING OF SPACE As an external boundary, a trellis allows you glimpses of the view beyond. A border of low evergreens, including hellebore (*Helleborus foetidus*) with its two tones of green, gives a little privacy without excluding the wider horizons of the outside world.

block out the world and the wind, then one of overlapping vertical or horizontal boards is quick, easy, and cheap. Supported by wooden posts, it shuts out the world effectively and is a barrier against wind. But its inflexibility can be a problem in severe weather — a good, strong wind gust can push the fence down. Solid-board fences resist the wind but offer no escape routes for it.

MAKE MORE OF YOUR FENCES

Trelliswork fences can be easily assembled from panels available in standard sizes at any lumberyard. A fence of this sort is an effective visual barrier and reduces wind force without causing turbulence. If you build the fence from panels that have been pressure-treated with a wood preservative, it will require no painting or staining.

Unpainted post-and-rail fencing looks rustic and informal, and it offers enough support for a flowering hedge such as the purple-leaved *Berberis thunbergii*. Or try *Rosa rugosa*, with its healthy foliage, large single flowers in pink and white, and bright autumn hips. It makes a stable hedge up to waist height, but grows higher if you give it space to develop a broader base.

Unpainted posts and rails will often outlast painted ones. However, painting the fence turns it into a more decorative feature, making it a good backdrop for herbaceous plants or low-growing shrubs. Herbaceous need not mean short. Some grasses, such as miscanthus, are capable of growing as much as 6 ft (1.8 m) in a single season, and the fading stems and leaves of many varieties are attractive in the first months of winter before the weather begins to damage them.

HIDING HOMELY FEATURES

Wire stretched between sturdy posts — called post and wire — makes a discreet support for a developing hedge or training climbers. Be sure that the wires are visible and that none is low enough to trip over. The same applies to post-and-chain fencing.

Chain-link fencing can be improved beyond recognition with a planting that covers it. It can even support herbaceous climbers in the summer, with golden hops and everlasting peas the best choices. The purple-flowered *Clematis × jackmanii*, which can be trimmed almost to ground level in winter, makes a per-

small flowers, clothed with foliage and blooms right down to the base. The orange 'Laura Ford' is typical in that it reaches a height of about 6 ft (1.8 m) and spreads about half that distance.

INSTANT BOUNDARIES

The joy of a fence is its immediacy. In a few days you can choose it, buy it, and erect it, gaining instant privacy. New wooden fences tend to be raw-looking, but they gradually weather, and plants in front of the wood soon mask the

color. Once the fence is put in place, most gardeners want to plant it with climbers or shrubs. There are a few self-supporting climbers such as ivy, Virginia creeper, and climbing hydrangea that can scale the fence themselves, but they make maintenance of the structure difficult. It is best to attach horizontal supporting wires to the posts. A fan of stakes fixed to the wires can support and train a host of plants, including fruit trees.

If your aim in putting up a fence is to

WOODEN FENCES TO SUIT STYLE AND POCKET

Fences can be peep-proof or see-through, head high or knee high, wooden or wire, painted or stained. With most garden centers offering only a limited selection, it is wise to look in specialty shops and mail-order catalogs for other options.

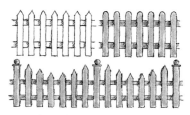

PICKET

The sight of white picket fencing, the tops pointed or more intricately shaped, conjures up visions of New England or country cottage gardens. Picket fencing looks good anywhere and need not be white. The wood can be stained and preserved, in which case it will need less maintenance than painted fencing.

RUSTICS

Post-and-rail fencing (above) is easy to erect, and you can vary the rail and post spacing. It gives little in the way of shelter, but makes a useful boundary marker. For more interest, have larch or other attractive wooden poles (top) constructed to the post-and-rail design of your choice.

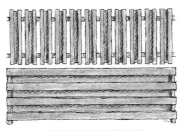

INTERFERENCE FENCING

Horizontal or vertical boards arranged on alternate sides of supports make for a sturdy fence. When constructed with gaps between the members, the fence provides a feeling of security and privacy, yet allows wind to filter through and permits glimpses beyond the garden. The rails come in a range of lengths.

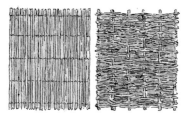

BAMBOO AND WATTLE

A bamboo screen (above left) looks naturalistic and gives a hint of the Orient. You can also grow a screen with bamboo plants. Suitable varieties range from dwarfs to tall, clump-forming kinds. Wattle fencing (above right) suits rural areas, where the woven stems blend into the surroundings. It is very compatible with wildflowers and cottage gardens and makes a good windbreak, but is neither inexpensive nor long lasting.

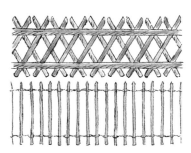

PALINGS AND SPLITWOOD

Wooden paling (above bottom) is ideal as a temporary fence when planting hedges — it looks better than wire alone and is quite cheap. It is sold in rolled-up lengths. Splitwood fencing (top) is made from softwood stakes fastened with galvanized wire. It buffers the wind but is not very durable.

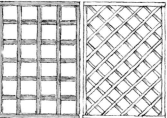

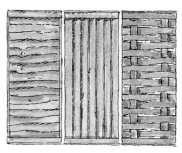

TRELLISES

Available usually in brown, green, or white and in a square or diamond pattern, trelliswork is sold as panels in a range of sizes. You can order a custom version to be made from your own design, as well as decorative posts (top). You can also buy panels with arched, open, or even fan-shaped tops. Trelliswork makes an attractive boundary in its own right, but creative choices expand once you start growing plants on it.

BOARD FENCING

Close-set boards give total privacy but need to be softened with plants. Horizontal overlap (above left) is economical, but often has skimpy overlap; check for sound construction. Vertical overlap (above center) is more expensive, but usually better made; the vertical boards are either feather-edged or square, which is the most expensive. Basketweave panels (above right) feature interwoven timber slats that offer a good deal of privacy.

CREATING SWAGS OF COLOR A two-tone climbing rose will transform a metal post-and-cable fence that marks the boundary between two gardens. The spectacular 'Climbing Masquerade,' a reliable variety with a long flowering period, smothers the post before spreading out along the cables.

fect companion to thread through the golden leaves of the hop.

Wrought-iron railings often mark the boundary of the front garden in a city dwelling. They are usually attractive in themselves and need only a little dressing up with shallow planting beds or troughs.

MAKING USE OF SMALL SHRUBS AND CLIMBERS

Many wall shrubs that need just a little support are at their best against a fence, if the spot is not too drafty. Some wall plants, such as *Garrya elliptica*, are well-mannered, while others, including *Solanum crispum*, sprawl at will and need supervision to keep them within acceptable bounds. When the plant is still young, train the main shoots in the desired direction. But after the solanum has matured, just cut away the shoots growing away from the fence once the multitude of mauve flowers has finished. A little pruning keeps the shrub fresh and young, with successive growths giving the maximum cover. In winter the solanum looks less appealing, so you may prefer the garrya, or you can grow both.

BE FIRM WITH CLIMBERS

If a climber is getting too top heavy, cut it back ruthlessly to stimulate new growth. Avoid the temptation to plant another climber to cover the bare base. It will follow the first to the top of the fence in a rush to find the light, leaving you with the same problem. This is why espaliered shrubs often make better screens than climbers, whose nature is to grow quickly to the top of the support, where their flowering and new growth happen out of sight.

When you combine climbers, choose those that can be maintained with ease. Climbing roses and clematis look lovely together, but make sure the clematis is one that can be pruned to near ground level each winter, as for example the late-flowering *Clematis viticella* or *C. texensis* hybrids can. Pruning and training are a nightmare when brittle clematis stems and thorny roses have to be separated.

Tangles of growth at the top of a fence, especially a light one such as trellis, can make it unstable and more likely to be damaged by wind. Avoid the most vigorous honeysuckles such as *Lonicera japonica* 'Halliana,' which is evergreen, and use deciduous types instead.

KNOW THE VIRTUES OF FACING NORTH OR SOUTH

The way that a wall or fence is positioned influences what grows well near it. One that runs from east to west has south- and north-facing sides. A wall to the north of the house faces south, which can be a big advantage — many wonderful plants thrive in the warmth radiated and reflected by the wall. But on the north side of the wall is an area

PLANTINGS FOR RAILINGS

If you are lucky enough to have ornamental railings at the front of your garden, draw attention to their decorative detail with judicious planting. In a back garden, use plants to fill in the gaps in the ironwork and provide more privacy.

IRON RAILINGS, which give a garden instant elegance, are more common in towns and cities than in rural areas. They are expensive to install, but lend a garden a timeless, classic look. Formal planting schemes work best, as they suit the geometric precision of railings. Climbing plants can use the slender bars for support, and a narrow border of low-growing seasonal specimens in front of the railings will soften their strong lines.

The ironwork requires more maintenance than a wooden fence. Paint it frequently to prevent rust from taking hold — peeling paint quickly makes railings look shabby instead of sharp.

Majestic spikes

The eye-catching bear's-breeches (*Acanthus mollis*) shows to advantage when planted alone. It blooms in summer with tall spires of purple-and-white flowers, and its large, deeply cut, glossy green leaves attract attention in any season.

Summer glow

Humulus lupulus 'Aureus' twines up the railings. *Philadelphus coronarius* 'Aureus' fills the middle ground with golden foliage; its creamy flowers smell of oranges. *Spiraea japonica* 'Goldflame' edges the border with bright leaves and pink blooms.

Purple splendour

In August and September, the feathery flower heads of *Liatris spicata* are at their best, set off by the darker leaves of the grapevine (*Vitis vinifera* 'Purpurea') and *Weigela florida* 'Foliis Purpureis.' While the colors harmonize, the shapes contrast — the stiff stems of the perennial liatris alternate with the bushy, arching forms of weigela, in turn interwoven with snaking vine tendrils. The weigela shrubs bring the bonus of rose-pink flowers as spring turns to summer.

A duet of roses

Few plants offer such diversity of form as roses. Plant a ground-hugging shrub rose to nestle at the feet of the old-time climber *Rosa* 'Albertine.' This triumph among ramblers looks its best in June, when the coppery buds burst into scented blooms. When it is not in flower, enjoy its vigorous growth and red young leaves, but beware of the sharp thorns.

Hydrangea petiolaris has lacy heads of small white flowers in summer.

Jasminum nudiflorum has bright yellow flowers in winter and early spring.

WIDE CHOICE FOR SOUTH-FACING WALLS

The southern exposure encourages early growth, and the risk of possible frost damage is offset by the advantage of a full growing season that usually allows new shoots to mature completely.

This gives the maximum flowering potential among plants from warmer climates such as fremontodendrons, with their flamboyant yellow saucer-shaped flowers, and the equally showy trumpet-creeper, grown for its funnel-shaped orange or red blooms.

Ceanothus has racemes of blue flowers in late spring, early summer, or autumn, depending on the type.

Chimonanthus praecox bears fragrant winter flowers that are cup-shaped and pale yellow with a purple center.

Pineapple broom (*Cytisus battandieri*) produces racemes of pineapple-scented yellow flowers, early to midsummer.

Mimosa (*Acacia dealbata*) produces round, fragrant, bright yellow flowers in spring. It is not very hardy.

Rosa banksiae 'Lutea' bears fully double yellow flower rosettes in spring.

PLANTING AN EASTERN OR WESTERN EXPOSURE

A wall or fence that runs north to south will have west-facing and east-facing sides. Of these the west-facing side is liable to be hotter and drier, since typically the hottest part of the day comes in midafternoon.

A west-facing wall supports a wide range of plants, though they may flower earlier than normal.

False acacia (*Robinia hispida*) has hanging racemes of pink flowers in late spring and early summer.

The Chilean potato tree (*Solanum crispum* 'Glasnevin') bears clusters of lilac-purple flowers in summer.

Wisteria produces drooping racemes of scented, pea-like mauve flowers in late spring or early summer.

Honeysuckle (*Lonicera*) is grown for its deliciously fragrant flowers.

Jasminum officinale has fragrant white flowers in summer and autumn.

The east-facing position is typically cooler and, in the North, should be planted with hardy specimens. Afternoon

---

BEST PLANTS

ALPINES FOR WALL CRANNIES

Alpines, which by nature anchor in rock crevices, scree, or pockets of gritty soil, are perfect for adorning a wall.

• *Aethionema* 'Warley Rose': evergreen subshrub with pink flowers in spring.

• *Alyssum montanum*: perennial with fragrant yellow flowers in summer.

• *Campanula poscharskyana*: spreading perennial with soft blue, star-shaped summer flowers.

• Maiden pink (*Dianthus deltoides*): evergreen, mat-forming perennial with white or pink flowers in summer.

• *Erinus alpinus*: semi-evergreen perennial with purple, pink, or white flowers in late spring and summer.

• *Parahebe lyallii*: semi-evergreen prostrate shrub with pink-veined white flowers in early summer.

• *Ramonda myconi*: evergreen perennial with blue or white flowers in late spring and summer.

• Saxifrage (*Saxifraga cotyledon*): evergreen perennial with yellow flowers in early summer.

• *Sempervivum montanum*: evergreen, mat-forming perennial with dark leaf rosettes and red flowers in summer.

PLANTING ON A WALL Tumbling gray-green aubrietia dresses the wall with purple flowers every spring while cushions of springy, white-flowered candytuft (*Iberis sempervirens*) bulge over the top. Both are evergreen.

that is shaded for most of the day. On a boundary this can cause problems if your new wall or fence shades your neighbor's sun-loving plants. In your own garden, regard shade as a positive boon. It creates a cool area to grow woodland plants. Indeed, they will grow in the shade of a wall far better than in most areas under trees, which are too dry and full of tree roots.

A position on the cool north side of a wall or fence delays growth until later in the season, which is a bonus since plants are less likely to have their new shoots damaged by late frosts.

CHOOSING PLANTS FOR NORTH-FACING WALLS

The colder north side of a wall is often the best place for frost-sensitive plants because temperatures fluctuate little and, after a frost, the thaw comes slowly. When morning sun strikes frost-bitten plants, it can do great damage, especially to flower buds and young growth.

Several intriguing plants are suited to a north-facing wall.

Silk-tassel bush (*Garrya elliptica*) has gray-green catkins dripping from its branches from midwinter to early spring.

shade is an advantage in the South, especially for heat-sensitive plants such as clematis. Generally, the east side of a wall does not suit sun-loving plants or plants that are sensitive to frost damage.

🌸 *Clematis* 'Ernest Markham' has large single flowers with magenta petals and chocolate anthers.

🌸 Japanese quince (*Chaenomeles japonica*) bears many orange-red flowers in spring, then spherical yellow fruits.

🌸 *Kerria japonica* 'Pleniflora' has large, pompon-like yellow flowers in spring.

CREATING IMAGINATIVE WALL DESIGNS

Walls give a garden a sense of maturity and stability, even when new. Few features look more satisfying than a wall made from native stone or traditional brick — both of which will age gracefully, soon acquiring a lived-in patina.

Conventional materials, however, can be used in attractive new ways. For example, you can arrange bricks in a honeycomb pattern, leaving a gap between each brick and the next. This design makes a strong boundary, filters wind, and allows some of the outside world to be seen.

You can incorporate honeycomb sections into the upper courses of a standard wall to give variety. Achieve a similar effect by adding curved roofing tiles into the wall to create decorative motifs.

You can also use concrete blocks precast in various open patterns to create a screen wall. It is the cheapest and easiest type of wall to build, and it suits most modern houses. The blocks are usually stacked one directly above another between concrete uprights but can also be used singly as an occasional decorative feature in a brick wall. They then give glimpses beyond the garden without loss of privacy.

ENJOYING TRADITIONAL BEAUTY

Dry-stone walls, with their timeless beauty, complement many architectural styles but work best in informal gardens. They are a classic feature of the New England countryside and always look at home there. When set into the side of a slope as a retaining wall, such dry-stone walls offer a host of cool, moist niches that are ideal for rock-garden plants.

For a greater opportunity to plant, build two low parallel walls and fill the space between with soil. The height of the walls and the width of the space will

GARDEN OF CONTRASTS A dark-painted trellis stands out against the warm-colored wall, a contrast echoed in the planting. Yellow lupines look even brighter against the purple globes of allium, while the irises echo both colors. Cranesbill geraniums and mixed herbs fill the front of the border.

BLOOMS AGAINST THE BRICK Tone down the harshness of new brick by attaching a trellis and growing a rose such as 'Climbing Pompon de Paris,' which makes a wonderful display in June. The trellis alone, whether in its natural color or stained, improves the appearance of the brick.

FILLING THE CRACKS A covering of moss and neat clumps of primrose add even greater charm to a retaining wall of local stone. Always choose flowers to suit the conditions and plant the crevices as you build the wall.

MERGING A WALL AND HEDGE Grow a ruff of ivy over a stone boundary. Use rope swags to train the plant, clipping it ruthlessly to the shape that you want. Ivy is vigorous enough to grow back with renewed verve.

mals — and some even incorporate wall fountains. They are usually made of artificial cast stone, terra-cotta, or plastic. You might also consider using grotesque masks or gargoyles — which are particularly effective when lit at night. Although such wall ornaments take a while to weather, fast-growing climbers quickly soften the outlines and help the feature look established.

USING PLANTS TO TRANSFORM A WALL

When you have a wall that is not an asset to the scene, convert it into an enviable feature with plants that cover it fully. The best plants are climbers such as Virginia creeper (*Parthenocissus quinque-folia*), Boston ivy (*P. tricuspidata*), ivy, *Schizophragma hydrangeoides, Hydrangea anomala petiolaris,* and pyracantha.

Clothe an ugly brick wall with ivy, then fix a white, pale blue, or natural-wood stained trellis over it. Stand tubs and urns of plants in front of the trellis for an additional feature.

PLAYING TRICKS WITH WALLS

Walls offer the best chance to use mirrors in the garden. Fix one on the wall of a small courtyard garden and grow ivy around it — and suddenly the garden becomes twice the size.

Much can also be done with paint. If you are skilled, re-create a scene from a holiday location or, if this sounds a little too ambitious, paint one single stretch of color. A pale masonry paint, perhaps one that is pink or stone-colored, gives a new background to place your plants against.

Be bolder still and paint the wall yellow. This might be too startling for large areas but is perfect for walls enclosing patios that are as much a part of the house as part of the garden. A yellow wall looks sunny all year and pushes purple foliage and red flowers to the height of their brilliance.

Follow the idea into pastels and use a soft mauve or lavender. This could be the basis of a pastel flower scheme of blue and lilac or a backdrop for a white and gray border at the foot of the wall, the hint of color making the monochrome planting even more ethereal.

A deep-blue boundary wall is the perfect home for a collection of sun and star wall plaques in Mediterranean style, and also for a border of sunny flowers in tones of yellow and orange.

dictate the choice of plants. The lower and farther apart the walls are, the more choice you have; tall, narrow beds dry out fast and support only a few alpines. If the two walls share a concrete foundation, leave weep holes for water to drain away. Ask for help from a professional if you are building walls taller than 3 ft (1 m).

ADORNING THE WALL TO ADD CHARACTER

Whatever the style of a wall and the building material it is made from, you will probably want to dress it up with some plants or ornaments.

There is a wide range of wall plaques available — often depicting birds or ani-

HEDGES FOR NATURAL CHARM

◆

HEDGES ARE POPULAR for their attractive appearance and because they are usually cheaper than fencing or walls. They demand less thought in planting, even though trimming requires more skill to make the most of the hedge as a decorative contribution to the garden.

All hedges are excellent wind filters, allowing some air through but sheltering plants — and people — from icy blasts. Most deciduous hedges have close to the ideal proportions of three-fifths solid material and two-fifths air space. The shelter hedges give garden plants is vital. It reduces damage and slows down water evaporation from the leaves, which is increased by drying winds. The plants need less watering, and the warmer, sheltered environment encourages growth.

REDUCING THE WIND FACTOR

In exposed sites, whether in arid climates or coastal areas, it is essential to establish a shelter belt of trees and shrubs that breaks the wind. Exceptionally windy gardens will need a series of windbreaks if plants are to have a fair chance for growth. Make the outer windbreak from an informal, mixed belt of evergreen and deciduous plants of varied heights and vigor. The ragged profile filters wind much more effectively than a closely clipped hedge, which causes a certain amount of turbulence.

The direction of a hedge in relation to the prevailing wind is important. The hedge is more effective when you plant it nearly at right angles to the wind. However, the individual location is always a factor in the usefulness of any windbreak. A hedge planted across a slope tends to trap cold air as it travels down the hillside. This may cause problems for plants in the garden immediately above the hedge, but it gives protection from frost damage to plants in the garden below.

MAKING PREPARATIONS

Think carefully about how a hedge is going to affect views, how easy it is to clip, and how often it needs clipping.

If the hedge is to stand between you and a neighbor, check who is going to cut each side. You may need to put up a tem-

---

BEST PLANTS

RELIABLE FORMAL HEDGES

These frequently seen hedge plants are popular for a reason — they are easy to grow and tolerate clipping.

- Boxwood (*Buxus sempervirens* 'Suffruticosa'): a low-growing evergreen; needs trimming twice a year.

- Bush honeysuckle (*Lonicera nitida*): tiny glossy evergreen leaves; trim in summer. Good for small gardens.

- Common beech (*Fagus sylvatica*): the best deciduous hedge for well-drained soils, retaining foliage all year.

- Common hornbeam (*Carpinus betulus*): though deciduous, most of the rusty-brown leaves are retained through the winter on clipped hedges.

- Holly (*Ilex* spp.): excellent evergreen hedge. It grows slowly, but is long lived. Trim in late summer.

- Lawson cypress (*Chamaecyparis lawsoniana*): a huge range of evergreen shapes and colors.

- Privet (*Ligustrum* spp.): both evergreen and deciduous forms; foliage may be green, gold, or variegated.

- English yew (*Taxus baccata*): ideal, long-lived evergreen, well suited to topiary. Trim once in late summer.

EVERGREEN BACKDROP For a solid curtain of color, yew is hard to beat. Trimmed to a peak, the hedge draws extra attention to the magnolia in front, and the light flowers are etched against the dark drape.

eties ready for planting is greatest then. You can buy bare-root deciduous plants far more cheaply than specimens in containers, which are all that are available in summer. Buy evergreens, however, such as holly, laurel, and escallonia, either in containers or as balled-and-burlapped specimens, with the rootballs wrapped carefully in burlap.

THE IDEAL HEDGE PLANTS

Select an appropriate hedging plant to ensure success. The ubiquitous Leyland cypress (× *Cupressocyparis leylandii*), for example, is widely available, but you should think twice before choosing it. It rapidly achieves a height of 6 ft (1.8 m) but does not stop there and requires heavy pruning from an early age to make a small, dense hedge. Plain green forms of Lawson cypress are more suitable in small gardens.

Holly copes with some shade and pollution and so is good for an urban garden, but it requires formative pruning to ensure dense growth. Choose an evergreen privet for year-round cover, remembering that its hungry roots can deprive neighboring plants of water and nutrients. Do not plant yew within reach of livestock as the dried leaves and branches are poisonous to them. The berries will also poison humans, but there will be little fruit on well-trimmed hedges.

There is no need to stick to green for hedging. Copper or purple-leaved beech seedlings offer an unusual alternative to common beech and are no more expensive. To accentuate the color, plant a tapestry hedge of purple and green.

Osmanthus × *burkwoodii* is a slow-growing evergreen hedge worth planting for its sweetly scented flowers in late spring. As a garden shrub it is rather dull but is admirable as a fragrant, trimmed background. Prune it after flowering.

Cherry laurel (*Prunus laurocerasus*) offers glossy leaves and fast growth and is one of the best large evergreen hedging plants. Prune in summer, using a hand pruner, as hedge trimmers leave unsightly ragged leaf edges. Grow it as a semiformal hedge or trimming can be daunting.

ENSURING SUCCESS WITH FORMAL HEDGES

To make a smooth, dense curtain of color, a formal hedge must be clothed with branches down to ground level. These develop only when the plants are

CORDLESS TRIMMERS

EVEN EASIER TO USE than electric or gas-driven hedge trimmers are cordless ones. The battery-powered trimmers work for about 45 minutes before they need recharging. They are safe, with no cables to get in the way, light to hold, and manageable in size.

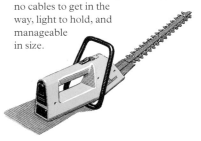

TRIMMING AND TOPIARY Carrying a clipped theme from hedge through to terrace gives the garden a unified style. A neat sphere of boxwood flanks the approach to a lawn backed by holly trimmed with dramatic scallops.

porary boundary of chicken wire until the hedge grows. Where it is difficult to reach the back of the hedge for cutting, high fence panels may be best.

Bear in mind that a hedge is a row of shrubs — a fact often forgotten when it comes to planting and preparation. These shrubs are to be in place for many years and need thorough soil preparation if they are to be given the best chance for long-term growth.

Clear the site of weeds in summer, dig in plenty of organic matter in late summer, and plant in October or November. Spring or mid to late fall are the best times to plant most shrubs: the choice of vari-

trimmed from a very early age. For this reason, start with small, young plants. Apart from being cheaper, they are more likely to establish a widespread root system that anchors the hedge soundly. It can then withstand the buffeting that wind causes on the top growth.

PRODUCTIVE TRIMMING

Conifers cannot stand such hard trimming just after planting as deciduous shrubs. Stems need to be clipped lightly and often as they develop. But leave the leading shoot of each conifer unpruned until the hedge is above the desired height, then cut it off about 3 ft (1 m) below the top. In subsequent years, the top of the hedge should fill out with side shoots.

Apart from this, do not be impatient for an evergreen or deciduous hedge to reach its full height. A stronger and more stable hedge results from trimming to encourage bushy growth. A tall, spindly hedge does not give privacy or stop the wind, and it will probably need some support to prevent it from blowing over.

From the start, shape the hedge to be wider at the bottom than the top. This makes it stable, helps prevent heavy snowfalls from damaging the top, and allows more light to reach lower parts of the hedge, encouraging sturdy growth. It is a particularly appropriate shape for conifers, as it echoes their natural growth habit.

WHEN AND HOW TO TRIM

To create an even profile, make a pair of wooden frames that can be set over the hedge as guides while you cut. Join the frames with strings to run along the top edges of the hedge.

Hedge trimming is laborious, but it is far easier if done regularly. Privet and bush honeysuckle need trimming about once a month during the growing season to keep them neat. Established conifer hedges need trimming once a year but look better if cut more often. Once a year is enough for yew, boxwood, and holly.

Hornbeam and beech both retain their dead leaves through the winter if trimmed yearly in late summer when the flush of growth is finished.

Nothing works so well as shears on soft growth like that of bush honeysuckle. An irregularly shaped evergreen hedge with large leaves needs trimming with a hand pruner. The goal is to take out whole shoots and avoid cutting a leaf in half, as the remnant will turn brown.

FORMALITY WITH A DIFFERENCE Golden buttresses are spectacular accents against the dark green "wall" and reinforce the imposing style of a yew hedge. Yew is ideal for such treatment — its small evergreen leaves tolerate close trimming, which is best done once a year in late summer.

TIDY NEED NOT MEAN STRAIGHT Closely planted columnar forms of Lawson cypress introduce curves and character into a formal hedge, accentuated by attentive clipping. The dark conifers are brightened by mats of aubrietia at the foot of the hedge and by flowering cherry above.

EXAGGERATING THE CURVES Formal meets informal with the scalloped edging of cherry plum (*Prunus cerasifera* 'Pissardii'). The plant is more often seen as a tree, but there are purple or green varieties suited for hedges. Left untrimmed, it bears white flowers in early spring.

SCULPTURAL QUALITY Once you master the arts of clipping and pleaching, exploit your skills to the full. The hedge, pleached halfway up, and the green arch over the entrance, look even better in winter, a rare achievement.

HEDGING ON STILTS A hedge need not be solid at the base. The technique of interlacing branches, called pleaching, requires different plants from hedging shrubs. Lime, which is pliable, is most often used. A pleached hedge is more a feature than a barrier, though it can serve both purposes.

When you keep a hedge no taller than shoulder height, trimming presents no problem. Use electric or gas-driven trimmers on firm and twiggy growth. Always keep safety in mind, preferably with someone else standing by to help and pass you tools.

🌪 Never use electric or cordless hedge trimmers in the rain or on a wet hedge.

🌪 Replace the cord if the insulation is damaged. Make sure the cord and electrical outlet are properly grounded.

🌪 If a hedge is too tall to reach from the ground, work from a scaffold of boards suspended between stepladders.

🌪 Never use trimmers with one hand; two hands provide a safe, steady grip.

🌪 Never overreach when cutting.

HOW TO SHAPE THE TOP

There are many ways to enliven the staid symmetry of a formal hedge. Use your topiary skills to express your individuality. The simplest form of topiary is varia-tion in the height of the hedge, which re-sults in a castellated top. Because this re-quires regular, matching notches along the top, measure carefully first and mark where you want the hedge to grow taller. You can mark with tape held by clothespins or, for greater accuracy, make a template from a thin board that includes at least one upper area and two lower. Lay it against the hedge and move it along as you cut. The upper areas will need only light trimming to take the tips off the shoots and encourage bushiness.

The top of the hedge does not have to be hard edged or regular. It could be trimmed in specific shapes, perhaps triangles or semicircles. You should make sure, however, that they rise in the right places to block out unsightly views or objects.

Another straightforward top is a crown. Find four or five strong shoots growing together in the center of the hedge at the top. Tie them together at their base, then to a vertical stake as they grow upward. When they are tall enough, take the tips and bend them gently down to their base, where they meet the hedge; tie them individually, to create four or five loops. In subsequent years trim the foliage closely so that each shoot makes a dense ring.

MORE AMBITIOUS SHAPES

The easiest ways to create topiary shapes are to make the basic form with chicken wire or to buy a ready-made frame and attach it firmly to a sturdy stake driven through the hedge in the desired spot. Tie strong shoots to this frame in the correct position on the underside. They will grow through the frame to fill the upper surface; in a time the frame will be covered. Trim the topiary a short distance outside the wire to keep it concealed.

Peacocks are a traditional shape for topiary, but you can cut more quirky, individual decorations — perhaps a ship or a car — into the top of an established hedge. Use clothespins to fix colored tape in the desired outline. Push stakes horizontally through the hedge to mark a matching outline on the other side, then fasten tape on the second side. Clip down to the marked outline on both sides and then across the width. You can leave some taller features, such as the funnels of a ship or locomotive, in the middle.

PLEACHING A HEDGE

For pleaching — which involves training adjoining plants horizontally to form a hedge on sticks — you have to plant larger specimens, but fewer are required. Put in a row of sturdy stakes tall enough to reach the top of the completed hedge and stretch wires horizontally between them.

The shoots are trained sideways, as with an espaliered fruit tree. The distance between the horizontal wires is usually 1–2 ft (30–60 cm). The height of the lowest wire depends on how much open space you want below the hedge. Place another stake or a sturdy pole at the end of the hedge for extra strength. Run the top wire diagonally down to the ground and peg it securely.

Under this hedge on legs, erect a white picket fence or a painted trellis supported by posts with carved finials on top. For a greener lower story, plant the fence with shade-loving plants such as hellebore, periwinkle, and cyclamen. This gives a definite boundary that is original and allows views of the outside world.

PATTERNS AND MESSAGES

Patterns cut into the side of a hedge give it individuality. They require less skill than pleaching and are definitely more vandal-proof than a row of peacocks on top of a boundary hedge.

You can even vary the pattern on each side of the hedge. On the inside it could be simple geometric shapes cut in relief or a favorite saying spelled out across the garden, and on the outside it could be the house number or your name. This decoration works best on very fine-leaved

PLEACHING YEAR BY YEAR

RAISING A HEDGE on "stilts" by pleaching gives it a new character. Little-leaf linden (*Tilia cordata*) is the best plant to use.

Make the framework taut and strong, as it must support the trees for at least three years until they are fully established.

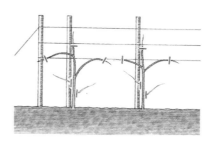

1. In the first winter after planting, tie the young trees securely to upright supports. Tie any suitably placed branches to the horizontal training wires and cut off growing tips to encourage bushiness. Remove all branches below the lowest horizontal branch, as close to the main trunk as possible. Trim the leader (main vertical stem) so that it is just below the next horizontal wire. Even if the leader does not reach the wire, trim it back by a few inches to encourage strong new growth.

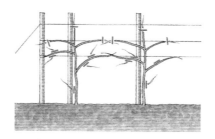

2. After a year, the first trained horizontal branches will have extended their growth. Once they overlap, twist the stem tips together. Remove or severely shorten side shoots to keep a clean framework of branches. There should now be two more branches to tie down to the second horizontal wire. Treat these in the same way as the ones the previous year, by removing the tips. Use the central, strongest shoot as the leader once again. Trim it just below the top wire. Remove any other stray shoots on the main trunk.

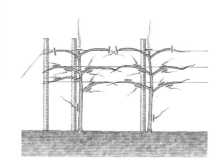

3. In the third year, the pleached trees will have reached the top of the support. Train two of the best side branches at the top horizontally as in previous years. Remove the leader, as you no longer need it to extend the height. Continue to prune the horizontal shoots of previous years, shortening the side shoots so that they are leafy and do not develop into woody growths that would interfere with the clean lines of the pleaching. In future years remove any strong upright shoots from the leader.

hedges, such as yew, bush honeysuckle, and conifers. Begin trimming with mechanical hedge trimmers and finish the details with one-handed shears.

Cut letter templates from cardboard strong enough to last for several years. Use them every time you trim the plants. With the template laid against the hedge, cut around the letter, working with hand shears to avoid making mistakes.

Alternatively, clip a message in relief on the top of a flat hedge so that it can be seen from above, perhaps a secret line to a loved one that can be read only from an upstairs window. To make the hedge let-

ters sturdy, lightly trim the tops of the shoots after removing the template. The shoots will branch and interlock. After several seasons the letters will be clear.

As with all aspects of hedge care, the success of topiary depends on continual attention. Occasional clipping is not enough. If you decide that the end does not justify the means, there are other ways to give a distinctive touch to a hedge.

CREATING A LIVING ARCH

Most people's idea of an idyllic country cottage includes a rose arch, preferably over the front gate, but an arch of leafy

HEDGE WITH ITS OWN FLOWERS It is easier to plant a flowering hedge than to apply color later. A climbing rose that repeat flowers is an excellent choice, and inexpensive if you raise plants from your own cuttings.

ONE-HANDED SHEARS

FOR TRIMMING low hedge shrubs, such as boxwood, or for sculpting intricate topiary shapes, one-handed shears permit a delicate touch. Unlike ordinary shears, where the two blades swing together, one blade remains fixed, which gives you much more control. The shears are lightweight and small, usually with a 6 in (15 cm) blade.

to it. The wire netting makes it easier to tie in the shoots as they grow up the frame. Pinch out the tips as the shoots grow to encourage better branching and trim the growths occasionally. Once the shoots reach the top, let them extend beyond the frame and carefully bend them over to cover the top. The living arch will take a couple of seasons to cover the structure and will soon blend in with the rest of the hedge.

Adapting this idea, you can increase the height of a hedge by several feet but still allow views into and out of the garden through "windows" left in the hedge. Make wooden frames that can be fixed in the hedge. Instead of squares or rectangles, the windows could be circles or diamonds, which are simpler because the shoots can be more easily trained up and around the frame.

THE INFORMAL LOOK

If you would like a more casual-looking boundary, or if the prospect of regular trimming is too daunting, an informal hedge is for you. Although some initial pruning is necessary to form a sturdy framework, the plants can be left to develop their natural shapes and to flower freely where appropriate.

Trimming an informal hedge is the same as if the shrub were growing elsewhere in the garden. For instance, trim *Berberis* × *stenophylla* in summer as soon as flowering is over to give the maximum bloom the following year.

If you take over a garden that has an overgrown hedge, take the opportunity to cut the plants back severely to renew the upper level. New growth is often very rapid, especially if you apply fertilizer, because of the substantial root system that exists. Such hard pruning is best done in early spring. New shoots then have a long growing season before the winter and can harden off sufficiently to withstand frost.

COASTAL CONTENDERS

Elaeagnus × *ebbingei* is fast growing and attractive, with deep-green leaves and scented autumn flowers. It is prone to die back and is not fully hardy below 5° F (−15° C), but it is ideal for mild areas.

Escallonia 'Red Hedger' is upright and fast growing, with glossy evergreen leaves. It needs shelter inland but is perfect by the sea. Trim it in spring to remove any frost damage and again in summer. If grown as an informal hedge,

plants is far more adaptable. Provided your hedge is not too old and lacking in vigor, you can train it into an arch over a gate or entrance.

A hedge of privet, for example, grows to 8 ft (2.5 m) and more, which is high enough for an arch, but it is not particularly stable at full height. Make a sturdy frame of wood about the desired size and shape of the arch. The frame can be square, pointed, or curved at the top, depending on your preference and woodworking skills. Give it a good coat of preservative intended for use in gardens and let it dry thoroughly.

Tie it firmly to the main branches of the hedge or to metal rods driven into the ground and staple a layer of chicken wire

WHERE HEDGE MEETS BORDER Shrubs such as *Philadelphus* 'Beauclerk' bridge the gap between herbaceous plants and high hedge, giving vigorous informal growth and a bountiful mix of flowers and heady scent.

it will flower more freely. *Griselinia littoralis* is another choice for the coast. It is a dense evergreen shrub with light-green leaves on yellow stems, and it makes an excellent close-clipped formal hedge.

Too often restricted to coastal areas, where it is indeed ideal, is the tamarisk (*Tamarix pentandra*); its willowy stems of tiny leaves end in fluffy pink flowers. Prune after flowering as hard as necessary to create a semi-formal hedge.

Ornamental willows such as *Salix alba* 'Chermesina' and *S. daphnoides* make interesting informal hedges when at least half their growth is pruned annually to promote tall, upright stems. They screen well during summer, and in winter, when the leaves are not present, the brightly colored young stems are visible.

THORNY HEDGE BARRIERS

Berberis × stenophylla grows strongly and is extremely prickly, making it suitable for keeping out animals and intruders. It occasionally suckers, which may be a nuisance, but the orange flowers in late spring are spectacular. Trim this evergreen informal hedge after flowering.

Hawthorn (*Crataegus monogyna*) produces a cheap deciduous hedge that tolerates hard clipping at almost any time of year. The white flowers are followed by red berries on the thorny stems. Hawthorn is a good hedge for attracting wildlife in rural areas — whether alone or mixed with privet, blackthorn, and elder.

Blackthorn (*Prunus spinosa*) makes a dense deciduous hedge suitable for rural areas. As its name hints, blackthorn is impenetrably thorny. It needs a yearly pruning in summer.

European elder (*Sambucus nigra*) tolerates any soil, air pollution, and some shade, and can be cut back hard. The two variegated forms with cream- or white-edged foliage make decorative semi-formal hedges if space is not too limited; they can be pruned at any time.

THE RIGHT FOREGROUND

Traditionally a wall, fence, or neatly clipped hedge is fronted by a border of other, lower-growing plants. To some gardeners a plain green hedge is a blank canvas on which to paint a picture. This is the purpose of the classic tall yew or

NEAT ALL YEAR Choose bush honeysuckle (*Lonicera nitida*) for a trim, year-round hedge. For brighter color, there is a yellow-leaved form, 'Baggesen's Gold,' or you can enliven the base of the hedge with honesty.

HARDY HORNBEAM For a deciduous hedge, opt for European hornbeam (*Carpinus betulus*). It forms as good a hedge as beech; its leaves are more strongly veined, toothed, and pointed, but as with beech, they don't drop in winter.

CHEAP AND CHEERFUL

IF YOU CANNOT WAIT for a hedge to grow and want a quick screen that need not be permanent, sow a row of sunflower seeds. They are fast growing and cheap. Along with the familiar tall yellow sunflowers, there are strains with colored or white flowers. The more branched plants are good for cut flowers as well as for a screen.

MIXING FLOWER AND FOLIAGE Growing a plant over the surface of a hedge adds an extra dimension to a plain backdrop. Starry pink *Clematis* 'Minuet' prettily partners 'Fletcheri,' a gray-green Lawson cypress.

beech hedge behind the herbaceous border. It provides a backdrop that throws the plants in the foreground into strong relief. But a hedge may run alongside the drive and is then a decorative feature in its own right. And it certainly needs to be this where it runs along the front of your property and is the first thing you see every time you come home.

Where space allows, make the planted area against a hedge as deep as possible. The hedge blocks light from one side, making it inevitable that the plants against it reach forward to the light.

PLANTS TO COVER THE FEET OF THE HEDGE

The soil at the base of a hedge can be dry and poor, making it hard for all but the toughest plants to survive. There are many attractive contenders.

Small-leaved English ivies (*Hedera helix*) in many guises — variegated, green, or with delicately cut leaves — cover the ground in even the deepest shade. They also scramble up stems. Avoid the temptation to plant a patchwork of several differ-

ent types that all vie for attention and may spoil the ordered form of the neat hedge.

Though the cyclamen looks so delicate and frail, *Cyclamen hederifolium* is a tough survivor. It is quite content under a hedge, especially if given a good mulch of compost during July, which is the only month it rests. August sees the start of its flowering, and, soon after, the prettily marbled leaves make close clumps that last until the following summer.

The periwinkles are often regarded as weeds, but they will grow anywhere, including dense shade, and are a blessing for alkaline soils. Their disadvantage is that they spread fast by creeping stems — or trailing stems in the case of the large periwinkle — to colonize better places. The variegated kinds are especially attractive and sometimes slower growing.

THREAD THE HEDGE WITH COLOR

With a flowering hedge you can combine more than one shrub type. A mixed screen that blends into smaller shrubs in the foreground, then perennials and

edging, is ideal for small gardens. Choose flowering times to coincide or to be staggered through the year, depending on whether you want a burst of seasonal glory or year-round interest.

If you already have a green hedge, give it color by growing plants on it. Plants that thrive in poor soil are best. The climbing nasturtium (*Tropaeolum majus*) is especially suitable. This hardy annual grows far more luxuriantly when given rich soil, but the plants can be very leafy at the expense of flowers. The roots of a hedge prevent any hint of lushness in the nasturtiums, so there are more flowers and fewer leaves. If the plants need trimming at the top, just cut them back — you will do little harm to the flowers.

Equally good is the closely related canary creeper (*T. peregrinum*), with small leaves and less showy, dainty yellow flowers but a greater ability to cling.

The everlasting pea (*Lathyrus latifolius*) makes a good show of warm rose-purple flowers. It will set seed and needs a good trim by the end of August when the hedge needs clipping. Other vigorous annual climbers include *Mina lobata,* which has racemes of little red flowers that fade to orange then yellow, and the Chilean gloryflower (*Eccremocarpus scaber*), which also has orange-red racemes.

The half-hardy cup-and-saucer vine (*Cobaea scandens*), with blooms that open yellow-green and age to purple, is another choice, or you could try the Japanese hop (*Humulus japonicus* 'Variegatus'), which has unusual foliage that is blotched and streaked with white.

DECIDUOUS FLOWERING SHRUBS

Fuchsia magellanica is the toughest of the hardy fuchsias, often retaining a woody framework all year. The small flowers are red and purple. The peeling rusty bark in winter is pretty, and plants can reach 6 ft (1.8 m) or more in mild areas. The pink-flushed white 'Molinae' is a good alternative to the common form, and there are variegated kinds, too.

Forsythias are a familiar delight in the spring landscape. When well pruned, by taking out old stems at the base instead of trimming back to the same twiggy framework each year, they flower profusely.

Serviceberry (*Amelanchier*) is usually used as a small tree, but it withstands pruning and makes a pretty screening plant in informal sites. Profuse white flowers in spring and brilliant autumn color give it two seasons of interest.

EVERGREEN WITH FLOWERS

Mexican orange (*Choisya ternata*) creates a year-round hedge of medium height with small, scented flowers in spring and a few in summer. It withstands heavy trimming but may be damaged by very cold weather and wind.

Hebes are dense evergreens for mild climates. Some spectacular flowerers, such as 'La Séduisante' and 'Midsummer Beauty,' are not reliably hardy, but *Hebe salicifolia,* with long leaves and narrow flower spikes, is suitable for tall hedges. Prune it in spring, when any branches damaged in winter can be removed.

Mahonia aquifolium is useful for shade but grows only to about waist height. It has holly-shaped leaves, clusters of lemon flowers, and purple berries.

All the pyracanthas make superb hedges, trimmed formally or left to grow naturally, when they produce more foamy cream flowers and scarlet berries. They perform well in cold and windy locations. Always plant named varieties, mixed if necessary, to ensure

that the flowers and berries are what you wanted.

Among the huge group of viburnums is *Viburnum tinus,* which flowers very early in spring. It will adapt to almost any conditions, and there are improved forms with bigger flowers, pink buds instead of the usual white, and attractively variegated leaves.

MINIHEDGES

As a simple boundary marker rather than a screen for privacy, low hedges allow you to grow a wide range of plants.

❧ Lavender can be clipped neatly and looks lovely around beds of pink and

HEDGE OF GRASS The ornamental *Miscanthus sacchariflorus* reaches 10 ft (3 m) and is sometimes sold as a hedging plant. Cut down the dead stems in late winter, and new growth will make a hedge by summer.

QUICK-FIX COLOR Add ravishing color to a screen by letting the long, flowering shoots of nasturtium (*Tropaeolum majus*) trail over a hedge. Other suitable choices to blend with different color schemes include sweet peas and morning glory.

IVY AS A HEDGE Cover lengths of a low trellis or wire netting with English ivy (*Hedera helix*) to form a vigorous green hedge that needs no clipping until the trailing stems travel too far. Ivy cuttings taken from pot-grown specimens are an economical way to plant a trellis.

white roses, where the combination of color and scent is a pleasure. 'Hidcote' and 'Munstead' are the most common varieties. Trim lightly from the outset to keep plants compact. There are also white- and pink-flowered lavenders.

- Use roses as a low hedge; there are many dwarf varieties that you can choose from.
- *Brachyglottis* 'Sunshine,' grown for its attractive gray leaves, makes a tough little evergreen hedge.
- Lavender cotton (*Santolina*) has silvery foliage that tolerates regular clipping. It enjoys a site in the sun.
- Sage, an aromatic sun-lover, comes in gold-splashed or purple-leaf forms as well as in gray-green.
- Hyssop, also an aromatic herb, has deep-green leaves and small blue flowers in summer, which you can leave or clip off for more formality.
- In shade, dwarf boxwood, neat and evergreen, is the best choice.

Ways to Combat Drought

If all goes according to plan, your hedge will be a long-term boundary of beauty and utility. But things can go wrong.

In very dry conditions hedges suffer as much as any other plant. As a preventive measure, mulch with mushroom compost, garden compost, manure, or other organic matter to help conserve moisture and improve the soil.

If individual plants in a young hedge die of drought, replace them in autumn. First study the soil to determine the reason for failure and improve the soil to foster good growth. Give the replacement plants every opportunity to thrive, with well-prepared soil and plenty of water. Unlike the original plants, they have to compete with strong root systems from the existing hedge. Cut away some branches of adjacent plants to let light and water reach the replacements.

Moving a Hedge

It is sometimes necessary to move large plants, when the line of a hedge has to be shifted or a gate or path is to be altered.

Prepare the root system of the plants a year in advance. Cut the main roots to encourage new fibrous roots to form. Make the cuts when the plant is dormant, cutting down on both sides of the hedge with a spade and then removing a trench of soil so that you can cut under the plants and sever at least some of the main roots. Mix compost with the soil and replace it, watering well and firming.

The following autumn the new site should be well prepared and ready to receive the plants. Have a large sheet handy to help move the large rootballs. Digging up the plant should reveal some new roots in the enriched compost where the soil was dug the previous year. Cut back branches where necessary to disentangle them.

Rock the plant to one side in the trench, tuck the sheet under it, then pull the plant back again; unfold the sheet and drag or lift the plant without disturbing the roots too much. Check that the receiving hole is the correct size and depth

SAFETY FIRST

SAFE TRIMMING

GOGGLES AND GLOVES are vital when you use a power tool on a hedge. Without them you risk cutting your hands and having bits of hedge clipping fly into your eyes. A mask prevents you from inhaling dust, and ear plugs muffle the noise. Some manufacturers sell all four items in a single safety package.

TO THE RESCUE

SAVING A BROKEN HEDGE

THE WORST DAMAGE to a hedge usually occurs if a traffic accident causes it to be broken at ground level. It is rare that any plants are killed altogether; if cut back, they often sprout again quite quickly. Water in a general fertilizer, put in temporary netting for security, and trim adjacent plants to let light and air reach the new shoots. Then let the old and new blend.

MIXED HEDGE Combine different shrubs for an informal boundary in a country setting. Two dogwoods, *Cornus alba* 'Elegantissima' and 'Westonbirt,' give winter interest with red stems and remnants of autumn foliage.

before putting the plant in position. Carefully work the soil among the roots, lining the plant up with the existing hedge. Firm the soil as you plant and water well. Trim the plant as necessary. Support tall plants with stakes or guy wires for the first season to prevent wind damage. Keep the soil moist.

REPAIRING SNOW DAMAGE

Heavy snow causes damage when it is left lying on top of a flat hedge. The weight eventually becomes so great that the hedge splays open or falls to one side.

Take the damage as a warning that you have let the hedge reach too great a height too quickly. It is best to cut off the damaged section with a saw and loppers and allow it to regrow, regularly clipping back to promote bushy growth.

If conifer hedges splay apart, wire them together, as they will not regrow from hard-pruned branches. Remove the center stems to achieve a narrower profile and allow for fresh growth on the outside and a more stable shape.

Apart from rare problems, the pleasure of all boundaries — living ones in particular — is that they improve with age. As hedging plants mature, the screen becomes denser. What starts out as a few stick-like saplings becomes an integral and creative part of the garden design.

ROSES AROUND THE GARDEN GATE The arching growth of *Rosa* 'Complicata' makes a thorny hedge that will reach at least head height. The cupped flowers are slightly fragrant and appear in profusion in midsummer.

The Lay
of the Land

Some of the most inventive and exciting gardens are made on the most challenging of sites. Your garden may have steep slopes, an unpromising exposure, too much shade — or simply be a featureless flat rectangle — but there are many imaginative solutions. You can introduce steps, terracing, a rock garden, raised beds, or sculpted mounds; less energetic measures will let the plants themselves do the work, perhaps with tall growers creating those missing contours or roses and clematis scrambling over grassy banks.

A creamy burnet rose with prickly branches grows wild in a seemingly inhospitable coastal region.

IN SYMPATHY WITH THE SURROUNDINGS Make the most of a sloping site to create changes of level that add character. Choose plants that, if not native, are in tune with what grows wild locally.

SUITING GARDEN TO SITE

ONE OF THE HARDEST TASKS for any gardener is to pause from cultivating plants long enough to take stock of the land they grow on. Even with a new garden the temptation is to buy plants immediately and set them out. But a garden is about more than growing a collection of plants. The longer you take to determine what the site has to offer and what plants will establish themselves best, the more harmonious the result is, and ultimately the more satisfying.

Such restraint is the equivalent of living with a minimum of furnishings until you decide what will suit you and suit the room, rather than buying odd chairs and a table, then a sofa and a lamp, and finally having some curtains made to match. A room based on impulse buys seldom works as a visual entity, while one in which every piece of furniture fits into a strong scheme does. The same applies to the garden.

PLANNING AHEAD

Resolve what it is that you want from your garden tomorrow, next year, and five years on. Look even farther ahead if you have a large piece of ground to plan and plant, and if you intend to grow trees.

The growing garden represents a complex process of development. As it matures, so your needs, and even your tastes, may alter. Your garden requires well-thought-out management and some general principles or rules for its development to make it work.

In creating a garden, there are layers of considerations that, taken in proper sequence, help you to achieve your ambition. Things go wrong when you break or confuse the sequence.

What your own particular garden is for — the roles you require of it — comes first. Choosing specific plants comes last. In the middle comes the all-important accommodation between you and what nature decrees. What the soil is like, which way the garden faces, whether it is exposed or sheltered, and whether the site is level or sloping are crucial to your plans. You can put money and effort into changing them, but for a garden that thrives and is easier to maintain you will do far better to recognize and work with the characteristics of the land.

GETTING TO KNOW THE SOIL

◆

THE SOIL IN YOUR GARDEN is the end product of a particular climate — rain, wind, heat, and cold that have worked upon rock over many millions of years. Whatever type of garden you ultimately achieve, you are dependent upon the soil. The best idea for your garden is to fall in with nature and follow its clues as to what you should grow.

WHERE SOIL COMES FROM

Wherever you live, the soil has had a long and complicated history, and so has the Earth's structure beneath it. What has been left over time is a remarkable diversity of ages and types of rock.

Our mountains and highlands are often piles of the hardest rock, but softer rock appears in elevations too. Areas of limestone are deposits carried from ancient sea or lake beds and made up of the shells of myriad sea creatures. Deposits of clay, boulders, and gravel — drift ma-

COUNTRYSIDE PLANTS Wild roses (*Rosa* spp.) are found on soils as diverse as clay, loam, and sand. Their generous flowering without any gardener's help indicates that these "species roses" are trouble-free choices for the garden.

terials as they are called — were carried far from their original bedrock and became the lowland landscapes.

Rain, frost, and heat broke down the parent rocks into particles of various grades known as sands, silts, or clay in which plants eventually grew — and died. The decomposing plants added organic matter to the rock particles, water and air clung to the organic matter, and the whole created a layer of soil on the surface

of the land. The more plants grew, the greater the amount of plant debris (humus) and the thicker the soil layer.

The types of plant that grew depended on soil and climate. Temperate forest covered most of eastern North America; this was replaced by boreal forest in the colder north and by grassland to the west. Only in the last few centuries has man changed this with logging, irrigation, and enclosure of land for graz-

BRINGING NATURE INTO THE GARDEN Hybridized forms of species roses share the robust growth of their native cousins, but have been bred to give an even greater profusion of larger flowers. Make gardening easier by choosing shrubs and perennials that thrive in your soil of their own accord.

TESTING FOR SOIL TYPE

To TREAT YOUR SOIL successfully, it is crucial to know what type it is. Testing its pH tells you whether the soil is alkaline (chalk or limestone), neutral, or acid (some loams, sand, or peat).

Soil-testing kits are widely available. Fill the small container with soil from your garden and add a capsule and water or the solution from the kit. By matching the color that the liquid turns against a chart you can see whether your soil is acid (orange), alkaline (dark green), or somewhere in between. Test soil from different parts of the garden because the pH can vary even over a short distance.

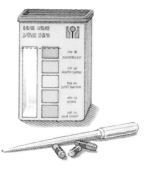

FLOWERY GLADE A walk through woods in spring illustrates the ease with which bulbs will spread. Scatter a few native bulbs in your garden and plant them where they fall. In a few years you will have a carpet of color.

ing. Each region developed its own character because of the nature of its underlying rock. In some areas the rock was suitable for building, and the color and style of the buildings arose from it. Where the rock was not suitable, brick and timber were used, giving a quite different look from stone areas.

The color and consistency of the soil, too, varied according to the rock that it originated from. Particular plant associations developed on different soils, emphasizing the character already established by local building traditions. It is only comparatively recently that building materials, crops, and garden plants have lost their strong local ties.

BEFORE YOU PLANT

Start your garden by studying what sort of vegetation is native to your area. This will keep you from making costly mis-

RUSSET WOODLAND Beech (*Fagus sylvatica*) can succeed in acid soils as well as alkaline; it thrives in all but heavy, wet soils. Beech makes a good hedge, or you can grow a weeping or colored variety as a specimen tree.

HOW TO TREAT YOUR SOIL

SOIL TYPE	PROBLEMS	SOLUTIONS
Clay soil	Difficult to cultivate, cold and heavy in winter, dry and cracked in summer	• Add well-rotted organic matter to improve drainage, aeration, and root penetration. It also feeds the soil and makes it easier to work. • Grow green manures such as field beans, white clover, mustard, winter rye, or winter barley. They aerate the soil, remove excess water, and protect the soil from compaction. Dug in, they increase humus. • Add mulches to protect the structure of the soil, to conserve moisture, and to prevent drying and cracking. They also help to keep soil warm in winter. • Improve drainage by double digging, breaking up compacted layers with an iron bar, adding gypsum at the manufacturer's recommended rate, introducing raised beds, or digging a drain.
Sandy soil	In summer suffers from drought; in heavy rain susceptible to erosion and loss of valuable nutrients	• Add organic matter to feed the soil, to help retain nutrients and water, and to improve structure. • Grow any plants to prevent leaching of nutrients from the soil and erosion. • Grow green manures such as alfalfa, buckwheat, crimson clover, phacelia, annual ryegrass, white lupine, and winter vetch to protect the soil. Dig them in to enrich the soil. • Add mulches to reduce drying and to prevent the washing away of nutrients. • Add lime if your sandy soil has become acid, but apply with caution.
Peaty soil	May become waterlogged	• Construct raised beds to improve the drainage. • Grow green manures such as field beans, white clover, mustard, phacelia, and winter rye to reduce waterlogging. • Add lime with caution if soil is acid. • Improve soil drainage by adding grit at two bucketfuls per square yard or meter, or by digging a drain.
Chalk and limestone soils	Thin, dry, alkaline; lacks organic matter	• Construct raised beds to increase the depth of topsoil. • Grow green manures such as alfalfa, buckwheat, winter vetch, winter barley, and phacelia to prevent leaching in deep beds and to add nutrients. • Add mulches to retain water, to prevent leaching in winter, and to protect the soils from rain.

takes and help you plan a garden that enhances the natural beauty of the site. After all, one reason you live in an area is that you like its appearance. On the piece of land you own you have the opportunity to maintain the existing look, so that your gardening seems at home in its site and does not impose something alien upon the land.

Apart from the pleasure of creating such a harmonious garden, there are practical benefits too. Lower maintenance is the major one; plants at home in the site need far less care than strangers. Go with the nature of your land and you make life easier. Fight it and you double the work. This is true whatever the size of your garden.

The land you work is the key to the garden you can devise — not only in terms of what will grow but also in its exposure and contours. Abrupt changes of level or a damp corner may seem insuperable challenges, but take heart from the fact that no matter how bad you think your soil is, it does naturally grow something.

WHAT GROWS ON YOUR SOIL?

In the wild, nature does not dig, but lets the canopy of trees and the vegetation beneath take generations to develop. Nature abhors a void in its green carpet and tries to fill it up as soon as possible, whether in the wild or in a garden.

What grow first after soil has been disturbed or cleared, as for example on a building plot, are annual weeds. Their growth is encouraged by soil cultivation. If you leave this first growth alone, a generation of native perennials will emerge and gradually take over. After the perennials come shrubs and eventually trees, developing all the way up to forest vegetation. The natural state of much of the countryside before the land was disturbed can reestablish itself.

Each soil and situation, no matter how limy, how clay, or how acid, originally had its own range of plants. This range, from annual to forest tree, is called a plant sequence. It helps if you know what your area's natural sequence would have been, but you are not bound to copy it in

EASY COVER FOR SLOPES

Clothing a bank with plants prevents soil erosion in the garden as efficiently as in the wild. Choose perennials and evergreens that need little care.

• *Cotoneaster dammeri*: prostrate evergreen shrub with dark green, glossy leaves, white flowers in June, and red berries in fall.

• St.-John's-wort (*Hypericum calycinum*): shrubby carpeter with bright green leaves, and golden flowers from June to September.

• *Rosa* 'Paulii': prickly thicket-forming shrub rose that roots as it spreads, with white fragrant flowers all summer.

• *Clematis heracleifolia*: sprawling growth bears purple-blue tubular flowers in August and September.

• Dead nettle (*Lamium maculatum* 'Beacon Silver'): mid-green leaves with overlay of silver, and pinkish-purple flowers in May.

• *Pachysandra terminalis*: hardy evergreen for shade, with rich green leaves and tiny white flowers in April.

• Lesser periwinkle (*Vinca minor* 'Aureovariegata'): unlimited spread of low growth with scattering of blue flowers all summer and yellow rims to the leaves.

• Blue fescue (*Festuca glauca*): ornamental grass for sunny banks with bristly blue-gray leaves, and little purple-gray flower spikes in summer.

• Blood-red cranesbill geranium (*Geranium sanguineum*): deeply lobed leaves with crimson flowers all summer. 'Album' has white flowers.

• Lungwort (*Pulmonaria officinalis*): shade-lover with large, white-spotted leaves, and clusters of pink and blue flowers in spring.

HEATH AND MOORLAND Damp, acid soil on a scrubby moor provides ideal conditions for heath and heather. In other situations, look for rhododendrons that have spread from tended land into the wild as indicators of soil acidity.

the garden. It makes a valuable yardstick, however, against which to check whether or not a plant is likely to settle comfortably where you want to put it.

LOOKING AT LOCAL PLANTS

Make your own survey of what grows naturally in your locality. Walk in local woods, study the open spaces, whether they are conservation areas or simply patches of waste ground. Any ground that is left virtually untended will give you clues about which plants like the local soil.

There might be neglected graveyards, unkempt corners of fields, a riverside wetland, and sites that have waited years for some new road or building project. Railway embankments are often wonderful wildlife habitats, where trees and smaller plants are left undisturbed over a length of time.

For a garden receiving full light, use the open spaces as your guide, and for a shady, tree-lined garden pay more heed to the wooded areas. A local field guide (usually available in a public library) helps with identifying the plants. Never take plants from the wild; take some close-up photographs instead for identifying plants later. It is surprising how many of their botanical names you will recognize as being similar to those of plants in your own garden.

Assess your site, particularly its soil, and keep at the back of your mind the range of plants that would grow naturally upon it. Stay close to this range and build up a collection of plants that grows with least fuss. You can veer either side of this, but knowing the list of what is suitable helps control impulsive buying of tempting exotics that will never like your site and will require a good deal of time and care to make them grow.

ACID OR ALKALINE?

Soil analysis is a basic requirement for making the right choices of what to grow. Uncultivated ground in your area is a good guide but when there is little of it use a soil-testing kit. A test also takes account of any treatment that may have altered the soil to some degree.

What greatly affects your soil is its acidity or alkalinity. Limestone in a soil creates alkalinity. The degree of alkalinity varies from limestone soil, which has the highest count, through "normal" soil

CLINGING TO A SLOPE Even the seemingly hostile environment of a shady rock face is home to plants such as ferns and primroses, which adapt well to damp or craggy gardens. Hybrid forms of *Primula* come in colors other than yellow. Cowslips, a meadow flower, prefer sunnier sites.

ACID SOIL IN THE GARDEN Conifers and heaths (*Erica* spp.) flourish in a garden with naturally acidic conditions. The fleece-flower (*Polygonum affine*) in the foreground thrives in any soil as long as it is moist.

having some lime, to soils totally free of lime, known as acid soils. A neutral soil is in the middle of this scale and gives a reading of pH 7 on a soil-testing gauge. Anything above is limy, while anything below gets progressively more acid. A good reading for most plants is pH 6.5.

Extreme acidity or alkalinity in a soil restricts the range of plants that grow, but helps to create the strongest regional idiom. Most plants, however, grow in most soils, apart from the extremes. While it is possible to adjust a soil, this entails arduous work — and the work may be wasted, for the roots may eventually penetrate the unaltered layer beneath.

Far better than "correcting" an alkaline soil for growing acid-loving plants such as azaleas and rhododendrons is to mix soil that is suitable for acid-lovers (add a generous dose of peat) and grow them in pots and tubs. Note that watering has to be of collected rainwater only, as tap water in limy areas will be alkaline and will harm acid-loving plants.

SAND OR CLAY?

Other factors such as poor drainage or cold are just as likely to inhibit growth as pH value. The soil's physical condition is important. The size of grain your soil is composed of depends on the source below ground. A coarse-grained soil is usually sand, and often acid too. The finest grained soil is clay or silt. The grains stick together when wet in a way coarse grains never do. The result is that clay soil drains badly and is heavy to work. As it is close-textured, it contains little air and remains cold in spring.

Sandy soil drains freely, and its open texture contains plenty of air, so it warms up quickly. Sand is light to work, but often poor because all the nutrients as well as water drain through it quickly.

HOW TO IMPROVE
THE SOIL STRUCTURE

A plant obtains nutrients in soluble or liquid form from the "skin" of moisture around each grain of soil. In a light soil your task is to hold those nutrients around the plant; in clay you need to open the soil to let in air between the grains and help the plant put down its roots. In both light and heavy soils, organic matter improves the structure.

When you have a garden on a newly developed site, dig in some form of organic matter at an early stage. The decaying strands of vegetation in manure or compost bind a light sandy soil and push

BEST PLANTS

SUITED TO ALKALINE SOIL

There are plants of all types and sizes that thrive in limy soil.

• Judas-tree (*Cercis siliquastrum*): small, deciduous tree with pink flowers in spring, heart-shaped leaves and dark red pods in late summer.

• Juniper (*Juniperus* × *media* 'Pfitzeriana Aurea'): low, spreading conifer with golden-tipped foliage.

• Sargent crab apple (*Malus sargentii*): spreading small tree with white spring flowers and deep red fruits in fall.

• *Rosa rugosa*: vigorous rose with single purple-red flowers followed by large flask-shaped red hips.

• *Ceanothus impressus*: evergreen bush with deep blue flowers in spring and small crinkled dark green leaves.

• *Iris variegata*: bearded yellow iris with purple veining on the lower petals.

• Scabious (*Scabiosa caucasica* 'Clive Greaves'): perennial with summer-long violet-blue flowers with centers like pincushions.

• Maiden pink (*Dianthus deltoides*): ground-hugging evergreen with white or pink flowers in summer; good for rock gardens or banks.

• *Lavatera trimestris* 'Silver Cup': tall annual with trumpet-shaped, veined pink flowers from summer to autumn.

• *Triteleia laxa*: bulb with purple-blue flowers in early summer.

• *Cyclamen hederifolium*: spurred, pink flowers in fall and ivy-shaped leaves with silver-green patterns.

ĐECIDUOUS WOODLAND Under the dappled shade of leaf-shedding trees, the spring-blooming wood anemone (*Anemone nemorosa*) carpets the ground. In the garden, plant this delightful perennial in part shade or sun.

NATURAL BEAUTY ON THE FRINGES Where weed-killers miss field edges, wildflowers spring up even when near urban areas. Corn chamomile (*Anthemis arvensis*) and poppies (*Papaver rhoeas*) are common in the wild, so you can count on success when you plant garden varieties.

apart the close, often waterlogged, grains of a clay one. Organic matter also provides minerals to feed the soil. It enriches alkaline soils, which commonly are too porous to retain nutrients without regular and generous additions of humus. There may be a complex pattern of sublayers, where a hard layer of lime overlies clay, or gravel overlies the lime. But still the best treatment you can give is to work in plenty of well-rotted organic matter.

The darker the color of a soil, the richer it is in organic matter. Dark soil is also warmer than light, for it absorbs more heat from the sun. A warmer soil makes for earlier development of plants in spring.

A handful of soil should be crumbly and dark, and it should smell fresh. By the continued addition of organic matter to a soil over a long period you can bring even the poorest soil up to good fertility

SOUTHWEST SOIL

Many parts of the American Southwest, especially those regions with an arid climate, have soils that require special management. Commonly, these soils are alkaline, often strongly so, and they tend to be very low in organic content. Often, too, these soils are salty — rarely does enough rain or snow fall in these areas to wash the soil clean. In areas with abundant water, the classic remedy for a salty soil is to flood the garden area repeatedly, but that of course is not possible where water is precious and scarce. Besides, the water that comes from the tap in such areas is often salty, too, so that irrigation only aggravates the soil poisoning.

An added difficulty in many arid regions is the presence of "caliche." This is, indirectly, a product of drought. When rain or snow does fall in these areas, the meager ration of water soaks only a short way down into the ground before evaporation off the soil surface draws the moisture back up. As it moves downward, the water carries dissolved lime with it; when it moves back upward, it leaves the lime (calcium carbonate) behind. Over the years this collects into a grayish layer that can be as hard and impenetrable as concrete. By barring the downward growth of roots, that layer prevents garden plantings from tapping into reservoirs of moisture lurking deep underground, and it makes the garden extra vulnerable to drought.

One treatment for caliche is to break

FAVORITES FROM THE WILD Some popular garden plants such as the blue meadow geranium (*Geranium pratense*) are wildflowers that have preserved a simple, natural charm. The yellow common St.-John's-wort (*Hypericum perforatum*) likes sunny, well-drained soil.

SECRET GARDEN Railway sidings provide a haven of undisturbed ground for wildflowers. Foxglove (*Digitalis*) and broom (*Cytisus*) typically grow on sand but tolerate lime and so do equally well in chalky, alkaline soil.

up the buried layer with a pick, but this may involve tremendous labor. An alternative is to garden in raised beds set over the caliche. The soil inside the beds is enriched with generous amounts of organic matter and treated with sulfur to reduce the pH if that is excessively alkaline. With the addition of a drip irrigation system, a nearly ideal environment for plant growth is created.

THE SCOPE OF SAND

Sandy soil, often acidic, is easy to work, but tends to be dry and nutrient poor. This makes it inhospitable to many traditional garden plants, but ideal for duneland natives and for plants that require good drainage.

Wild-type rugosa roses (*Rosa rugosa*), often found on beaches, thrive in sandy soils. Many ornamental grasses also flourish on sandy soils, and most rock plants thrive in sandy soils too if the location is cool. Mountain ashes, birches, and pines are all trees that tend to do well on sandy soils.

PRODUCTIVE CLAY

Gardening on clay is heavy work, but the soil can be extremely productive. In the wild, plenty grows upon it even though no one digs it. Clay soil can be acid or alkaline or somewhere between, so its vegetation includes the plants from limy and sandy soils. A further range of plants thrives since the soil can be waterlogged at certain times of the year and may be in woodland shade.

Many hardwood trees such as ashes (*Fraxinus* spp.), oaks (*Quercus* spp.), and maples (*Acer* spp.) do well in clay soils if it is not too dense. Plants that require good drainage (most spring bulbs, for example, many of the western natives, and virtually all rock and alpine plants) find clay a trial unless it has been well dug and heavily amended with gypsum or coarse sand and organic matter. Once clay has been treated in this fashion, its natural richness makes it excellent for most roses and perennial flowers.

Plants such as willows that relish moist soils, however, generally thrive in poorly drained clays.

PUTTING PLANS INTO ACTION

◆

MOST GARDEN EXPERTS now recommend that a new garden should be in close harmony with its setting. This gentle approach to a garden's design contrasts with the traditional style of clearing, draining, and deep digging the land. That produced magnificent results in many cases, but only at tremendous cost to the environment. Maintaining such a garden also demanded tremendous amounts of labor.

DRAWING ON A COMMON HERITAGE

The kind of garden desired in years past was formal in layout, with statues of Greek, French, or Roman origin, and its chief merit in the owner's eyes — even above that of its layout — was the number of alien plants displayed in it. Imported species spoke of knowledge, travel, and wealth, as well as of a love of plants. The garden was protected by hedges, with the location all but blotted out in an attempt to realize a dream in which mundane considerations were not allowed to fetter the imagination.

The gardens of this sort that still survive, usually as parks, are frequently period pieces of great beauty. They recall an age when gardens were maintained by staff for owners, often highly informed owners who vied with each other for supremacy in the size of their rhododendron collection, their camellias, or the conifers in their pinetum. But a garden of this kind is not a practical proposition for most garden owners today.

A SHIFT IN INTENTION

During the last century, there has been a shift in thinking about the nature of gardens. The wisdom of planning a garden based on exotic species rather than native plants is questioned.

Not just the wisdom but the aesthetic and environmental value of such gardens is doubted by modern designers and a growing number of garden owners. For that style of garden and the wide range of foreign plants it contains is patently at odds not just with the landscape in which it sits, but with native flora and fauna. It entails suppressing the natural in layout and plant material and replacing it with an unnatural form. In an age when a

SEASIDE SURVIVORS A walk along the clifftops reveals the rich variety of plants that cope with the exacting conditions. Pink thrift, oxeye daisies, yellow kidney vetch, and wild carrot hug the slope, flowering in the face of salt breezes on this exposed headland.

STEEP-SIDED PLANTING Take advantage of dramatic changes of level to grow plants such as tumbling yellow roses (*Rosa banksiae* 'Lutea') that relish a wall-top position. Tuck in geraniums for a dash of summery pink.

COASTAL GARDEN Thrift (*Armeria maritima*) rises to the challenge of an exposed seaside site. More familiar in a rock garden or border front, its grassy cushions of leaves and dense flowers also suit a wilder part of the garden.

TEMPORARY TERRACING

WALLS, PATHS, AND PAVING must be strongly constructed to stay sound. This can be costly, and it is better to spread the work over a few seasons than have a quick job poorly done. Paths and paving have to take priority, but you can make temporary low walls to create level areas on a slight slope.

Cut a slit in the slope, taking out the soil from the bottom to make level ground. Use a row of peat bales as the wall, securing them with short stakes driven in along the front. Level the upper surface with the soil taken from the lower level.

Nasturtiums, lobelia, aubrietia, and other trailers cover the wall until the permanent one is built — and the bales' contents dress the soil. Landscape ties — or, for shallow terracings, cinder blocks — are alternatives to peat bales.

more easygoing style of living prevails, it is in keeping that a more natural attitude to gardening should win favor.

An earthier approach to the garden did exist in former times alongside the artificial styles imposed by the well-to-do. Cottage-dwellers' employment, building materials, and house style continued for generation after generation to come di-rectly from the immediately surrounding land. Local work and materials were the only practical possibilities.

The garden too was largely dictated by practical demands, with vegetables and herbs growing next to fruit trees, and flow-ers barely removed from the wild. Gardens such as this rarely survive now, even in rural areas, and are a curiosity where they do. But the traditional cottage plots have more relevance to the current thinking on gardens than the grand aristocratic layouts. Their smaller size is similar to the extent of average modern plots.

BLENDING HARD AND SOFT

Apart from establishing a broad theme of planting based upon your soil, you can link your garden to its locality by choos-ing appropriate hard materials. Look at old homes in the area to see what material has been used to build the fence, the steps, and the path and its edging. If the stone or brick used is now expensive, use just a little of it as insets among cheaper material that is in sympathy with your region. If there are no old homes in the areas try an old churchyard. One ap-proach is to decide what would definitely not be right and then work backward by elimination.

The larger your site the more influ-ence the region should have upon your garden. In a smaller garden you can link the hard materials back to the house itself, choosing them to match or harmo-nize with brick or stone, with the color-ing of walls, or with the slates or shingles on the roof. These are the colors and textures to consider for a terrace, for steps, for path edgings, and driveway surfaces. But before you design in detail, pause to think a moment longer. A garden lasts for a long time, and it is best to get the look of it correct from the start. Although you can change a garden, you can do so only at a cost.

ASSESSING THE SITE

One way to cut the initial cost, especially in terms of labor, is to pay heed to what the site dictates. Must the site really be level, or will the garden be better with some dips and rises? If the site is already level, can you introduce some contours with skillful planting rather than embarking on major earth-moving? Which parts receive the most sun? Where does the prevailing wind strike?

Draw a plan of the garden, note what is there already, such as sheds and trees, and influences from outside the garden such as sun and wind. Include on your plan the views into and out of the site. Often with a light trim of a hedge you can enjoy a neighbor's pear tree in flower or catch a glimpse of a church spire.

SKILLFUL USE OF WIND FILTERS

Removing a gloomy conifer opens up a site and lets sunlight into it, completely transforming the feel of the place. Similarly, bold clipping can improve Leyland cypress planted as a high hedge. Often, evergreen hedges have been planted to keep out the wind, but the necessary screen has now become far too high and can be reduced in its height by half. But bear in mind that opening up an outward view may bring in gales, particularly if you live in an exposed position or near the sea. Before cutting anything down, ask yourself why it was planted.

Wind can be reduced by filtering it. Some standard trees with a light head

---

SAFETY FIRST

THE RIGHT SITE FOR A TREE

BEFORE PLANTING A TREE be sure that you know its ultimate height and spread, below ground as well as above. Choose a site where the tree will not damage underground pipes and cables or get caught in overhead wires. Do not plant trees too near the house, especially in clay soils. Apart from shading the windows, some trees, especially poplars (*Populus*) and willows (*Salix*), have strong, far-reaching roots that can damage drains and a building's foundation.

FROM BARE PLOT TO BEAUTY

A blank plot can look unpromising, but starting from scratch gives you the chance to work with the site and the soil and put your imprint on the garden.

TAKE YOUR TIME in assessing the site at different times of day and in different weather conditions; consider what to hide and what to enhance — a few plants work wonders. Then list your priorities.

After seeding in a lawn, the first task is to soften the harsh lines of raw masonry. Balanced groupings of dwarf conifers and broad-leaf evergreen shrubs should be planted to mask the foundation; climbers such as the hardy Boston ivy are superb for tempering the blankness of new brick walls.

The next task is to block the open view to the house next door. A board fence and pyracantha hedge on one side of the driveway and, at the other, two pyramidal hornbeams save the situation.

Virtually the whole garden is at the front of the house, looking straight onto the street, so the next priority is to shut out the traffic and give some privacy. Fences are quick to put up and mark the boundary, but they need their straight lines softened with plants.

COMPLETING THE CHANGES

After five years' growth, evergreen hebe and eleagnus have made an informal hedge, with swaths of caryopteris at the front. On the flat site, the higher rim of shrubs and the lower plants within add contours. The sweeping curve of the border lends movement to the otherwise static square layout.

The dull northwesterly corner turns into a shower of gold when the leaves of the fast-growing black locusts flutter in the breeze. As the wind is funneled down the road from the north, the taller plants in the deep border serve as a filter for wind as well as noise.

The swoop of the lawn is reflected in a circular bed, a later addition that adds color near the house with cluster-flowered (floribunda) roses that bloom all summer and into fall.

BLANK CANVAS When taking on a new site, you can create the garden you want, rather than adapting someone else's ideas.

Enhancing the view

The neighboring house is screened by a board fence and a pyracantha hedge, close-clipped near the garage so as not to obstruct the doorway. Farther away it is left to flower.

Blocking traffic noise and pollution

The front-line shrubs are sturdy evergreens, forming a mixed flowering hedge capable of filtering car fumes and muffling street sounds. The more the hedge matures, the better it screens.

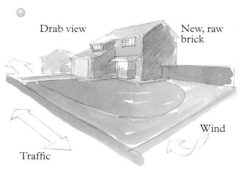

PINPOINTING DRAWBACKS List the plot's flaws and decide what to do about them. Give these solutions priority before fine-tuning details.

Making the most of the sun

The house and garden face east, so morning sun is plentiful. By the afternoon, the house casts shade over much of the garden. But keeping the style as open as possible, with no high evergreens to cast oppressive shadows, makes the garden seem light and airy.

Softening new bricks

Self-clinging climbers such as ivy quickly brighten a blank expanse of wall. Contrary to popular opinion, they do not harm the brickwork — as long as it is sound, they protect it from the elements.

Reducing the wind

The dense, shrubby border filters chilly breezes so that people and plants alike enjoy the sheltered conditions.

1. *Pyracantha atalantioides* 'Aurea'
2. Hornbeam (*Carpinus betulus* 'Fastigiata')
3. Boston ivy (*Parthenocissus tricuspidata* 'Veitchii')
4. Rose (*Rosa* 'Allgold')
5. Persian ivy (*Hedera colchica* 'Dentata Variegata')
6. Black locust (*Robinia pseudoacacia* 'Frisia')
7. *Hebe* 'Midsummer Beauty'
8. *Caryopteris × clandonensis* 'Kew Blue'
9. *Elaeagnus × ebbingei* 'Limelight'
10. *Hydrangea arborescens* 'Grandiflora'
11. Portugal laurel (*Prunus lusitanica*)

PLANTS FOR DAMP SITUATIONS *Ajuga reptans* grows most vigorously in wet ground, so add it to your plant list if you need ground cover to clothe an awkward, boggy corner. Some species are evergreen, others semi-evergreen, and all are fully hardy and tolerate sun or shady conditions.

WINTER CHEER Many apparently wild plants have naturalized from gardens. They include the common snowdrop (*Galanthus nivalis*) and winter aconite (*Eranthis hyemalis*), two welcome signs of the new growing season.

near the house — European birches, for example — filter the wind as efficiently as a tall hedge planted a distance from it. In smaller town gardens and walled gardens, you often have to cope with a blast of air that whisks around a corner or between two properties; it may become a vortex when trapped in an enclosed space. Such wind tunnels need to be blocked, either by planting or, even better, by a wall or fence.

The vortex effect of the walled enclosure is harder to deal with. You cannot apply the best remedy, which is a shelter belt outside the enclosure to divert the wind over the top of the garden. A tall line of open plants to lift and filter as well is some help. If you are fortunate, a neighbor will grow such a belt, and this will be much more help. Many small urban spaces are sheltered by neighboring properties as well as their trees.

IMPROVING AN URBAN GARDEN SITE

In built-up areas, you can be troubled by views into your garden. A solid fence or hedge is one way of providing privacy, but an alternative is to position plants strategically as baffles within the site. This gives a feeling of greater space than an extensive barrier. Use baffles to block out headlights or to muffle traffic noise if you live on a corner.

Think very carefully about getting more light into the garden. By cutting down taller, older vegetation you allow more sun into your garden. But consider first where newly admitted sunlight will fall and whether it will be the right place for the layout that you are planning.

If you live in a town and your garden is surrounded by tall buildings, it can be sunny and sheltered in summer but very dark in winter when the sun never rises above your skyline.

Choose the plants with this firmly in mind; they must be tolerant of shade and unspoiled by full sun. If this will rule out too many plants you long to have, create permanent plantings of evergreens to suit the winter conditions and enliven the summer scene with pots and troughs of sun-loving plants. This is the plan to follow also in suburban areas where trees in a neighboring garden blot out the low winter sun.

SUIT THE PLANTS TO THE SUN

The ideal garden has plenty of sun and little wind, but whether it is morning, noon, or evening sun affects how you use your garden, where you like to sit, and which plants you grow. Many plants like sun all day long, from sunrise in the east to sunset in the west. Most herbs, flowering shrubs, and perennials require sun; very often, bright flower color is an indication of the need for ample sun.

SAFE AND STYLISH STEPS

All garden steps should be shallow for easy use, with plenty of room from front to back to give firm footing. They need to be soundly constructed, with care to ensure that water drains off — otherwise steps become slippery in freezing weather. Suit the material to the house and the design to your style of garden.

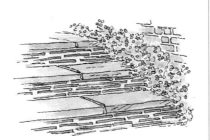

TILE AND STONE

Large tiles cemented together form the risers and stone slabs make stable treads in steps that suit any garden, casual or formal, large or small. Use materials with a slightly roughened, nonslip surface.

RUSTIC STONE

Where there is a local stone, chunky slabs of it fashioned into steps blend naturally with a rural garden. Make sure that the surface of the treads is generous and not too uneven so the steps are easy to negotiate.

LAYERS OF BRICK

For a sophisticated town-garden look, lay bricks side by side over a lower, lengthwise layer. You could also set them in a running bond of alternating layers. Brick steps fit well next to a raised brick bed or retaining wall.

TIMBERS AND GRAVEL

Landscape ties make generously wide steps. Combined with gravel, they form a softer-looking feature than stone or brick steps, especially when edged with plants. This mixture of materials suits a modern, informal layout.

RANDOM PAVING AND BRICK RISERS

Steps can be rounded instead of straight-edged. It is easier to make the curve smooth with random paving or irregular stone slabs of various sizes instead of rectangular tiles. A single layer of brick makes the shallow risers.

PAVING AND CONCRETE

Bring steps out to a point if there is a corner to tuck them in. Stone pavers or concrete slabs are much cheaper than natural stone, especially if you live in an area without a local stone.

TIMBER AND TILES

Treated timber joists are narrower and smoother than landscape ties, giving a sleek rather than rustic appearance. Pair them with handsome tiles, softening the rigid lines with plants at the sides if you wish.

GRASS AND BRICK

Lead onto or from a lawn with springy steps of grass on brick risers. You have to clip with shears, but the effect is decorative. Matching low side walls of brick make a stronger feature of the short flight of steps.

Few sites allow full sun; your house, a neighboring house, or a big tree probably gives partial shade. Nearly all plants can cope with this, as long as they receive some hours of sunlight.

Some plants truly enjoy light shade all day. Shade-loving plants often have large leaves, which give them a greater area to catch light. All plants need some light to convert the nutrients taken from the soil into food. Flowers on shade-loving plants tend to be pale colors, to show up in the shade and attract pollinating insects.

Shade is urgently needed in many exposed new gardens. As well as giving somewhere pleasant to sit, it creates a point of interest and adds texture to the scene. A pool of shade in an otherwise sunny site always attracts the eye.

There is a small range of plants that open their flowers at night and have a fragrance to attract moths. Flowering tobacco and evening primrose work this way and give great pleasure on summer evenings when planted near your garden bench.

COPING WITH POOR DRAINAGE

It is entirely possible that within a single garden you may have both well-drained land and a boggy area. The waterlogged patch may not be in a spot where you want a pond or bog garden, and it may not respond sufficiently to your digging in coarse sand and liberal amounts of moisture-absorbing compost.

The solution could be to install some drainage, but consider carefully before you take on the work. Few gardens need complex systems of drainage. The house itself is probably on a part of the land that is well drained, with a surrounding apron

---

SAFETY FIRST

INSTALL A HANDRAIL

WHERE YOU HAVE a flight of more than three steps or a steeply sloping bank, think about putting up a handrail. The simplest way is to drive a series of posts into the ground and attach a length of rope, securing it to the top of each post. Alternatively, you can buy elegant, ready-made handrails in wrought iron. For steps beside a wall, attach iron rings to the brick or stonework. Thread a stout rope through them, knotting it securely to each ring.

TRANSFORMING A NARROW GARDEN

Many houses in built-up areas have long strips of garden. The key is to break up the length, dividing it into rooms. Turning an existing slope to your advantage helps to achieve this.

WHEN TAKING OVER A PLOT, start by analyzing the site and the features that are already there.

The shade down the left-hand side of this garden is balanced by sun drenching the right. The rectangular shape of the site has straight sides that need to be broken up. Mature trees bring the planting a step forward. All of them can stay except for the dominant conifer near the house, which makes the shadiest part of the garden seem gloomier and sucks up moisture in the nearby soil. A bank slanting a third of the way down suggests a natural break in both style and function.

The owners want a place to sit and relax in the sun, a bit of lawn, and a play area for the children, unified in a straightforward planting scheme — one that avoids fussiness in both looks and maintenance.

CHANGING LEVELS

A hard surface is laid for putting out chaise longues, chairs, and a table. Concrete paving harmonizes with the color of the house. Shade-loving plants jut out from the left while herbs, conveniently near the kitchen, soak up the sun that bathes the area on the right.

A flight of steps is cut across the slope, one of the many diagonal features in the new layout that help to make the shape seem wider and not so long. A solid handrail prevents the children — or anyone else — from falling, and a cupboard built in underneath the top level holds outdoor toys.

With a new level comes a new material — gravel. A gravel area is less formal than paving and breaks up the expanse of grass, providing a neat transition from the hard surface to the soft lawn. The tone of the garden

becomes more casual the farther away it is from the house. Another step down separates the children's "room" from the rest of the lawn. The surrounding trees and shrubs are robust enough to take a few knocks as well as provide playhouses. Tucked away at the end of the garden, the children can run around without disturbing the adults, but the area is in view of a watchful eye from the terrace.

TAILOR-MADE PLANT SCHEME

The planting is designed to need a minimum of care. Ground-covering santolina, rosemary, senecio, meadow geranium, and hostas help to keep the weeds down, and shrubs and small trees need just an annual trim.

The yellow, blue, and gray plan is in sympathy with the yellow-beige of the house and hard surfaces. In June many of the plants are in bloom, but at other times of the year flowers come from viburnums and mahonia. Pyracantha gives fall interest with its vivid red berries, and dogwood's red stems brighten the winter scene. The white-variegated foliage of ivy and silvery senecio is welcome all year, alongside the shimmering bark of European birches.

THE EXISTING PLOT The owners take over a garden that contains the elements they want — paved area, lawn, and space for the children to play — but it looks stark and has little charm.

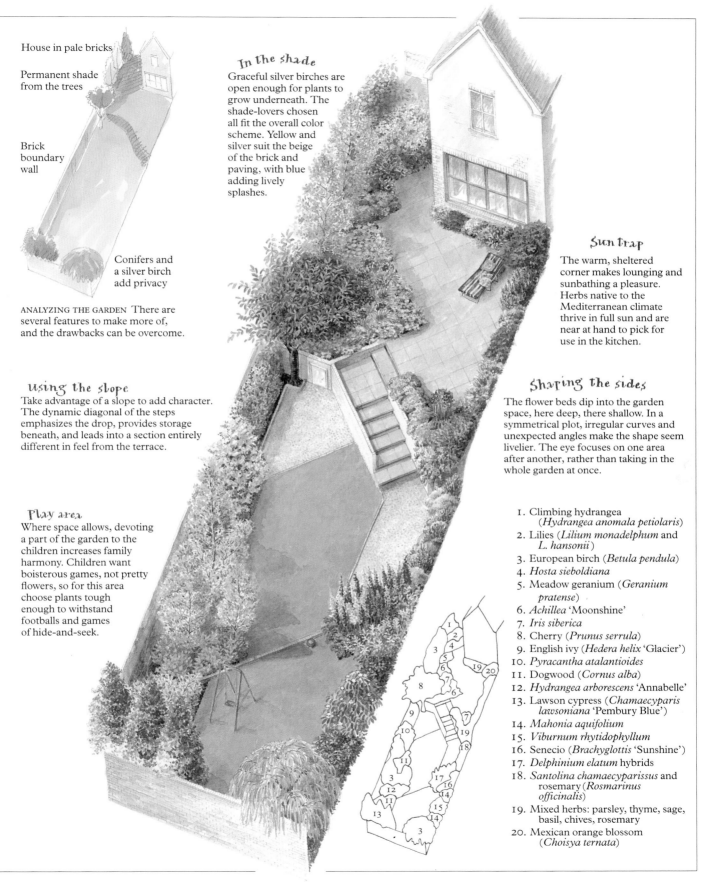

House in pale bricks

Permanent shade from the trees

Brick boundary wall

Conifers and a silver birch add privacy

ANALYZING THE GARDEN There are several features to make more of, and the drawbacks can be overcome.

In the shade

Graceful silver birches are open enough for plants to grow underneath. The shade-lovers chosen all fit the overall color scheme. Yellow and silver suit the beige of the brick and paving, with blue adding lively splashes.

Sun trap

The warm, sheltered corner makes lounging and sunbathing a pleasure. Herbs native to the Mediterranean climate thrive in full sun and are near at hand to pick for use in the kitchen.

Using the slope

Take advantage of a slope to add character. The dynamic diagonal of the steps emphasizes the drop, provides storage beneath, and leads into a section entirely different in feel from the terrace.

Shaping the sides

The flower beds dip into the garden space, here deep, there shallow. In a symmetrical plot, irregular curves and unexpected angles make the shape seem livelier. The eye focuses on one area after another, rather than taking in the whole garden at once.

Play area

Where space allows, devoting a part of the garden to the children increases family harmony. Children want boisterous games, not pretty flowers, so for this area choose plants tough enough to withstand footballs and games of hide-and-seek.

1. Climbing hydrangea (*Hydrangea anomala petiolaris*)
2. Lilies (*Lilium monadelphum* and *L. hansonii*)
3. European birch (*Betula pendula*)
4. *Hosta sieboldiana*
5. Meadow geranium (*Geranium pratense*)
6. *Achillea* 'Moonshine'
7. *Iris siberica*
8. Cherry (*Prunus serrula*)
9. English ivy (*Hedera helix* 'Glacier')
10. *Pyracantha atalantioides*
11. Dogwood (*Cornus alba*)
12. *Hydrangea arborescens* 'Annabelle'
13. Lawson cypress (*Chamaecyparis lawsoniana* 'Pembury Blue')
14. *Mahonia aquifolium*
15. *Viburnum rhytidophyllum*
16. Senecio (*Brachyglottis* 'Sunshine')
17. *Delphinium elatum* hybrids
18. *Santolina chamaecyparissus* and rosemary (*Rosmarinus officinalis*)
19. Mixed herbs: parsley, thyme, sage, basil, chives, rosemary
20. Mexican orange blossom (*Choisya ternata*)

that is also dry even when it is built on low-lying land. There is then the problem of where to drain water to — and draining too well also takes away a plant's natural food, which is held in the water.

SIMPLE DRY WELL SOLUTIONS

Far more necessary than a complicated herringbone pattern of underground drains are one or two dry wells in crucial positions — but they must be at least 16 ft (5 m) from the house. Site a dry well at the trouble spot itself or conduct water to it with a pipe that receives excess water runoff from the trouble spot.

On heavy soil, pick up surface water this way from a terrace, for instance, or at the foot of a change of level such as a bank. Make sure a slight fall in the hard surface leads to a gully that drains into the pipe leading to the dry well. Steps, too, need to throw off water easily, or they will be covered with ice in frosty weather.

A house sitting on a hill gives you more serious problems with levels, for while water flows away from the house on one side, the flow is toward it on the other. You have to decide whether to treat the fall toward the house as one straight fall or as a series of terraces. You must also consider how you are going to catch water runoff at the bottom.

First of all you need a clear and level surround to the house. A gully between it and the sloping land can simply conduct water right and left of the house; half-round piping concealed by gravel will suffice. It is often illegal to lead rain runoff into the main drainage system.

How you treat the bank above the drain depends on its importance. If the driveway has to be on the slope you do not want it too steep. Anything with a gradient steeper than 1 in 3 will be hard

to negotiate in wintry conditions, and the junction with the road needs the gentlest slope. Where the land is very steep, consider laying the driveway in a gentle curve across the site to give greater length, which then allows you to have a shallower gradient.

Terracing beside the driveway gives many attractive possibilities for planting and need not be too much work to maintain. Grow large spreads of a few plants for the best effect. Make more terraces and keep the maximum slope 1 in 3 if the land is light and sandy or it may shift down. Where soil is heavy and sticky, a gradient as steep as 1 in 2 will hold.

PLANTING A GRADIENT

For extra stability grow plants that root as they spread and thus hold the incline. Ivy and periwinkle do this naturally. More decorative plants include the climbing hydrangea (*Hydrangea anomala petiolaris*) and rambler roses whose tips, if pegged down, take root and put out more stems. Ramblers sprawl down or up a bank equally well, and clematis clambers eagerly through them. Grass is another possibility; a fine, low-growing turf that you trim only a couple of times a year serves unless you want trimmed neatness — but this would require more care than ground-cover shrubs.

Some evergreens do not root as they go but spread out horizontally, keeping close to the ground and making excellent cover where the soil does not need to be stabilized. *Juniperus sabina* 'Tamariscifolia' or, for partial rooting, *Cotoneaster dammeri* are among the best.

Terracing is not a task to take on yourself unless the retaining walls are shallow. Any structure more than 3 ft (1 m) high should be checked by a structural engi-

SOFTENING STEPS Dwarf, spreading species such as *Campanula poscharskyana* are ideal for tucking in the crevices around steps and paths. The star-shaped blooms are usually blue — but almost white in the form 'E.H. Frost,' which adorns the stone retaining wall behind these steps.

TO THE RESCUE

DRAINAGE TO A DRY WELL

WHERE WATER LIES on the ground, you can install a dry well. Make it on the spot or, if it is near the house, at least 16 ft (5 m) away. Dig the dry well 3 ft (1 m) square and deep. If it is at a distance from the damp spot, make a V-shaped trench 20 in (50 cm) deep at the wet place, sloping down to the dry well. Lay perforated piping in the trench. Fill both trench and dry well with rubble, gravel, and then topsoil.

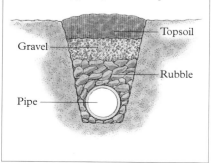

PERFECTING THE STEPS

TO CHECK whether a surface is absolutely flat or on a slight slope, use a spirit level. Just lay it on the surface. The bubble in the spirit level is central on a flat surface, but moves right or left on a slope to whichever side is higher. Steps should have the tiniest slope down from back to front so that water runs off — the bubble should move nearer the back. If steps are flat or slope the wrong way, water forms pools on the tread, making it slippery underfoot, especially in freezing weather.

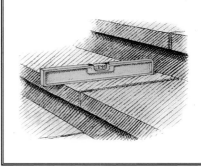

AVOIDING A FILM OF ICE Water may gather at the bottom of a flight of steps. Solve the problem by putting a narrow band of gravel up to 1 ft (30 cm) deep in front of the bottom step to act as a simple dry well.

DRAMA FOR DAMP GARDENS Whether your garden is boggy by nature or design, there is scope for striking planting. White-sheathed calla lilies (*Zantedeschia*) behind mauve and white *Iris kaempferi* adorn the edge of a pond.

neer. The weight of damp earth pushing against a retaining wall is enormous. Your retaining wall, whether it is of reinforced concrete alone or faced with brick or stone, must both have a foundation of the correct depth and be the proper thickness to do its job. This is not work for the amateur.

BUILD IN CONTOURS FOR MORE APPEAL

A completely level garden takes on more character when you introduce contours. Raising one part by just one step, creating a small sunken area as a sun trap, and using the spoil to make a bank for wildflowers in a corner, add not only drama but apparent size. The eye has different levels to dwell on instead of taking in the whole flat area in one sweep. When you can construct mounds using surplus soil from the excavation of, say, a pool, you

save the cost of removing it from the site. Make sure, however, that you remove any precious topsoil from the mound site before dumping your subsoil there and set aside the topsoil from the pool site also. It can be used again over the subsoil, but the depth may end up less than the original.

Grass can grow in a topsoil depth of 4–6 in (10–15 cm), whereas shrubs need at least 12 in (30 cm) if they are to thrive. Standard trees need an even greater depth of topsoil, 18 in (46 cm) or more.

Creating contour changes is one of the most satisfying jobs, for you achieve an instant effect. Try to make a finished mound or hollow look as natural as you can. Avoid too much regularity or too abrupt a change. Be sure to blend the edges carefully with the natural level so that your creation does not seem to be a waste pit or a soil dump.

Where the garden is bordered by a noisy road, a mound can help provide quiet. A mound 7 ft (2 m) high will block noise if you are sitting in its lee. But the higher the mound, the greater the width needed at the base, so it could easily dominate a small garden. And always remember that the more you go with the natural character of the land, the easier your garden will be to maintain.

SETTING THE STYLE

TIME AND PERSONAL TASTE are the key factors when you are starting or reshaping a garden. The best garden is the one that suits your particular needs, so choose from the ideas of other gardeners and other ages to compose the style that pleases you. Create a garden that runs on a few hours' work a month or one that is an all-consuming passion. Design it to be childproof or easy for a disabled gardener to manage. Make it simple and modern or follow the cottage tradition; and if you want to experiment, evoke the mood of the Orient or the Mediterranean in a corner of your plot.

A classic symmetrical pattern of clipped boxwood scrolls around a central urn in a mirror image designed to be viewed from above.

THE RIGHT STYLE FOR YOU

DECIDING ON A STYLE for the site is as exciting to a gardener as decorating a home is to someone who is passionate about interior design. There is a rich heritage to draw on, demonstrated in many great gardens of the past that have been maintained from their heyday or re-created in the style of the period.

Gardens in a modern style, suited to today's space and pace, also inspire with examples of architectural lines and hard surfaces softened by fuss-free plantings. Travel abroad, too, introduces new ideas for touches of the exotic. Stimulated by influences from all sides, enthusiasm for growth and change is likely to mount ever higher, whether the garden is embryonic, in its infancy, or mature.

You may like a naturalistic, or informal, garden in keeping with the surrounding landscape, or prefer everything in neat rows with clipped hedges and straight paths. Personal taste, the age and habits of those who use the garden, and the tones of the local earth and stone are all factors affecting the choice of plants and materials, layout and mood.

REMAINING REALISTIC

You could combine different styles in the garden, with perhaps a soothing Japanese corner, a sizzling Mediterranean area, and an English kitchen garden plot. But it is vital to be practical and to channel your dreams into the realm of the realistic. Remember that the enormous herbaceous border you saw in a public garden last June is maintained by an expert staff and may not look as good during the rest of the year.

Your aim should be to stay within your bounds, so that when you achieve the desired image, it is manageable and appropriate. It is a gardener's nature to aspire upward, but too much grandeur, too many urns or hard stone benches, too many period planting schemes or mixtures of style can look pretentious and overdone in a private garden. So if the chosen style is not quite working, resist the urge to add more — it is much better to take away.

NOVEL WAYS TO GROW PLANTS A mulch of gravel over soil creates a marvelous growing medium for pockets of pansies and aromatic herbs, and you can walk on it. This informal style makes the most of hard materials without looking as severe as some modern architectural garden designs.

GARDENS TO SUIT TIGHT SCHEDULES

THE AMOUNT OF TIME you want to spend gardening is a factor in determining how elaborate your design will be and which style you choose. Formal layouts, for instance, need the most time for clipping and restraining the plants, since you are imposing an unnatural idiom on a site.

Whether the garden is planned for low maintenance or is labor intensive, it saves time in the long run to prepare the site thoroughly and construct the layout properly. Take the chance to banish perennial weeds when the plot is bare. The time to get rid of ground ivy or mugwort is when preparing the beds; digging the soil exposes the roots, which must be removed.

Another consideration early on is the hardscape. Spend a sizable portion of your garden budget on laying down hard surfaces solidly, with the correct base and sub-base. If you skimp on this, in a few years' time the paving will crack, wobble, and be infested with weeds.

Establish a realistic budget and build the garden accordingly. You may have just bought a house and paid for its decoration. If the garden comes last in your financial priorities, do a small part of it well to start with. In the short term, seed the remainder of the garden with grass or, if it is in the shade, plant it with a ground cover that you can remove later on. Dead nettle (*Lamium*) covers the ground fast, as do ivy and periwinkle. You can complete the desired layout in successive years.

YOUR PERSONAL STYLE

When you have assessed the site conditions, and thought about a style compatible with your house, turn your attention to the most important matter — what you want. If the garden is to be practical, it must please you. A list is probably the easiest way to clarify your needs, particularly when more than one person uses and tends the garden.

Perhaps develop a second list of questions, such as, who is going to look after particular parts of the garden? And how much time is available for it? If the answer is that you are the one who has to do the work, how much do you like gardening? The less time and enthusiasm

AN ATTRACTIVE STOPGAP Fast-growing turf is a superb cover-up for areas you can't afford to landscape right away. Over time, you can remove the grass and add more beds.

KEEP A GARDEN DIARY

A GARDEN DIARY helps you to keep track of which plants are where and is fun to look back on as your design develops. Make a note of each new plant, when you set it out, and where it came from. Then you can repeat successes as well as learn from any mistakes.

Jot down, too, when different plants flower or look their best, to help you plan new groupings or extend color schemes. It is also interesting to see from year to year how early or late the same plant flowers or bears fruit.

you have, the more you need a strong, simple layout with the minimum of frills. In any case, there is beauty to enjoy in a garden that is not always immaculate.

GARDEN PLANNER

Now, while the canvas is still bare, is the time to work out your style ideas. To clarify your requirements, divide a sheet of paper in three. In one column write what you must have, in the second what you would like to have, and in the third what you do not want. For example:

What you must have:
Place for garbage cans near the kitchen door, but covered up.
Place to hang clothes out to dry.
Convenient faucet for watering and for a hose to wash the car.
Place to make compost, preferably in constructed bins.
Place for tool storage.
Place for storing barbecue gear, play equipment for children, and bicycles.

What you want to have:
Place for a few herbs in summer.
Terrace to provide somewhere to sit, read, sunbathe, entertain, and eat.
Place for wildflowers; bulbs naturalized under a tree, perhaps.
Play space for children.

SHORT CUT TO DRAMA Growing just a few huge plants cuts down on maintenance chores. For banana, red-flowered canna, and variegated giant reed, you need a very sheltered garden that is not touched by frost.

What you do not want:
Rock garden — requires too much site preparation at the outset.
Meadow — it is too untidy and takes up too much space in a small garden.
Fruit trees — not enough room.
Ornamental pool — a hazard for children.

Most arguments are over the features you dream of having rather than those you must have. Once you have decided what you must keep in, what is desirable but not essential, and what is definitely out, pencil in the items on a scaled plan of the garden. A plan helps you to resolve precisely what it is you want and how much you will be able to look after without the work's overwhelming you.

Before you commit yourself to a design, get estimates for any work proposed. You can even have a design drawn up. Professional or homemade, it becomes the blueprint from which to work.

INCLUDING DREAM FEATURES

Gardens started from scratch often revolve around one particular feature that you can't live without. Many gardeners long for a pergola, for instance. It conjures up images of dappled light filtering through the leaves of a climbing rose decked with scented flowers, of the evening fragrance of honeysuckle, and bunches of grapes temptingly beyond reach. Provided that you get the dimensions right, a pergola will soften the abrupt transition from indoors to out.

Most gardeners hanker after a lawn when conditions allow. A typical, rectangular plot lends itself to a lawn with beds on either side. A few informal curves soften the rigid lines, but avoid too much weaving in and out, as intricate shapes are tricky to mow.

☙ Make sure that the lawn will be in sun or only partial shade so the turf will thicken up satisfactorily. Otherwise seek out a turf or seed specifically designed for shade. Site the lawn away from large trees if possible.
☙ Leave a grass-free strip all around the lawn, which makes edging much easier than if it goes right up to a wall or a fence.
☙ Lay paths to take the quickest route across the lawn; otherwise people will take short cuts and wear bare patches in

the grass, making an unwanted path.
☙ Banks should have a slope of less than 30°. It is hard to mow a steeper slope; grow ground-cover plants on it instead.

A pond is often another priority, and when well stocked and managed, a water feature is a joy. The larger it is the more easily you can establish enough flora and fauna to keep the water clear.

Where to put it is the next concern. A favorite spot is near a paved sitting area,

SOW SEED FROM ANNUALS

THERE IS NO NEED to buy new plants each year. Save seeds of annuals such as cosmos or phlox and sow them thinly in early spring in washed-out yogurt cups or ice-cream tubs filled with seed compost. Keep them on a warm windowsill until the danger of frost is past. The young plants may not be identical to the parent plants; you may have some color surprises.

✿ Mix shrub roses with smaller roses; this adds interest by way of autumn hips and gives a variation in heights.

✿ In a formal garden, alternate rose beds with beds of perennials or low shrubs to create a far more interesting place for strolling.

REDUCING MAINTENANCE

For an easy-care garden tailor-made to your needs, think of what to leave out. Maybe you could forgo a lawn and do without vegetables and soft fruit. Instead of a formal hedge, choose an informal one that does not need clipping. Cover as much bare soil as possible with garden plants to keep out weeds. Roses, except shrub roses, need frequent care; perennials may need staking and dividing. You could instead have a garden of shrubs and trees alone.

After deciding where you want the items on your "must have" list to go, think about incorporating some hardscape features that add visual interest without causing extra work — for example, the mixing of surface textures, such as gravel with granite slabs, pavers with bricks, or cobblestones with tiles.

One of the joys of gardening today is the blurring of old distinctions between different types of border. Instead of separating herbaceous, bedding, and woody plants, you can now mingle roses, shrubs, bulbs, perennials, and annuals, and even edible plants. The mixed border gives year-round interest with little effort.

To minimize the workload, choose a few shrubs, preferably evergreens, and put clusters of the same species together. For instance, a group of rhododendron varieties needs little attention if you have acid soil and has a unity of form enlivened by different flower colors and leaf details. Add the occa-

where you can watch birds, insects, and small animals attracted by the water. Such a placement usually calls for a regularly shaped pond that will work with a paved area's geometry, which in itself should echo the shapes and proportions of the house. This is the way to build up a relationship of shapes that gives proper unity to a garden's design.

A plot for many people, particularly traditionalists, is not complete without a rose garden. The flowers of hybrid tea and floribunda roses (also called cluster roses) are superb, but the plants themselves are not. From autumn until late spring they offer only twigs. You can relieve this situation in several ways.

✿ Blend rose bushes with herbs — sage, lavender, and rosemary have foliage interest through winter in mild areas. Grow them somewhat apart, as roses need feeding and herbs do not.

MAKING A RAISED BED WITH LANDSCAPE TIES

A RAISED BED lets you garden from the comfort of a sitting position. When you build your own, you can make it the precise height you want. It also lets you control soil and drainage.

Landscape ties blend with nearly all types of hard surface and provide a complementary frame for plants. They are sold at large garden centers and lumberyards around the country.

Ties are stable but heavy and cumbersome; you can have them sawn in half before use. A two-layer raised bed requires no additional support, but a three-layer bed needs metal rods driven into the ground to brace the outside of the ties.

Spread a layer of gravel at the base to aid drainage

Staggered layers make a strong frame

sional tree if there is the space. Use architectural plants such as *Yucca filamentosa* for interest against a shrub background, limiting massed color to spring bulbs in tubs or summer annuals spilling from pots.

RAISED BEDS TO SAVE BENDING

Easy-care styles are well suited to older people as well as busy ones, and indeed to any gardener who likes to take it easy. Even devoted gardeners appreciate a layout that minimizes hard labor, leaving plenty of time for enjoyment. A garden made up entirely of raised beds fits the bill perfectly, as it reduces bending or kneeling. Rectangular or square beds are suited to a formal design and are especially attractive when surrounded by paving or gravel. If you prefer an informal look, oval or kidney-shaped beds are more effective.

Allow access to each raised bed from at least three sides if it is 5 ft (1.5 m) wide or more, so that you can reach across. Use brick, stone, landscape ties, or paving slabs on edge, with the soil level about 18–24 in (45–60 cm) above ground.

You can also grow roses, which will be at a good height for deadheading and pruning. Include herbs with them to conceal their legginess, which is even more noticeable when they are raised. Herbs are valuable for both the kitchen and the ornamental garden; they are fragrant and decorative in flower and foliage, and need

RETAINING WALL The low wall raises the bed so that low-growing plants such as aubrietia, arabis, lamium, and pulmonaria are easy to see and tend. The weathered brick blends with the stone wall in the background.

MODERN LOOK Compact raised beds filled with self-sufficient, spreading foliage plants such as lamb's-ears and tarragon leave you time to relax in the garden. Climbers will soften the wooden arch as they mature.

WOODLAND GLADE At the other extreme from raised beds is a garden allowed to imitate nature, with bluebells carpeting the ground in spring. In a smaller garden, a few bluebells planted informally under a deciduous tree will soon self-sow and naturalize to create a similar effect.

little care. Many herbs are evergreen — lavender, rosemary, hyssop, and savory, for example — which reduces maintenance even further and provides winter interest in mild regions. Alternatively, design a raised herbaceous planting spilling over with woolly leaved lamb's-ears or blue-flowered catmint or make a scree bed of gravel for alpines.

RAISED VEGETABLE PROFILE

When you have a vegetable plot, there is no need to banish it to the end of the garden, farthest from where you want to use it. The foliage of such vegetables as blue-green cabbages, broad beans, and carrots is handsome enough to mingle with ornamental plants and herbs. The best design is a square layout, if you want

COASTAL PRIVILEGE If you live in the warmest climate — for instance in southern California or on the Gulf Coast — you can grow frost-tender plants such as the spiky *Echium pininana* and subtropical *Cordyline,* which would perish in a colder region.

vegetable patches of a manageable size.

Raise vegetable beds by 12 in (30 cm) or so with a frame of timbers. Raise the soil level to correspond by placing well-rotted organic matter on top, which has the added advantage of improving the vegetable-growing potential of poor soil. The effect of raising the bed is to make a feature of the vegetables, and they are at a handy height for harvesting. Add an arch or two for runner beans and squash, and you create a stylish garden. Raised beds and arches will also screen unattractive views or outbuildings.

SOFT SURFACE IDEAS

A garden of raised beds, whether for vegetables, decorative plants, or a mixture, needs no grass — the most common medium for the floor of a garden. The lawn is an American institution but is unknown in the gardens of many other countries. It does not even feature in traditional cottage gardens for, if you are surrounded by green fields, why have another on your side of the hedge?

There are ways to cover the ground with "soft" surfaces other than a grass lawn that give your garden a different mood and require less maintenance. The best choice is to plant areas with a low-growing evergreen ground cover. Swaths of periwinkle, ivy, or wild ginger resemble a woodland floor, and you can grow other plants through them.

ADAPTING AN EXISTING STYLE

Another range of considerations arises when a garden is not new but established, even neglected. What should you keep, and what should you take out? It is best not to rush into a decision. Live with your new site to get the feel of what is needed in both summer and winter. Remember that a predecessor put things where they are for a reason. The cause may now be gone, or perhaps the solution is now too big, but you should think before renovating.

With most overgrown shrubs, your best course is to cut them back hard after flowering. After a year you know when their best season is, and whether you like what they have to offer. Even if you are not won over by a shrub, it may be worth keeping as a backdrop to a border.

When large trees need attention, check with the local government in case they are protected by an ordinance. Old trees may be blocking too much light, using up too much space, or impoverishing the soil around them. Call an arborist for technical advice before cutting down trees or lopping off branches.

An old greenhouse may be in place. If you do not want it and it is sound, sell it and use the old base as the foundation for a terrace. Do not keep a greenhouse and fit a garden plan around it if you find the structure unattractive. The same applies to any garden feature, whether a fence, hedge, fountain, or wall.

FINDING A STRONG THEME

When you take over an existing garden, you may find that the basic design has been diluted with a haphazard mixture of plantings, colors, periods, and materials. When this is the case, pick out the features you like best and build the garden around them.

Once you have decided what you are going to keep in the garden, draw up a scaled plan showing these features but excluding existing elements you want to remove. Use tracing-paper overlays placed on the plan to try out the possible positions for new items. Try the most appropriate places and work out every possible permutation until you resolve the garden's layout.

The layout can be interpreted in a number of ways. The location of your property may give the first clue to the style. If you are surrounded by woodland, for instance, a garden of bulbs growing in the dappled shade cast by a blossom-covered fruit tree would be suitable. A coastal garden, too, may make the decisions for you. Trees such as pine, tamarisk, and sycamore filter the wind, with escallonia, hebe, and gorse filling the middle ground. Buddleia, cistus, and fuchsia add color and interest.

Exposure and soil type also dictate the plants you grow. Some plants naturally thrive in shaded, north-facing places oozing with water; others prefer a hot, sunny exposure.

Develop any naturally boggy areas into ponds of water that can become wildlife sanctuaries; plant them with flags, reeds and rushes, and some yellow-flowering marsh marigolds.

AN INFORMAL MODERN GARDEN

Beauty and practicality characterize this simple design. Drifts of plants punctuated with trees and imaginative use of the sloping site create a low-maintenance garden.

IMMEDIATELY OUTSIDE the house, an L-shaped terrace wooden deck provides a transitional area with steps leading to the rest of the garden. The straight lines of the timber contrast with the curving contours of the garden, where fluid lines lead the eye easily from one part to the next. Under the decking is a shady spot studded with cobbles, which makes an ideal environment for ferns.

A lawn carpets much of the garden. The mowing differs according to where the grass is and what its function is. Where the ground is flat, the grass is closely mown for easy walking. On the banks, rough grass is dotted with bulbs. Autumn crocus and cyclamen bloom in September, followed by groups of heaths and heathers, which provide year-round foliage and flower interest.

CREATIVITY WITH SHRUBS

Above the mid-garden bank, European mountain ashes, also called rowan trees, line a mowed path that meanders alongside a bed planted with rhododendrons. The shrubbery makes a pleasant vista, filters northerly winds, and screens the neighbors from view.

The size of the shrubs varies from tree height to ground cover. Some of the leaves have differently colored undersides, so you catch glimpses of brown, purple, and blue-white. The theme continues with a group of azaleas, relatives of the rhododendron.

With evergreens blanketing much of the ground all year, there is hardly any weeding to do. Any weeds that crop up in the grass banks can be left to mingle with the naturalized bulbs.

This garden is on sandy, acid soil, ideal for growing heathers and rhododendrons. In a limy, alkaline soil, a similar design could be carried out with whitebeam (*Sorbas aria*) and viburnums.

Rowan trees are decked with bright autumn berries

Heathers nestle on the bank, giving colour all year

Azaleas clothe the slope with contrasts of foliage

1. Rowan tree (*Sorbus aucuparia*)
2. Irish heath (*Daboecia cantabrica*)
3. Tree heath (*Erica arborea*)
4. *Rhododendron bureavii*
5. *Rhododendron calophytum*
6. Mixed bulbs (*Colchicum speciosum* 'Album' and 'Rosy Dawn'; *Crocus speciosus*; *Cyclamen hederifolium*)
7. Darley heath (*Erica × darleyensis*)
8. Heather (*Calluna vulgaris* 'H.E. Beale')
9. Heather (*Calluna vulgaris* 'Darkness')
10. Heather (*Calluna vulgaris* 'Cramond')
11. Heather (*Calluna vulgaris* 'Serlei')
12. Azalea (*Rhododendron* 'Lemonora')
13. Azalea (*Rhododendron obtusum*)

A FLAVOR
OF THE PAST

Y OUR HOUSE is a guide to possible styles that would suit the garden. The date of the house might inspire you to incorporate historic features or classic plants in the layout — perhaps a colonial-era split-rail fence or 19th-century bedding annuals. Even in the modern garden, a corner devoted to a particular period is enough to recall the past and echo the heritage of the house. A little knot garden of santolina, hyssop, lavender, and boxwood pays homage to the Tudor inspiration of a half-timbered house, for instance.

While the style of your house provides some pointers to your garden design, the materials it is constructed from are equally important. Using some of the materials of the house in pavings, edgings, and other features helps unify the design. A fieldstone farmhouse, for instance, would be complemented by a rugged dry-stone wall.

Most gardens are maintained by one or two people pressed for time. When adapting ideas from an earlier period, it is possible to keep the flavor of the original without its continual maintenance demands. That is the secret of re-creating the past: interpreting it in an imaginative way that brings together the best of old and new.

ECHOES OF TRADITION

The roots of American garden tradition lie in Europe, and it is both easy and pleasant to create a sense of that heritage in any enclosed space. Typical traditional features include arbors and trellises clothed in scented climbers, as well as fountains and pools, where ladies used to dabble their fingers. Lawns were once strewn with flowering plants or made up of fragrant ground cover.

A chamomile lawn makes an aromatic as well as old-fashioned alternative to grass and needs mowing only once or twice a year. It has feathery foliage and a pleasantly sharp smell when crushed underfoot — but it is for the occasional stroll, not for regular foot traffic, and looks dull in winter. Choose the form 'Treneague,'

TRANSLATED IN TIME Tiny squares of clipped boxwood filled in with pinks revive in miniature the grand schemes of Old World knot gardens. Scale the design depending on how much space you want to devote to one style.

COLONIAL DAYS Ranks of tulips, enclosed beds bordered with clipped evergreens, tidy brick paths, and picket fences mark a garden at Colonial Williamsburg, in Virginia. Such formal, geometric layouts are typical of the garden style in fashion in early America.

ANTIQUE SPLENDOR Formal knot gardens look their best seen from a raised vantage point, where the pattern of plants clearly shows. An intricate design is labor intensive — you may need to be less ambitious in today's garden.

ORDERLY STYLE Evoke the a flavor of the Renaissance by planting in blocks. Such a layout is particularly striking with low hedging plants, but it is also suited to vegetables, which can be decorative as part of a strong design.

which does not flower. Set out the plants about 6 in (15 cm) apart during spring in well-drained soil. Replant any bare patches that appear and weed as necessary. Pearlwort, thyme, or clover can also be used as alternative lawn plants.

To make an arbor in Old World style, train an arch of old-fashioned roses and honeysuckle over a wooden frame, with lavender and pinks at the climbers' feet. For pleasant scent, mix *Rosa centifolia* and *R.* 'Alba Semiplena' with *Lonicera periclymenum* 'Belgica' for early summer flowering or 'Serotina' for later blooms. Place a bench underneath the arbor — perhaps with a turf "seat" of chamomile, so you are cushioned by its springy, aromatic greenery while you sit.

As the influence of the Renaissance spread, the focus of European gardens shifted. Vistas, pathways, and avenues created strong geometric shapes, linked by focal points such as fountains and sculptures — all ideas that are still fundamental to many of today's garden styles.

TRIM AND FORMAL SCHEMES

The first gardens in the American colonies were formal, with the basic materials of yew or hornbeam clipped and trained into walls or colonnades. Gardens were trim and neat with rectangles, squares, or canals of still water and hardly any flower color. Topiary work was immensely popular. If you adopt this soothing style, the time you spend clipping hedging plants is countered by the hours you save on weeding and tending herbaceous plants. This is the garden for a pleached hedge (*see p. 47*) as a boundary or divider or for incorporating a water feature when the hard surfaces are put in.

While most gardens in the thirteen colonies were quite small, they were gracious, fitting surroundings for the well-proportioned houses. Excellent examples of this style may be seen at Colonial Williamsburg in Virginia, as well as other museum villages. Typically such gardens were formal, with an emphasis on gravel and clipped greenery. If you feel more at home with flowers but like an ordered layout, adopt a similar style and combine a geometric design of hard surfaces with pockets of bulbs, annuals, and perennials.

ENHANCING A NATURAL LOOK

As the frontier moved west in the 19th century, American landscaping turned to a romanticized vision of the wilderness. This movement produced such elaborately contrived "natural" landscapes as New York City's Central Park. Reproduced on a smaller scale in the garden of today, this natural look becomes a haven for wildlife and native plant species, particularly trees, and may feature a pond set in a meadow-like lawn dotted with wildflowers.

In the hands of romantic designers, the garden was regarded almost as a landscape painting, and buildings in Gothic or rustic styles completed the pic-

ROMANTIC FREEDOM The landscaped garden of the late 18th century let nature roam, but controlled by the hand of man. To capture something of this spirit, think of opening up a view hidden by a fence or dense shrubbery.

ture. You can give something of the same atmosphere by building a little folly or shell grotto or by adding fanciful details to a garden shed.

The naturalistic look changed with the arrival of Victorian attitudes. In the second half of the 19th century, gravel paths were snaking through lawns edged with somber shrubberies of laurel, boxwood, and aucuba.

DIFFERENT THEMES FOR LOVERS OF COLOR

Slowly, the desire for color crept in to the Victorian garden — not the soft tones of cottage garden perennials, but the vibrancy of geraniums and begonias set within edgings of alyssum and lobelia. The advent of the conservatory, heated by a steam boiler, allowed the propagation of half-hardy plants for the garden.

The 19th-century passion for these "bedding" plants brightened summer scenes then as now, whether in beds of circular or diamond shapes in public parks or as island beds or hedge-backed borders in private gardens. For a modern version of such a labor-intensive style, you can devote some of the space to permanent plantings. Introduce interest for winter with shrubs such as *Cotoneaster horizontalis* and pyracantha for their attractive berries and mahonia for its flowers.

When reaction against industrialization sparked the changes known as the Arts and Crafts movement, garden design was rethought along with all other aspects of design. Designer-craftsmen and writers began to draw their followers away from vivid annual color toward wildflowers and the cottage-garden style.

Late Victorian gardeners included fruit trees with herbs and simple perennial flowers on a grand scale. The great country houses built during the late 19th and early 20th centuries were surrounded by gardens in the form of hedged rooms decorated with non-native materials mixed in the cottage style. The goal was to fill the garden with as many different exotic plants as possible — an ambition that long persisted.

At the end of the 20th century gardeners are questioning this precedent. The emerging style is more concerned with native plants and a more relaxed manner

FORMAL AND ORDERLY In contrast to the naturalistic look, gardens of the 19th century were symmetrical. Immaculately clipped evergreen hedges enclosed color-coordinated planting schemes and formed interesting pathways. Ornaments were placed in strategic locations.

of growth. Informal plantings of native species fit into a strong basic design, which makes the garden functional, beautiful, and not too time consuming.

PLANTING IN PERIOD STYLE

You can pursue the idea of planning a garden in the manner of an earlier epoch and choose plants that were in vogue during the period when the house was built. For instance, ferneries were very Victorian. They thrived on the estates of wealthy industrialists and are well adapted to any northern exposure. Many planting schemes in their day were nostalgic reminders of travels abroad. The moist, warm conservatory recalls expeditions to the tropics, while part of the fashion for rhododendrons sprang from their exotic Himalayan origins.

Rhododendrons were hybridized extensively all through the early 1900s, while Japanese cherries arrived in the 1930s. The widespread × *Cupressocyparis leylandii* made its first appearance in the 1950s, while the gold *Robinia*

CARPET BEDDING Victorian-style patterns of planting are fun to re-create. Try arranging blue *Echeveria* and purple *Iresine* among mixed foliage plants. An agave encircled with sempervivum graces the center.

TIMELESS AND AGELESS This cherub steps out of classical myth but has a playful air that is equally suitable for a less controlled, informal style. Swaths of ivy make an appropriately wild and natural garden floor.

pseudoacacia 'Frisia' was widely planted in the 1980s. Flower arrangers within the last 20 years have also popularized certain plants, such as variegated eleagnus, the blooms of astrantia, and gray-green hosta leaves.

There is no need to be rigid in your selection according to era, but knowing when plants became popular casts an interesting sidelight on them. Observing the style of your house and corresponding materials and plants can give you pointers to a satisfying result.

COTTAGE OR COUNTRY-HOUSE STYLE?

A cottage may well come with an overgrown, mixed muddle of the nostalgic ideal — a medley of gnarled apple trees, rosemary, thyme, nasturtiums, holly, hawthorn, and hollyhock, campanula, pinks, and wallflowers, sweet William, and sweet pea. Such a garden may need extensive pruning and clearing but little stylistic change unless you want space for some new features.

The country-house style, which originated on grand estates, changed with the period. In Victorian times, the garden could be either formal, with beds of colorful annuals around a central purple cordyline, or naturalistic, with

TO THE RESCUE

MAKING A FERNERY

MANY PLANTS cannot tolerate damp, dense shade. But do not despair if your garden has a boggy, dark corner: one group of plants — ferns — relishes such a site. Ferneries were popular during the Victorian era, so you can create a period piece at the same time.

Choose hardy ferns, for example royal fern (*Osmunda regalis*) and the sensitive fern (*Onoclea sensibilis*), for the boggiest areas, and *Adiantum venustum*, which needs neutral to acid soil, on slightly drier land. Dig rotted manure or compost into the soil before planting. Then enjoy the tender green and bronze-red young leaves, unfurling into rich green mature foliage.

COTTAGE GARDEN The charm of a small country garden lies in its seemingly unplanned miscellany of old-fashioned, often scented, herbaceous plants including catmint, clary (*Salvia sclarea*), *Campanula latifolia* 'Alba,' and foxgloves, backed by clambering honeysuckle and roses.

BEST PLANTS

LOW-ALLERGEN CHOICES

If you suffer from hay fever or similar allergic reactions to particular plants, choose from the many "safe" species.

• Serviceberry (*Amelanchier lamarckii*): tree with leaves that unfold bronze, turn dark green then orange-red; sprays of white flowers in spring.

• Judas tree (*Cercis siliquastrum*): clusters of pink spring flowers and purple-red pods in late summer.

• Double wild cherry (*Prunus avium* 'Plena'): dark green foliage shaded red and yellow in autumn; reddish-brown bark and white flowers in spring.

• *Hebe* 'Autumn Glory': moderately hardy, with purple stems and violet-blue flowers from summer to autumn.

• *Viburnum tinus*: evergreen, with flat white, pink-budded flowers all winter and spring.

• *Weigela florida* 'Aureovariegata': golden-edged leaves; arching branches and pink flowers in early summer.

• *Delphinium elatum* hybrids: closely packed upright spires of white, blue, or purple flowers, usually with an eye of contrasting color.

• *Campanula persicifolia*: forms spreading rosettes; nodding, bell-shaped papery white or blue flowers.

• *Bergenia cordifolia*: forms evergreen ground cover; large, rounded, crinkled leaves and pale pink spring flowers.

• *Epimedium perralderianum*: forms semi-evergreen ground cover; large, toothed glossy leaves and yellow flowers in spring.

gravel paths sweeping through dense beds of shrubbery.

The Edwardian look, which developed in Britain before the First World War, features smaller areas within a garden divided by hedges of yew, holly, or hornbeam. The garden pattern extends from the geometry of the house, using borders of perennials. Favorite flowers include asters, phlox, hollyhock, and delphinium, arranged in the manner of that doyenne of color harmonies, the plantswoman Gertrude Jekyll.

Jekyll's style still works well when it is adapted to lessen the maintenance. Typical are wide paths, ending in a feature. Borders on each side of the path are

GARDENS WITHIN A GARDEN The Edwardians introduced the notion of outdoor "rooms," where each compartment had a separate character or color. The White Garden at Sissinghurst, Kent, is one room in a larger scheme; in a small garden, you could color-coordinate each section.

color graded — strong in the foreground, paler in the distance. Pot-grown lilies and foxgloves supplement the borders.

In their original form, these borders lasted for six weeks, while a family was at its summer home. Such schemes are impractical today. Copy the adaptations that were devised in the 1950s and add shrubs to the perennials to make a mixed border and reduce the work load.

IN AND OUT OF TOWN

In town, smaller Edwardian terrace gardens were filled with similar flowers and often had a vegetable patch at the farthest point from the house. Paved areas were separated from planting beds with rope-pattern edging tiles or bricks set on edge to create a zigzag line. This is as charming now as it was then.

The style and form varied in the 1920s and '30s as more people took to gardening. Layouts dating back to those decades contain elements of the Victorian and Edwardian gardens before them, in a scaled-down form of gracious living.

In the 1960s, outside rooms, barbecues, and play space for children became major requirements — as they continue to be. People with small urban gardens were readier to do without a lawn as they relished the convenience of hard surfacing, offset by architectural plants such as yucca and New Zealand flax. This style, too, is one to continue today.

Herbs, and their merits as garden specimens, were appreciated as foreign cuisines and healthier diets became popular. The cycle is completed with these Old English regulars again in high favor. Full sun is best for herbs, although chives and mint grow in shade too; plant them near the house for easy picking. Apart from their culinary use, herbs are lovely to brush against as you walk through the garden.

A GARDEN FOR CHILDREN

There is no need to turn your garden into an unbroken spread of lawn for children: formal hedges and knot gardens are superb for games of hide-and-seek and tag, while a cottage garden can cope with baseballs landing in a flower bed, and the branches of a mature apple tree can be trimmed for safer climbing.

However, you may want to set aside one area for children and their toys. Apart from enjoying sunflowers, nasturtiums, and a few other plants that offer dramatic results, children tend to want

an extended playroom, not flowers and foliage, scent and seasonal interest.

A layer of wood chips provides the softest surface to cushion falls from swings, jungle gyms, and slides. Grass tends to become bare in spots that are subjected to a lot of foot traffic. A path can be a tricycle course, and paving a hopscotch area.

When the children grow up, it is easy to convert their play areas into "grown-up" features. Transform the sandbox, which you want near the house so that you can see what is going on, into a pool; use the swing and jungle gym area for training runner beans and sweet peas, perhaps using the original features as supports.

THE ESSENCE OF A STYLE

Give your garden an instantly recognizable character inspired by distant places or times past. You can evoke the original style with a single feature or a collection of plants.

MIDDLE EAST OASIS
Water gushing from an intricately shaped and inlaid fountain gives relief from the heat of the day. The windmill palm (*Trachycarpus fortunei*) will conjure a tropical look. A Persian rose opens wide in the warmth of the sun.

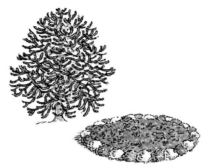

VICTORIAN PATTERNS
The distinctive monkey-puzzle tree (*Araucaria araucana*), with its branches like furry tails, was introduced from Chile late in the 18th century and was in vogue by Victorian times. Island beds of annuals in precise patterns also evoke the era.

MEDITERRANEAN HEAT
In a sheltered sun trap, plant terra-cotta or cement pots with an agave or an orange tree, plants often seen in southern France. A mural of gaily colored tiles gives a white wall a Spanish flourish.

MODERN OUTDOOR LIVING
The golden leaves of *Robinia pseudoacacia* 'Frisia' rustling in the breeze are one of the most visible legacies of recent decades. The patio became an outdoor kitchen and living room, with built-in barbecue and sitting areas.

JAPANESE TOUCHES
Bonsai — miniature trees — are an intriguing Japanese idea and never fail to provoke comment. Raked pebbles imitate the flow of water, dotted with "islands" of rock under the aloof pose of a stone stork.

TUDOR TIMES
An arch of sweet-smelling roses, a mulberry tree with crooked branches and late-summer berries, and a quince tree bearing pear-shaped or round fruit all conjure up the times of the English royals Henry VIII and Elizabeth I.

HOLLAND AND NORTHERN FRANCE
The royal garden of Versailles gave its name to a container much used in this formal style, often with a bay tree clipped into a standard "lollipop" shape. Spirals were another popular topiary shape. Beds of tulips were a Dutch passion.

CLASSICAL ROME
Classical statues and a pebble-and-paving mosaic recall the heyday of Rome, when it was the center of artistic inspiration. Try out mosaic patterns on paper first, before buying pebbles in contrasting colors to make them up.

INFLUENCES FROM ABROAD

INSTEAD OF CREATING a piece of nostalgia, you might like to adopt the idiom of another country. As travel becomes easier, people see more styles and long to capture their character at home.

Gardens in northern France have a distinctive mood that resembles the formal styles of the colonial tradition. Set the scene with gravel paths and border them with clipped boxwood topiary and low boxwood hedges. Place a statue or ornament at the end of each vista. Hang painted shutters at the windows and set out matching café tables and folding chairs on a paved area.

Fill window boxes and pots with geraniums and find a place for a piece of French pottery. Install a stone trough for a centerpiece. Such a garden is far easier to lay out than an informal, rambling one, but it takes more time to maintain.

THE MEDITERRANEAN LOOK

Whether Spanish, Italian, or Provençal, the Mediterranean look appeals to those who yearn for steamy summers, where the garden is hot and sunny and the owner likes to sunbathe. You need a site facing south or west. A seaside garden is ideal, as long as it is sheltered, because tender plants are easier to grow where hard frosts are rare; the light is bright and clear, and the views are magnificent. Forget the lawn and install instead small corners of paving, partially shaded by pergolas draped with wisteria and vines. Add the cooling sound of trickling water and pack in some decorative terra-cotta pots brimming with geraniums.

Lay terra-cotta tiles on the terrace and grow vines over the white walls. Scatter around amphorae (two-handled, narrow-necked jars), filled with trailing plants or left empty and sculptural. A fig tree, cape plumbago (moved indoors for the winter), and *Convolvulus cneorum* add to the southern atmosphere. Culinary herbs, along with lavender and cistus, come into their own. Ceramic plaques make attractive wall features.

The Mediterranean look may surround a swimming pool, where flowers of clear blue and yellow work best. This is a tricky area to style, particularly if the pool is an insistent blue. Stick with bright colors, which suit an area of activity. This

SOUTHWEST STYLE Seeing the fleshy growth of cacti and succulents instantly transports you to hotter climates. These plants store water in their tissues to carry them through dry spells and cope with infrequent watering even when grown in pots. Most need to winter indoors in the North.

is a good place to build a barbecue into the wall, for outdoor eating after a day of swimming and sunbathing.

ASIAN HARMONY

Japanese-style gardens are highly popular, although most of those seen in this country under that name bear little relation to the original. Rock, water, and plants are the core features and should evoke the natural landscape. Surface texture, subtle coloring, and shape all contribute to their style and appeal.

Make a restful oasis, planted with bamboo, other foliage plants, and small-leaved evergreens, all set among drifts of gravel, pebbles, and small boulders. Add a bonsai tree in a beautiful pot, a Buddha strategically placed, or a stone lantern. Plants that lend the right mood include the

JAPANESE SERENITY Rocks and stones are the most dramatic features in an area that is planned according to traditional Japanese style, where space, texture, and form predominate. Use rocks as a sculpture, in an asymmetric arrangement, to set beside paths and swirls of raked gravel.

BAMBOO CLOCHES

COMBINE FUNCTION and form in an Eastern-style garden with bamboo cloches. Place the cover over a plant for shelter from frost and wind. To give more protection, cover the cloche with landscape fabric or newspaper held in place with clothespins. The woven dome lets rain through while creating a warmer microclimate.

angelica tree (*Aralia elata*), with large, deeply divided leaves, and its relative, *Fatsia japonica.* Clipped Sawara cypress (*Chamaecyparis pisifera*), grasses, ferns, and mosses are also appropriate. A Japanese maple (*Acer palmatum*) adds autumn color. The bamboo *Nandina domestica* and shrubby *Pinus mugo* — indeed all pines — add an Oriental air. Enhance the oasis with hummocks of clipped azaleas.

In a Chinese garden, plants have significance beyond their visual appeal. Grow peonies for wealth and grace, and magnolia, crab apple, and laurel for wealth and contentment. The bamboo is flexible yet strong; the peach brings fertility and longevity. Intersperse plantings with mosaics of pebbles or tiles that depict plants or animals.

Indian and Persian gardens can be suggested in your own plot. Such gardens are always formal, with cisterns of water as centerpieces and gently play-

ing fountains running along the length. Pots of geraniums stand symmetrically around the water. A palm, cordyline, or citrus tree in a tub helps to create the mood, although none of these is hardy in areas where temperatures regularly drop below freezing. The windmill palm (*Trachycarpus fortunei*), though, is hardy through zone 8.

Use precise, symmetrical plantings, perhaps in sunken beds with flowers at path height. Persian gardens are associated with roses, and the richness of all yellow roses has come from their *Rosa foetida* 'Persiana,' a double yellow old-fashioned shrub rose. Eastern styles and plants suit a small, enclosed town garden.

MODERN STYLES AT HOME AND ABROAD

In the rocky landscape of Scandinavia, gardens created from natural stone groupings studded with European birch are popular.

MODERN MIX AND MATCH Plants such as shrubby potentilla provide plenty of detail to hold interest, and they soften the hard surfaces. The gravel mulch suppresses weeds. Landscape ties support changes of level.

To echo this easy-living style, make an informal arrangement of lawn, conifers, and ground-cover plants, enlivened with spring bulbs and a few flowering shrubs. Add heathers for extra-trouble-free planting if you have acid soil.

In a town, try a totally architectural garden, in the style of modern French designers. Emphasize the paths, walls, and containers rather than the plants for a year-round no-work garden. Put the plants you do include in raised beds for changes of level. For satisfying shapes choose *Mahonia lomariifolia, Juniperus × media* 'Pfitzeriana,' or *J. scopulorum* 'Skyrocket.' Shrubs with good leaf color include *Euonymus fortunei* 'Silver Pillar' and *Ilex × altaclerensis* 'Lawsoniana.'

You could make separate sections of the garden reminiscent of the styles of other countries. One section could have the contemplative character of Japan, another the formality of France, and a hot area could have the flavor of Spain.

Gardeners are often conditioned by tradition to expect a certain look in a garden, and new ideas — even convenient ones — are accepted only slowly. The modern emphasis on subtle plantings overlaying hardscape is offering a distinctive new style, which is catching on gradually just as bygone styles once did.

MOORISH COOLNESS The sound of playing water, so welcome in an arid climate, the arches created by the jets, and the whispering of dark citrus leaves cool the sizzling atmosphere in a sun-drenched garden.

TOOLBOX

COPPER TAGS

WHEN SETTING OUT new shrubs, it is wise to label them, particularly if you have selected a specific variety and want to remember its name.

For an unobtrusive but permanent marker, use a copper tag and tie, which weather to a greenish color that blends in with the stems and foliage. Just write on the tag with a ballpoint pen and the name becomes indented. Attach it carefully to the chosen plant, making sure to leave plenty of slack for the stem to grow with age.

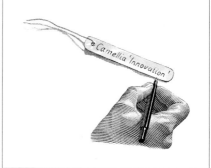

UNCLUTTERED LINES Unified by decking used for surfaces, seating, and planters, this modern garden has a no-frills simplicity. The fresh white argyranthemum and cheerful yellow chrysanthemum offset any starkness.

GARDENING BY DESIGN

FLOWER BEDS AND LAWNS, paving and gravel, paths and screens — what is the best combination for your garden? With so many possible shapes, patterns, and textures, ideas abound for striking a balance among the garden's major features. The plants will be the crowning glory, but the basic plan plays a crucial part in making your garden a success. It turns a static site into a dynamic design, builds in layer upon layer of interest, and ensures that, as the seasons pass, the garden gives lasting delight.

A richly planted bed of pinks, foxgloves, roses, and wallflowers is one component in a well-balanced composition of lawn, paving, and flowers.

BEDS, BORDERS, AND BETWEEN

CREATING A GARDEN happens over the years, reflecting the changing needs and tastes of its owner — and it is never finished. Often, ideas may come from visits to other gardens, both public and private. Public gardens are usually designed on a scale beyond the means of a private individual, but still may be thought-provoking. What works well in them can be adopted and adapted for sites that are often very different.

Commonly, however, it is the visits to private gardens that are most inspiring. In these more modest landscapes you see what a limited budget can achieve when joined with imagination and hard work. Any walk down a leafy street or through a village provides ideas — the flow of a border, the materials of a path, or a particularly pleasing combination of plants.

Back gardens are less easy to "visit." Perhaps the best chance to see them is from a train, when you may catch glimpses of all sorts of gardens. Traveling from a commuter rail station, you might see inner-city yards give way to the manicured lawns of suburban developments, and even to grand estates that may have matured long before the coming of the railroad.

REALISTIC PLANNING

Gardens often seem to have grown out of the life-styles of the owners, partly by need and partly by intention. The two vital questions in garden design — what do you want, and what do you have — impinge upon each other. There is no point in craving herbaceous borders with great drifts of color when you have a small town courtyard — but color harmonies are still important. It is equally futile to covet rhododendrons and camellias when you have alkaline soil, but raised beds and containers of an acidic well-drained soil mix can solve the dilemma on a small scale.

It helps to look at three major components of most gardens: grassed areas or their various alternatives; the beds and borders, specifically their shaping, planting, and edging; and the features that link or screen, such as paths, internal hedges, pergolas, and trellises. How these interact to form a satisfying whole is at the heart of garden design.

SHAPES AND SPACES Most gardens are developed around a choice of varied plant materials contained in a flower bed or flower border. You can use the garden's shape imaginatively — for example, on a square site, mow a daisy-free circle out of a round lawn surrounded by curving borders.

GREEN SURFACES

FOR MANY PEOPLE a lawn is central to the idea of a garden — it is where much activity takes place, both work and play. To maintain its perfect appearance you must feed, water, and mow it, as well as rake, weed, and aerate it. You might even have to treat it for pests. The close-clipped putting-green effect obtained is often its own justification — it is a design feature in which color and texture are as consciously contrived as broadloom carpet indoors. Its edges are as impeccably finished as its surface.

Other gardeners, however, while admitting its beauty, regard a perfect lawn as nearly unattainable and even unnecessary — and "green" gardeners consider the chemicals commonly used to achieve it as ecologically unacceptable. But most gardens of any size have some form of lawn.

Like other ground surfaces, a lawn has several roles to play.

❧ It provides open, flat space that contrasts with the densely planted borders that meet it.

❧ It is the best place from which to view the borders and to work on them.

❧ It offers a place to stroll, relax, and play games.

❧ It leads the eye and the feet to other parts of the garden.

❧ More than other surfaces, a lawn is forgiving and soothing in feel and color.

DIVIDING A LAWN INTO "ROOMS"

The use of different patterns of cutting helps distinguish the separate parts of the garden. Typically, garden spaces progress from formality around the house to ever-increasing informality where, for example, a field or an orchard meets the boundary hedge.

Give the first section of grass, quite small in area, as much care as you have the time to provide, in order to link the outdoor and indoor carpet effects. This will also demonstrate that the less carefully groomed effect elsewhere is intentional. After a divider such as an arch, a pergola, or an opening in an internal hedge or trellis, grow a stretch of less pampered lawn.

Where there is space, let this in turn, after a further divider, lead into an orchard area of fruit trees or specimen shrubs in rough grass. Such a meadow

HEART OF THE GARDEN A path flanked by spheres of boxwood marks the entry to the main "room" of the garden — the lawn. The grass should be smooth, but tough enough to walk on and take hard wear without damage.

effect — heightened by drifts of daffodils and poet's narcissus (*Narcissus poeticus* var. *recurvus*) from March to early June, oxeye daisies and lupines in summer and autumn crocus (*Colchicum*) to follow — makes a major feature in its own right.

Vary the planting to include your favorite bulbs and native species, which will determine how much maintenance the area needs. Usually a meadow — which comprises a mixture of herbaceous plants, not all of the grass family — can be maintained with one annual mowing. It needs no feeding, virtually no weeding unless some perennial becomes

GRASSY PATHS Like a path through a woodland, a strip of cut grass runs across a meadow-like area of long grass spangled with daffodils.

invasive, and certainly no spraying. Lovely as meadow grass looks, it is not easy to walk in, is slow to dry after rain, and needs a path mown through it. Where there is room, make the path wide enough for two people to walk abreast. Single file makes for tedious strolls.

Remember that a path cut through high grass lets stems flop inward across the path, especially in wet weather. This ruins the appearance and the convenience of walking. Cut a band about 1 ft (30 cm) wide to intermediate height on each side of the path; it will prevent lank stalks from brushing your legs and add another dimension to the design.

WHERE LAWN MEETS BORDER

Just as long grass falls across paths, plants bordering carefully tended lawns often flop. Plants tumbling forward in their natural habit show their beauty to the fullest, but the grass beneath suffers.

Except in the most formal spots, shrubs spilling onto the lawn do not matter, for the effect is yearlong and therefore the dead grass never shows. But removing herbaceous growth in autumn reveals entirely unacceptable edges and damaged turf that barely recovers by the following season. On the other hand, impeccably edged grass results in a bare rim of soil around the flower bed. Installing a border edging is the answer.

Variations on low retaining walls can help separate grass and border gardens.
❧ Ready-made edgings of plastic, wire, concrete, and wood are available at most garden centers. Just line them up and push them into place.
❧ Make miniwalls of local stone, brick, or paving slabs set on edge.
❧ Use landscape ties or redwood stripping, or logs set vertically or horizontally.
❧ Grow low hedges of boxwood, thyme, germander, or lavender.

It does not matter if a raised edging is not itself very attractive, because carefully chosen plants for the front row — such as arabis, aubrietia, *Gypsophila repens*, or pinks — tumbling over the rim hide much of the face. The advantage is that the edge plants do not meet the grass.

Even a bed edging that is only 3–4 in (7.5–10 cm) high lessens the problem; and a support higher than this contributes

MOWING MADE EASY A strip of paving bricks beside the lawn, butted up to terra-cotta edging, separates the soil and plants in the border from the grass. As well as looking neat, the arrangement greatly simplifies mowing.

A ROLL-OUT PATHWAY

IF YOU ARE GOING back and forth across the lawn with a wheelbarrow, perhaps with grass clippings or leaves, avoid making tracks or ruts in the grass by using a lightweight instant pathway made of wooden fencing. Simply hose the pathway down to clean it after use, and roll it up into a bundle for storage.

INVITING AUTUMN APPEAL In wilder parts of the garden, a scattering of maple leaves adds informal charm. A stepping-stone path tempts you to stroll around the shrubs and offers a firm footing on the grassy slope.

in other ways. Beds raised 1 ft (30 cm) above path or lawn level are markedly easier to weed. Raising bed edges is also a simple way to level a sloping grade and to prevent heavy rain from washing soil and seeds down onto a lawn or path.

MAKE LIFE EASIER WITH A MOWING STRIP

The hard vertical surface of a border edging prevents the mower blade from reaching the very edge of the grass, so you have to clip it by hand or use an electric trimmer. Insert a band of flat paving slabs just below lawn level at the base of the miniwall or bed edging, and the problem is solved. This band, known as a mowing strip, is equally important for a flat border.

Lawns require maintenance, and the shape of a lawn can both determine and

TRIM BORDER EDGINGS

A raised edging keeps plants and soil away from the lawn or hardscape and, when coupled with a mowing strip, makes cutting grass much easier. Some materials are so decorative that they become features in their own right.

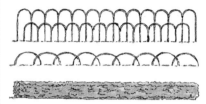

WIRE OR GREEN EDGINGS
Drawn wire edging was popular in the 19th century. Now more familiar in parks, it still makes a good separation of surfaces in the home garden. Clothe the wire with small-leaved ivy for a living edging or grow an entirely green one of clipped boxwood or neat dwarf hebe.

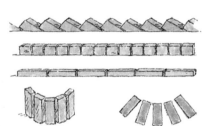

BRICK
Antique or modern, brick edging has a pleasing texture and can be laid in a variety of patterns. It works well around a circular bed. A dogtooth pattern, with bricks set on the diagonal, catches the eye. Choose a color of brick to suit the house or garden walls.

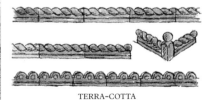

TERRA-COTTA
Glazed and shiny or unglazed and matt, terra-cotta edging tiles add a distinctive Victorian feel to the border. They come with little corner posts and in various patterns and colors. There are also plastic imitations available.

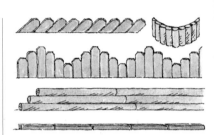

WOOD
Depending on their height, small logs can take on the character of a low retaining wall to hold a semi-raised bed. Wooden edgings come with rounded or flat faces. Combine different heights for added interest or paint the wood.

HOMEMADE OPTIONS
In a woodland garden, use small branches or sawn logs as a suitably rustic and informal edging. At seaside, pebbles, cobblestones, or shells set in mortar to hold them in place are in keeping with the coastal theme.

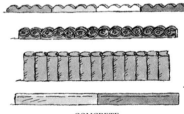

CONCRETE
Edge blocks in concrete are cheap and versatile. The plain ones can be laid on their ends or sides. Many have a decorative scalloped, fluted, or rope-motif top. They come in a range of colors, many agreeably muted.

be determined by the way it is mown. Large areas that require a riding mower should have curves, not sharp corners. On a lawn cut with a walk-behind mower, a rectangle is possible.

ALTERNATIVES TO GRASS LAWNS

Grass is the most adaptable living material for a lawn and is a plant family of amazing diversity. No other plants stand up to such foot traffic and wear. It is a delightful fantasy to wander down the garden path in a haze of crushed thyme or chamomile, and, indeed, it can be done — occasionally. Both thyme and chamomile (and pearlwort in heavier soils) have their

place; they can be introduced as additional species in a grass lawn and can combine and coexist with the finer grasses. Alternatively, put them in the gaps of paving and other hard surfaces.

Beyond this, "turf" composed entirely of such broad-leaved species soon gets tired and shabby. Simplicity of maintenance is also a promise not borne out in practice. Regular mowing is not needed, but grass becomes a persistent weed in such a lawn, and selective herbicides for it are hard to find.

In areas where there is little or no foot traffic, easier solutions apply. Ground-covering shrubs such as creeping junipers

may be planted at intervals of a couple of feet and surrounded by a thick mulch of shredded bark. In a few years the shrubs will meet in a sea of textured green.

PLANTING GROUND COVER

Use ground cover where lawn will not thrive — in damp, dark areas or thin, dry soils where you do not want to walk but would like to see an expanse of green. Make them into elements of the overall design, planting in geometric shapes, bold swaths, or informal groups.

🌿 Evergreen ivies, periwinkle, and pachysandra grow well in sun or shade and in most soils. All three have variegated forms to add interest.

🌿 Wintergreen (*Gaultheria procumbens*), with red berries in autumn and bell flowers in summer, thrives in light shade and acid soil.

🌿 In a sunny, dry place, try the silver *Hebe pinguifolia* 'Pagei,' lamb's-ears (*Stachys byzantina* 'Silver Carpet'), thrift (*Armeria*), most pinks, sunroses, and two aromatic herbs — chamomile (*Chamaemelum nobile* 'Treneague') and creeping thyme (*Thymus serpyllum*). All of these plants tolerate alkaline soil.

FRAMING A RECTANGLE OF LAWN Around a small area of grass, a mowing strip acts as a frame and gives a hard edge on which to turn without stepping in the soil. Border plants can dip forward without damaging the turf.

USE A GFCI

WHEN YOU WORK with a power tool such as an electric mower or hedge trimmer, always plug it into a circuit protected by a ground fault interrupter. It cuts off power instantly if you cut the cord. Drape the cord over your shoulder to keep it at a safe distance from the blades as you work.

A SUCCESSFUL BLEND OF GRASSES Lawns need a mixture of several grass species; even an impeccable putting green is made up of two or three. Your cooperative extension office can advise on the best grasses for your region.

HARD SURFACES

P AVED AREAS are likely to be permanent structures in the garden, and their design and construction require the utmost thought and care. You will need to balance aesthetic considerations — you look at these areas all the time — with convenience and durability. Surfaces should be smooth but not slippery, quick to drain and dry after a rain, and easy to maintain.

The choice of materials, both natural and manmade, is vast. There are marble, slate, and stone; bricks, granite setts, pavers and tiles of all kinds; cobblestones, pebbles, gravel, and sand; wooden decking, planks, landscape ties, sections of tree trunks, and wood chips or shredded bark. Any is effective in the right setting.

ONE MATERIAL OR SEVERAL?

The use of similar materials throughout various areas and levels unifies the garden. Laying a range of surfaces, however, has the opposite effect: each part of the garden displays subtle differences in character, which are emphasized by the choice of plants and ornaments.

When you are mixing materials, use the most formal, such as flagstones or brickwork, nearest the house. Farther away, install a more casual surface, such as gravel dotted with stepping-stones and informal plantings. Farther away again, build a path of, perhaps, landscape ties to a dappled glade, where bluebells, primroses, ferns, hostas, and other shade-lovers grow through bark mulch.

IMAGINATIVE USE OF BRICK AND STONE

Stones and pavers of all kinds are made to suit every style, budget, and situation. Lay them butted close together, either set in sand or pointed with mortar; you can edge them with bands of timber, brick, cobblestones, grass, or low-growing plants. In any case, leave some gaps to fill with plants.

Use granite setts in a similar fashion. They are handy for curves and circular designs because of their small size. In a modest area, a circle is dramatic enough

SUBTLE WAYS WITH BRICK Lay materials to direct the eye or to star in their own right. The zigzag herringbone pattern suggests movement down the path, while the circle draws attention to the central pedestal.

CONTRASTING SHAPES, TONES, AND TEXTURES For a small garden, dispense with lawn and use an imaginative mixture of surfaces instead. Loose gravel lightens the brick in color and form, with evergreens providing year-round shades of soft green on the ground and up poles and trellises.

to need little more than a few peripheral plants to set it off. A spiral of setts, like a jelly roll filled with, say, creeping thyme, would dramatize a plant or ornament at its center.

Bricks come in many colors, from soft yellow to dark purple-blue, and several varieties. Make sure you select bricks that can be used for paving and are frost resistant. When possible, use those that complement the house walls, perhaps banded with another color for contrast in a large area. Coordinate them with nearby plants, too. Honey-colored bricks and somber gray-purple ones are compatible with most flowers, but vibrant red brick, on the ground or as a wall, clashes with French marigolds, scarlet roses, and geraniums.

There are many patterns of brickwork, from herringbone and basketweave to simple courses, both straight and curved. Lay bricks alone or with any other surfacing material. Laying them diagonally or in overlapping squares and circles creates interesting effects, particularly useful when a break in pattern draws attention to a change of level.

If you can get it, native stone looks best for paths and paving. Many areas of the country have their own type to offer. In a neighborhood of brick houses, use stone to relieve the large expanses of brick surfacing.

Precast concrete slabs, which vary from stone look-alikes to unrelieved blocks of gray, can be almost as good as natural stone. Use colors to harmonize with the plants and soften further with bands of other materials.

Random paving is best laid in sections framed with brick or redwood stripping to give form to the broken stone slabs.

CREATIVE WAYS WITH CONCRETE

For large areas, poured concrete is comparatively inexpensive and very practical, needing no cutting or trimming to fit into tricky corners. It is the quickest material to lay, but hard to remove once in place. Concrete requires imaginative handling, even if colored. It gains more character when interspersed with other materials. Its appearance is improved when it is given texture by brushing to expose the aggregate or raking to create shallow grooves, both of which also prevent it from becoming slippery.

In a small informal garden, press shells, fossils, stones, or tiles into the concrete just before it hardens, putting them in a variety of shapes and designs. Alter-

CHECKERBOARD PATTERNS Lay concrete squares, filling some of the spaces between with smooth cobblestones and planting others with grasses and herbs. Add a central urn and you have a very sophisticated look.

natively, stamp patterns into the concrete at the same stage by pressing down firmly on pastry cutters, shells, leaves, or bits of ironwork. For fun, make hand prints or walk up the path in bare feet or flipflops (the larger the better). Fill the resulting impressions with some colored gravel; plant them with baby's-tears (*Soleirolia soleirolii*), moss, grass, stonecrop (*Sedum*), or creeping thyme; or leave them empty to catch water and reflect the sky.

There are other ways to relieve the starkness of concrete. Frame formal areas with bands of brick or stone (ideally exactly the same color as those of the house) or insert panels of granite setts, cobblestones, pottery shards, or tiles.

In a modern setting, insert lengths of timber and groups of low-growing plants

PLAIN BUT BOLD The stronger the paving pattern, the simpler the planting should be to work with it. Furry leaves of lamb's-ears (*Stachys byzantina*) enliven the flat texture of the bricks and color of the stones.

BEST PLANTS

CREVICE PLANTING

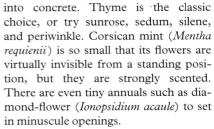

Soften the lines of a hard surface and keep the weeds out by sowing seeds of low-growing plants you want.

• Aubrietia (*Aubrieta deltoidea*): evergreen with pinkish-lavender flowers in spring.

• Maiden pink (*Dianthus deltoides*): evergreen and mat-forming with small white or pink flowers in summer.

• *Erigeron karvinskianus*: daisy-like flowers open white, turn pink, and fade to purple in summer and autumn.

• Diamond-flower (*Ionopsidium acaule*): lilac or white flowers flushed deep blue in summer and early fall.

• Corsican mint (*Mentha requienii*): tiny semi-evergreen leaves smell of peppermint when crushed; little lavender-purple flowers in summer.

• *Pratia angulata*: evergreen, with star-shaped white flowers in late spring and purple-red berries in autumn.

• Pearlwort (*Sagina subulata*): mat-forming perennial with starry white flowers in summer.

• Creeping thyme (*Thymus serpyllum*): aromatic, with leaves from olive to bronze to yellow and silver; pinkish flowers in summer.

into concrete. Thyme is the classic choice, or try sunrose, sedum, silene, and periwinkle. Corsican mint (*Mentha requienii*) is so small that its flowers are virtually invisible from a standing position, but they are strongly scented. There are even tiny annuals such as diamond-flower (*Ionopsidium acaule*) to set in minuscule openings.

Brushed concrete is a comparatively cheap surfacing, created by watering and brushing newly laid concrete when it is nearly dry to expose its gravel aggregate. Poured concrete areas, unless reinforced with mesh or coarse chicken wire, should not be more than 10–13 ft (3–4 m) across, because the expansion and contraction that occur in changing temperatures cause cracks. Create a pattern that allows for the concrete to expand and contract by containing it in separate areas framed by treated softwood or cedar strips, brick, or slabs.

ORNAMENTAL USES FOR SAND, PEBBLES, AND GRAVEL

Sand and gravel, being cheap, adaptable, and easy to install and maintain, have few drawbacks, except that gravel is not kind to bare feet or high heels. Letting plants grow and self-seed through gravel gives a pleasing sense of change and development. Sand and gravel are much used in Japanese-style gardens — raked into swirling patterns around groups of plants and boulders to suggest the movement of water. As the patterns are broken when the area is walked upon, put in some stepping-stones or wooden "bridges" for strollers to use.

Cobblestones or disc-shaped stones make unusual paved areas. Smaller, flat stones, set on edge in mortar, make a charming circle for a central feature. Use clay tiles, also set on edge and sunk flush with the ground, to make circles and patterns among paving.

GRAVEL PRACTICALITIES

Gravel has been a staple covering for stretches of garden since gardens were first made, and it remains useful. There are local colors and textures. Take care not to use too great an expanse or you end up with a pebble beach over which it is almost impossible to push a loaded

WINNING COMBINATIONS Stone or concrete slabs can seem unwelcoming until rimmed with plants. Primroses, pansies, pinks, and lady's-mantle quickly make a cold gray expanse look friendly and approachable.

wheelbarrow. Loose gravel is also easily picked up underfoot and carried onto grass, where it subsequently meets the mower with a crash.

Some sort of bonding is essential; it can occur naturally with crushed rock mixed with stone dust (obtainable from most gravel suppliers). This, rolled in over a firm, level base, gives a hard-wearing, long-lasting surface. Resin-based bonding agents are also available to settle the layer of loose surface stones. Plants will seed themselves into gravel, but they are easy to pull out. Do not pull too hastily or you risk losing desirable plants that appear. Many find an untrodden bit of gravel a perfect seedbed. Transplant them later or even leave them where they are.

VARIETY IN WOOD

Wood is compatible with many garden styles and is easily trimmed to size. Decking works for a level area or as a walkway over broken ground. It can be laid in straight or diagonal runs, and small sections can be laid in squares. Planks of rot-resistant hardwood or of pressure-treated softwood make unusual hard surfaces in corners or damp places.

Discs cut from a tree trunk can be used for a path in wild gardens, winding among low plants. Decking has a nonslip coating, but planks, tree slices, and landscape ties get mossy and very slippery and must be cleaned regularly.

Landscape ties are effective with bold plantings and also make low retaining walls. Two will bridge a small stream.

MIXING MATERIALS IN A COMPACT SPACE

Given enough space, most gardeners want a lawn. But in a small urban space you are better off mixing hard materials to create a courtyard atmosphere. This cuts down considerably on the labor, although the initial outlay is higher.

The smaller the space, the more important it is to consider the winter months. Little lawns of muddy grass in a town garden are depressing, while crisp paving with a winter-flowering cherry or winter jasmine, a beautiful camellia, sculptural conifers, and some tubs promising early-spring bulbs look encouraging through the bleakest time of the year.

A mixture of squared flagstone and brick gives a classic look. Substitute cast

A GROOVE KNIFE

FOR GRUBBING OUT WEEDS from between paving stones, a specialized tool makes the work easier. A groove knife has a right-angled blade that can be turned over to provide a narrow hook so you can poke into crevices to remove moss and the roots of unwanted plants.

CONTRASTS IN SIZE Show-stopping plants such as gunnera are set off by rugged granite setts with moss between. Rising from a sea of foliage plants in a confined space, the vast leaves look all the more dramatic.

WOOD AND GRAVEL Landscape ties are tough and useful both for making strong lines in a design and for edging and containing gravel.

IN VOGUE WITH DECKING Wooden decking is both stylish and comfortable; and if made with treated wood, it will need little maintenance.

CURVES AND COLOR In a garden defined by austere brick, straight lines, and monochrome, contrive some pleasing curves and cheery accents with plants. Pink cranesbill geraniums tumble over the edging, pansies beam toward the light, and a dusky red clematis drapes the wall.

stone or slabs of concrete to cut the cost while retaining the elegant style and run rivulets of brick through the design to create a more mellow effect. Blended with soft herbs, paving and planting like this give a Mediterranean air that lasts all year if you include plenty of evergreens.

STARKER COMBINATIONS

Hard gray granite chips and granite setts create a starker effect than brick and stone mixes. In regions where granite is the native rock, such surfacing looks at home. Beware, however, of introducing such assertive materials into other landscapes.

To soften a design of granite setts and chips, plant low-growing *Pinus mugo*, a gray-leaved senecio *Brachyglottis* 'Sun-shine'), or broom (*Cytisus*) with some low junipers. Introduce color with annuals or bulbs planted in half-barrels set on the paving.

TAKE CARE OF THE DRAINAGE

Lay all paving on a well-tamped 6–8 in (14–20 cm) layer of coarse sand. In small areas this is usually all the drainage necessary, and plants grown in the cracks soften the scene.

The larger the area of paving, the greater the need to drain it. Slope it very slightly away from the house, picking up surplus water at the edge of the paving in a drain run below the soil in the flanking border. Lead it to a dry well if the ground is not porous enough to absorb most of the water runoff.

STONE PAVING In a chic, urban garden, team the elegance of stone with a symmetrical design, graceful foliage, and clipped evergreens.

PLANNING BEDS AND BORDERS

Besides housing plants, beds and borders serve to surround and divide garden areas. The height and bulk of the plants protect you from wind, screen you from neighbors, and even help muffle the noises of traffic or children playing nearby. Frequently borders are backed by a boundary or internal hedge, or they run alongside paths.

What is seldom seen in photographs of grand country-house herbaceous borders, which appear so completely of a piece with the setting, is that a narrow service path runs between the hedge and the flowers. The hedge can be clipped without the plants being hurt, root competition is reduced, and the border itself is easily maintained from both front and back. Even in a small garden, the virtues of such a path are clear.

Similarly, in the country, garden borders frequently back onto pasture, and people go to great trouble to erect barricades that prevent animals from browsing on their choice shrubs. Failure is frequent. It is much better to bring the border forward by, in effect, taking a yard or so off the lawn in front and slipping it in at the back. Maintenance is helped, weeds from the field no longer creep in, and animals cannot reach the plants.

ACCESSIBLE ISLAND BEDS

An island bed does not have to follow a path or boundary, so it can have a more flowing shape. Cut two, three, or more areas out of the lawn, and the areas between double as paths allowing passage for maintenance and appreciation.

The size of island beds is determined partly by the scale of the garden and partly by what you want to grow in them. Sweeping, flowing edges are more difficult to mow or to provide with a mowing strip, so aim for gentle curves. As with curved lawns, avoid irrational, fussy wiggles and swirls.

First sketch shapes of island beds on paper. Use garden hose or a piece of rope to try out the shape on the ground before you do anything irrevocable. When you

MIXED BORDER Compose a wide border with classic herbaceous perennials such as sedum, agapanthus, crocosmia, and dahlias, backed by shrubs and yucca. Cordylines add a touch of the exotic in warmer gardens.

are cutting beds out of an existing lawn, you can help soil fertility by digging the turf in face down to rot gradually. You must remove some soil so that the final bed level is not much above that of the grass. Mounded beds are seldom successful; soil is apt to be washed down in periods of heavy rain.

Grade the plants' heights from the edge to the focus of the bed. Island beds have clear advantages: as they are never backed by higher hedges or fences, their plants are less likely to become thin and leggy. This virtually eliminates the need to stake herbaceous perennials, especially when you choose plants with robust stems rather than the dwarf varieties, which often lose the typical form and charm of the species.

An island bed faces in all directions but is completely open to light. There is little need to be concerned with exposure unless the central plants are large enough to cast considerable shade. There is room for surprise, too. Break a too-even grading of plants by placing some taller ones toward the front; select early-flowering plants so that, when they are past and clipped back, a shorter plant behind comes into view.

VISTA BORDERS

A view from a door or a window often needs framing so that the eye is led away — for a few feet or a hundred — to a focal point at the end. That framing is wonderfully executed with a pair of narrow borders flanking a walk.

The walk itself, regardless of the size of garden, is unlikely to be less than 4 ft (1.2 m) wide, but the vista borders can be of any width. Narrow ones might hold just a single line of Hidcote lavender or, for color in August and September, *Caryopteris* 'Kew Blue,' thickly underplanted with crocuses and *Scilla siberica* for spring. As with island beds, the open aspect of double-sided borders reduces the need for staking, especially where the central walk is hard and mowing strips on the outside edges catch front-row plants that flop forward.

CONSIDER EXPOSURE

Formal straight borders face a particular direction. The exposure determines the range of plants a border can contain.

Borders that face south, especially where soil drainage is good (and it is well worth ensuring that it is), call for sun-loving plants. Choose species from warm

WALK OF DELIGHT The pleasure of wandering through a garden reaches new heights when Himalayan blue poppies (*Meconopsis × sheldonii*) flank the lawn. These short-lived perennials need plenty of water in summer.

COMBINING PLANTS Concentrations of color against a permanent frame achieve the best result. The clematis provides a splash of pink between the background *Solanum crispum* and bluish grass *Helictotrichon sempervirens*.

MONEY · SAVERS

SEVERAL PLANTS IN ONE

WHEN YOU BUY young perennials in containers, look for robust, bushy specimens. You can usually turn one such plant into at least three. At home, take the plant out of the pot. Tease the roots apart, and divide the plant with a sharp knife, making sure each section has plenty of roots. Plant the pieces in separate holes in their flowering positions. Tamp them down and water in well.

climates, such as the Mediterranean cistus, the tree poppy (*Romneya coulteri*) from California, and red-hot pokers from South Africa, as well as spring bulbs.

A north-facing border is the mirror image. If the soil does not dry out, it provides a happy home not just for all the subtly beautiful plants that accept shade but also for water-lovers, often considered the prerogative of gardeners with a pond. Waterside marginals such as primulas, rodgersias, and astilbes flourish.

West-facing borders have many of the advantages of south-facing ones but never get as hot, since the sun comes in midafternoon. Plant sun-lovers such as *Jasminum officinale* and peonies. There is no need to restrict your choice to drought-resistant specimens.

East has the chill of a north border but alleviated by morning sun, which passes before the full heat of the day. Plants to avoid are those that bloom early in the year such as peonies or camellias. Frosts may strike first thing in the morning, and sun on frosted plants browns them. A clematis such as 'Ernest Markham,' with magenta flowers in summer, is suitable.

Fortunately many garden plants will flourish in a wide range of conditions. However, no rhododendrons or camellias do well in alkaline soils, and no sun-loving types thrive in poorly drained clay. Apart from basic concerns like these, the choice is up to you.

SHRUBS FOR THE BACKBONE OF THE BORDER

Develop your ideas bearing two points in mind. First, in most American climates, no plants flower continuously. Second, green is a color, not simply a backdrop. Accept that the form, texture, and foliage of your plants often offer more to the garden scene than masses of temporary color. Wonderful effects can be obtained with the formality of the simplest materials such as walks, hedges, and topiary. Keep vibrant color to annuals in pots, as in southern European gardens.

The most permanent border plants are woody shrubs. Usually you make a choice based on the beauty or brilliance of flowers — for instance, golden forsythia for spring, the headily scented lilac or mock orange for early summer, buddleia for later. The transient season of each is part of the joy of the garden — one plant's moment of glory leading on to the next. But what about lilac or mock orange during the other eleven months of

PROPAGATING INDOORS

YOU DO NOT NEED a greenhouse or a propagator to raise shrubs from your own cuttings; an indoor windowsill provides a protected environment.

Screw two cup hooks into the wall on either side of the window, about halfway up, and rest a dowel across them. Set a short wooden board on the windowsill. Secure this shelf with strings fastened with tacks on its underside and tied to the dowel above. Lay tinfoil, shiny side up, on the shelf and up the sides of the window recess.

Pot the cuttings and place them on the shelf. Attach a sheet of heavy-gauge plastic film to the dowel, draping it over the front of the shelf. The cuttings should soon take root.

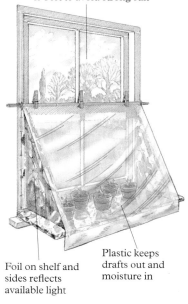

Northeast-facing window is best to avoid strong sun

Foil on shelf and sides reflects available light

Plastic keeps drafts out and moisture in

the year? Consider whether an alternative would earn its keep for more of the year. A shrub such as *Mahonia aquifolium*, with glossy evergreen leaves that bronze in winter and bunches of purple fruit that follow the yellow flowers, gives twelve months of interest.

CHOICE OF A COLOR SCHEME

Begin planning a bed by listing "must haves" and their color or by checking off irresistible plants in a catalog. If you have no preconceived idea of the desired look,

study the list to see if any theme suggests itself — maybe a white border or a blue-and-gray bed.

Perhaps there are a number of yellow-flowering plants — forsythia, *Cytisus × praecox*, *Rhododendron luteum*, *Spartium junceum* — and a couple of pink or red shrubs such as weigela or *Rhododendron* 'Mars' on your list.

It is now a matter of choice whether you keep the happy miscellany or develop a deliberate scheme. For instance, you could keep the yellows and, instead

A SHOW FOR THE FIRST YEAR

Use annuals to give a long-term border early character. Hardy types often self-seed and come up the next year.

- Love-lies-bleeding (*Amaranthus caudatus*): bushy, with plush tassels of red flowers from summer to autumn.

- Pot marigold (*Calendula officinalis* 'Art Shades'): double apricot, orange, or cream daisy-like flowers.

- Cornflower (*Centaurea cyanus*): double, daisy-like flowers in blue, pink, red, purple, or white; good for cutting.

- Godetia (*Clarkia unguiculata*): generous trumpets of pink, salmon, red, purple, or white flowers.

- *Convolvulus tricolor* 'Royal Ensign': intense dark blue saucer-shaped flowers, with yellowish-white throats.

- California poppy (*Eschscholzia californica*): cup-shaped, vivid yellow or orange papery flowers.

- Sunflower (*Helianthus annuus*): huge, daisy-like yellow flowers with dark centers.

- Mallow (*Lavatera trimestris*): white, pink, or red trumpet-shaped flowers.

- Love-in-a-mist (*Nigella damascena* 'Persian Jewels'): semi-double flowers in blue, pink, or white; ferny leaves.

- Opium poppy (*Papaver somniferum*): large single or double flowers in red, pink, purple, or white.

- Corn or field poppy (*Papaver rhoeas* 'Fairy Wings'): red, pink, and white single and double flowers.

FILLED WITH COLOR Pink lupine spikes tower over a clump of blue-purple *Centaurea montana* while, farther along, poppies burst into bloom. Rustic poles allow for growing climbers at the back of the border.

of the pink flowers, bring in *Cotinus coggygria* 'Royal Purple' and *Rosa glauca* to paint a picture in gold and purple.

Continue such a theme by adding gold and purple herbaceous perennials to fill out the garden at a lower level — still remembering the value of foliage. You might consider *Acanthus spinosus*, gold-variegated *Yucca filamentosa*, or the late-flowering purple-leaved variety of *Cimicifuga racemosa* to put with a group of asters. Provide spring interest with golden daffodils, coming through purple ajuga, 'Apricot Beauty' or 'Black Parrot' tulips, and *Lysimachia nummularia* 'Aurea.' Plant the bulbs deeply to remain as permanent plants. A similar theme can be pursued through any choice of colors.

BRIGHTENING THE BORDER IN THE FIRST TWO YEARS

The early days in a border's life can seem interminable before your ideal vision starts to show, so temporary plants are the answer in the first two years. Spring hardly lives up to its name in the garden without wallflowers (*Erysimum*), sweetly scented as nothing else. 'Harpur Crewe' fits the bill to perfection. Choose polyanthuses and primroses at the same time; they stay in flower for months if deadheaded regularly.

Common stocks (*Matthiola incana*) overlap with wallflowers and last into June. Like all true cottage garden plants, they are strongly scented. In late summer perennials such as rudbeckia and sweet peas can take over.

(continued on p. 112)

DEVELOPING A BORDER

A border planted in autumn is already taking shape the following spring. Bulbs and annuals fill it out while the permanent shrubby and herbaceous plantings mature.

THIS BORDER is the main planting area of the garden and extends about 12 ft (3.7 m) from the back fence. A low retaining wall separates the border from the lawn, and a path, which will be virtually hidden by the mature plants, lets you reach the middle and back of the border for weeding and pruning.

Shrubs form the framework of the planting, supplemented by perennials and bulbs, both of which flower reliably year after year. The taller shrubs are near the fence at the back, the smaller ones in front. Set the young bushes one-and-one-half times their mature spread apart, so you do not fall into the trap of plant-ing too close. The color theme is blue and purple with flame-bright accents. Purple and gray foliage complements, cools, and contains the floral display. Planting relatively few species heightens the effect, so there are single plants of the large shrubs, several perennials, and as many bulbs as possible.

Color and even height can come from annuals and biennials in the first year, but it is still vital that the permanent plants go in at the beginning. The temporary plants follow the planned color scheme, and these easy-come-easy-go plants give a foretaste of how the mature bed will look in its full glory.

Silvery artemisia sets off purple sage

The first spring

With autumn preparation and planting, you can expect color and interest from early spring, only four or five months later. The contribution of bulbs is short but spectacular. Bright red tulips and pastel-tinted daffodils and wallflowers reflect the overall color scheme. Crocus and scilla provide early color, and forget-me-not comes into flower slightly later.

The first summer

In the first and second years, before the shrubs fill out, there is ample space to add splashes of summer color. Annuals planted in early summer over the bulbs include cornflowers and California poppies, petunias, nasturtiums, annual mallow, cosmos, and love-lies-bleeding. In a mild winter a few cushions of cold-tolerant pansies can provide welcome color.

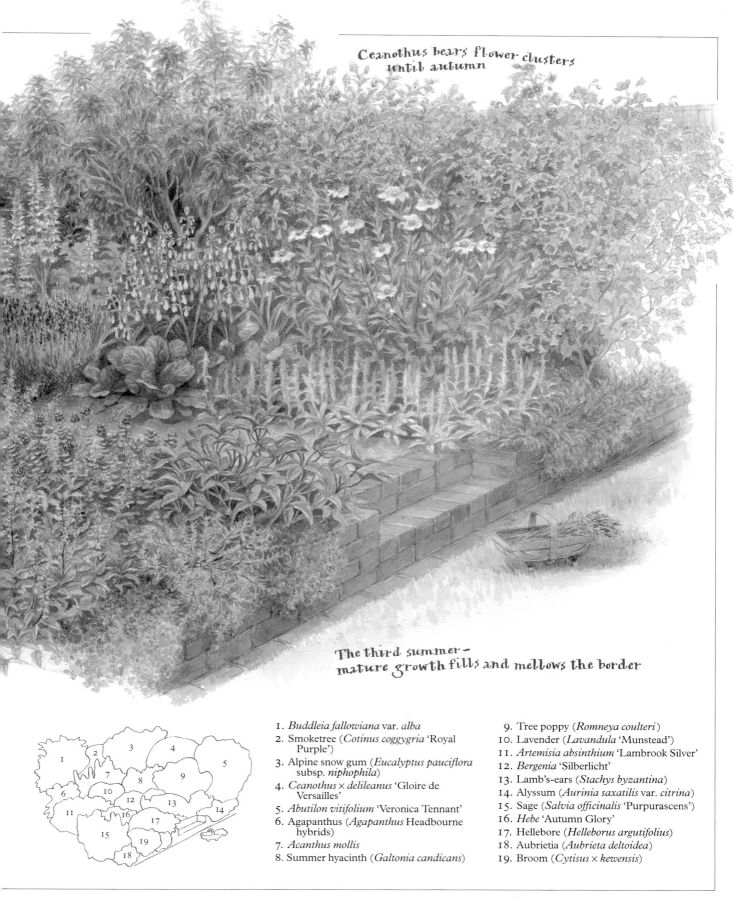

Ceanothus bears flower clusters until autumn

The third summer — mature growth fills and mellows the border

1. *Buddleia fallowiana* var. *alba*
2. Smoketree (*Cotinus coggygria* 'Royal Purple')
3. Alpine snow gum (*Eucalyptus pauciflora* subsp. *niphophila*)
4. *Ceanothus* × *delileanus* 'Gloire de Versailles'
5. *Abutilon vitifolium* 'Veronica Tennant'
6. Agapanthus (*Agapanthus* Headbourne hybrids)
7. *Acanthus mollis*
8. Summer hyacinth (*Galtonia candicans*)
9. Tree poppy (*Romneya coulteri*)
10. Lavender (*Lavandula* 'Munstead')
11. *Artemisia absinthium* 'Lambrook Silver'
12. *Bergenia* 'Silberlicht'
13. Lamb's-ears (*Stachys byzantina*)
14. Alyssum (*Aurinia saxatilis* var. *citrina*)
15. Sage (*Salvia officinalis* 'Purpurascens')
16. *Hebe* 'Autumn Glory'
17. Hellebore (*Helleborus argutifolius*)
18. Aubrietia (*Aubrieta deltoidea*)
19. Broom (*Cytisus* × *kewensis*)

LINKS AND DIVIDERS

TURNING A CORNER Inset strips of concrete are simple to lay around a curve and are easier and quieter to walk on than slightly shifting gravel.

FOUR-SQUARE FORMALITY All paths lead to the central focal point, and the continuous line of chamomile adds a visual and fragrant lure.

BRICK MOTIF The brick pattern has a practical purpose: it stops gravel from being carried to the lawn. Landscape ties make handy steps.

PATHWAYS SHOULD BE just one part of a garden layout, not the reason for it. Imagine two identical neighboring gardens. One has a T-shaped path to link the key elements of the layout, leaving three little plots to cover with grass: one on either side of the path and one along the top of the T. The other, filled with flowers and shrubs, has a single path weaving among the masses of color and fragrance and joining every element of the design without dominating it.

Either approach is valid, but regarding the hardscape as just another element in a tapestry tends to produce a more versatile, less rigid layout, giving you scope to develop the garden.

There are no rules stating that a path has to be such and such a width or even that it must be straight. The path may take a diagonal route across a wider paved area scattered with planting or zigzag through shrubs.

THE BEST MATERIAL FOR A PATH

The length, and therefore cost, as well as the look you are seeking are factors in your choice of path. Service paths, which lead to, say, the garbage cans and are in frequent use, need to be usable at all times of the year — preferably textured and well drained so that they do not become slippery in winter. But bear in mind that stone paving, even when well laid, becomes slippery under trees or in shade unless you scrub it regularly.

Bricks take a lot of beating as a surface. Use wire-cut pavers, which are thinner and harder than building bricks. Building bricks need to be set on edge to expose their hardest sides, and are extravagant as pathways for that reason. The way you lay bricks influences how the eye sees the path.

❧ Bricks laid lengthways emphasize a long, narrow look.

❧ Bands of bricks laid crossways with another material break up the length, suggesting greater width.

❧ A diagonal pattern acts like an arrow, urging walkers down the path.

Textured concrete or cast stone slabs come in an enormous range, are nonslip, and, when coordinated with their surroundings, are pleasing to the eye. Edging is not necessary when you pave with a hard surface, as long as the levels are correct on either side of it. But install either a brick-on-edge curb or a wooden one when you use a fine path medium such as pea gravel or, in a woodland setting, shredded bark.

PUTTING PATHS ON SLOPES

A path on a slope needs even greater care. When crossing a slope, any walkway should be horizontal, making in fact a terrace. Ground above the path must be graded gently so that soil does not wash down — quick-spreading ground cover such as periwinkle, wild strawberry, *Lamium galeobdolon*, or *Hypericum calycinum* help. Alternatively, the slope needs a retaining wall to support it. This results in one of the best and most convenient of all garden features — a raised bed. The path itself must also have sound support, such as bricks set in a cement base, on its lower side.

Paths on a slope have their own problems. Loose gravel or stone chips are unsuitable surfaces, as they move under the feet and are washed away by heavy rain, though a diagonal gutter set across the path between two boards every so often helps. Surfaces can be slippery regardless of material once the slope exceeds about one in ten. There is then no alternative but for the path to have a step every stride or so.

SCREENS WITHIN THE GARDEN

Part of the function of borders is, as the word suggests, to "border" — to edge a space. But they also link and divide garden areas. Think of the border across the garden that conventionally separates lawn and flower beds from a vegetable garden, wild garden, or the compost and storage areas beyond.

A screen in this spot is often one of the first requirements of a new garden, but a fully living division takes several years to achieve. Some hedges are quite quick — Leyland cypress does the job wonderfully but never knows when to stop. But more satisfactory for immediate effect is a built divider. Walls and fences, especially if they match or harmonize with existing buildings in the same material, are seldom bettered.

Lighter screens are usually less expensive to construct but less permanent. Diamond-pattern or squared trellises have an honorable tradition — the grandest 17th-century gardens in Europe, from Versailles downward, used latticework

END IN SIGHT Part of the function of a path is to divide borders, but it also works to lead the eye to a distant object such as a bench.

DYNAMIC DIAMONDS The zigzag of gravel and slabs feels more energetic than a straight line, suitable for a path leading down the garden.

IN COTTAGE-GARDEN TRADITION Roses and catmint tumble softly over a path with a white picket gate at the end. Laying the bricks horizontally across the path makes it seem wider, and even with plants narrowing it, two people can still walk along comfortably side by side.

UNDER A CANOPY Scented roses overhead add pleasure to a walk, with an intriguing glimpse of distant lawn and plants to draw you on.

extensively. When a trellis is firmly anchored — perhaps as panels within a solid fence or wall frame, reducing visual weight and cost at the same time — it is to be highly recommended. It provides perfect support for climbers, the quickest of all plants to grow, soon making the screen between garden areas effective.

That end-of-garden area where all manner of unsightly objects, pieces of equipment, and piles of debris accumulate needs to be screened, but also reached. A simple service path down one side of the main garden area — itself screened from general view — is one option. When the central lawn is intended to be impeccable, such extra access is essential to keep a worn track from developing, though wear can also be reduced by setting paving stones into the grass at vulnerable points.

But more often, you want to take pleasure in passing from one area to another. Where there is only a yard or two between the screen and the end of the garden, frame an eye-catching pot on a pedestal in the gap, leaving just enough space left and right to get a wheelbarrow to the compost bin. When there are more spacious garden areas to go on to, make a bolder focal point with a statue or large architectural plant.

Frame this important sight line with the edges of a border, cut through by a path to provide access. Mark it with a matching pair of sentinel features, made from pillars, obelisks, simple posts, or from statuesque plants. This is just the place to practice the gentle art of topiary, whether a pair of simple obelisk yews, a peacock and another creature, or abstract flights of fancy.

MAKING OVERHEAD FEATURES OF LINKS

Screens and paths act as frames for the garden as well as links and dividers. To complete the frame, link a screen on the left and right with an overhead section. Join the top beams of a trellis or train topiary pillars to become an arch.

Unlike a two-dimensional picture, a garden has real depth. You can project an arch backward or forward to become a pergola. At once you reintroduce the link between architecture and plants that makes gardening so satisfying.

Visits to large garden centers and flower shows demonstrate the range of materials from which to make garden screens, pergolas, arbors, and tunnels. Stone, concrete, wood, iron, and even

A FOLDING WHEELBARROW

LIGHTWEIGHT AND COMPACT, a folding wheelbarrow takes up hardly any storage space and is much less cumbersome than a conventional metal type. Despite the lightness of its woven fabric, the wheelbarrow is sturdy enough for most garden jobs and ideal for transporting weeds, prunings, or lawn clippings. The fabric and the rubber wheel are replaceable, and the frame is rust resistant.

VERSATILE TRELLIS The open diamonds make an excellent garden divider, separating different areas without closing them off. Where the panels meet in an arch, clematis turns the trellis into a stunning feature.

PULLING TOGETHER The reward for meticulous planning is a garden where surfaces, borders, and dividers all work to make a satisfying whole. The paving leads around soft plantings of euphorbias and yellow alyssum to the steps in the balustrade, which make the link to the raised lawn.

wire constructions are available. Base your choice on existing features, what you expect its life span to be, what you expect to pay, and, specifically, its job.

Is the feature to be a tunnel you walk through? Is it to support climbers or trained plants? If so, think very carefully about height; it should be 7 ft (2 m) to be sure that errant growths of climbing rose do not catch in your hair. The width must be at least 4 ft (1.2 m) if you are not to get soaked by strands of sodden clematis. Do not choose a wire arch and expect it to support a wisteria; be prepared for rustic poles to rot just when the plants they support are at their best. The better the quality, the more successful the tunnel will be.

SCREENS FOR PROTECTION

Pretty though a pergola is as a divider, it gives little shelter, and many gardens need internal divisions that offer protection, usually from wind, sometimes from sun. A lightly planted trellis casts dappled shade that filters sun pleasantly, but wind often takes more defeating.

Hedges, or for immediate protection securely fixed latticework fencing, are better than a wall, as they filter the wind and reduce its speed. High walls within a garden can block you in and look intimidating unless the area is very large.

Seaside gardens are sometimes enviably frost free, and many grow an almost subtropical range of plants. But taking advantage of the moderating influence of a maritime site is only possible once the sea winds are tamed. Plant a screen of robust, wind-tolerant shrubs — such as *Cotoneaster simonsii*, which has white flowers and orange-red berries, or the evergreen *Pittosporum tenuifolium*, with honey-scented, purple spring flowers — to shelter the patio or seating area.

Other plants will flourish on the lee side, many of them from the Southern Hemisphere — for example, escallonias, *Hebe salicifolia*, *H. brachysiphon*, and the compact *H. × franciscana* 'Blue Gem,' which flowers almost all year and looks wonderful in summer with catmint.

Keep in mind the need to select plants to suit each site, rather than attempting to change the site to suit the plant. There is a plant for every place and a place (though not necessarily in every garden) for every plant. Choosing plants that are already adapted to your conditions — shade or sun, dry soil or bog — increases your success in creating a garden.

HERBAL LINK When a border is composed of large drifts of just a few species, it becomes more of a hedge than a flower bed. Lavender and purple sage line the border, making a low hedge that divides the garden in two, yet echoes the herbal knot garden and boxwood circles by the house.

Through the Window

SHIVERY WINTER DAYS and steamy summer downpours alike put the garden out of bounds for all but the most devoted gardeners. Yet it can still be enjoyed. With a well-planned design, you can admire the dainty flowers of winter while sitting in your snuggest armchair and have a grandstand view of the first spring butterflies basking on the blossoms. A hallway window might permit a quick glimpse at flowers too daringly gaudy for longer contemplation. Even washing the dishes will have more appeal when a few choice blooms are nodding at you through the kitchen window.

SPECIAL FEATURES

A sunlit vine frames the window view onto a shady garden corner planted with red nicotiana.

THE GARDEN FROM INDOORS

WINDOWS ARE THE EYES of a home, opening on the world and seeing it from a unique point of view. But how many gardeners, as they are designing and planting a plot, give any thought to how it is going to look when viewed through the windows? There are some parts of the garden, however, that are far more frequently viewed from inside the house than from outside.

Most people spend the greater proportion of their time indoors, even during the summer months. Whether preparing meals or cleaning up after them, relaxing in the living room or watching television, almost every indoor occupation, except sleeping, is likely to be punctuated by glances or lengthy stares through the window. In fact the first move in the morning is usually to open the bedroom curtains and take a peek outdoors to judge the state of the weather and check on that private small patch of the world outside.

BRIEF OR LINGERING LOOKS

Since gardens are so frequently viewed through the windows, it makes sense to ensure that every pane of glass provides not merely an inoffensive view, but a tableau of delights that prolongs the pleasure through the changing seasons.

With a little forethought, a dash of imagination, and a handful of clever ideas, you can make each window the frame for an absorbing picture of a section of the garden. Some windows are in sight for much of the day, while others seldom draw the eye. Some constitute the chief focus of a room used all day long, while others are seen often but only in passing. As you walk by a window on a stair landing, for example, you are unlikely to scan the view carefully, but one simple item of beauty that can be taken in at a glance provides enormous pleasure.

A window in more constant view, however, needs to offer much more. Here you want a satisfying outline and a wealth of detail — and you expect it to please every day through the seasons. A well-designed garden has year-round interest built in, but the seasonal drama can be staged to enhance the performance you watch from your favorite window.

CLOSE INTEREST When used as a focal point near a window, a plant should offer at least two seasons of interest and have a pleasing shape, attractive foliage, or fragrance. Hydrangea flower heads last for a long time and take on pretty rosy or metallic tints and a papery texture as autumn advances.

DESIGNING
TO SUIT
THE VIEW

THE TIME SPENT looking through a window is an influential factor in planning the scene outside, but not the only one. The window's size and shape cannot be ignored, since they create the frame. Windows that are tall and narrow, round-topped, or broad and spacious all create specific design opportunities. A tiny porthole might look on nothing more than a single potted plant outside, while a tall window can encompass a soaring, statuesque plant, and a huge picture window takes in virtually the whole expanse of the garden.

Light levels outside the windows are another unalterable fact to be taken into consideration when you plan the picture.

ANGLES OF LIGHT AND SIGHT

The light may vary from the comparative gloom outside a basement window to the glare outside south-facing patio windows. Each situation has advantages to

MAKING · IT · EASIER

HIGH
PLANTING

A PLANTER with an attached trellis solves the problem of supporting tall plants or climbers on a roof garden or balcony, where you cannot drive in posts. Such elevated sites are surprisingly breezy, and a flowery trelliswork screen makes a pretty windbreak.

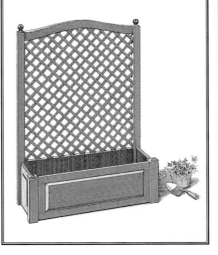

COLOR IMPACT Planting the same types and shades of flower in big clumps, thereby creating blocks of color, makes far more visual impact than intermingling a few of this and that. Arrange perennials in drifts, sited to be seen through a side window in a swift but stunning glance.

offer, and the disadvantages need not lead inevitably to a disappointing view.

Bear in mind that strong light from one side encourages plants to bend toward it, so make allowance for this when positioning them. Many flowers — roses and daffodils, for example — generally turn to the sun; so if they grow to the south of a window, they face away from it.

Bright sun and hard shadows are unkind to delicate colors. Only the bold and bright make an impact in dazzling sun, so save the subtle palette for shadier spots. Many foliage plants love shade. Those with variegations make their own pools of light, but intricate leaf shape, glossy surfaces, and a bold outline overall add further interest to a shaded scene.

Two or three windows may have the same dimensions or the same amount of light outside, but no two share exactly the same view. Indeed it is astonishing how two windows separated by only a yard or so of wall have quite different views onto the same patch of garden. One might show the curving line of a lawn between jutting beds of tall plants, while its neighbor looks out between the beds into a recess that frames a fountain or statue.

VIEWS FROM ABOVE OR BELOW

Perspectives change even more markedly from above. Much of the contour goes, and plants lose their silhouettes. More of the surface and the ground plan are visible, however, so you can arrange plants as if they were patterns in a tapestry.

A lawn seen from above looks cool, green, and weed-free. Its size and lines are exaggerated, while the planted areas

MAKING PLANTS STAND TALL

UNOBTRUSIVE SUPPORT for a tall herbaceous plant ensures that it will hold its flowers upright — and visible from the distance — rather than drooping in a bedraggled heap. For maximum benefit, put the stakes in early, soon after the first growth appears.

Use stakes that link to form a flexible "wall," which you can wind around or among the stems. As the plants shoot up and bush out, they quickly hide the supports from view.

seem to shrink. On the other hand, "carpet gardening" has an impact from above rarely equalled at ground level. A blend of low-growing thymes, with flowers of different purples and pinks, is dramatic from above and holds its impact when the leaf colors deepen in winter.

Equally effective from above are formal low hedges grown in squares around blocks of contrasting foliage or single-color flowers.

When the garden is on a balcony, you have large windows or doors looking onto a tiny area. Space is tight, but with large enough boxes and troughs, you can create your own micro jungle. A roof garden has more potential still, as you can add a layer of soil for small flower borders or shrubbery — but check first to make sure the building will support the extra weight.

If your window looks up from a basement, relatively small objects such as plant pots or dwarf shrubs become dominant because of their positions. This is something you can turn to advantage, adding drama to even the dullest spot.

FOLLOWING ORTHODOX STYLE

Although every window benefits from a specially tailored view, the design will draw on the same elements that go into any beautiful piece of scenery — line, form, texture, and color. You have to evaluate what satisfies you most in the garden — be it long vistas, surprise views, secret corners, a symmetrical or informal design, artful touches of drama, or well-composed color schemes.

Long views are easy to create from a window vantage point. Even from a large window, the view is more limited than when you stand outside. This has the effect of making features that lead away from a window more dominant. A path, a narrow lawn between borders, pairs of matched shrubs flanking ground cover, or some pillars supporting climbers become special features when aligned with a principal window.

When one of your windows looks out across a border to a lawn on the far side, carve a path to draw the eye through the border and set a sundial, birdbath, or other small feature at its end.

A distant point of interest, perhaps a specimen plant or structure near the boundary, is as effective as one close by. It draws the gaze farther, giving the illusion of more space, and leads the eye across the garden or even to a pleasant vista beyond the boundary.

SOFT EDGES Lady's-mantle is an ideal plant for softening the hard lines of paving and toning down more showy companions. Its scalloped leaves and sprays of tiny lime-green flowers reward close scrutiny, especially when they are spangled with raindrops.

the interiors and the style of the house. Just a little effort with the foreground immediately increases the sense that the garden is an extension of the room — especially where there are large windows or patio doors. If the color scheme in a room is, say, pink and blue, use compatible colors in a window box and in containers or beds nearby. To strengthen the link even more, grow houseplants on a windowsill inside that complement the leaf form or echo the flower color of the plants outside.

A period house usually looks better if its garden has at least a flavor of the same age and style. Small knot gardens, for example, have just the right blend of geometry and formality to blend with a colonial farmhouse. Victorian town houses, on the other hand, look comfortable with neat lawns and colorful flower beds in their gardens.

You can make harmonious links easily with modern houses. Patios or terraces, for example, are often separated from interiors by no more than large glass doors, so you can have great fun matching floor color and clean-lined furniture inside and out, even before you plant outdoor pots with hardy ferns and fatsias to echo the dainty ferns and weeping fig (*Ficus benjamina*) indoors.

Above all, with large windows revealing everything, your patio must remain attractive in winter. Plant some evergreens in the beds around it, even if you have room for only a few. In some climates chrysanthemums, hellebores, and early-flowering bulbs thrive on a sheltered patio, giving it color until spring.

VERSATILE CONTAINERS

Housing winter plants on the patio is only one contribution that containers make. Balconies, roof gardens, decks, and entry steps would be barren without an assembly of troughs, boxes, tubs, urns, and pots teeming with plants. The expanse of a city roof can be masked, or a sunken patio can become more luxuriant, with lovingly tended container plants.

At ground level, an elaborate empty pot or an overflowing tub of petunias or nasturtiums creates a focal point or brightens a dull area. Being movable,

A careful layout provides much more than focal points. You want to inspire window gazers to absorb the broader picture. Punctuate large, curving borders with eye-catching plants at irregular intervals and place pools of color around them for the eye to explore before being swept into the orbit of the next scene-stealer. You can even tantalize viewers by having a path or lawn meander onward.

Arrange your plant combinations with even more care than usual. It is the broadbrush effect that is visible from most windows, not the fine detail. Big drifts of plants, not tiny dots of this and

that, work best in the foreshortened view. Variations in height let the plants show their colors to advantage, and plenty of foliage allows pools of brightness to stand out even more. Mercilessly evict any plant that does not earn its keep throughout the year with flowers, shape, fragrance, autumn berries, winter foliage, or, preferably, several of these.

HOW TO HARMONIZE DESIGN

Garden design is much more successful when it fits in with its surroundings. Through-the-window design works best when it harmonizes, to some extent, with

SHAPES AND SHADES This predominantly green-and-gold planting scheme is punctuated by striking architectural foliage plants — elegant hostas and a huge rheum. Impatiens, tall lilies, and other white flowers in the distance create pools of light that draw the eye along the path.

containers let you vary the scheme and add beauty wherever needed. The beauty may be provided by color or shape or, in summer, when windows are often open, also by fragrance. Place some pots of mignonette or basil under a sheltered window; though not colorful, they emit a heavenly scent. Lilies, lavender, and miniature roses will all provide fragrance as well as color.

SCREENING THE VIEW

Imaginative planting is often needed when the view from a window is spoiled by an eyesore — perhaps an intrusive streetlight or sign, or a neighbor's shed. You can hide most eyesores with the help of a cleverly positioned hedge or fence or even an ingenious use of mirrors. With through-the-window gardening, subtler ploys can work. The objective is narrower when only the unique view from a particular window has to be considered.

You can arrange screening plants to line up with the window, then create a vista and take your eye to a distant focal point. A flowering or evergreen arch that leads nowhere or a tall white fence decorated with climbers will conceal a tall eyesore. If a neighbor's window overlooks yours, place a single tree or shrub where it breaks the direct line of vision without blocking the light or the remaining view for either window.

SPECIAL WINDOW SCENES

A LTHOUGH THE WINDOW must never be a tyrant, dictating the design outdoors, you can tailor the garden so that the views from particular windows give as much pleasure as a stroll outside.

Tall, narrow windows work well with a view that is long and thin, but it need not be a narrow pathway, bordered by flower beds. Such windows are ideal for allowing a fleeting glimpse of a beautiful object — an ornament, perhaps, or patterned bark on a specimen tree — that comes into view only at certain angles.

Windows that reach almost to floor level, whether sliding patio doors or French doors, do not cut off your view of the garden but bring it right up to the house. Create a foreground of small features — a shallow trough of tiny alpine plants, pots of winter bulbs, and a long-flowering, dainty-leaved potentilla — that will add beauty on even a drab day, whatever the season.

VIEWS FROM GROUND FLOOR

Gardeners often have a favorite chair near a window, where they draw up new plans in winter, review the garden's progress in fall, and welcome new blooms or plot the day's chores in spring. And on summer evenings, they find nothing more pleasurable than watching the colors gently fade in the garden as the twilight deepens.

When the view is so familiar, an observant eye can spot even the slightest changes, generally in the individual plantings rather than the overall design. Every day there are slight alterations in colors as flowers emerge or in silhouette as growth increases at midsummer. Larger changes are seasonal: the spring transition from browns to leafy green or the big winter cleanup when the spent vegetation is carted to the compost pile, leaving just the bare bones.

All the layout needs to do is provide a pleasing outline and an arrangement of beds, borders, pathways, or features to show the plants to their best advantage from indoors. A window box gives sharp focus to the foreground. Set the box low enough to let you look down onto the tops of the plants. Informal design allows the greatest scope for continuous interest in the middle distance and background. Arrange curving borders, strategically

PLANT FRAMES

Choose plant frames, or "tuteurs," that not only provide support for climbing plants, but also become features in their own right. When viewed from indoors, the vertical structures vary the horizon line and lift specimens up so they are visible at a distance.

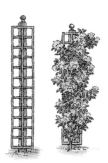

HOMEMADE PILLAR
Attach to a post two panels of trelliswork 6 ft (1.8 m) long by two squares wide; top with a finial. The lattice gives the post width and provides a foothold for plants.

PYRAMID PROP
You can buy fan-shaped trellises to attach to a wall. But turn four fans upside down and tie them together with twine, and you will have a pretty pyramid for a climber.

DOUBLE HOOP
Two simple hoops crossed and secured with wire create a three-dimensional arch; the metalwork will disappear from view once overrun by a flowery climber.

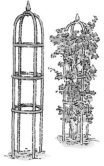

MAJESTIC OBELISK
Turn a flowering shrub into a triumph by training it up an obelisk. Select a deciduous plant if you wish, as the frame is handsome enough without winter foliage.

UMBRELLA SPOKES
Use an umbrella frame for weeping shrubs or trailing roses, as its shape mirrors their growth habit. A small frame, no more than 4 ft (1.2 m) tall, will work in a small garden.

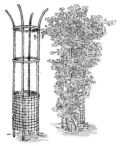

FOUNTAIN COLUMN
Ideal for sprawling climbers such as honeysuckle, this column makes an impressive sight — especially if your garden is large enough for a tall frame.

placed trees, and lawn or paving in naturalistic lines that are easy on the eye.

If you opt for a formal look, make sure that the design is not too static. Let border plants grow free and unclipped — even if you impose a symmetrical layout and have such formal features as clipped hedges or topiary. Whatever the design, tall features add scale and contour to the scene. Plants trained on umbrella-shaped frames, pillars, obelisks, and arches all act as punctuation marks.

PLANTS TO SOFTEN PAVING

There is often a hard surface outside the window — part of the driveway or path at the front of the house or a paved terrace

---

BEST PLANTS

CLIMBERS FOR TALL FRAMES

Tall climbers, which can be ideal for viewing through the window, offer attractive foliage, profuse flowers, and rich perfume.

• Kiwi (*Actinidia deliciosa*): heart-shaped dark leaves studded in early summer with white flower clusters that age to buff.

• Bird's-foot ivy (*Hedera helix* 'Pedata'): narrow-lobed, pale-veined evergreen leaves of metallic green.

• Maidenhair vine (*Muehlenbeckia complexa*): tangled reddish or dark purple stems with bright green leaves and tiny greenish flowers in summer.

• *Clematis montana* 'Elizabeth': covered with large clusters of pink flowers in spring.

• *Clematis* 'Huldine': summer-flowering variety with large white blooms, mauve beneath.

• Rose (*Rosa* 'Albéric Barbier'): yellow buds opening to scented white blooms in high summer.

• Chilean potato tree (*Solanum crispum* 'Glasnevin'): glossy semi-evergreen leaves and profuse purple flowers in midsummer with a scattering into autumn.

• Woodbine honeysuckle (*Lonicera periclymenum* 'Graham Thomas'): sweetly scented cream flowers followed by red autumn berries.

• Star jasmine (*Trachelospermum jasminoides*): shiny evergreen leaves and heavily fragrant white flowers in summer followed by seedpods.

---

at the back — but it need not be bare and bleak. Just a few plants poking up among the flagstones or sprawling at the edges of the paving change the look completely.

Slip in some dwarf irises to blaze in spring and sunroses to take over later. Strong reds and yellows stand out against the neutral tones of gravel and stone. Double sunroses, such as the crimson 'Mrs Earle' or the yellow 'Wisley Primrose,' are ideal because the flowers last a day longer. Singles are fine in the morning but often shed their petals by afternoon on a hot day; even so, their long succession of flowers is a joy.

Saxifrages also thrive in crannies, as do flat mats of Mt. Washington dryad (*Dryas octopetala*) and mounds of the evergreen candytuft (*Iberis sempervirens*), which make pools of rich green year-round. For winter flowers that shine like little jewels, plant *Cyclamen coum* and the early yellow crocus *Crocus ancyrensis*.

COLOR SCHEMES FOR EDGING PAVED AREAS

At the edges of a hard surface, you can add to the strong summer color theme with shrubs such as *Ribes sanguineum* 'Brocklebankii,' a currant with deep-rose flowers and golden leaves, and the yellow-leaved *Physocarpus opulifolius* 'Dart's Gold.' In winter some willows and dogwoods still look spectacular. The willow *Salix acutifolia* 'Blue Streak' has winter stems brushed with a bluish-white bloom, while the gold-leaved dogwood *Cornus alba* 'Aurea' has twigs that shine red in the winter sun. If you prune these dogwood shrubs early in spring, you will get leafy displays in summer followed by a forest of colorful wands in winter.

Herbaceous plants and bulbs complete the scheme through the year. Stick to a strict color scheme against which bold accent plants will stand out. Blue, gold, and yellow with an occasional white flower look fresh but not dominating.

At the first hint of spring, enjoy the cheerful yellow cups of winter aconite, nodding white snowdrops, and the heart-shaped foliage and yellow-spurred flowers of *Epimedium alpinum*. Fill out the season with jonquils, yellow and blue primulas, long-lasting saucers of geums — especially creamy 'Lionel Cox' — and vivid yellow leopard's-bane (*Doronicum*). Soon after, euphorbias add an acid-yellow contrast for blue monkshood (*Aconitum*) and Siberian iris. Plant

---

A PICTURE WINDOW IN SPRING

When winter is almost over, but warm days are rare, you can still take great pleasure in a well-planned garden — all without setting foot out-of-doors.

EARLY SPRING IS a confounding time for gardeners. It teases with some bright, balmy days, but the weather can turn chilly and damp in an instant. So instead of venturing out, plan a garden that can be surveyed from the comfort of your favorite armchair, strategically placed beside the window.

To ensure maximum enjoyment of the outside from the inside, bring the brave early blooms — low-growing little hepatica and cyclamen as well as the wide cups of hellebores — to the front of the bed near the window.

To provide contrast, place the twiggy viburnum and dark-leaved camellia at the back. They will tower over their low-lying companions and emphasize the soft flowers around their feet.

COMPLETING THE PICTURE

Be sure to take the distant vista into account, as it helps to accentuate the foreground. Shape and texture are as important as color.

The green solidity of a conifer stands out against the fading russet line of a hedge, both of them serving as a foil for the brighter colors of the flowers at the front of the stage. The pretty cherry tree in the center of the lawn links the more neutral distance with the bright, busy foreground. It bears a delicate, pale covering of blossoms, which recalls the recent coverings of snow.

For extra interest and color close up, there is a cluster of flowering and foliage plants immediately in front of the window, raised on upturned pots to ensure that they are in full view.

The cheerful colors of the irises and hyacinths, heralds of spring, brighten up the dreariest day. The attractively bushy pussy willow bears numerous twiglets, each crowded with swelling buds that hint at the display of the fuzzy little catkins to come.

Palest pink cherry blossoms open throughout winter

Dainty cyclamen, hepatica and anemone fringe the raised bed

Hyacinths and dwarf irises bloom close up

Green and pink hellebore cups face the window

1. Autumn cherry (*Prunus × subhirtella* 'Autumnalis')
2. *Viburnum farreri*
3. *Camellia* 'Freedom Bell'
4. *Cyclamen coum, C. hederifolium,* and *Hepatica transsilvanica*
5. Spring snowflake (*Leucojum vernum*)
6. Bethlehem sage (*Pulmonaria saccharata*)
7. Windflower (*Anemone blanda* 'Radar')
8. Lenten rose (*Helleborus orientalis* hybrids)
9. Pussy willow (*Salix caprea*)
10. Common hyacinth (*Hyacinthus orientalis* 'Ostara')
11. Danford iris (*Iris danfordiae*)

PLANTING AND STAKING A TREE

TALL PLANTS such as trees catch the eye first in a scene through the window. Make sure that young trees get off to a good start. Supporting a newly planted tree with a short stake leaves most of the trunk free to bend with the wind. Such movement stimulates the production of a substance called lignin, which strengthens the trunk and gives the tree a speedier natural anchorage in the ground.

1. Dig the planting hole wide and deep enough to accommodate the roots and sprinkle a handful of slow-release fertilizer at the bottom. Place the tree in the hole, spreading the roots to ensure they are not congested, and put enough soil on top to hold the tree upright.

2. Drive the sharp end of a stake into the soil at a 45° angle, with the point facing the same way as the prevailing wind. Drive it in until half the stake is in the ground.

3. Fill the hole with soil and tamp it down firmly. Fasten the stake to the tree, making sure the tie is tight around the stake but slightly loose around the tree, leaving room for it to expand.

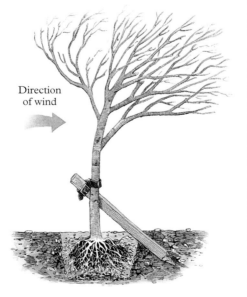

Direction of wind

ADJOINING CIRCLES Seen from a window above, pattern becomes prominent in a garden, while detail is obscured. This strong, simple design is based on repeated circles, reinforced by the design of the flagstones.

masses of blue pansies along with pale, butter-colored *Potentilla recta* 'Citrina' and white 'Mount Cook' scabiosa. Add a scattering of evening primrose, blue cranesbill geranium, campanula, and yellow yarrow to extend the gold and blue theme throughout the summer. In autumn, the colors will soften as the foliage turns a rusty color and eventually dies back.

VIEW FROM THE KITCHEN

In many houses the kitchen vies with the living room for the title of most used room, since long hours are spent there every week on inescapable chores. Most of the planning and tricks used outside a living-room window work equally well outside the kitchen. But the kitchen has its own character, which needs to be considered if the view from the window in front of the sink is to offer an escape for the eye and imagination.

Soften the stark outline of kitchen windows by framing them with plants such as rockspray cotoneaster, climbing roses, and *Viburnum rhytidophyllum*. These plants can do double duty by giving support to early and late clematis species, such as *Clematis macropetala* 'Markham's Pink' and *C. viticella* 'Alba Luxurians.' For scent, plant lily-of-the-valley, lavender, and old-fashioned pinks below the windows.

UPSTAIRS LOOKING DOWN

Most formal designs are seen to advantage from above, since their symmetry is at least as effective in two dimensions as in three. The pattern may be a knot or parterre, an arrangement of flower-filled circles with crescents around them, or a rectangular assembly of clipped hedges, grass walks, gravel, and bedding displays. Other elements might include pools, statues, topiary, and paving.

Paving is one of the garden features that looks even better when viewed from above. An intricate pattern — whether of various-sized pavers or bricks, in one of the traditional bonds such as Flemish or herringbone — gains impact when you see the overall design.

Formal designs and paving are particularly suitable for a front garden in town, which tends to be glimpsed rather than gazed upon. If you soften it with imaginative plantings, it will stand up to a much longer look and even make a satisfying layout for a small back garden.

For an airy feel, team the loose spires of pink-red penstemons and the frilly-leaved cranesbill geraniums, whose saucers of pink or mauve seem to float on air — and because cranesbills are repeat-flowering, the effect is long lasting. Inject more soft color and profuse flower and foliage with mauve and purple salvias, white and pink *Argyranthemum*, the more muted annual geraniums, and lilac and rose-red verbenas. Let the plants tumble over the edges of their carefully shaped beds or froth at will within neatly clipped boxwood minihedges. For color early in the season, plant bulbs — especially tulips, whose stateliness is lightened in the double and lily-flowered forms.

The pattern of beds looks equally good when set in lawn, paving, or gravel. Make clear paths through the beds — not just to emphasize the design from above, but to walk along for a closer appreciation of the plants. A statue provides the perfect finishing touch.

Informal layouts are now more common than formal ones, but they do not make a satisfying picture from above

SWEEPING CURVES A sinuous expanse of lawn seen from above is more elegant than a rectangle and, at ground level, reveals the garden gradually rather than at a glance. The small dovecote draws the eye across the lawn to explore the dense beds packed with focal plants.

when they present a shapeless jumble of flower beds, paths, and tiny dabs of color that merge into an overall blur.

Boldness and line are the essential ingredients, and the choices are almost infinite. The lines may be straight or curved, but they should create pleasing shapes that balance one side of the garden with the other. They should carry the eye toward points of interest — a clump of sunflowers, a pool, a seat under a rose arch, or a tree ripe with apples.

In the planting, use large sweeps of color — a swirl of purple acanthus, a big circle of lupines, a patch of hostas wider than your outstretched arms, a whole bed of white petunias. It is only broad strokes

that stand out when you look from upstairs. The strong structure of trees and shrubs stands out too, so use them to set off the brighter colors and give a change of height sufficient to be evident from above. Serviceberry, Japanese maple, holly, magnolia, tulip tree (*Liriodendron tulipifera*), Judas tree (*Cercis siliquastrum*), rhododendrons, and mahonias all offer plenty of visual value.

SIDELONG GLANCES

A glimpsed view requires special treatment. Such a view is most likely to be seen through a window on the stair landing or along a hallway; you pass it often but never linger. There is no time to see

COMPOSING A SCENE In the right setting, planting on a lavish scale is not necessary. A gold-leaved shrub against a velvety dark green hedge makes an ideal backdrop for seasonal highlights such as stately tulips.

SAFETY FIRST

COVERING BAMBOO STAKES

IT IS EASY to forget there are stakes in a garden bed when you are focusing on the plants beyond. But you can easily injure your face or eyes by bending over a stake. Protect yourself by putting tops on the stakes. Buy green PVC tops, which are cheap, easy to fit, and discreet, or use green tape.

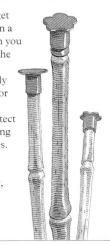

FRAMING THE PICTURE Plants that change with the season provide an ever-evolving scene as you pass a window. After wisteria's blooms have faded and the leaves have fallen, the gnarled stems continue to draw attention.

detail; simple, forceful features are all you take in as you move past.

A single tree branch can be of sufficient interest for a quick glance from above. Most branches are always changing: sometimes in full bloom, sometimes in fall color, sometimes motionless, but more often moving gently in the breeze.

At ground level a few square feet of fertile soil widen the choices for delighting the senses. A design statement that can be spotted, noted, and enjoyed in an instant is vital, so plants need to shout to be noticed. Support the taller herbaceous plants for maximum effect and keep in mind year-round interest.

🌢 A brilliant patch of tulips is eye-catching in spring. The bolder the color or mixture of colors, the better.

🌢 For summer, choose the 'Beauty of Livermere' red poppy or the double pink peony 'Sarah Bernhardt.'

🌢 For autumn, plant double asters such as 'Andenken an Alma Potschke' or 'Harrington's Pink.'

🌢 A Japanese maple offers colorful buds and leaves in spring, a graceful form in summer, and gorgeous autumn color.

🌢 Let a clematis run up a shrub that lacks summer appeal, such as a conifer. Once established, the violet *Clematis × jackmannii* or the wine-red 'Madame Julia Correvon' will clamber to the top.

🌢 Grow a rose, such as coppery pink 'Albertine' or golden 'Emily Gray,' up a tree with handsome bark, perhaps a cherry or hawthorn.

🌢 Put a windmill palm (*Trachycarpus fortunei*) in a large tub in a sunny spot. Its pleated fronds become particularly dramatic against a white wall.

BELOW-GRADE GARDENING

When you have a worm's-eye view of the world, the challenge is to provide good reason to look outside at all. However,

A VIEW FROM BELOW

Although often dismissed as gloomy and impossible to work with, a below-grade area becomes a verdant little jungle when wisely planted.

IF YOU HAVE A VIEW below grade level — whether through a window in a finished basement or sliding doors opening onto a sunken patio that is bordered by retaining walls — you can still enjoy a lush garden, aglow with green and gold.

The key is to choose plants that thrive in shade and offer varied textures and light colors. When staged in front of a pale blue wall, to suggest the open sky, the foliage and flowers will seem to pop.

The holly's sculptural form and glossy leaves show up boldly against the wall. The small tree contrasts with the lacy ferns, both evergreens that unfurl their bright green fronds in spring.

Do not forget the changing seasons. It is important to create year-round interest, within the limitations of the light and space. Make sure there are always stars to take center stage.

In spring the stars are the luminous white and yellow flowers of oxlip primrose, dainty lily-of-the-valley bells, and the fluffy heads of false Solomon's seal. The sweet perfume of the lily-of-the-valley wafting in through the window delights even the most jaded senses.

PLEASURES TO COME

During summer, golden Welsh poppies, yellow loosestrife, creamy foxglove, and deep blue willow gentians will take center stage. The ground-covering epimedium, which blooms early with snowy white spurred flowers, bears pretty heart-shaped leaves that open with a bronze flush, then turn green in summer and ruddy in fall.

Silver vein creeper looks attractive throughout the year — especially when grown in shade, which deepens the leaf color. But it really comes into its own in autumn, when its variegated leaves change to scarlet. In spring the vigorous climber serves as a backdrop for its more delicate and earthbound companions.

Virginia creeper extends its tracery with new shoots

Sculptured holly leaves stand out boldly

Lily-of-the-valley spreads a rich scent

Fern fronds soften the edge of the low wall

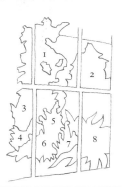

1. Silver vein creeper (*Parthenocissus henryana*)
2. English holly (*Ilex aquifolium* 'Madame Briot')
3. False Solomon's seal (*Smilacina racemosa*)
4. Lily-of-the-valley (*Convallaria majalis*)
5. Oxlip primrose (*Primula elatior*)
6. Epimedium (*Epimedium × youngianum* 'Niveum')
7. Hart's-tongue fern (*Asplenium scolopendrium*)
8. Soft shield fern (*Polystichum setiferum* 'Acutilobum')

GARDENS BELOW To turn a boxy sunken space into a verdant jungle, build up a strong framework of evergreen architectural plants such as fatsia and mahonia. Add seasonal color with containers of flowering plants.

with a little imagination and some prudent choices, a vertical garden can bring a green oasis to a basement window.

The first task is to alleviate the gloom when the window is only a few feet from a high wall and sunlight is brief or nonexistent. Select light-colored paving for the ground and paint the wall white or pale blue, which not only reflects light but also provides a contrasting background for the plants. If you want a warmer atmosphere, use a lemon or or soft ochre paint color.

In such a restricted space, the plantings must be largely vertical: vines to climb the facing wall and trailers to cascade down it. Plants whose nodding flowers "look down" — as the Lenten rose's do — or that trail without being trained are particularly useful.

Climbers respond best to a cool, roomy root run in rich soil, so a vertical garden needs fertile beds or large containers at the base of its wall. Where there is a narrow bed above the level of the window, enrich it to make a nourish-

ing home for trailing plants. *Clematis macropetala* dangles its blue stars, the broom *Cytisus × kewensis* makes a creamy cascade, and small-leafed ivies drape beautifully into evergreen curtains.

If there is no soil at the top of the wall, more ingenuity is needed. Hang small pots in brackets fixed to the wall and plant them with aubrietia, saxifrage,

lobelia, and campanula. Fill some tall jardinieres with ivy-leaved geraniums, whose stems will trail exuberantly. Do not forget the steps leading down to the area; they are a ready-made stage for displaying pots of plants.

Increase decorative value by turning practical plant supports into design features. You can use lattice, for example, to

GARDENS ALOFT Balcony gardens can be
exposed to drying winds, and plants will need
big containers and frequent watering. The
geraniums will not collapse as soon as they
dry out and have a long flowering period.

is simplified, since it has to be planned
from the vantage point of the window; no
other view is possible.

The chief way to grow plants on a
balcony is in containers, which you can
shift around as the mood strikes. With
only a small area needing your time and
care, you can afford to replace plants regularly for a fresh, healthy look all year.
Each plant must be at its best to earn a
place in this miniature garden.

The bigger and roomier the containers are, the better the plants do and the
greater the number and variety you can
grow. Small trees and shrubs need a particularly generous root space but, if
grown in suitable planters, reward you
with vigorous growth and opportunities
for pruning them into desired shapes.

If you have room for a small tree,
Japanese maples, which have more than
one season of interest, lend themselves to
container culture. The trees stay healthy
if fed regularly and placed in a well-lit
part of the balcony. Prune to develop a
mature shape by judiciously removing
whole branches, encouraging limbs to
bend and arch as if with age, and keeping
the trunks as clean as possible.

Shrubs are easier to grow, especially
if you select small varieties such as
Sarcococca confusa or *Daphne retusa*, both
shade-tolerant evergreens with fragrant
flowers. On a well-lit balcony, a wisteria
gives generous rewards with the heaviest
flowering after a hard summer pruning.

Evergreens such as boxwood or
lavender assume denser, fuller shapes
when kept clipped. Citrus trees are good
candidates for training into topiary standards, but you will need to take them indoors for the winter if you live in a cold
climate. Taller plants such as this vary the
outline of a balcony garden, while easily
changed perennials and annuals form the
bulk of the planting.

For year-round pleasure, vary the
plants as much as you can.

☙ Good-value perennials are pinks, car-
nations, penstemons, hostas, and ornamental grasses.

☙ For disposable summer planting, use
salvias, strawflowers, petunias, nemesias,
osteospermums, and heliotropes.

☙ 'Angel' geraniums are especially valuable for balconies. Their profuse maroon,

create arches along the wall, bringing
them forward a little to suggest depth.
You can also buy ornamental ironwork
trellises in a variety of shapes.

Single spot supports, perhaps with
wires between, can be adornments, too.
Wooden, porcelain, glass, or metal
doorknobs are easily screwed into anchors driven into the joints in the wall.

Invisible supports, such as wires held by
vine eyes, are another choice.

MAKING MORE OF A BALCONY

Balconies vary in size, but even with the
roomiest, space is at a premium. And yet
the opportunities to create an interesting
garden are many. Although there is a
wide choice of plants, their arrangement

mauve, and pink flowers appear over a long season and, being small, last longer in breezy conditions.

- Herbs give you a pinch of fresh flavor for the kitchen and thrive in poor, dry soil. Silver thyme, golden marjoram, and purple sage make a pretty collection.
- Plant bulbs for early color. Although some are pricey, bulbs give a showy display for little effort. Scilla, chionodoxa, snowdrops, and crocus have tiny flowers that benefit from close viewing.
- Narcissus planted in groups give dense color, and many are fragrant.
- For easy-care spring displays, grow violets or pansies. These undemanding plants bloom profusely, come in numerous colors, are deliciously fragrant, and provide posies for indoors.
- Autumn bulbs for strong splashes of color are the golden *Sternbergia lutea* and the lilac-blue *Colchicum speciosum.*

TO THE RESCUE

REPAIRING A BROKEN POT

YOUR BALCONY OR BASEMENT garden may seem so much like an extra room that you forget your display of pots is exposed to the elements. If a wind gust blows a pot over or a cold snap strikes while a pot that is not frost proof is still outdoors, you may end up with a broken container.

Do not throw it away; the break is not difficult to repair and may be the push you need to repot a root-bound plant. Remove the plant and tease out the roots; prune the roots and the top growth by a third before repotting it.

Clean the broken pot thoroughly, moisten the edges to be bonded, and coat them with an epoxy that matches the pot color. Press the edges together, letting any excess adhesive squeeze out of the crack. After an hour, cut off any surplus with a sharp, wet knife, then leave to harden overnight.

The next day, wrap wire around the pot below the rim and twist the ends together with pliers to tighten it.

HOW TO IMPROVE SHADY VIEWS

Dense, dry shade presents one of gardening's most taxing challenges. In town gardens, the condition often exists in sunken back yards enclosed by fences or buildings, which block light and rainfall. In the countryside, dry shade is generally found on slopes under trees, where greedy roots and runoff leave the soil parched. What can be done?

First, try to reduce the severity of the conditions. Make the garden as open as possible to admit maximum light. Thin out or limb up overhanging trees or remove the less attractive ones. Next, use a light paving material and paint walls and fences a pale color to help reflect available light. Instead of having a solid fence or wall, make the top strip from lattice, which admits some light while preserving privacy. You can dress it up with a pale-flowered climber.

Before installing new plantings, amend the soil generously and perhaps install soaker hoses or a drip irrigation system for easy watering. Moist, well-fed soil gives the plants a better chance of fulfilling your expectations of them.

Choose plenty of plants with pale or white flowers or variegated foliage — they seem to shine in low light. For contrast, intermingle them with striking architectural plants. Fragrant white lilies blooming above *Hosta sieboldiana* give a summer mix of flower and foliage. The handsomest foliage belongs to *Gunnera manicata,* which in the wild grows to vast sizes, with a single leaf sometimes reaching more than head height and spreading like a beach umbrella. This is a bold choice for a small space and needs a good deal of moisture, but it would always draw your eye to the window and lend drama to the scene.

If you prefer something less dominant, try *Rheum palmatum,* a relative of rhubarb whose leaves grow to about 18 inches across and make it a superb showpiece. In the right conditions, rheum sends up spikes of white flowers.

Underplantings of snowdrops, the white snowflake (*Leucojum vernum*), the white Christmas rose (*Helleborus niger*), and white crocus would brighten late

Tassels of itea drape the side screen

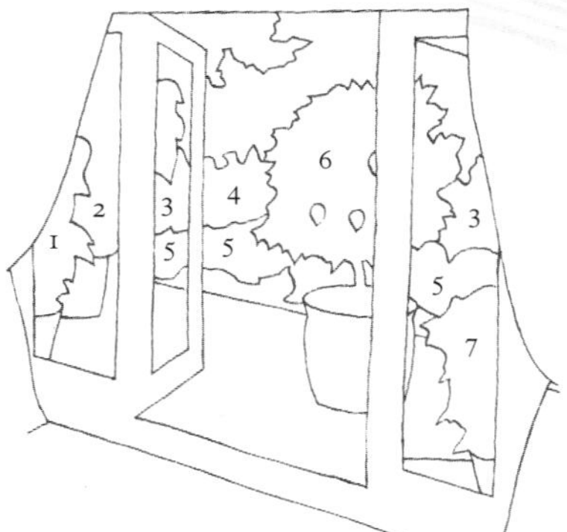
1
2
3
4
5
6
7

Scented, starry jasmine blossoms frame the door

Glossy, dark leaves set off the ripening lemons

Purple-centred clematis nods outside the window

1. Common white jasmine (*Jasminum officinale*)
2. *Itea ilicifolia*
3. *Salvia patens*
4. *Datura inoxia*
5. *Plectranthus coleoides* 'Variegatus,' coral gem (*Lotus berthelotii*), and ivy-leaved geranium (*Pelargonium peltatum* 'L'Elégante')
6. Lemon tree (*Citrus limon* 'Meyer')
7. *Clematis florida* 'Sieboldii'

THE BALCONY AS A FRAGRANT OASIS

Gardening above street level provides a unique opportunity for experimenting with plants that are less hardy, as well as enlarging and enhancing your living space.

IF YOUR OUTDOOR SPACE is a few stories above the street, you can still make it feel like a more conventional garden. In fact you have a special advantage, because your balcony can easily be transformed into an extra room.

What could be more delightful than being greeted by a rush of fragrance as soon as you open the French doors? Or than looking out onto a refreshing tangle of lush green foliage that helps block out the hustle, bustle, and odors of a busy street below?

SUMMER BLUE AND GOLD

Plants framing the doorway link the balcony with the room indoors, while the handsome lemon tree in the Oriental-style container provides a strong focal point that can be moved as needed to vary the design. The mass of plants in the troughs lining the balcony railing screens the outside world and offers protection against the strong breezes that often swirl about at this height.

Shown in summer, this southwest-facing balcony provides such good shelter that the container, which can be moved indoors for the winter, is more ornate and delicate than those generally used in an open garden. A stylish pot or urn becomes part of the decorative scene in its own right.

The trumpet flowers of the datura, with their rich, deep fragrance, and the sweetly scented lemon tree and jasmine will fill the room with their perfume.

The clematis, with bicolored blooms, and the *Itea*, with its dramatic long catkins, are beautiful climbers, both adding an unusual touch to the scene.

The variety of colors and shapes are an irresistible draw. The plants are pleasing at a casual glance, and their intricate details make them even more interesting the closer you view them.

PLANTING FOR YEAR-ROUND VIEWING

◆

Planting is a creative art, and as in the other arts, a sense of beauty and an ability to imagine the finished result are a great help. Successful planting, however, does not need years of hard-won experience. Even with the first attempt you can produce satisfying results, and that feeling of satisfaction continues to grow as your experience deepens.

In gardening there is no need to bow to another's taste. You are free to choose the shapes, colors, and textures that please you — provided the site is right for the plant. Despite different tastes and aims, however, gardeners share the basic goal of wanting to make their plots look as good as possible year-round. This is particularly important in through-the-window gardening, where you cannot move from one point of interest to another but must take the view presented. Forethought, practice, and some corrective transplanting will compose scenes that work outside and from indoors.

HIGH-PERFORMANCE TREES

If there is room, plant a tree. There is no better way to draw attention from a distance. When your eye falls on an attractive or distinctive trunk, it is drawn upward and then along the outline of the limbs until you enjoy the tracery of the smaller branches and twigs.

Look for trees with more than one attribute: the gleaming trunk of the Chinese cherry, *Prunus serrula*, resembles polished mahogany and is as outstanding in winter as in summer, when it bears single white blooms. *Prunus sargentii*, the popular Sargent's cherry, has a shapely outline, shiny bark, and looks beautiful all year. In spring the russet foliage emerges after the deep pink blossoms have faded, and in fall the leaves turn to orange and scarlet.

Among evergreens, plants with generous berries, such as hollies — especially the heavy fruiting 'J.C. van Tol' or the variegated 'Handsworth New Silver' — give year-round pleasure and help feed wildlife in winter. In milder areas a wonderful window tree is the slender *Eucryphia × nymansensis* 'Nymansay,' which has shiny evergreen foliage and is smothered with waxy white blooms in

LEVELS OF INTEREST A clear area of paving creates a feeling of space that is extended toward the lawn as the urn draws the eye onward. Two contrasting surfaces, hard and soft, are separated by a change of level, which adds a further dimension of interest.

winter. The evergreen shrub *Osmanthus × burkwoodii* keeps its glossy, dark leaves all winter long, making it an ideal backdrop for white spring blossoms. Pale *Colchicum* 'Lilac Wonder' and *C. speciosum* 'Album' will continue the theme in autumn.

If you have paving, which suits the setting much better than sparse grass,

create highlights in the crevices with impatiens, shade-loving annuals that last till first frost. You could also slip in some mint or chervil to use in the kitchen.

Complete the summer scene with a climbing rose that can thrive in dim light. *Rosa* 'Madame Alfred Carrière' offers an abundant succession of heavily scented white blooms.

autumn. Perhaps the most spectacular tree of all for mild areas is the Chilean firebush (*Embothrium coccineum*), whose tall, narrow shape is perfect for viewing through a long window and whose light, glossy evergreen leaves disappear in summer beneath a blazing mass of orange-red spidery blooms.

DISTINCTIVE SHRUBS

An arresting silhouette is the feature to look for in shrubs. The pleasing shapes of many dwarf conifers, for example, make bold, permanent features in the garden. And glossy, solid camellias, handsome all year but ravishing when in bloom, also lend a garden strong shape.

Position key specimens so that when viewed through the window, preferably from armchair level, they enhance the garden's outline. To be sure you get the position just right, do some tests, placing stakes as markers where the shrubs are to be located. Keep moving in and out of the house to make adjustments until you are sure you have positioned them to maximum advantage.

You will be glad you took the trouble later on, when you can admire from indoors a perfectly placed blossom-wreathed shrub rose, the long arrays of holly-like leaves on a *Mahonia × media* 'Charity' crowned with spires of yellow flowers, or the long, pale catkins of *Garrya elliptica* dancing among the dark-green leaves in the early spring breezes.

GENEROUS FILLINGS

Between high-profile specimen plants, fill in with a lush foundation of foliage. Although relatively constant in its coloring, this groundwork gently increases in luxuriance as the growing season advances, then fades or dies back in autumn. Pulmonarias, some with silver-specked foliage, and lady's-mantle, with its scalloped light green leaves, are ideal choices. Bergenia leaves persist and retain their color well in winter before vivid heads of pink blooms provide a splash of early spring color.

In partial shade, *Euphorbia amygdaloides* var. *robbiae* is a key contributor, making a green carpet all year but giving its chief delight in spring, with intense lime-green blossoms. The plant is inva-

sive, so do not shrink from pulling it up if it rambles too far.

Add more muted splashes of color with low-maintenance drifts of honesty, foxglove, sweet William, and forget-me-not. These all look as pretty from the distance as from close by, and they frequently self-sow into colonies.

Include some plants with spectacular flowers, intense colors, strong architectural shapes, and for summer, when the windows are open, a beguiling fragrance. Their function is to spur the observation process — to clamor for attention but not hold it too long. They

SIGHTS OF SPRING The level of the soil next to this window means that plantings can be brought up close, at eye level. Bright, contrasting colors, as seen with these tulips, primulas, and arabis, make for a vivid scene.

INTO THE DISTANCE This garden is designed to accentuate distance and conceal its narrow bounds. The paving pattern adds breadth in the foreground, while the honeysuckle arch tempts you into the alluring space beyond.

NATURAL TEXTURES Warm-toned gravel and mellow stone provide a soft setting for sunny-colored shrubs and flowers. The lilies planted by the window will join the display later in the year and send their heady perfume indoors.

the window — raised on a pedestal if necessary — and plant it with crocuses for late fall and hyacinths for spring. Fill such bowls with as many bulbs as you can — of course allowing for proper spacing — and stick with one variety at a time for each bowl.

You might try the purple-striped crocus 'Pickwick,' for instance, which could be followed by the soft blue hyacinth 'Myosotis' or the apricot-colored hyacinth 'Gipsy Queen.'

SUMMER STARS

To attract attention in summer, position fragrant plants beside an open window. A climber on the wall, preferably framing the window, will fill a room with perfume and allow tantalizing glimpses of the flowers. Summer jasmine is perfect for this, with its pretty flowers and strong scent. In a shadier position, use honeysuckle instead, especially the Japanese species; look for the variety *Lonicera japonica* 'Halliana.' Roses also make lovely window-framing plants; the pink, thornless 'Zéphirine Drouhin' will not scratch you if you lean out the window, and its flowers are intensely fragrant.

Lilies are elegantly formed flowers to enjoy close up near a window and bring much-needed color to the summer garden. Many are fragrant as well as lovely, and they are as happy in pots as in the ground.

A conventional but still irresistibly eye-catching choice for a container is a collection of geraniums, of fuchsias, or of petunias. Look especially for some of the new hybrid geraniums: 'Eroica,' for example, is a hot pink, and 'Ecco' an intense orange-scarlet semidouble with darkish foliage. A generous clump of any of these plants maintains its bold color throughout the summer.

SUSTAINING THE DISPLAY

Windows in frequent use must offer constant interest, regardless of the season. You need some changes of mood and of color, not only from season to season but from week to week.

Nowadays, bedding plants tend to be changed only twice a year — once for the spring display and again for summer. Victorian gardeners were far more ambitious, revising or replacing their schemes several times each season. This could be expensive on a large scale, but in a modest-sized planting you can easily follow their example to sustain through-

must not be too intrusive in the general design, but should allow the eye to move at leisure to other elements in the scene.

In winter something as simple as a clump of snowdrops can be spectacular if you choose the extra-large Crimean species, *Galanthus elwesii*, and bring them right up to the window so that they gleam in the light. Lenten-rose hybrids, especially those with pale pink or white spotted flowers, are stunning in a raised bed near the window; sun behind them gives them a particular glow. In a small courtyard, place a large bowl in view of

LONG SEASONS
OF INTEREST

Select trees and shrubs that make strong statements — especially when viewed from a far. For maximum effect, look for specimens with more than one ornamental features.

• Giant dogwood (*Cornus controversa* 'Variegata'): tiered branching habit, flat heads of white summer flowers, vivid autumn leaves, and blue-black berries.

• Red maple (*Acer rubrum* 'October Glory'): Red flowers, leaves, and fruit and brilliant scarlet autumn color.

• Sargent's cherry (*Prunus sargentii*): smooth, ruddy-brown bark, rose-pink blooms, black fruits, and foliage that turns from purple to green to red.

• Moyes rose (*Rosa moyesii*): tall shrub with deep red summer flowers and vivid scarlet, flask-shaped hips in fall.

• *Fuchsia magellanica*: bushy shrub with bright green foliage and a profuse show of dangling crimson and purple flowers from midsummer to fall.

• Smoketree (*Cotinus coggygria* 'Purpureus'): feathery purplish plumes in summer and deep purple leaves lightening to red in autumn.

• Judas tree (*Cercis siliquastrum*): pink spring flowers followed by heart-shaped leaves flushed red at first, then turning yellow in autumn.

INVITING ASPECT The slightly random paving in the foreground and the circular shape of the central bed invite the onlooker to travel around the path and into the unknown. The canopy of foliage leaning in from both sides changes with the seasons, giving varied color and light.

the-window interest. Select potted chrysanthemums for autumn, bulbs and pansies for late winter, wallflowers and forget-me-nots or primulas for spring, and sweet peas, pot marigolds, snapdragons, or impatiens for summer.

Unconventional bedding plants, such as aubrietia, arabis, or the heavy-blooming annual *Limnanthes douglasii*, contribute pools of clear color to temporary plantings. Gladiolus, a tender summer favorite, is bold in color and form; try the fragrant *Gladiolus callianthus* 'Murielae,' with white and maroon blooms.

Herbaceous plants that grow tall very quickly can play a dual role. A scattering of tall mulleins, for example, provides a series of focal points when in flower, but their large rosettes of woolly foliage add a distinctive texture to the background. *Veratrum nigrum* is a slower-growing plant whose leaves, huge and pleated, add texture to the scene before the curi-ous, though not conventionally beautiful, brownish flowers emerge on towering stems in later summer.

THE BEST OF INSIDE AND OUT

Gardening through the window is a special culture with its own set of design and planting considerations. You can tailor the garden to suit each unique window view, but the basic gardening principles still apply; only the point of view changes. With a shifting focus on star performers set against a general picture that develops through the seasons, the view through the window will remain of constant interest.

This does not detract from your outdoor design in any way. Indeed, the extra thought that you devote to the planning will improve the views both inside and out, and the result will be a garden of double delight.

PLANTING TO PLEASE THE SENSES

ONE OF THE CHIEF JOYS in gardening is weaving together the colors you love most to create atmosphere and impact. Cool whites and lemons, gentle pinks and mauves, deep reds and crimsons, rich blues and violets, sophisticated greens, or a fresh and cheerful mixture may be what you long for — and with a little practice you can match your dream to the reality of your site. But gardens delight more than just the eye; a drift of sweet fragrance as you stroll along a path and a crisp rustle as leaves stir in the breeze add to the magic. And who can resist touching the furry catkins of a pussy willow, the soft plumes of fennel, or the satiny bark of a cherry tree?

*The deep color of the fragrant sweet pea flowers emphasizes
their velvety texture.*

EXPLORING EVERY DELIGHT

◆

O F THE FIVE SENSES — touch, taste, hearing, smell, and sight — the last sense is the most finely attuned. So it is no surprise that even the most creative gardener devotes the most attention to color, shape, line, form, and movement.

The sense of smell runs a close second to the joy in visual satisfaction, and as a result many gardeners devise planting schemes that incorporate the rich scents from spring's awakening and summer's abundance right through to the late months of winter. But plants offer more than just fragrant flowers: aromatic foliage, ripening fruit, and pungent seeds all contribute to a garden's sensual atmosphere. Even the smell of gentle decay as the garden declines at the end of the year can add its own sweet hint of melancholy.

And what about touch, sound, and taste? Almost any planting scheme is enriched when it includes something to satisfy these three senses, as well as the two more dominant ones. Have you ever thought, for instance, of siting a bamboo where you can hear its whisperings through an open window or of planting artemisia beside a favorite garden bench simply for the pleasure of running your hands through its silky foliage?

There are many simple, and cheap, design features planned around the senses that will help intensify the sudden bursts of pleasure, the lifting of the spirit, and the sheer delight engendered by a successful garden.

PLANNED TO SPARKLE With their subtly diverse shades of white, variegated hostas, fresh-faced pansies, and the heavily scented shrub *Viburnum carlesii* create the monochrome effect of this planting scheme. The cups of the tulips, catching the light, seem to float against the green background.

VISUAL SATISFACTIONS

◆

COLOR HAS INSTANT IMPACT, but shape gives its own subtle, enduring pleasure that should not be neglected. It may be the shape of an individual leaf or plant or the structure composed by the planting as a whole that satisfies the gardener's creative energies.

In the historic formal garden, such structures as pleached avenues, knots, and parterres played a far greater role than color. Patterns were bold and geometric, styles were rigid, and the scale was often stately. Strong geometry is just as effective in modern private gardens, however — even in small, informal ones.

Clever planting must lead the eye deliberately to specific points. To get people to look upward to a treasured plant, for example, guide the eye through a crescendo of lower ones, leading it to follow the outline higher and higher.

Contrasting shapes that are carefully composed allow rounded, tiered, upright, or creeping plants to be enjoyed to the fullest. Color then becomes an extra device used among the different shapes to highlight, embolden, tone down, or shift the pattern with seasonal change.

When shape and color are also combined with plants chosen for their special qualities — a strong architectural silhouette, perhaps, or spiky foliage — a planting takes on yet another dimension.

PLANTS FOR TEXTURE

Use some of the bold, even brash, architectural plants that are irresistible to the eye. The giant thistle (*Onopordum nervosum*) grows at an impressive rate and has alluringly soft felted leaves, although its spines are vicious. The plant scatters seeds prodigiously, but seedlings are easy to hoe out or transplant. The mullein, too, is gray-white and woolly, and its knee-high rosettes of large leaves send up spires of crowded blooms resembling those of the hollyhock.

Plants with enormous leaves — gunnera, for example, or the rhubarb-like *Rheum palmatum* — make compelling shapes from a distance but are also fun to look at close up.

You can plan overall schemes that marry and enhance visual pleasures. The narrow grassy leaves of a brown sedge, for example, create a silky effect when

NATURAL SCULPTURE The expansive, eye-catching leaves of *Rodgersia tabularis* spread like a crowd of opened umbrellas over the dense mauve flowers of *Montia sibirica* that carpet the ground beneath.

combined with the foliage of California poppies (*Eschscholzia*), while the satiny, vivid orange poppy flowers give a bright edge to the bronze grass blades.

The character of a planting changes according to season. The tender green growths of spring dry to crisp textures and starker brown shapes in autumn.

BEAUTY OF FORM WITHOUT FLOWERS

It is satisfying to compose plantings where flowers are not used at all, and where all the interest comes from leaf, stem, and trunk, relying on their variations in outline, color, and texture.

A mixture of evergreen shrubs and woody plants with an attractive bark or pattern of bare twigs provides interest in the winter. Plants with lots of small leaves — periwinkle and the low-growing hebes, for example — present a soft background for more conspicuous characters.

Tall fans of sword-like iris leaves, spiky clumps of yucca and striped New Zealand flax, and huge purple hands of

---

TOOLBOX

KEEPING A FULL RECORD

AN INSTANT CAMERA keeps the best record of what is flowering and when in your garden. Take a series of shots over the seasons to use when planning what changes to make.

Before you make any decisions, spread out the photographs and place illustrations of interesting plants, cut from catalogs, with them. This gives a good idea of what a new plant will look like in a certain position.

leaves gleams all the more brightly when teamed with the woolly foliage of *Ballota pseudodictamnus* or *Senecio cineraria*. A dense ground cover of gray-green *Sedum spectabile* does wonders for the dark foliage of Portugal laurel or pittosporum, while the lighter-leaved *Weigela florida* 'Variegata' looks its best standing out from a dark underplanting of evergreen candytuft (*Iberis sempervirens*), common thyme, or even plain ivy.

Bamboos combine shimmering leaves and graceful height. The shiny leaves of *Pleioblastus auricomus* shiver in the slightest breeze, drawing attention as they catch the light. In winter, little can divert the eye from the wildly twisted twigs of Harry Lauder's walking stick (*Corylus avellana* 'Contorta'). Place this where you can see its fascinating silhouette and enjoy its dancing catkins in late winter.

HOW TO MAKE COLORS WORK

Different hues and combinations produce different effects on the viewer. Intense color tends to heighten the emotions; gentle, pastel shades relax; reds and yellows are urgent and restless together; blues and whites create a cool setting, but the warmer contrast of blues and golden yellows is invigorating. Being aware of how colors work, together and on their own, helps you achieve whatever effect you want.

The abrupt impact of a strident bed of hot tones, for example, distracts from a less than satisfactory outline or feature elsewhere in the garden. Conversely, a foliage garden with variations of green and subtle gray, lime or olive undertones merges into one dull mass unless something bolder is placed in it to make the viewer focus more sharply and notice all the subtleties. A group of red tulips among spring greenery, for example, shouts for attention and invites the beholder to take a second look.

Once an initial flash of color has drawn the eye, the viewer then begins to observe other colors and shapes, perhaps the brown and gray wrinkles of tree bark, the vivid green spikes of young crocosmia foliage, and the pleasant contrast of softer, more muted green foliage behind.

USING COOL, PALE COLOR SCHEMES

Pale colors, especially lemon yellows, blues, and whites, work especially well in low light levels, gaining a luminosity that can be missing in the full glare of the

---

TO THE RESCUE

ENDING A COLOR CLASH

IF IT SUDDENLY strikes you that two flowering plants are clashing and you need to take one out, do not hesitate to do so. Simply dig out the offender with its roots and as much surrounding soil as you can lift and put it immediately into a prepared hole in a spot where it will show to greater advantage. Firm the plant in well and water it frequently until it is established.

Fill the gap left in the border on a temporary basis with a bland-colored herbaceous plant such as a white pansy or petunia. Either of these will provide adequate ground cover until you find a permanent replacement.

CLEVER COLORS A clump of bright pink *Geranium sanguineum* is planted in front of *Stachys macrantha* and the red *Knautia macedonica*. This unusual combination is bold and dense enough to seize the gaze and keep it from an unattractive wall behind.

Rodgersia pinnata 'Superba' provide dramatic shapes. Less commonly seen but equally striking are the toothed cream and dark green leaves of *Scrophularia aquatica* 'Variegata.'

Maples, and especially the Japanese species, also have beautifully shaped leaves in many subtle colors including bronze, red, and purplish hues. The delicate points of the maples show to advantage above a drift of bolder, broader foliage. Hostas are good here, especially in fertile, moist soil.

Try contrasts of pale and dark, shiny and matt, as well as of differing shapes. The glossy sheen of holly and camellia

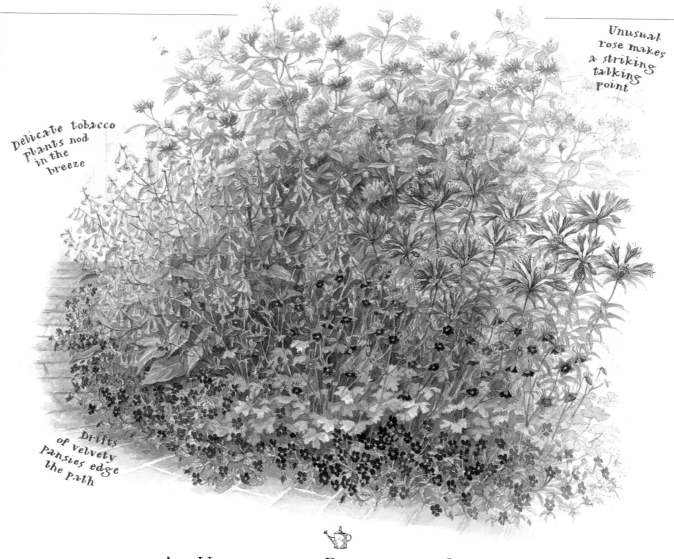

Unusual rose makes a striking talking point

Delicate tobacco plants nod in the breeze

Drifts of velvety Pansies edge the Path

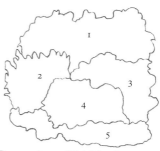

AN UNEXPECTED PALETTE OF COLORS

Startle the senses with an unashamedly novel slant on old favorites, in which green, red, and, surprisingly, black mingle to create an effect that is strong yet harmonious.

A CARPET of self-seeding black pansies (*Viola tricolor* 'Bowles' Black') sets the tone for this adventurous corner. The small black flowers are dotted around the front of the bed, while tall *Nicotiana langsdorffii*, with its clusters of flaring green flower tubes, provides contrast in color and height.

The reddish-brown tinge on the petal edges of the unusual green-blossomed rose, *Rosa × odorata* 'Viridiflora,' echoes the combination of red and green in the flowers of *Alstroemeria psittacina* — which are also streaked with black. Under these two impressive examples of nature's way

with color, the striking brown-and-green columbine *Aquilegia viridiflora* makes its early summer display.

EXTENDING THE THEME

Many other plants would fit into the scheme. The pansy 'Mollie Sanderson' has larger flowers, and the burgundy tulip 'Queen of the Night' would add spring excitement to the border. Follow the columbine with bells of Ireland (*Moluccella laevis*), which looks like a short green delphinium, and try the willow *Salix gracilistyla* 'Melanostachys,' with black catkins, in the background.

1. *Rosa × odorata* 'Viridiflora'
2. *Nicotiana langsdorffii*
3. *Alstroemeria psittacina*
4. Columbine (*Aquilegia viridiflora*)
5. Pansy (*Viola tricolor* 'Bowles' Black')

COOLER TONES Glancing sun accentuates spires of white foxgloves, which enliven the intense blue of *Meconopsis betonicifolia.*

FRESH SPRING BLEND The distinctively green-streaked white *Tulipa* 'Spring Green' rises above the daisy-like flowers of *Anthemis cupaniana* and the fragrant cup-shaped blooms of *Anemone sylvestris.* This pale grouping is offset by the bright green of spring's emerging foliage.

sun. Flowers are important, but don't underestimate the contribution that foliage plants make. You can do nearly as much if you use plants variegated with white or yellow in among leaves of green or blue-green.

For spring the coolest tulip variety is 'Spring Green,' whose white petals are broadly streaked with green. Late white narcissus, especially the sweetly fragrant *Narcissus poeticus recurvus*, blend in well. In partial shade the spreading perennial *Anemone sylvestris*, with its cup-shaped creamy white flowers, puts on a long display and has attractive foliage. Add white violets and primroses for extra charm, along with plenty of small bulbs such as grape hyacinth (*Muscari armeniacum*) in both white and blue varieties, perhaps preceded in late winter by a flush of dainty snowdrops.

Link spring to summer with a white-flowered honesty with cream-splashed leaves (*Lunaria annua* 'Alba Variegata') or with *Pulmonaria saccharata* 'Cambridge Blue,' a beauty whose leaves are generously spotted with silver. Later, use the subtle tones of hostas to continue the cool theme throughout summer. Their flowers, usually lavender-mauve or near white, look washed out in full sun, but in dappled shade enhance the cooling theme. The bold, blue-gray foliage of *Hosta sieboldiana* is especially useful and contrasts well with variegated species such as 'Thomas Hogg' and 'Albopicta.'

Summer formal displays are often composed of warm colors, but when the choice is restricted to a cooler range, the result is refreshing, even on a sunny site. Silver foliage works especially well; indeed, many species that have evolved silvery or woolly foliage have done so as a defense against excessive sun.

COOL BUT NOT COLD

To avoid too white an effect, include at least one other cooling color in the design. Supply more pale or medium blues with *Brunnera macrophylla*, forget-me-nots, or bluebells in spring and, for late summer, the easiest of the gentians, *Gentiana septemfida.*

Lemon tones are also attractive. Try *Achillea taygetea* or the variety 'Flowers of Sulphur.' Seeds of the primrose-yellow *Potentilla recta pallida* will produce progeny that bear pale yellow blooms. White *Cyclamen hederifolium* continues the display into autumn, and for late winter, plant the pale forms of *Helleborus orientalis*, many of which are greenish white with just a hint of pink.

SKILLFUL WAYS TO USE WHITE

The white garden works especially well on a small scale, occupying a single border or even just a small corner. By day the whites can be almost dazzling, and the viewer depends on contrasting foliage plants for relief. But in low light, the white border takes on a magical quality when the white flowers appear to float on invisible stems.

☀ Take care when combining white flowers. Shades range from the cream of

MAKING HOT COLORS HOTTER A touch of cool contrast increases the intensity of a bright color, as seen with these orange California poppies backed by blue *Geranium × magnificum*. Such striking colors are especially effective in full sunlight, which makes subtler hues fade.

emerging white tulips to the pink flush found in most white roses, and one shade can make another look dingy.

🌸 Roses that are particularly good for white borders include the hybrid musk 'Prosperity' and the floribunda 'Iceberg,' both of which fade away gracefully. Deadhead frequently to keep the petals of fading flowers from showing up too markedly against the white background.

🌸 Keep the different plants apart with plenty of silver or gray foliage to lighten the display and ensure that one white flower does not make another look dirty.

🌸 Every ensemble needs to have its star performer, so be sure to have one white plant that is bigger, better, and more showy than the rest — for example, the great heads of the hydrangea or the sculpted stateliness of the calla lily.

BRIGHT HERBACEOUS BEDS

Single colors are almost always more dramatic than a mix. Hot colors work exceptionally well against a drab, gray building or in a front garden that might otherwise be featureless. Abandon all thoughts of compromise and choose the boldest, brightest colors.

Vivid gold and orange French and African marigolds (*Tagetes patula* and *T. erecta*) are among the easiest half-hardy annuals to grow. They flower over a long period and are as good in single colors as in the more usual mixtures. Ever-flowering begonias in brilliant red, orange, or yellow also thrive out-of-doors when they are treated as half-hardy annuals.

For a discordant but effective note, put pink with orange — *Alstroemeria ligtu* hybrids with poppies, perhaps — and pay special attention to foliage, which is important even in the brightest displays. Red blooms and purple-bronze foliage make the dahlia 'Bishop of Llandaff' an excellent center plant for a fiery border.

BUILDING A HOT SCHEME WITH SHRUBS

Golden-leaved shrubs make an essential contribution to a glowing hot scheme, and the best are those that do not scorch in direct sunlight. *Physocarpus opulifolius* 'Dart's Gold' drops its golden leaves in autumn but has pleasing winter twigs with flaky tan bark, while the smaller, evergreen *Choisya ternata* 'Sundance' keeps its yellow leaves all year.

Choose shrubs that maintain the hot scheme in autumn when the herbaceous plants have disappeared. Berry bearers such as pyracantha or cotoneaster, dwarf maples with their rich autumn color, or the dark, purple foliage of *Cotinus coggygria* 'Purpureus' that lightens to red in autumn are all eminently suitable.

Under the shrubs grow some euphorbias. Scarlet bracts make the statuesque

SUBTLE IMPACT A foaming urn of silvery artemisia makes a cool combination with the woolly leaved lamb's-ears at the base.

STAND-UP WEED BAG

A FREESTANDING OPEN BAG is ideal for tossing weeds and debris into as you work in the garden. Such a receptacle can be fashioned from a sturdy tote-bag; stiffen it by stitching heavy-gauge wire along the insides of the bag's seams. Wire salvaged from old clothes hangers works well and may be attached to the material with heavy thread or light monofilament fishing line. The result will be a bag that is light, strong, and easy to carry.

Euphorbia griffithii 'Fireglow' and its stockier relative 'Dixter' attractive. The ground-hugging *Euphorbia polychroma* is smothered in spring with a profusion of tiny flowers in golden bracts.

MAINTAINING HOT COLOR THROUGH THE YEAR

Euphorbias are interesting for most of the year, but they peak in spring and early summer. Combine them with deep red blooms — perhaps the tulip 'Couleur Cardinal' or scarlet anemones — to make an arresting highlight.

American columbine (*Aquilegia canadensis*) would also look good in a hot planting scheme, flaunting its bicolored red-and-yellow, long-spurred flowers in early summer. In midsummer *Inula magnifica* grows huge leaves, sending up 8 ft (2.4 m) stems topped with big yellow daisy-like flowers. In more restricted plantings, tiger lilies (*Lilium lancifolium*) are lovely in summer, coming in yellow, red, or orange forms, and the hybrids of the Peruvian lily *Alstroemeria ligtu* offer a range of glowing salmon pink, scarlet, and yellow flower shades from June into early fall.

Kniphofias and crocosmias are wonderful for a splash of orange in mid- and late summer, perhaps with coreopsis to

precede them. Yarrow and goldenrod enrich the yellow range, and are followed by chrysanthemums later in the season.

VIVID ANNUALS FOR SUN

Sometimes a garden bed has fertile soil and receives almost constant sunshine. The range of plants that thrive in such conditions is vast, but hardy annuals, many bred from agricultural weeds, are particularly suitable.

An open, sun-drenched site begs for a joyful mix of strong colors. A traditional choice would be deep blue cornflowers teamed with flame-red poppies. Larkspurs in blue and pink add further

VIVID CONTRASTS In strong sun, strident colors often work where pastel blends might be lost. The late summer combination of yellow rudbeckias and dusky pink chrysanthemums is striking in its own right, but also coordinates well with yellowing autumn foliage as the seasons change.

MELLOWER MIXES Color schemes that are warm without being too insistent provide an early summer feast for the eye. A drift of red-and-gold columbines, rising from their dainty foliage, sprawls across the paving stones, while richer notes are added by a group of purple irises.

BURNISHED REDS AND GOLDS Nasturtiums grown against a wall provide a vivid backdrop to a late summer bed of richly colored flowers interspersed with cooler foliage. Reddish-orange heleniums contrast with spiky phormium leaves, and crocosmias and roses add bright shades of red. The orange blooms of the dahlia 'Ellen Houston' stand out against its purple-bronze foliage.

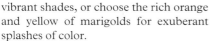

vibrant shades, or choose the rich orange and yellow of marigolds for exuberant splashes of color.

Color clashes also work well in bright sunlight. The strong orange of California poppies, for instance, combines beautifully with the purple-blue of *Convolvulus tricolor* 'Blue Flash,' and the deep yellow

Ursinia anethoides blazes magnificently against blood-red dahlias.

To set off such contrasting flowers, add the fast-growing castor-bean plant (*Ricinus communis*) for its huge, palmate leaves, which are borne almost head high. The green form is strong and fresh in color, but there are also varieties with

bronze or red-purple foliage; the red-leaved 'Impala' would be striking among a display of vividly colored annuals.

SUBDUED SCHEMES

Soft blends of pink and mauve spiked with a little blue are among the prettiest color combinations. Roses cannot be bet-

TWILIGHT DRAMA Placing a large-flowered plant at the front of the border provides a powerful focal point to capture attention. In this case, the pale spires of lupines rising from fresh green leaves contribute architectural interest and seem to hold the last rays of the afternoon sun.

PASTEL PRETTINESS Soft pink oriental poppies (*Papaver orientale*) with frilled papery petals combine with the starry white flower heads of *Anthemis cretica*. Such muted colors come into their own in fading light.

tered as a centerpiece, and some of the classic cultivars are the loveliest. Their flowers are pinker than many modern counterparts and have a sweet fragrance.

Such historic cultivars as the two-tone pink-striped *Rosa gallica* 'Versicolor' and old forms of *Rosa alba* such as 'Maiden's Blush' and 'Queen of Denmark' have vigor, fine flower shape, and rich scent. Since they bear only one flush of flowers, mix them with modern shrub roses, which have all the charm of old roses and flower longer, but are less fragrant.

Underplant the roses with lavender, silver mounds of lamb's-ears, and pinks, especially the crimson-eyed blush-pink 'Doris' and the maroon-laced 'Dad's Favorite.' At intermediate height, sweet William (*Dianthus barbatus*) adds old-fashioned charm in midsummer. For foliage grow meadow rue (*Thalictrum*), which has decorative, finely lobed leaves.

For spring use bulbs, especially pink tulips such as 'Greenland' or the later 'Clara Butt,' to follow drifts of purple crocuses and blue grape hyacinths.

PLANTS TO TOUCH AND TASTE

HANDLING PLANTS just to see what they feel like is one of the great joys of gardening. Some are irresistibly silky, some velvety; there are trees with polished bark, flowers whose petals form firm bowls, and leaves whose quilting of veins has to be traced with a finger.

Apart from stinging nettles and obviously spiny or thorny growth, most plants feel pleasant, but certain species are worth growing especially to touch. Many of them are pleasing to look at, too, and not just in the summer but right through the drabbest months of the year.

SOFT TO THE TOUCH

Eminently touchable plants are best placed near sitting areas or beside paths so that they can be plucked, tweaked, or stroked by passersby. Many grasses are especially useful here, but take care — some have sharp edges to their leaves. Among the silky grasses that are handsome to look at and safe to finger are the Japanese *Hakonechloa macra* 'Aureola,' with striped green and gold leaves, and *Helictotrichon sempervirens*, which is much taller. This excellent grass forms distinctive sage-green clumps and sports summer flower stems that dance gracefully in the breeze.

The aptly named feather grass (*Stipa pennata*) bears its long silvery plumes

---

AWAITING RELEASE A generous bush of thyme encroaches on a garden bench, its profusion of delicate pink flowers inviting a sitter to grasp and gently squeeze a handful to release the herb's aroma. Behind, the whimsical "ears" and feathery foliage of French lavender are also irresistible.

BRILLIANT CONTRAST The white bark of *Betula utilis* var. *jacquemontii* stands out dramatically against the autumn foliage of an *Acer palmatum*. The leaves of this striking tree may turn clear yellow before they fall.

SKELETAL CONTORTIONS Once its summer foliage has gone, Harry Lauder's walking stick (*Corylus avellana* 'Contorta') reveals its intricate corkscrew twigs, which are festooned in late winter with dancing yellow catkins.

SUMPTUOUS WINTER BARK The copper-tan bark of the Chinese cherry *Prunus serrula* shines as though treated to a daily polishing and provides a sturdy column of gleaming color to warm the view in the colder months.

BEST PLANTS

A PLEASURE TO TOUCH

Grow one or several of the plants below so that you can enjoy the sensual, textural qualities they provide.

• Lamb's-ears (*Stachys byzantina*): low, mat-forming perennial with leaves like silver felt and woolly stems.

• *Prunus serrula*: a Chinese cherry whose glowing, satiny bark peels off each year to reveal a new, shinier skin.

• *Abies pinsapo*: a conifer with stiff, blunt needles that feel like a comb's teeth when you run a finger over them.

• *Rosa* 'Zéphirine Drouhin': a thornless rose — which makes it the perfect climbing rose for pruning and training.

• *Carex flagellifera*: a grassy sedge with narrow brown or tan leaves and stems that feel almost like hair.

• Snapdragon (*Antirrhinum*): when the blooms are pinched gently at the sides, the petals open like jaws.

• *Verbascum bombyciferum*: the most densely coated of all mulleins, with rosettes of gray leaves and tall, woolly flower spikes the following season.

• Pussy willow (*Salix caprea* 'Kilmarnock'): a weeping willow with silky gray, and later yellow, catkins borne in early to mid spring.

• *Salix hastata* 'Wehrhahnii': a small willow with silver-gray catkins.

---

through midsummer, while *Pennisetum villosum* has creamy-white hairs that fluff out from the cylindrical flower head. Squirrel grass (*Hordeum jubatum*) waves long golden-tinged silky threads, but the white flower heads of hare's tail (*Lagurus ovatus*) have a furry softness.

The unusual pasqueflower (*Anemone pulsatilla*) has silky seed heads that extend its beauty through May, after the flowers have faded. The downy leaves that accompany the seed heads are lovely to brush with the hand, too. The yellow-flowered *Clematis tangutica* offers its shiny seed heads to be stroked in fall.

It is a close contest between fennel and some artemisias as to which has the softer foliage. Fortunately you do not have to choose; the two make a beautiful combination when the spidery bronze fennel (*Foeniculum vulgare* 'Purpureum') soars above a foaming silver mass of *Artemisia schmidtiana* 'Nana.'

Altogether cozier is the sensation of touching lamb's-ears (*Stachys byzantina*), whose thick gray-green leaves have a comfortably fleecy feel, or giant pussy willow (*Salix chaenomeloides*), which has fuzzy silver catkins that can grow up to three inches long.

The plush-covered young shoots of the staghorn sumac (*Rhus hirta*, syn. *R. typhina*) are soon hidden by graceful ferny leaves that turn fiery when autumn comes. This small tree is eager to colonize the garden with suckers, however, so the velvet tassels of love-lies-bleeding (*Amaranthus caudatus*), which dangle in long crimson bunches from midsummer into fall, may be preferable.

The chief joy in touching snapdragons (*Antirrhinum*) is seeing the "face" open its mouth wide when you squeeze the sides of the flowers gently. With the Chinese lantern (*Physalis alkekengii*), it is the papery orange globe hiding the berry-like fruit that is so tempting. And with love-in-a-mist (*Nigella damascena*), it is the brown balloon of the seedpod.

More sedate pleasures are offered by magnolias and tulips, whose exquisitely smooth petals, gleaming slightly, form cool, firm goblets.

WINTER WOOD TO CARESS

Some trees and shrubs are so ravishing in winter that they are worth growing just for their twigs or bark.

The Chinese willow, *Salix fargesii*, has twigs like polished mahogany, with deep chestnut-red buds. Paperbark maple

(*Acer griseum*) has thin bark that peels off in flakes, and several species of madrona, especially *Arbutus menziesii*, have light tan bark that gleams in the sun. The two trees with the loveliest winter bark are *Prunus serrula*, with a gleaming copper-tan trunk, and the whitest of all birches, *Betula utilis* var. *jacquemontii*.

Trees like these are prettiest if the lower part of the branches are kept clean of shoots. This gives the maximum area of gleaming bark for your enjoyment.

GARDEN TASTES

As you stroll around the garden picking a growing tip here and there, it is tempting to test it with the tip of your tongue as well. Many plants are good to taste — not grown specifically as food for the table but added to the ornamental garden for their decorative qualities. The cherry tomato is a sweet little mouthful to eat straight from a plant grown against a sunny wall. Tender green peas, sugar snap peas, and green beans all make a crunchy tidbit and grow contentedly in an informal bed. Even in the smallest garden you can find room for a dwarf pepper, and in a large one you might let a thornless blackberry sprawl along a boundary fence; you will have to be quick, though, to beat the birds to the fruits.

Alpine strawberries are dainty plants to use as bed edging, but to save you from stooping to harvest the luscious fruits, grow them higher up — perhaps in a trough garden, at the front of a raised bed, or even in a pair of hanging baskets. The fruits are incomparable for flavor, and both leaves and flowers are pretty.

PETALS AND LEAVES
TO NIBBLE

More unexpected pleasures come from familiar flowers that are regarded as purely decorative. Pink rose petals and violets are frequently crystallized to use as garnishes and have a sweet taste even before the sugary coating. Pansies and nasturtiums add a colorful flourish to salads, and the orange rays of pot marigolds, slightly bitter in taste, will spice up a bowl of soup.

Herbs are the most promising plants for plucking, sniffing, and nibbling. Grow herbs beside a garden path where you can brush against them as you pass by or plant a selection beside your favorite garden bench, so you can pick off leaves with ease and rub them between your fingers to release their aroma.

GROW STRAWBERRIES IN A POT

CULTIVATING STRAWBERRIES in a strawberry jar or planter rather than in a bed keeps the fruit off muddy soil and away from slugs. You can select any variety that is adapted to your region.

Use a terra-cotta or plastic pot designed for growing strawberries or a small wooden barrel drilled with several holes. If you want, install a simple watering system. Place a length of perforated plastic hose or pipe down the center of the container as you plant it, leaving the top end open. Fill the tube with water, which will seep out through the soil.

1. Put a thick layer of pot shards or foam packing "peanuts" in the bottom of the pot, then fill it with sandy, organically enriched potting soil up to the first holes.

2. Push the roots of a plant through each of the lowest holes from the outside, cover them with soil, and firm it over the roots. Repeat for the remaining holes.

3. Once all the holes around the pot are planted, set several strawberry plants on the top, placing them about 6 in (15 cm) apart and firming them into the soil.

4. Stand the pot on bricks for good drainage and in a sunny location. Water immediately after planting, then water regularly during the summer.

Each of the many varieties of mint has its own flavor. Some are rather rank, others sweet; apple mint and orange mint are delicious when snipped into a salad or floated on a refreshing drink.

Basil is startlingly powerful tasted on its own, and lovage leaves have a sharp, celery flavor. Thymes are, without exception, decorative, so be sure to plant a selection, including golden or variegated forms. Lemon thyme, *Thymus × citriodorus*, is both aromatic and delicious.

Chamomile and feverfew are good to nibble, though the latter leaves behind a bitter aftertaste. Young coriander foliage has an intriguingly peppery fragrance and, unlike so many herbs, tastes exactly as it smells. Be cautious, however, when nibbling, as some plants that smell tempting are quite unsuitable for culinary use. The curry plant, for example, smells of curry only by coincidence and should not be used to flavor food at all.

Other plants are positively harmful. Rhubarb leaves, laburnum seeds, and yew berries are all poisonous, as are the blossoms of foxglove, iris, daffodil, and sweet pea. You should also never eat any flower or foliage that has been treated with pesticides.

FRAGRANCE AND AROMA

E VERYONE ACKNOWLEDGES the impor- tance of fragrance in a garden, but few gardeners fully exploit this rich and rewarding resource. Scents are potent revivers of memories, the same smell evoking a different recollection in each person. Perfumed flowers are an obvious source of fragrance, and herbs are famil- iar favorites. But with a little gardening experience you can create a much wider range of sensations to savor.

Evergreen shrubs such as cherry laurel, holly, and aucuba carry a mildly acrid aroma that goes with shady plant- ings. Boxwood has a sharp smell — en- joyed by some, loathed by others — while walnut leaves smell spicy. Emerging poplar foliage has a hint of honey or musk, and on a hot day, eucalyptus pro- duces a marvellous clean aroma.

Certain plants, such as the oak-leaf geranium, have foliage so pungent that it overpowers the delicate scent of the flowers. A woodland planting where wild garlic predominates is unmistak- able but not at all unpleasant, even in midsummer when the garlic leaves are beginning to die back.

There are also quirky plants that are fun to grow for their unique aroma. If you have a sunny indoor space, grow the tender senna plant (*Cassia didymobotrya*), whose dark brown buds at the end of the flower spikes smell just like peanut butter. It is one of many flowers with a smell of food. In warm rain, sweet briar foliage has the fragrance of ripe apples, while the red- flowered *Salvia elegans* has foliage that, when bruised, smells so strongly of pine- apple that it makes your mouth water.

FRAGRANCE THROUGH THE YEAR

Even when you are planting chiefly for fragrance, do not forget that the overall aim in any garden is to delight all the senses. Sight and sound are as impor- tant here as anywhere, so careful plan- ning is needed to create a garden that weaves these elements together — and not just for high summer but for the whole year.

Among the hundreds of beautiful and scented plants available there is some- thing for every month, every week of the year, from winter-flowering shrubs such as witch hazel, to summer's sweet peas

WELL-PLACED FRAGRANCE The heady scent of the tall *Lilium regale* wafts out on the lightest breeze, spreading over the garden and inside the house when the windows are open in summer. The lily's impressive clusters of flowers stand out best when surrounded by foliage plants.

and Madonna lilies. It is always possible to have a flowering plant to provide fragrance, either where it grows or once it is picked and brought indoors.

WINTER AND SPRING SCENT

Most gardens have room for only a few large shrubs or small trees. Choose ones that bear scented blooms at a time when herbaceous plants are resting, such as *Viburnum × bodnantense*, with pink winter flowers, or the equally fragrant white *V. farreri*. The intensely perfumed *Chimonanthus praecox* and the untidy winter honeysuckle (*Lonicera fragrantissima*) are good alternatives.

For the spring plant the evergreen *Osmanthus delavayi*, whose small white blooms are richly perfumed. The evergreen *Daphne laureola*, a lovely shrub that is hardy to zone 7, will surprise you early in the season, when its small green flowers exude a pervasive scent on mild afternoons. Strew the ground beneath the shrubs with a selection of violets, such as the vigorous *Viola odorata* 'Admiral Avellan' and the pink-flowered 'Coeur d'Alsace.'

SUMMER PERFUME

If you have the space, a mock orange provides waves of fruity perfume in early summer, while a repeat-flowering rose such as 'Roseraie de l'Haÿ' or 'Fragrant Cloud' would be perfect for later.

Foliage makes a valuable foil for flowering fragrant plants, and if it is aromatic as well as decorative, so much the better. Rosemary and thyme meet both these requirements, and mints, despite being rather invasive, excel in their aroma — especially the dark eau-de-cologne mint (*Mentha × piperita citrata*).

Lavenders keep their aromatic silver-gray leaves all through the year and make lovely companions for garden pinks. Mix old and modern pinks for flowers and scent. Old-fashioned cultivars, such as *Dianthus* 'Dad's Favorite' or 'Sops in Wine,' have a tang of cloves but tend to bear only one flush of flowers. Modern border pinks — such as 'Doris' — are sweeter but less clove-like and stay in flower for much longer.

Some peonies have a distinctive sweet smell, especially strong in the cultivar 'Sarah Bernhardt,' while lupines have a spicy undertone. For late in the season, plant the herbaceous *Clematis heracleifolia*, whose small, pale blue flowers have a fresh narcissus-like scent. Scented geraniums

A BLEND OF APRICOT AND CHOCOLATE

When there is a moment to pause and reflect, a quiet spot planted to please all the senses is sure to lift the spirits.

IN THIS SUNNY CORNER, mouth-watering smells of chocolate mingle with a sweet, full fragrance reminiscent of tea, while shades of apricot yellow and velvet brown delight the eye.

The large, loosely formed flowers of the tea rose *Rosa* 'Lady Hillingdon' appear with gratifying regularity through the summer. When combined with the glossy buds and dark, velvety flowers of the sprawling chocolate cosmos (*Cosmos atrosanguineus*), which stretch up from the ground on a profusion of tall, spindly stalks, it completes a natural frame for a simple bench.

'Lady Hillingdon' is the most reliable of the climbing tea roses and overwinters reliably to zone 7, especially against a sunny wall. Chocolate cosmos also flourishes in full sun, flowering through the summer season but succumbing to the first moderate frost in fall.

Light tea fragrance surrounds the rose

Velvety flowers release a chocolate aroma

WINTER SCENTS

Growing just two or three of these attractive, scented plants livens up the garden during the dull and dormant autumn and winter months.

• Sweet violet (*Viola odorata*): garden varieties such as 'Coeur d'Alsace' and 'Quatre Saisons' produce flowers in autumn, winter, and spring.

• *Viburnum farreri*: a Chinese shrub with delicate, fragrant white blooms flushed with pink on leafless twigs.

• Witch hazel (*Hamamelis mollis*): a shrub with winter flowers resembling yellow spiders; their warm fragrance has a slightly metallic undertone.

• *Mahonia japonica*: prickly evergreen shrub with sweetly fragrant yellow flowers in late winter. Its perfume is reminiscent of lily-of-the-valley's.

• Wintersweet (*Chimonanthus praecox*): parchment-colored flowers on bare twigs have the strongest fragrance of any winter shrub.

• *Sarcococca humilis*: low, evergreen shrub with tiny, cream, late winter flowers that smell distinctly of honey.

• *Daphne mezereum*: small shrub that produces purple flowers in late winter. Their fragrance is sweet and strong and hangs in mild, still air.

• Hyacinth (*Hyacinthus orientalis*): the scent of the numerous hybrids can be almost overpowering inside the house, but outdoors this bulb is a great contributor of fragrance.

A PLACE OF REPOSE The heavily scented honeysuckle *Lonicera × americana* overhangs a secluded bench tucked away in the garden against a sheltering wall. Cushions of lavender add further fragrance.

and verbenas can be put out for summer, but need to overwinter indoors; there you can pinch the leaves to release their perfume whenever you wish.

Among annuals, little can match for strength and sweetness the fragrance of stocks and white nicotianas, both of which release their scent in the evening. Even sharply aromatic plants such as marigolds and pot marigolds add to the overall fragrance with their pungency.

Bulbs for a scented border must include jonquils or pheasant's-eye narcissus for late spring and species lilies for summer. *Lilium regale*, *L. candidum*, and *L. speciosum* have outstanding beauty and a perfume that far surpasses that of hybrid lilies. In contrast to such sweetness, a few species of allium add an arresting scent. In autumn a bulb usually sold as *Acidanthera murielae* (but correctly known as *Gladiolus callianthus* 'Murieliae') has a soft, clean fragrance.

CREATING A FRAGRANT BOWER

A bower is a bewitching, romantic spot — a seat for two under a canopy of fragrant climbers. The climbing rose 'New Dawn' is perfect for midyear freshness of perfume, and white jasmine for late summer fragrance. In warm, sheltered gardens, where frost is a rarity, try the jasmine-like *Trachelospermum jasminoides*, which offers evergreen foliage and a delicious scent from its cream summer flowers.

Another possibility for growing over bowers is the dependable honeysuckle, especially the vigorous *Lonicera japonica* 'Halliana,' which is the longest blooming. From summer to late fall, the sharply scented blossoms just keep coming. Other honeysuckles include the early-

blooming *Lonicera periclymenum* 'Belgica,' or 'Early Dutch,' whose tubular red flowers open to reveal a yellow center, and *L. p.* 'Graham Thomas,' whose lemon blooms fade elegantly to a deep shade of parchment.

A stronger-colored rose than the shell-pink 'New Dawn' is needed to complement the honeysuckles. Grow the thornless climbing Bourbon 'Zéphirine Drouhin,' which is vigorous with a succession of fragrant, deep pink flowers.

At your feet grow chamomile, lemon thyme, or even coriander. Each of these has foliage with a sharp tang to balance all that sweetness, and their pinkish-white, lacy flowers are extremely pretty.

Place your bower in a bright spot, so the sun will bring on the flowers of the climbers while the seat will be shaded and cool. Stand a container or two of heliotrope or lemon verbena at the entrance to the bower in early summer and replace it with a pot of lilies later on.

AROMATIC RECIPES FOR SUNNY CORNERS

The favorite part of your garden is often the sheltered nook that traps most sunshine and where you take a stroll during a moment of leisure. Make it an extra source of pleasure by putting two or three well-chosen scented plants there.

Herbs are ideal for sun-baked spots. Many of them are natives of hot, dry regions and give their best when these conditions are re-created for them. Traditionally herbs were utility plants, grown for their culinary and medicinal value, but many have a discreet beauty.

Most herbs are aromatic rather than fragrant: their smell, and indeed flavor, is in the leaves. This is a bonus since the smell is not limited to flowering time but is much longer lived, waiting to be released by anyone brushing against or crushing the leaves.

Thyme is lovely for bright carpets of color — in pink, purple, and white — and is gently aromatic, especially in late spring. Its young foliage adds zest to the delicate fragrance of cowslip flowers.

In summer place pots of Madonna lilies, with their clean perfume, among mounds of sage, tarragon, southernwood (*Artemisia abrotanum*), wormwood (*A.*

WINTER COLOR AND SCENT Witch hazel brightens up the dreary months with a splash of color early in the year. Its limbs are lined with little tufts of thread-like yellow flowers that spread a sweet scent with a sharp edge.

BEST PLANTS

SUMMER FRAGRANCE

Beautiful plants abound to keep your garden fragrant all spring and summer.

- Pheasant's-eye narcissus (*Narcissus poeticus recurvus*): a white-petaled flower with a shallow, frilled red cup and a fresh, clean fragrance.

- Wallflower (*Erysimum cheiri* 'Harpur Crewe'): a double yellow form with twice the usual generous scent.

- Peony (*Paeonia delavayi*): an Asian tree peony whose blood-red single blooms have a powerful fragrance.

- Mock orange (*Philadelphus* 'Beauclerk'): a sharp, green, citrus-scented bloom, strong in early evening.

- *Rosa rugosa* 'Roseraie de l'Haÿ': a species rose whose purplish-pink blooms, produced in flushes all summer, have a strong, sweet scent.

- Sweet rocket (*Hesperis matronalis*): sweet-scented with a spicy note halfway between wallflower and stock.

- Pink (*Dianthus* 'Sops in Wine'): an old-fashioned pink, maroon with white markings, with an aroma of cloves.

- Lavender (*Lavandula angustifolia* 'Hidcote Pink'): one of the most powerfully scented of the lavenders with purplish-pink flowers.

- Summer jasmine (*Jasminum officinale*): a climber with white flowers and a rich, dark fragrance.

- Flowering tobacco (*Nicotiana alata*): droops by day but lifts its white trumpets to blast out waves of rich fragrance by night.

- Golden-rayed lily (*Lilium auratum*): heavy fragrance wafts from the yellow-striped white flowers freckled with dark red spots.

---

absinthium), and rosemary — all of which delight with their silvery-gray foliage, as well as with their different smells. Plant a purple sage underneath an old rose such as the Bourbon 'La Reine Victoria' for a softer summer look, adding a purple lavender for its flowers as well as its invigorating scent. Lavender also combines well with clove-scented garden pinks and an aromatic marjoram.

Stocks add a touch of spice, as do some other annuals such as mignonette (*Reseda odorata*) and sweet rocket (*Hesperis matronalis*). The fragrance of sweet

SWEET AND SPICY Sight and smell are engaged by this ravishing bed of clove-scented border pinks backed by *Rosa × odorata*. The rose and the many varieties of pinks, which are treasured for their fragrance and lacy beauty, are a traditional combination in cottage-style gardens.

SOUND AND NOISE

HEARING IS THE SENSE least catered for in most gardens. Gardeners look, smell, touch, and sample the taste, but seldom listen to a plant. And yet the ambiance of a garden is so important that you should consider sound at least as carefully as the other senses to make your enjoyment as complete as possible.

In a water feature, for example, it is the tinkling of a fountain or waterfall that appeals just as much as the appearance, and on a dreamy summer afternoon, it can be positively hypnotic.

Unwanted noise is an unfortunate feature of many gardens. There are ways to reduce noise with plantings and to enhance the natural sounds that help distract from the unwelcome and make the garden a place of private enjoyment.

NATURAL SOUND EFFECTS

Plants make some remarkable sounds of their own accord — cranesbill geraniums release their seeds with a slingshot action that makes an audible ping, and broom pods pop in July sunshine like distant pistol shots. Most sounds, however, are caused by the weather.

Of all the elements, wind has the most effect. Quaking aspen, for instance, is pretty for its shimmering foliage, but the patter of its leaves in a breeze sounds so like rain that hearing it makes you glance at the sky, even on a cloudless day. Grasses, especially those whose foliage persists in winter, whisper dryly, while conifers sigh and mature willows moan, groan, and creak.

The wind makes even sweeter music if you hang wind chimes where a gentle breeze blows or set up a wind harp, whose strings thrum as the air moves across them.

Rain also makes pleasant sounds, varying from soothing to sad. In classical Chinese gardens, it was common to plant broad-leaved species beneath the eaves of a building so that the sound of raindrops on them could be heard inside. To imitate this, plant *Rheum palmatum* or some of the larger hostas, such as 'Sum and Substance' and 'Snowden,' near a window or door.

Birdsong, even in city gardens, makes early mornings and spring evenings a joy. Songsters that are commonly found in

rocket carries strongly on still evening air. The flowers are in a range of delicate colors, from white through palest lavender to mauve, and in twilight the pale hues show up well. They make an attractive combination when interplanted with tall, feathery, bronze fennel and round-leaved apple mint.

For an altogether bolder composition, mix the vivid greens of basil and crisply curled parsley with the bright golds and scarlets of a non-trailing nasturtium.

PLANTING FOR SCENT AT DOORS AND WINDOWS

Seize every opportunity to place fragrant plants near the house. It is easy to concentrate on appearance when dressing up a doorway, but there is an added delight in garden scent wafting in through a door or window. Wherever there is a window that is opened in mild weather, plant a scented climber outside. All the favorite climbers — roses, honeysuckle, jasmine, clematis — work well for framing a door or window.

To those you can add a number of wall shrubs. Train wintersweet (*Chimonanthus praecox*) on a south- or west-facing wall, where summer sun can mature the twigs to ensure good flowering the next winter. Wisteria has a special fragrance,

and the Japanese apricot (*Prunus mume*) on a warm, sheltered wall will sometimes release its gentle almond scent early in winter. To relieve the summer mediocrity of these shrubs, use their branches as supports for sweet peas, especially the strongly fragrant *Lathyrus odoratus* 'Painted Lady.'

Even routine summer bedding provides plenty of opportunity for fragrance at the door or under a window. Heliotrope has a rich, almost cloying scent and brooding purple flowers that look pretty dotted among a formal planting.

When you make a bed of geraniums, add a few scented types. There are many to choose from besides lemon-scented *Pelargonium* 'Graveolens.' Try the black-and-green-leaved *P.* 'Chocolate Mint' and the musky oak-leaved *P. quercifolium*, and do not overlook the most aromatic of them all, *P.* 'Fragrans.'

At the kitchen door grow something useful as well as fragrant. A big pot of spearmint, pineapple sage, or even pungent chives presents opportunities for pinching and sniffing. Keep a steady supply of coriander seedlings germinating indoors through the winter months so that you will have fresh herbs to use and can enjoy their sharp fragrance every time you brush past them.

the garden include mockingbirds and catbirds, as well as doves, finches, flycatchers, sparrows, and wrens.

The best songbirds are encouraged by soil and lawns in a healthy condition with a high worm population, plenty of cover, and branches they can use as song posts. Birds love rummaging about, under shrubs for example, but it is worth remembering that they can make quite a mess in the process, scattering mulch onto paths and lawns — and they are inveterate fruit robbers.

If the birds do not come, it is always possible to cheat with recordings of birdsong. Keep the volume low, and you soon forget the stratagem in the relaxing atmosphere. The sound may even help attract the real songsters. The same trick can be used to re-create a playing fountain, a trickling stream, or even the surge and retreat of the sea on a pebble beach.

Just take care to consider your neighbors. What is pleasant to you might be annoying to another.

BARRIERS TO DEADEN NOISE

Noise is different from sound. Noise is nuisance, something to be kept out of the garden or to be masked if it cannot be shut out entirely. Unfortunately it is seldom feasible to cut noise out altogether, so clever ways of insulating and

SHIMMERING SEED HEADS A dense growth of quaking grass (*Briza maxima*), with its slender stems and dangling flower heads, will rustle softly as it responds to the elements — whether harsh winds or soft breezes.

BACKGROUND SOUNDS

Pleasant sounds can set the mood for lazy days in the garden. Warm air currents or summer rains can stir hanging chimes to life, the hypnotic hum of a wind harp is awakened by fresh breezes, and a simple birdhouse can attract cooing doves.

BELL CHIMES
Bell chimes are light, delicate, and often oriental in style. As the wind blows, the clear, melodic tones of the bells chime, their unique sound evocative of Eastern temples.

DEER SCARER
Originally Japanese, deer scarers feed water into pivoted hollow canes. Once full, the canes tilt over, empty, and return to the original position, making a metallic chink as two studs strike each other.

DOVECOTE
The gentle cooing of doves is a welcome sound on summer afternoons. A dovecote amplifies the low sounds of its inhabitants and makes a pretty focal point in the garden.

WIND HARP
This ancient instrument is also known as an Aeolian harp, after Aeolus, Greek god of the winds. As the wind blows, strings stretched across the simple, open box vibrate with a mellow hum.

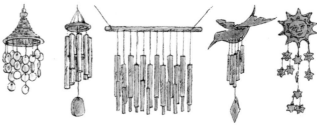

WIND CHIMES
Wind chimes create a soothing atmosphere, their sound varying according to the material used, generally wood or metal. Hang them from trees, under a balcony, or from a post in the garden — but well away from neighbors who may not enjoy the sounds.

masking it are essential. You can insulate your garden from outside noise without compromising the overall design.

The most obvious way is to develop barriers that soften or deflect sound. Walls, screens, hedges, even loose groups of shrubs and trees all help. You can turn each of these barriers into a design feature, even a key focal point.

Try lining a wall or fence with a row of pillars linked by trelliswork panels and smother it with climbing roses or wall plants. Together, the wall, trellis, and planting create a triple layer of insulation that helps muffle noises coming from outside the garden.

A straightforward evergreen hedge reduces noise well enough but can look rather ordinary. However, there are many alternatives to a standard hedge. A tapestry hedge is particularly attractive, made up of such different foliage plants as beech, holly, and golden cypress. By incorporating flowering currant (*Ribes*), sweet briar, escallonia, and other flowering plants, you can make a mixed hedge to provide a pleasing view year-round as well as fulfilling the original intention of screening out unwelcome noise.

A tough species such as *Clematis montana* is too vigorous to thread in a mixed hedge, but you do need some extra-strong characters. *Chaenomeles speciosa* is a sturdy grower and is also a useful protection for a more delicate treasure such as the beautiful *Clematis florida* 'Sieboldii,' with its resemblance to the passion-flower. These plants look lovely grown against a screening wall, fence, or thick, dark hedge.

Some roses can grow beneath trees, as long as they are not too densely shaded, but in poorer light, evergreen viburnums, mahonias, or low-growing cherry laurels are more suitable. At their feet, plant ground covers or perennials such as cranesbill geraniums, hellebores, or the creeping *Euphorbia amygdaloides* var. *robbiae*. The denser the growth, the more effectively it will absorb intrusive noise.

RUSTLING GRASSES The tall, feathery stems of *Miscanthus sinensis* produce a soft whispering in the breeze, while its graceful arched leaves produce a drier, rustling note. The fluffy, pale seed heads of *Pennisetum villosum* in the foreground add variety in height, texture, and sound.

HARMONIES IN THE GARDEN

Planting to add a background of agreeable sounds gives the garden a dimension that is all too easily neglected, but completes the charmed world you are creating.

COMBINE THE VISUAL DELIGHT of a leafy corner with the sighs of foliage, the gentle rattle of stems, and the soothing trickle of water. Gentle sounds not only delight the ear but also help divert attention from any intrusive noises beyond the boundary of the garden.

Tall bamboos stand guard at the back of this summer border, screening the garden from the outside world. Their apple-green leaves sway on hollow stems that rub together, making quiet background chatter. A wren, light enough to perch on a leaf, adds its tune. Despite their slender appearance these evergreen bamboos are quite resilient.

The pots of grass and sedge and the dwarf bamboo behind contribute color as well as sound. The reddish-brown leaves of *Hakonechloa macra* 'Aureola' emerge in spring as yellow blades with green stripes — a bright complement to the small, variegated bamboo.

The tree peony takes up the Eastern theme started by the bamboos. The huge, crimson-blotched lemon-yellow flowers are at their peak in summer.

THE MUSIC OF WATER

The fountain, rising above glistening pebbles, also evokes the Orient, since water and gravel are integral features of many Japanese gardens. The water spouts just high enough to tinkle as it falls and serves as a "sculpture" to punctuate the soft mounds of plantings. A songbird looking for worms or drawn by the water will add counterpoint to the music with its gentle scratching or splashing sounds.

As raindrops begin to fall, they patter rhythmically against the firm foliage of the rheum and collect in the deeply veined leaves. Rain or shine, the orchestra in this lush, green corner lends a melodious note to the garden.

Tall bamboos click busily in the breeze

Grass and small bamboos whisper as they stir

A fountain patters like gentle rain

1. Muriel bamboo (*Fargesia murieliae*)
2. Tree peony (*Paeonia* 'Argosy')
3. Dwarf white-stripe bamboo (*Pleioblastus variegatus*)
4. *Hakonechloa macra* 'Aureola'
5. Sedge (*Carex flagellifera*)
6. *Rheum palmatum* 'Atrosanguineum'

CAPTURING A MOOD

Most gardeners have a favorite time of year or style. For some, the fresh greens of spring have unmatchable beauty; others can never get enough of autumn's glowing colors. Cottage profusion is the essence of a garden to some people, while others consider orderly formality essential for providing the sense of peace they seek in the garden.

If your choice is a garden of several moods, with a single section or a corner devoted to each one, you can use a low barrier — a hedge, wall, or fence — to divide a formal corner from a wild one or sharp greens from mellow golds. The barrier will change depending on its location in sun or shade, which will also help establish different moods.

MEDITERRANEAN GARDEN

If you have a dry garden area, seize the opportunity to create a fragment of the Mediterranean. With gravel or pebbles of different sizes and discreetly placed stone or concrete pavers, you can intensify the arid nature of the site. Stones push summer ground temperatures up, intensifying the release of aromatic oils from the foliage of typical Mediterranean shrubs, among them many silver-leaved beauties such as *Convolvulus cneorum*, lavender, lavender cotton (*Santolina*), and artemisia.

For more spectacular herbaceous plants, choose from mulleins, blood-red poppies, or some of the more dramatic irises. You could even increase the desert flavor by planting dryland natives, such as spiky agaves and aloes or fleshy aeoniums and echeverias. In all but the warmest regions, these plants need to overwinter indoors, but you can still enjoy their exotic beauty in the summer garden. Simply sink potted specimens in the ground and mulch with a layer of gravel; when frost threatens, lift them out and set them in a sunny room.

SPRING LEMONS AND GREENS

The fresh yellows and greens of spring that are so cheerful after a drab winter can be continued, to prolong the mood of bright optimism. Allow foliage to predominate and choose flowers to echo the color theme. The spring plants are easy — variegated periwinkle and euonymus

ETERNAL SPRING The freshness of light green, golds, and pale yellows makes spring a season to gladden the heart and lift the spirits. Here, a sunny combination of wallflowers and euonymus starts the year on a cheerful note.

MOOD IN MINIATURE If the autumnal color range of russet shades gives you the greatest pleasure, create the same red-gold scheme throughout the year with a wooden tubful of pansies in gold, orange, and brown.

OVERLAID WITH GOLD Yellow *Iris pseudacorus* 'Variegata' rises above the light green *Tanacetum parthenium* 'Aureum' in the foreground and golden *Filipendula ulmaria* 'Aurea' in the corner. The shrub *Philadelphus coronarius* 'Aureus' adds to the air of spring in this July border.

CHANGING SEASONS The warm colors so loved in autumn sing out in this late summer border, with red-hot pokers towering over dwarf red dahlias, bronze *Helenium*, orange crocosmia, and golden rudbeckias.

studded with winter aconites, leopard's-banes, celandines, primroses, and daffodils to give some height. As spring turns to summer, ferns such as the ostrich fern (*Matteuccia struthiopteris*) or, in drier sites, *Polystichum setiferum* or hart's-tongue (*Asplenium scolopendrium*) reveal a spring-like green.

Grasses and bamboos prolong the feel of spring. *Milium effusum* 'Aureum' has soft, waving foliage and feathery flowers in summer, and the fresh green leaves of the dwarf bamboos *Pleioblastus auricomus* and *P. variegatus* look youthful throughout most of the year.

Lady's-mantle is an essential part of the display. Its lacy green flowers last for weeks. Lemon roses, potentillas, dahlias, and chrysanthemums can maintain the mood into autumn.

SUMMER PURPLES ALL YEAR

The natural flower colors of summer in the wild are mainly in the mauve, purple, and wine-red range, found in knapweeds, scabiosa, thistles, willow herb, and tufted vetch. In a garden, summer purples and cerises are readily found in shrubby plants such as roses, buddleias, and hebes, perennials such as centaurea and cranesbill geraniums, and bedding annuals such as petunias and heliotrope.

The warm purples of summer look just as effective at other times of the year. In autumn, asters, colchicums, and late Korean chrysanthemums such as the plum-pink 'Mei-kyo' take up the theme.

In spring choose purple or cerise tulips — try the beet-purple 'Negrita' or lily-flowered 'Springtime.' The easiest outdoor primula in cultivation is *Primula juliana* 'Wanda,' whose bright purple-red blooms pop up in profusion beginning early in the season.

The chervil *Anthriscus sylvestris* 'Ravenswing' is a contributor to this mood, producing dark ferny leaves in spring and then delicate, white, lacy blooms. Rodgersias are perfect if you have plenty of moisture and space, and for drier conditions, *Euphorbia dulcis* 'Chameleon' is pretty, with deep bronze foliage and dainty green flowers.

The warm effect can be heightened by adding splashes of apricot and orange. In spring the tulip 'Apricot Beauty' looks gorgeous with purple, and the gentle apricot rose 'Buff Beauty' or the foxglove 'Sutton's Apricot' makes a ravishing

LATE SPRING PURPLES Although warm purple is a characteristic color of a midsummer garden, it can be used to equal effect, as here, in late spring. Mauve wallflowers (*Erysimum* 'Bowles' Mauve') face a bed of bearded irises that are edged with aubrietia.

EFFUSIVE COTTAGE GARDENS Foxgloves, delphiniums, and lupines tower above a happy jumble of color and foliage in this typically generous cottage garden, where the plants spill out to take over the paths.

summer companion. Yellow Welsh poppies and early spring pansies in warm orange are stunning with purple aubrietia, purple or mauve tulips, and dark purple crocuses.

MELLOW FRUITFULNESS

The glowing tones of fall foliage blunt the sting of approaching winter. Color is warmest during these autumnal months, when green gives way to yellow, gold, and red. The familiar late border plants, such as chrysanthemums, dahlias, and orange and yellow crocosmias, are particularly vivid.

Re-creating the red-gold scheme in other seasons is easiest in the summer. Red and yellow gaillardias flower for months on end and look good alongside the fiery scarlet of *Euphorbia griffithii*. In moist soil, orange and yellow Asian primulas — *Primula bulleyana*, *P. sikkimensis*, and *P. florindae* — create the desired atmosphere. In dry spots, the red or bronze varieties of the sword-like New Zealand flax (*Phormium tenax*) have an autumnal feel; choose 'Bronze Baby' or 'Aurora' for the warmest colors.

Winter is the most challenging period because there is so little foliage remaining — although you can compensate with gold-splashed evergreens. Among the brightest of these is the variegated holly 'Golden King,' which also fruits heavily.

Berries and fruits that hang on through the winter warm the scene.

Cotoneaster horizontalis colors beautifully in autumn with little red leaves and abundant berries clustered on the herringbone branches. One of the brightest winter shows is put on by the crab apple 'Red Sentinel,' whose cherry-like red fruits hang on until the harshest winter days and beyond.

In spring deciduous azaleas can provide a range of autumnal colors, many with the bonus of fragrance. Columbines are available in several brilliant reds, pinks, yellows, and combinations; choose *Aquilegia canadensis* and *A. formosa*.

COTTAGE GARDEN PRETTINESS OR FORMAL SYMMETRY

Whatever the mood you aim to create, bear in mind the potential of leaf, stem, and fruit as well as flower. In a cottage garden, the end result should be a happy tumble of mixed plants, whereas a formal garden relies on shape, line, and form as well as plant interest.

The bulk of cottage perennials flower between late spring and midsummer. Back up your main display with long bloomers — penstemons, geraniums, osteospermums, verbenas, and mignonette. You will have color in the garden that lasts well into autumn. Fill out the design with fall favorites such as chrysan-

themums, azure monkshood (*Aconitum carmichaelii*), Japanese anemones, cimicifuga, and crocosmias.

Lilies are outstanding among late performers, especially *Lilium auratum*. Plant gladiolus late — up to the end of April — for prolonged flowering. Colchicums are useful too, and their foliage, following in spring, will fill gaps between such early flowers as crown imperials (*Fritillaria imperialis*) and honesty.

In a well-designed formal garden there is often as much opportunity for skillful planting as in an informal scheme. Every plant, including those used for outline,

GENEROUS SELF-SEEDERS

AMONG THE PLANTS that give the best return in the garden are the natural self-seeders that flourish in increasing numbers year after year. Many of these are found growing in the wild, adding color to meadows and fields, but they look equally at home in the garden.

Foxglove (*Digitalis purpurea*) is a biennial that blooms once. If you leave the seeds to ripen and germinate, however, they provide a springtime display of large pink bells year after year.

TROUBLE-FREE CHOICES
A woodland flower that grows best in half shade and in clay soil is primrose (*Primula vulgaris*), which flowers in spring and self-sows to come back stronger every year. Deadhead some of the plants, and in milder regions they often provide another, lesser display in the fall.

For brilliant yearly color, Welsh poppies (*Meconopsis cambrica*) are not only persistent perennials, but also prolific self-seeders. They germinate best in part shade, even in the poorest soil, their clear yellow or orange flowers popping up in cracks and crevices.

Love-in-a-mist (*Nigella damascena*) has deep blue or white flowers that turn into balloon-like seedpods; once they open, you can be assured that more of the annuals will appear the next year.

Another prodigious self-seeder is forget-me-not (*Myosotis*), with blue flowers in spring. Seedlings should be thinned out or moved to a nursery bed to mature for later transplanting.

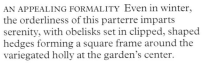

AN APPEALING FORMALITY Even in winter, the orderliness of this parterre imparts serenity, with obelisks set in clipped, shaped hedges forming a square frame around the variegated holly at the garden's center.

can provide interest. Knot gardens or parterres with low boxwood or lavender hedges and clipped hollies are set off by blocks of colorful plants. In spring augment lasting performers such as pansies and dead nettle (*Lamium maculatum*) with tulips and wallflowers.

In summer add height to nemesia, geraniums, or osteospermum with late-flowering *Phlox paniculata*. As the summer bedding begins to tire in September, add polyanthus or more pansies to bloom while the senior partners — chrysanthemums and dahlias — reach their late autumn climax.

SOMEWHERE TO SIT

THERE IS NOTHING MORE RELAXING than sitting outside on a shimmering summer's day in the comfort of your own garden, so create a sunny haven for a picnic or afternoon tea, make a sheltered spot for breakfast where the early sun is warmest, or provide some shade to shield a Sunday gathering of friends and family from the lunchtime sun. A perfect patio for a quiet read, or a hideaway where you can enjoy the sun, will offer a place for purely private pleasure. Whether your garden furniture is permanent and weatherproof, elegant and fragile, or simple and homemade, find a place for it — and surround it with your favorite plants.

An elegant weathered bench, a trellis to provide shelter, and judicious plantings of scented flowers and shrubs that act as a screen create an invitation to linger.

MAKING A HAVEN FOR LEISURE

O F ALL THE PLEASURES that a garden offers, perhaps the greatest is the simplest — that of just sitting for a while and absorbing sights, sounds, and scents.

Good garden furniture is an investment in comfort and enjoyment and can be an added adornment. So take care with your choice of furniture — it should be in keeping with the surrounding architecture and the overall atmosphere of the garden. The best furniture may be expensive, so allow time to consider the disadvantages, as well as the advantages, of whatever strikes your fancy.

The placement of furniture is as important as its style and construction. Some people are more relaxed sitting in an enclosed area — an arbor or a glade, for example. There are many ways to create a sense of intimacy and privacy, from simply surrounding a bench with scented plants to placing it in a patch of dappled shade while all else is in full sun.

While many garden owners see their plot as a retreat from the world, others have their most enjoyable gatherings with friends and family in a garden that serves as an extra room, complete with comfortable seating, a table for mealtimes, and a barbecue for cooking.

SITTING IN THE SHADOWS An accommodating chair in a shady spot on a hot day is the perfect place to enjoy the fruits of your gardening labors. From a quiet and secluded corner, you can observe the dappled sunlight and the brightly lit stems of vivid yellow-green euphorbia.

CHOOSING AND CARING FOR FURNITURE

B EFORE YOU BUY FURNITURE, think about storage space. If you have none, seating and tables will have to stay out all year and must be sturdy and weather resistant. Where there is a little storage room, folding and stacking furniture is the most practical. When you have a garage or large shed where the pieces can overwinter, your choice is wider.

Some furniture comes complete with protective covers that help keep it clean (particularly useful in city gardens and under trees) and prolong its life, but the shrouded shapes lend a rather gloomy look to the garden in winter.

Those fortunate enough to have an enclosed porch or a sun room are free to choose all kinds of charming and delicate furniture that can be enjoyed inside and brought out when the weather is good.

SUITING THE SURROUNDINGS

Choose outdoor furniture that will complement its surroundings, just as you would when buying furnishings for inside the house. Plastic stacking chairs may seem brash on a formal terrace, while an ornate stone bench looks pretentious in a simple country garden.

Any piece, no matter how comfortable, detracts from the atmosphere of the garden if it is shoddily made, awkward in style, or fitted with garish cushions. Plain dark blue is particularly pleasing in the sun, whereas a splash of bright color brings a shaded corner to life. By the sea or a pool, turquoise looks fresh, while striped canvas is agreeable for deck chairs and hammocks; just two colors, and wide stripes, make for a crisp look. Floral patterns compete with nature's display but come off badly beside it.

GOOD FOR OCCASIONAL USE

Comfort is important, of course, but to varying degrees. A chair used as a temporary stopping place, so you can rest or admire the view, need not offer the same comfort level as one at a table used for meals outdoors, while those used for sunbathing and drowsing should be very comfortable indeed.

In a small garden, with room for just a few pieces, it is useful to select things that are easily moved. Movable furniture is

STATELY STONE Sunlight and shadow make an inviting pattern on the surface of a solid, curved stone seat. Stone is weighty and has to remain in one place, but it is robust enough to be left there permanently.

inconvenient if too heavy, but lightweight furniture will have a shorter lifespan if left outside. A good compromise would be sturdy wooden pieces with wheels to make moving them easier.

DESIGNS IN STONE AND METAL

Benches and tables of stone or simulated stone can be left out in all weathers and look the better for it, becoming patterned with a textured layer of moss and lichen. To speed weathering, brush on a coat or two of yogurt or of buttermilk mixed with a little corn syrup.

Stone seats are handsome, durable, and at home in most gardens, but also cold, hard, and virtually immovable once set in place — better for visual impact and occasional perching than comfort.

Metal furniture comes in an enormous range of designs. Pieces in cast iron are heavy, while those made of wirework or cast aluminum are lighter but more likely to tip. Cast iron with elaborately raised patterns is uncomfortable unless covered with cushions — which obscures the design. Without cushions, all metal seating pieces are a little hard, except those with backs and seats of fabric, woven plastic, or flexible metal strips.

Metal furniture can stay outside, but unless made from aluminum it will need regular maintenance to keep rust at bay. Remove any flaking spots with a wire brush and repaint, using a rust-inhibiting primer and any paint that provides a protective, corrosion-resistant finish. Spray the metal framework of folding chairs with a rust inhibitor before you put them away for the winter.

VARIETY IN DURABLE WOOD

There are designs in wood to suit both formal and cottage gardens, clean-lined styles to complement a modern setting, and informal pieces for romantic, rambling gardens. Most are equally at home in town or country.

Picnic tables, which are rectangular with a fixed bench along either side, are sturdy and serviceable for the barbecue

SCENTED SHADE Under a canopy of holly and roses, this inviting bench has mellowed to a soft silver gray. The weathered wood merges naturally with the underplanting of variegated ivy, the hosta, and the white *Rosa* 'Nevada.'

HOW TO SECURE A SEAT

LIGHTER BENCHES, whether wooden or metal, will tip if children clamber on them, or if adults fling themselves back too heartily. The consequences can be painful, but you can prevent accidents by securing the piece to the ground with a galvanized iron bracket.

One end of the bracket fits over the rail of the bench, and the other is hammered into the ground.

area, informal outdoor gatherings, or places where children are likely to climb and play on them.

Wooden furniture can be heavy, but it is comfortable and durable. Pieces made from weather-resistant hardwoods, including such exotics as teak, bubinga, iroko, and shorea, will give years of use, even when kept permanently outside, though you may want to cover them in severe weather.

Oil can be rubbed into hardwood, but its purpose is purely cosmetic — to restore wood color. It is not necessary for keeping the wood in good condition; untreated hardwood develops distinguished silvery tones as it ages.

Some softwoods, such as cedar, cypress, and redwood, resist rot and can be left to weather naturally. Most other softwoods, however, need to be treated with a decorative and preservative stain or paint. While a high-gloss paint finish gives a traditional look, it also peels and flakes, requiring frequent touch-ups. Wood stain, which is available in a wide range of solid and semi-transparent colors, is less demanding.

SEA, TOWN, OR COUNTRY STYLE

Folding "steamer" chairs of slatted wood are sturdy and comfortable; some have armrests and leg rests, as well as fitted cushions for added luxury. Adjustable loungers are even more comfortable; they are made from slats of hard- or softwood, sometimes with wheels, armrests, and fitted cushions, and are at home on a large terrace or beside a swimming pool.

Café tables and folding chairs of wooden slats on metal frames are light and practical and look good in all but the grandest gardens. But they are strictly for sitting in demurely, not for lazy sprawling. The slats need to be varnished, stained, or painted regularly, and metal parts need rustproofing and painting.

Rustic furniture particularly suits cottage, woodland, and other naturalistic gardens. Twig furniture, with or without the bark left on the wood, is sold at many garden centers and through some mail-order companies.

SIMPLICITY WITH CANVAS, CANE, AND WICKER

Folding chairs of canvas on metal or wooden frames include the familiar deck chairs. Director's chairs impose a more upright position than deck chairs, but some have a tiltable backrest that

ROOM OUTSIDE A secluded sitting area has been created in a sunny spot, using trelliswork dividers, paving, careful planting, and elegant metal benches. Clipped boxwood in pots helps to define the perimeter of the area.

WHEN THE WEATHER SUITS Lightweight and comfortable, folding canvas chairs are also easy to move — whether to a spot in the sun, to an outdoor dining table, or to the basement or shed for storage in bad weather.

TO THE RESCUE

NEW LIFE FOR A DECK CHAIR

SUN AND RAIN weaken the canvas on a deck chair. When it tears, replace it with new deck-chair canvas or double lengths of strong upholstery fabric sewn together. Attach it with a staple gun.

Canvas is available in ready-cut lengths — use the old piece as a pattern. Allow 3 in (7.5 cm) of extra material at each end to wrap around the rails.

Staple the fabric first to the bottom rail, at 1 in (2.5 cm) intervals, then wrap it once around the rail to cover the staples. Stretch the fabric as tightly as you can and turn under the raw edge before stapling it behind the top rail.

TAKING THINGS EASY

A place to sit adds to your enjoyment of a garden. Choose the pieces with care to suit the setting and function, whether it is a lounger on the lawn, a bench to put in a secluded corner, or a dining chair for a convivial meal out-of-doors.

VERSATILE WOOD
Wood is warm, solid, attractive, and versatile. Hardwood furniture can be left out to weather with the seasons and take on a silver sheen. Café chairs with wooden slats fold up flat and can be stored in a small space for the winter.

LIGHT BUT TOUGH
Plastic chairs are inexpensive, light, strong, and easily transportable. Those made of synthetic resin also withstand the elements. Stacking chairs are useful in saving space when they are not required for entertaining.

STURDY RUSTICS
A storage bench, a farmhouse bench, and a twig bench made from peeled poles all have an appropriate rustic charm for less formal gardens. They look good in cottage-style gardens and those with an old-fashioned atmosphere.

GENTLY SWINGING SEATS
The ultimate luxury in garden leisure is a seat that swings. Two sturdy trees will support a hammock; if you have no trees, use a hammock stand. Gliders offer the added indulgence of soft cushions and shade from the sun's bright rays.

TRADITIONAL FAVORITES
This stylish selection includes a painted wooden bench that can be wheeled to the most advantageous site, a sturdy and inviting Adirondack chair with wide armrests and a sloping back, and a wicker chair, an old favorite for appearance and comfort.

DURABLE ELEGANCE
Metal furniture, both wrought iron and cast iron, combines strength with an elegant fragility of detail. Long lasting, it can be left permanently in position to draw the eye and enhance a site, giving interest through the year.

RECLINING IN COMFORT
For putting your feet up to enjoy the warmth of a summer's day, there is an array of choices in style and materials. Pick a classic wooden "steamer" chair or a plastic frame with padded cushions that adjusts to varying degrees of inactivity.

SIMPLE CANVAS
Director's chairs are comfortable and attractive. Easily folded, they provide useful extra seats for entertaining. The adjustable deck chair is better suited to a more relaxed position. Both are readily transportable and storable.

LAZY DAYS You do not need a large garden to enjoy the use of a hammock — just two strong, well-spaced branches will suffice. Hammock stands are also available, although they are rather unwieldy and are no substitute for the shade and sound of trees.

allows for some reclining. Similar to director's chairs are campaign chairs, with armrests and leg rests, a tiltable canopy, and, often, slots in the arm for a glass.

All look unpretentious, suit any style, and take up little room when folded. Move them indoors for the winter and in wet weather to keep the canvas from rotting. Varnish, stain, or paint the wooden parts annually and oil all hinges and other parts susceptible to rust.

Give individual style to your humble deck chair by abandoning bright stripes and using plain canvas that you have decorated with an appliquéd pattern. Cut out simple motifs such as leaves or scalloped circles from colored fabric and oversew the edges to prevent fraying. Stitch the decorations to the canvas or attach them with fabric glue.

Careful handling and winter shelter are essential to help make rattan and wicker furniture last. Usually very comfortable although rather creaky, they look attractive virtually anywhere you put them, indoors or out. Both rattan and wicker can be attacked by insects, so watch out for telltale holes and treat immediately with insecticide.

In warm and humid climates, mildew may be the biggest threat to wicker and other natural materials. A rash of black specks spreading over the surface is a sign of mildew. Wash the furniture with a solution of 1 part bleach to 10 parts water. Leave the furniture to dry in the sun, then paint it with a clear, weatherproof sealant.

THE VIRTUES OF PLASTIC

Furniture made from plastic or synthetic resin is durable, comparatively inexpensive, light, and unharmed by the weather, unless it is blown around by strong winds. Some rigid designs are stackable, others are hinged to fold up or recline.

White furniture shows dirt and stains but is easily cleaned; just wipe it down with soapy water. This is the only care it needs. Other colors are also available, including black, brown, and dark green; you can also buy cushions, although the pieces usually "give" comfortably.

With so many virtues, plastic furniture is on sale everywhere, but it does not suit every setting. In an elegant or romantic garden, you might want to drape the pieces with a decorative shawl or "throw." It is, however, perfectly at home in an informal garden and by the sea, and its lightness makes it ideal for roof gardens and balconies.

FANCIFUL METAL AND CLAY

Metal is worked into some curious furniture, from rustic "twig" benches of cast iron to filigree delicacies in galvanized wirework. Some designer-blacksmiths make chairs that resemble giant vegetables or are composed of horseshoes.

At a price, a metalworker can craft a custom piece to your own design — for

STACKING CHAIRS

PLASTIC MOLDED CHAIRS, available from most garden centers, are cheap and comfortable, as well as being light and easy to stack for storage. This is a great advantage, as it means that they take up very little room when stored — four or six stacked chairs take up no more floor space than one.

example, a pair of hands, one for the seat and one for the back, or a "spider's web" chair complete with spider.

Drum-shaped stools and tables made of porcelain or pottery are very decorative on a small terrace or in an enclosed courtyard. They must be brought inside during the winter to prevent cracking.

You can design a chinoiserie setting to suit these oriental-style furnishings, especially if they are blue and white. Set up a backdrop of lattice screens or an open wooden pavilion, painted lacquer red or a color to match the pieces. In front, make a pool crossed by a small bridge or a few stepping-stones; add sculptural rocks and plant bamboos around them.

SOOTHING MOVEMENT

Swings have a hypnotic appeal for most people, because the rhythmic motion induces a relaxed state. Metal-framed gliders with thick cushions and a canopy are popular and bring a quaint, innocent look to the garden.

There are also gliders available made from pine, pressure-treated with preservative to make the wood very durable. Their strong construction and simple design make them especially suitable for a contemporary or informal garden. A coat of wood preservative, applied every

FOR ALL WEATHERS Cool green-and-cream ivy is a complementary background for this durable cast-iron bench with ornate detailing. An antique storage drum has been planted with the blue bells of campanula for added color, and fragrance wafts from the mauve heliotrope behind.

other year, is all they need to help keep them weather resistant.

Much simpler and less costly is a plank of wood suspended by two lengths of rope from a sturdy bough. You can make a swing for two from an old wooden bench without its legs. Hang it by two lengths of rope at each end, to get the balance right, making sure that the bough is sufficiently strong to take the weight of two people. Alternatively, you could sling the bench from a crossbeam of a sturdy pergola.

A hammock is the ultimate in garden relaxation — once you master the art of getting in and out. If you do not have two stout trees to sling one from, buy a supporting frame — or hang it across the corner of two walls at right angles and train scented climbers around it.

SEAT WITH A VIEW Slabs of stone and a boxwood clipped to form a backrest make a low seat that is also a focal point to draw the eye down the grassy path. Situated at the end of a border of fragrant lavender, the seat offers an invitation to sit and enjoy the sights and scents of summer.

QUIRKY AND UNEXPECTED SEATING

CURIOSITIES ARE FUN in an informal design, and even a formal garden may have a hidden corner where a quirky chair surprises and amuses. Junk shops, auctions, antique shops, and tag sales are all good hunting grounds for potential treasures.

Trunks, barrels, school benches, tables, and church pews turn up from time to time, and all, with a little attention, make serviceable seats. Any low, wooden storage box has the makings of a seat; give it a back rail, supported by two short uprights. It doubles as a place to hide boots, hoses, and tools.

Slabs of slate or marble, including those from dismantled fireplaces and old washstands, can become seats when well supported by a plank raised on sturdy brick or stone piers. Practically any flat, strong material of the desired size has potential. Lay it on concrete blocks, which can be quickly concealed with ivy.

Let your imagination run free in transforming junk-shop finds into outdoor chairs and tables. Strip the baize top from an old card table and stick colorful tiles in its place. Finish off with wooden edging. Store the table in a shed when it is not in use.

Choose paint colors and fabrics to create an effect. Among bronze foliage and pink blooms put deep pink furniture with softer pink cushions. Place crimson seats with purple cushions beside matching fuchsias. For a hint of the East, use glossy scarlet or black paint on old chairs, decorate with gilded transfers, and use an oriental print for cushions.

TREE TRUNKS AND TOADSTOOLS

Weird seats and tables are easily made from oddly shaped tree trunks, roots, and branches — the more bizarre and twisted the better — to resemble something from a fairy tale. Quirky furniture looks best in a wild or informal garden.

Such pieces would suit a "gingerbread" garden house made from rustic logs, or split poles nailed over an existing shed, decorated with garlands and pine cones stuck on with a glue gun. Cover the floor with bark chips.

Children love such fantasy settings. Make "toadstool" seats and tables for them from log sections. Nail a large, flat slice on a longer, narrower piece whose bottom half has been soaked in preservative. Sink it into the ground and pour concrete around it for extra stability.

MAKING SEATS FROM LOGS AND BARRELS

Chairs and benches can be hacked out of upright sections of dead tree trunks, but a log seat is easier to make. All you need is a 3–4 ft (90–120 cm) length of a tree trunk, approximately 18 in (45 cm) across, with any branches cut off flush with the trunk and the cuts sanded smooth. Lay it down in long grass and mow a path to it and a circle around it for a rustic perching place.

Use trunks of lesser girth as supports for planks or sanded floorboards. Cut two lengths of trunk about 2½ ft (75 cm) long for the supports and sink them half their length into the ground. Nail on planks or floorboards with long galvanized nails. Or gouge hollows across the tops of the supports so that they cradle a length of tree trunk snugly.

Seats made from half-barrels look good everywhere except in the most formal setting. Top them with a painted circle of marine plywood and add a cushion.

GREEN, LIVING SEATS

"Green" seats date from medieval times. The simplest is just a low bank of turf on which to sit or sprawl. If you have a higher bank, then cut a seat directly into it and let grass cover it. Flat stones, concrete slabs, and landscape ties can also be used to form the base, sides, and back of such seats. They look particularly pretty with low plants trailing over them.

Another style of turf bench is easily made from a stone, brick, or timber planter, about 18 in (45 cm) high and wide and 36 in (90 cm) long. Fill two thirds with rubble or bricks, finish off with topsoil, and grow a cushion of grass on the top. Alternatively, grow creeping thyme (*Thymus serpyllum*) or chamomile (*Chamaemelum nobile*), both of which are pleasantly aromatic. They are also attractive to bees when in flower, so look before you sit down on such an herb seat.

As a longer-term project, train a hedge of boxwood or *Lonicera nitida* in the outline of a sofa or armchair, minus the seat, clipping it into a comfortable-looking shape as it grows. Fill in the seat space with brick piers topped with stone slabs or thick, well-sanded planks.

MAKING A DRAWER SEAT

LOOK CLOSELY at any battered old chest of drawers at a tag sale or junk shop. It is worth rescuing any with deep bottom drawers to transform them into seats.

Cut a piece of ¾ in (19 mm) marine plywood or medium-density fiberboard to fit on top of the drawer space as a lid. Brass hinges make it easy to open so you can use the storage space inside.

Paint the piece of wood and the drawer, inside and out, with gloss paint, let it dry, and place a cushion on top.

SEATING AS SCULPTURE This topiary sofa of clipped boxwood gains visual impact from its size and setting. A dense, dark green hedge makes the background, while the foreground of paving stones harmonizes with the stone seat. Adapt the idea for green "living seats" on a smaller scale.

TREE SEATS With some ingenuity and a few power tools, large logs and trunks can be adapted in a variety of ways to serve as seats. This log chair makes a rugged perch that is right at home in the woodland setting.

SAILOR'S REST The curved sides of half a boat upended create a sheltered seat for a seaside garden. Ivy planted at the base will quickly soften hard edges and make the boat seem a long-standing feature of the garden.

SETTINGS FOR TIME OF DAY

W HERE YOU PLACE your carefully chosen furniture depends not just on your garden but on your habits as well. Are you going to sit out during the day throughout the week or only on the weekends? Do you eat breakfast or lunch on the terrace or simply sip an evening aperitif on a garden bench? Are you an avid sun worshipper, or does the heat make you seek cover?

Seating should be easy to reach, welcoming, and sheltered from the wind. A delightful view also helps. Put a bench in a luxuriant oasis and plan an attraction beside it — a fragrant shrub, a small fountain, or flowers to attract butterflies.

In a large garden, there may be room for two or three sitting areas for different times of day, but where space is limited you might have to settle for just one. Since it is likely to be a main focal point of the garden, make sure the furniture is the most elegant and decorative you can afford. You can bring out a number of cheaper folding and stacking chairs when you have guests.

CATCHING THE MORNING SUN

There are few better ways to start a sunny day than by strolling into the garden and sitting there for a while, enjoying the gentle warmth of the morning sun and noting each newly opened flower.

There is a lovely freshness, especially if rain has fallen overnight, and the scents are faint but sweet. Honeysuckle (*Lonicera periclymenum*), flowering tobacco (*Nicotiana alata* 'Evening Fragrance'), and night-scented stocks (*Matthiola bicornis*) are still delicious in the morning. To take advantage of their last fragrance before the heat of the day suppresses it, place a seat among them facing east and back it with a protective semicircular wall or yew, beech, or hornbeam hedge.

The fragrant white climbing rose 'Madame Alfred Carrière' will flower through the summer. It tolerates plenty of shade, so it does well in an east-facing position. Plant the scented yellow day lily *Hemerocallis citrina* at its feet.

If you like to walk barefoot in the dew, set a seat on mown grass. If you prefer strolling well shod, set it by a crisp path of gravel, which dries out quickly and does not become slippery with moss and algae as pavers and bricks tend to do when they receive only the morning sun.

IN SEARCH OF SHADE AT NOON

As the day becomes brighter and hotter, you have to choose between sun or shade. While tan seekers are happy to stretch out on a deck chair or chaise longue placed in full sun, shade-lovers make for the lee of a north- or east-facing wall or seek shelter in the filtered light beneath a tree. Benches that encircle a tree trunk come in a variety of styles made in delicate-looking ironwork or wood.

You can create extra places in the shade with imagination and patience.
🌢 When a tree is grown in a raised bed,

SCENTED BREEZES Permanent seating needs careful positioning. Consider the direction of the sun's rays in the morning and evening — so you can make the most of early freshness or savor the late warmth when perfumed plants such as these roses give off their strongest scent.

give the retaining wall a broad, flat coping so that it can be used as a seat.

❧ For seating, place wooden decking raised on matching uprights around a tree.

❧ Grow a boxwood or privet shrub as a tall standard in a container beside your favorite sitting place. Train and clip it over a frame into a neat umbrella.

❧ To prevent a seat on a south-facing terrace from becoming unbearably hot at midday, put up canvas blinds or awnings and create an airy space.

For easy portable shade, a beach umbrella is ideal — you can sink it into the soil wherever you like. Most outdoor umbrellas are designed to fit into a weighted base, usually of metal or plastic, or into a central hole in a garden table.

Even in a small garden you can create a shady area. Many small spreading trees or large shrubs cast some shade and do well in a container for some years. Try a southern catalpa (*Catalpa bignonioides*), a golden-leaved robinia or maple such as *Acer negundo* 'Auratum' or 'Flamingo,' the flowering crab apple *Malus* × *moerlandsii* 'Profusion,' or such graceful rowans as *Sorbus cashmiriana*, *S. vilmorinii*, and *S. hupehensis*.

Evergreens for warm gardens include the variegated privet *Ligustrum lucidum* 'Excelsum Superbum,' the pineapple-scented broom *Cytisus battandieri*, and *Ceanothus arboreus* 'Trewithen Blue.'

Plant resinous conifers and aromatic herb plants near a seating area. In the warmth of midday, artemisia, rock-rose, catmint, lavender, rosemary, lemon verbena (*Aloysia triphylla*), sage, thyme, and many more release their fullest aromas in the hot sun.

HOARDING THE WARMTH FOR EVENING

A garden is often at its loveliest on a fine summer's evening when the light is soft, the air gentle, and a host of flowers give off their delicious fragrances.

A west-facing corner is the perfect spot to watch the sun as it sinks, throws long shadows, and gilds the trees. Here is the place for flagstones or brick paving, which stay free of the dew and retain some warmth from the day. However, any sheltered corner near the house gains warmth from the walls and makes a pleasant place to take an evening meal.

Where there is no sheltering wall or warm paving, set up movable trellis screens or arrange groups of container

MORNING WARMTH The color and texture of warm stone paving is the foundation for a morning seating area screened by fencing and brought to life by colorful planting. Plants include lady's-mantle, variegated ivy, Londonpride saxifrage, and the pink-splashed vine *Actinidia kolomikta*.

BEST PLANTS

SCENT TO WAFT ON THE AIR

Place scented plants so that their fragrance will carry on the breeze to your seating areas.

• Mexican orange (*Choisya ternata*): evergreen shrub with white spring flowers and a few in summer.

• Moroccan broom (*Cytisus battandieri*): silvery leaves; pineapple-scented yellow flowers in summer.

• Mock orange (*Philadelphus* 'Sybille'): mid-green leaves and white flowers in early to mid summer.

• *Rhododendron luteum*: yellow flowers in late spring.

• Sweet briar (*Rosa rubiginosa*): bright pink flowers in June and autumn hips.

• Lilac (*Syringa vulgaris*): deciduous shrub with large flower heads of white, mauve, or purple in early summer.

• *Trachelospermum jasminoides*: evergreen climber with waxy, very fragrant white flowers in summer.

• *Buddleia alternifolia*: arching shrub with mauve flower spikes in June.

• *Lilium* 'Pink Perfection': deep pink trumpet flowers borne in summer.

UNDER SPREADING BRANCHES In the heat of the midday sun, a tree bench offers shady relief. In the morning and evening, the rustle of leaves and the song of birds make it an ideal spot to enjoy extra pleasure in the garden.

plants, which you can change around for a succession of flowers and fragrance.

Plan a more permanent screen with a fixed trellis covered with roses, clematis, and summer jasmine, then plant sweet rocket (*Hesperis matronalis*), flowering tobacco, and night-scented stock (*Matthiola bicornis*) below them. Add lilies or verbena for even more scent.

To brighten an evening sitting area, plant it with as many white-flowered specimens as possible, as the blooms glow magically in the dusk.

Subtle lighting will transform this scene once darkness falls. Uplights, downlights, and spread lights show off the plants, and strings of lights draped overhead and in the trees look pretty. Use lanterns, candles in stable holders, oil lamps, and torches to illuminate a table and paths, leaving other parts of the garden in mysterious pools of darkness.

A PLACE FOR ALL
TIMES AND ALL SEASONS

One of the best places to relax is a sun room, as plain or fancy as your taste and budget dictate. Consult the local building inspector about codes before undertaking any work.

Crucial to your plan is the way the room faces, as every direction has particular drawbacks and advantages. A south-facing position is brightest in winter but may prove unbearably hot in summer. You would have to install an efficient type of shading and good ventilation, which would also provide the conditions that many showy, exotic plants need.

A north-facing site is comfortable enough in summer and requires no shading, but some heating is needed to make the room usable in winter. East- or west-facing positions are ideal, getting reasonable light but remaining a pleasant temperature for most of the day.

Use the walls and the roof area to increase the luxuriance of the plantings without occupying too much of the floor space. Purple-leaved vines and crimson bougainvillea make a richly colored start. Freshen the scheme with the blue-and-white passion-flower (*Passiflora caerulea*), pale blue *Plumbago auriculata*, and the soft sky-blue hanging bells of *Sollya heterophylla* — all of which will thrive in a sunny indoor space, especially an area that faces west.

For brilliant white flowers and rich scent, grow the climbers *Jasminum odoratissimum*, *J. sambac* 'Maid of Orleans,'

MOVABLE SHADE An airy, freestanding umbrella can create a shady sitting area where previously the sun was too dazzling or scorching for sitting out in comfort. Plants in containers are used to delineate the raised area, where slipcovered chairs look fresh and inviting.

SUNNY SECLUSION Hedges and shrubs give privacy to a paved area that is softened by low plants. Flowers in containers add color and leave the paving free so the chair can be moved around to follow the sun.

and *J. grandiflorum* 'De Grasse.' Many geraniums will rise to a reasonable height on a sun-room wall, while others, particularly the ivy-leaved geranium (*Pelargonium peltatum*), trail from hanging baskets, windowsills, and shelving. *P. p.* 'La France' has pinkish-mauve double flowers, and white-flowered *P. p.* 'L'Elégante' has pretty white-edged leaves. A minimum temperature of 45–50° F (7–10° C) must be maintained for all these flowering plants to flourish.

Complete the scene with foliage in contrasting sizes, shapes, and shades. The golden feather palm (*Chrysalido-carpus lutescens*), the drooping combs of Kentia palm (*Howeia forsteriana*), and the glossy, crimped-edge tufts of bird's-nest fern (*Asplenium nidus*) all help create lush green corners.

SOFT LIGHTS FOR SUMMER NIGHTS

When dusk falls and nights are balmy, illuminate your garden with the flattering glow of candlelight or torches. There are decorative ways of safeguarding the flame, though it is always sensible to have a bucket of water nearby as a precaution.

GARDEN TORCHES
Torches are best used in a sheltered spot and are easily positioned for scenic lighting. Anchor them in the ground or in a pot. The protected candle inside split bamboo can also be hung from a tree.

DECORATIVE CAST IRON
Candles inside cast iron are sheltered and also show up the ornate tracery of the metalwork. A Victorian stove and an ornamental Japanese lantern are shown to advantage when lit from within.

POTS AND PAILS
Garden candles in pails and flowerpots can be used time and time again. They have a long burning time, and as some have an insect repellent included, they are ideal for summer entertaining.

PROOF AGAINST BREEZES
A glass hurricane lamp and metal storm lantern provide candles with decorative shelter from garden breezes.

PARTY TIME
String up colorful lights for a festive occasion. Hanging on the rope are candles in colored glass holders with wire handles. Ship's lanterns hang from support poles to cast a brighter glow.

UNUSUAL CANDLEHOLDERS
Search out some unusual candleholders that fit in with your own garden setting. A stone gargoyle candleholder adds a touch of grotesque drama, while an old-fashioned metal bird cage is elegant and airy.

PRACTICAL AND ALLURING SETTINGS

A WELL-CHOSEN CHAIR is only the first requirement for comfortable relaxation in the garden. You will also need shelter, privacy, something lovely to look at, fragrant plants nearby, and perhaps some herbs you can touch or crush to release their aroma. Screens and hedges, bowers and pergolas, pavilions and gazebos all add form and depth of interest to the garden. Any one of them set in the right place and among elegant or informal plants, as befits them best, can become the garden's chief attraction.

MAKING PRIVATE CORNERS

An inexpensive way of creating a secluded glade is to design or reshape the lawn so that it flows out of sight around a corner into a small circular area screened by tall shrubs and perennials. Set the seat directly onto the grass or on a small area of paving at the edge of the lawn to avoid scuffing the grass.

For a similar effect on a smaller scale, plant a low screen of lavender and herbs around a comma-shaped space at the end of a winding path. The path need only be short, with just one bend before it disappears behind the lavender. Mark out the shape with a length of rope or hose. Put the hose in the sun or run it off the hot water heater for a few minutes to make it pliable.

In a paved garden, divide up the space with groups of plants in containers, using small trees and medium-sized shrubs for an instant transformation. A garden with parts screened off appears larger, as the eye is invited to travel around the plants into the unknown beyond. Include some evergreen plants in the screen — for example, bamboos, ceanothus, eleagnus, one or two conifers, fatsia, a strawberry tree (*Arbutus unedo*), *Rhamnus alaternus* 'Argenteovariegatus,' and privet. Add a few deciduous shrubs and herbaceous perennials, with some pots of bulbs and annuals to keep up interest.

For areas of luxurious retreat, follow the well-established practice of dividing the garden into separate "rooms," giving at least one of them a bench. The smallest garden is enhanced by such divisions.

Low clipped or informal hedges, pierced walls, fencing or trellises, and low

TRELLIS TRANSFORMATION Charm and privacy can be created from an unpromising starting point. A trellis, a comfortable bench, and skillful planting transform a low brick wall and paved yard. The bench is framed by twin containers of flowering annuals and by luxuriant hostas.

raised beds make satisfactory divisions and can take straight lines or a curve.

There are numerous plants suitable for a plant screen, from the larger hebes and smooth-leaved hollies, through the beautiful camellias and ceanothus, to the elegant, whispering bamboos.

In a very small garden surrounded by raised beds, one corner can be given a built-in seat and table to save space. The garden will appear larger if you plant the beds thickly to obscure the boundary walls and fences, so that it becomes unclear where the garden begins and ends.

Fast-growing plants for hiding the boundaries include *Phyllostachys aurea,*

Acer negundo 'Flamingo,' *Cornus alba* 'Elegantissima,' *Lavatera* 'Rosea' and *L.* 'Barnsley,' *Ceanothus*, and *Cotoneaster* × *watereri* 'Cornubia.'

A SHELTERED SPOT IN A WINDY GARDEN

For protection from the wind, bamboo screens and board fences are extremely effective, as are the more rustic woven wattles or split-pole fences.

There are elegantly ornamental trellis panels on bracket feet, while others come with attached planting troughs — both useful in paved areas, where climbers in containers or in the trough grow quickly

enough to decorate the panels. Two such screens set at a right angle will shelter a chair, three will shelter a bench.

To give an illusion of permanence to the design, place a container on either side of the screen and plant each with a small tree fringed with scented annuals.

White trellis is attractive, but also consider other colors — black or dark green for a sophisticated layout or a soft blue-green or dove gray for a romantic spot.

A BREEZY SEASIDE PLOT

The best shelter for a seaside garden is a barrier of tough plants. The hardy sea buckthorn (*Hippophae rhamnoides*) has narrow silver leaves on spiny stems, and provided you grow male and female plants, the females bear a heavy crop of berries that the birds usually leave alone through autumn and winter. Sea buckthorn grows in sandy or alkaline soils.

Evergreen *Griselinia littoralis* makes a pleasant hedge, as do two other evergreens, *Escallonia rubra* var. *macrantha* and *Euonymus japonicus*. On thin alkaline soils *Escallonia* 'Iveyi' is the best choice.

While these plants are establishing themselves, make use of a three-sided windbreak of trellis panels, attached to four wooden posts driven well into the ground. Set a chair inside the shelter with crushed shells or pebbles for flooring. *Crambe cordifolia* on each side of the seat foams with tiny white flowers in summer. Grow sweet peas (*Lathyrus odoratus*) up the trelliswork for exquisite scent.

Pots of the pink-flowered *Convolvulus althaeoides* make a charming alternative for such a spot; they like a dry, sunny site but need to be brought in during the winter, except in the mildest areas.

For unorthodox shelter at the seaside, use whatever is to hand. Folding screens of canvas on a metal frame or grass matting, woven bamboo panels, or tightly stretched burlap on an old wooden screen all make a movable shelter for a couple of deck chairs — and provide a hideaway for a bashful sunbather.

Another quick and attractive way to screen a seaside seat is to surround it with clumps of some fast-growing, tall ornamental grass such as Chinese silver grass (*Miscanthus giganteus*).

FITTING IN THE BARBECUE

A barbecue needs to be conveniently near the house, but, to make it an asset rather than an eyesore, screen it with plants or set it neatly in a rectangle of low

ROOM FOR ONE A niche in a raised bed is just the size for a bright chair that gives a private view of the geums and yarrows.

ROOTED INTO THE LANDSCAPE A permanent bench is built into a raised bed where marigolds can be appreciated at eye level.

THE WARMTH OF WOOD Decking is warm to the eye and the feet and its organic origin gives it a particular affinity with a garden. Properly constructed from treated wood, decking is long-lasting and hard-wearing. Wooden chaise longues are well suited to this type of setting.

SOCIABLE SEATING A circular seating area framed by lush foliage makes a convivial site for entertaining. This patterned brick floor is decorative and impervious to the wear and tear of summer barbecues.

on a sloping site. Lay the boards in straight or diagonal runs or in chevrons; ready-made squares create a checkerboard pattern. Straight runs that lead away from the house appear to lengthen a short garden, while those laid from side to side seem to broaden and shorten a long, narrow one.

Leave some gaps in the deck for trees or mature shrubs to grow through and raise a layer of decking around them to form a seat. Soften up all these strong lines with containers of lilies, hostas, and perhaps a heavily perfumed, trumpet-flowered datura (*Brugmansia candida* 'Knightii') — beautiful but poisonous.

THE PLEASURE OF PERGOLAS AND VERANDAS

Two rows of uprights, whether wooden posts, metal poles, or pillars of brick or stonework, crossed by beams overhead and set far enough apart to accommodate a bench, make a simple enough structure yet create a sense of gracious living. Entwine the pergola with roses and honeysuckle, clematis and jasmine, and there is no more enticing place to enjoy airy privacy.

The pergola can be freestanding or set against the house, where it makes a link between the building and the garden. It needs just one row of uprights to support the crossbeams; the other end can be fixed to joist hangers or to a sturdy beam attached to the wall.

In a south-facing garden, a veranda, which is covered, is a more welcome retreat than a pergola for those who prefer to sit in the shade. Running along the wall like a wide, open porch, it has a sloping roof resting on posts that can be either of serviceable wood or elegant cast iron depending on the surroundings.

The floor, raised up a step or two above ground level, gives plenty of space for seating and for containers of shade-loving plants. Sun-lovers will thrive in a bed at the foot of the veranda steps, where climbers, too, can start the ascent up the posts and along the roof edge.

If you have an extension built on a south-facing wall, consider letting the upper story jut out beyond the lower one. The shady gallery below — a loggia — with wooden or plaster pillars along it, is a comfortable spot for outdoor meals. In

walls and built-in seats. Make the walls double, with a gap in between to hold soil, and use them for growing marjoram, rosemary, sage, thyme, lemon thyme, tarragon, chives, parsley, and fennel for flavoring the barbecue food.

Make the seats of double walls, too, and top them with slabs, some of them left loose so that the space beneath can store the cushions in plastic bags, as well as barbecue fuel and utensils.

A similar design that is sunk into the

ground is an unusual alternative. Make the barbecue area circular, with built-in seating. At the center put a round table large enough to contain or support a small grill. Grow herbs in the surrounding beds and add an outer circle of plants for a windbreak if necessary.

CLEVER DESIGNS WITH DECKING

A seating area is easily made into a strong feature when you use wooden decking. It is particularly useful for making a level area

MAKING
AN ARBOR

A PRETTY PLACE to rest after the exertions of weeding is inside an arbor, furnished with a simple, comfortable chair. Whether freestanding or placed against a wall, it will look delightful, especially when covered by a rambling rose or another scented climber.

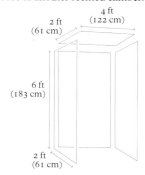

You need three 6 × 2 ft (183 × 61 cm) trellis panels to make the sides and the roof and a 6 × 4 ft (183 × 122 cm) panel for the back. Use four 6 ft (183 cm) lengths of 2 × 2 in (5 × 5 cm) lumber for the uprights.

Make a three-sided box by nailing the side and back panels to the outside of the four uprights with galvanized nails; drill holes in the trellis panels before nailing to prevent splitting.

Cut down the roof panel to 4 ft (122 cm) long and nail it across the top in the same way.

Attach the arbor to a wall with screws and lead anchors or bolt it to steel brackets set in concrete footings. Top the corner posts with wooden finials and crown the front with a shapely crest cut from marine plywood. Paint or stain the arbor.

DINING OUT This pergola provides support for climbing plants and some shade when the sun is overhead. The pleasures of eating outside are enhanced by the privacy created by the structure and the profusion of container plants, including the tall yellow spikes of *Ligularia przewalskii*.

summer the loggia is likely to be shady, but at other times of the year the lower-angled sun will light and warm it.

INTIMATE ARBORS

Pergolas, loggias, and verandas may have space for several people, but an arbor is made for one or two.

Ready-made arches of rustic poles, wooden lattice, or wirework are sold at most garden centers and, when placed against a wall, hedge, or fence, become an instant arbor. You can make your own with trellis panels and wooden posts, then smother it with roses for the full romantic aura. In a partly shaded site, clothe it with *Clematis alpina*, *C. macropetala*, runner beans, or the colorful annual black-eyed Susan vine (*Thunbergia alata*).

Set the arbor among such large-leaved plants as rodgersias, bergenias, fatsias, and the purplish ornamental rhubarb *Rheum palmatum* 'Atrosanguineum.' All have a solidity that emphasizes the structure's delicacy. Add woodruff (*Galium odoratum*) for a scented "floor."

Turn a walled corner into an arbor by attaching a strong trellis panel across the top. Make it more distinctive by raising the ground a little and laying an approach of a couple of semicircular steps.

If the garden is very sheltered and south-facing, grow the evergreen climber *Trachelospermum jasminoides*, which will look spectacular planted on each side of the arbor, where it will twine its way up support wires and over the trellis. Its glossy, dark green leaves are attractive all year, while in summer, the small, star-like flowers produce the most heavenly fragrance. In more exposed areas, the scented evergreen honeysuckle *Lonicera japonica* 'Halliana' is a good alternative. Put a silky-leaved *Artemisia absinthium* 'Lambrook Silver' at the foot of each honeysuckle as a finishing touch.

Against a white wall, an *Actinidia kolomikta* is lovely clambering up either side of the arbor. Its heart-shaped green leaves are generously splashed with white and pink, as if by a careless painter. For blooms and fragrance, add a few pots planted densely with pink and white lilies and flowering tobacco.

SIMPLE GREEN BOWERS

A striking, permanently green bower is easy to make with a strong wooden frame covered with stapled-on chicken wire or plastic mesh. Cover it with ivies, and it takes on a rustic character.

Try dark green *Hedera helix* and *H. hibernica*, the yellow-variegated *H. helix* Goldheart,' or some of the large-leaved ivies such as *H. colchica* 'Sulphur Heart,' *H. c.* 'Dentata Variegata,' and *H. algeriensis* 'Gloire de Marengo.'

While the ivy is still immature, plant annual climbers, such as runner beans, sweet peas, the cup-and-saucer plant (*Cobaea scandens*), or morning glory (*Ipomoea hederacea*) around your bower.

Experiment with other evergreen frames for your seating furniture.

❧ Plant a semicircle of boxwood or conifer hedging behind a curved bench.

❧ Carve out an alcove from a well-established hedge. Be sure it is one that sprouts again after a hard pruning, such as yew or privet.

❧ When planting a new hedge, make a recess long enough for a bench by setting one section of plants 2–3 ft (60–90 cm) farther back than the rest.

❧ Plant a hedging conifer at each side of a garden bench and train and clip the two to meet in a round or pointed arch.

TREE BOWERS

Weeping trees make delightful natural arbors. The weeping ash is very hardy and thrives almost anywhere the soil is not waterlogged. In time it forms a medium-sized tree whose leafy branches trail to the ground, providing the oppor-

TRANQUILLITY IN A SCENTED CORNER

By creating a calm but colorful corner, you can transform a terrace or patio into a special, private place where you can put a chair in the sun or shade and relax totally.

DOZING OR READING in the dappled shade of the garden, surrounded by your favorite plants and soothed by scented flowers, is the summer equivalent of curling up on the sofa in front of a fire. A paved corner serves as an extra "room" — an extension that offers all the delights of living outdoors. Set against a backdrop of permanent ornamental plantings, it has the added bonus of flexibility: you can move furniture in and out as required and shift pot plants from garden to paving as the mood strikes you.

This corner is set for one person to enjoy the solitude of a peaceful afternoon. The wooden folding chair is light and compact enough to be moved with ease. At present the chair faces east, cooled from afternoon rays by the partial shade of the climbing rose above and behind it.

The trellis gives privacy and divides the "room" from the lawn, while on colder days the wall blocks out chill northerly winds.

Creeping thyme thrives among the paving, softening the look of the concrete and releasing a sweet aroma as you walk over it. Containers of scented plants clustered around the chair offer a feast for the senses and are ready to release their aroma when touched.

EXTENDING THE PLEASURES

When evening comes, flowering tobacco starts to give out its scent, the pale star-like blooms — and those of the lilies — looking almost luminous in the dusk.

More flowering tobacco graces the raised bed tucked against the wall. The bed provides room for climbers, herbaceous plants, and herbs that can stay in place summer and winter and creates interest with a change in heights.

Climber-covered trelliswork keeps out breezes

Pot plants release a heady blend of scents

A hanging basket of trailing geraniums adds another level to the display. Wind chimes tinkle, and water trickles gently from a wall fountain.

Despite its small size, the outdoor room is more than merely ornamental. The scarlet-flowered runner beans will yield several helpings. The herbs are also for picking. Snuggled up to the pot of marjoram, sage mingles with the tendrils of periwinkle draping the raised bed. Hard and soft features combine to make the most of a confined space.

Runner beans complete a colourful niche

A raised bed holds plants to frame the fountain

tunity to trim away a small arch to frame a seating area.

Weeping willows are suitable for similar treatment and look lovely by water. However, they become large trees, so do not be tempted to plant them in a small garden — they lose their grace if they are chopped back. Much better are the weeping purple beech (*Fagus sylvatica* 'Pendula Purpurea') and the silver-leaved pear, *Pyrus salicifolia* 'Pendula,' both of which make charming arbors, one darkly glowing, the other airily pale.

For a quick result, plant two silver-leaved pears about 8 ft (2.5 m) apart, then tie the top branches together at the center and prune away some of those underneath to make a shady "cave"; a climbing rose such as 'Parade' or 'Pink Perpétué' and the purple-leaved vine grape (*Vitis vinifera* 'Purpurea') look lovely growing up through the branches.

Most of the evergreens that are traditionally used for topiary — yew, cherry laurel (*Prunus laurocerasus*), honeysuckle (*Lonicera nitida*), and a fast-growing boxwood (*Buxus sempervirens* 'Handsworthiensis') — form green "houses" with time and careful clipping. Plant bushes in a round, rectangular, or hexagonal shape, leaving one part open. Train the stems up and, once they have grown high enough, pull their tops over and tie them together to form the roof. Keep the bower well trimmed within. If you grow alternate green and gold privets in this way, they make a striking striped "tent."

PAVILIONS AND GAZEBOS

Similar to the living tent is a small garden pavilion, a pretty feature to look at in the garden as well as an elegant place to sit. On a breezy site, you can close the sides for more shelter, and on hot days, you can open them for ventilation so that the interior does not get too stuffy.

If you want something more substantial, invest in a gazebo, whether in a rustic or modern style. One of these wooden structures offers a shady spot to relax on sunny days. Some come with benches built-in along the low walls, and you can add your own furniture, which the roof will protect partially from the weather.

COURTYARDS OR PATIOS

Not quite so enclosed is a courtyard or patio. It is open to the sky but is sited within sheltering walls or fences.

Sometimes a courtyard has one wall, usually the back of a large building, that

4. Runner bean (*Phaseolus coccineus*)
5. English ivy (*Hedera helix* 'Glacier')
6. Flowering tobacco (*Nicotiana alata*)
7. Lavender (*Lavandula angustifolia* 'Munstead')
8. Easter lily (*Lilium longiflorum*)
9. Pink (*Dianthus* 'Houndspool Ruby')
10. Greater periwinkle (*Vinca major* 'Variegata')
11. Tricolored sage (*Salvia officinalis* 'Tricolor')
12. Golden marjoram (*Origanum vulgare* 'Aureum')
13. Thyme (*Thymus serpyllum*)

1. Rose (*Rosa* 'Aloha')
2. Honeysuckle (*Lonicera periclymenum* 'Serotina')
3. *Pelargonium* 'Mexican Beauty'

is tall and somewhat overwhelming, but the intimidating effect is lessened by placing your seating area at its foot so that you face away from it.

First paint a large arch or rectangle on the lower part of the wall. To draw the eyes down, make a raised semicircular or rectangular seating area in front and edge it with a low wall. Place a bench in the center with a pair of architectural plants — such as fatsias, figs, *Mahonia × media* 'Charity,' or Mexican orange (*Choisya ternata*) — on each side.

Instead of painting an arch, frame the seat by training a plant on the wall into a fan shape or by installing a decorative panel of metalwork, lattice, or bamboo screening. Or make a frame with a climber trained from each side to meet and form an arch. Mount a terra-cotta mask in the center and, beneath it, install a raised pool with a wide, flat coping on which to sit and admire the fish or water lilies.

On the lower level around the raised seating area, plant a narrow bed with a low evergreen hedge of hebes, lavender, or clipped boxwood. Roses, fuchsias, or bay laurel shaped into topiary standards and underplanted with pansies will give you a pretty view from the sitting area, especially when the remaining walls are planted with *Parthenocissus henryana*.

RETREAT ON THE ROOF

Every bit of potential garden space is an asset, so in cities, where space is at a premium, a roof garden is especially valued. Determine at the outset from your local building inspector and an architect what restrictions there are on the appearance, structures, and weight.

On a flat roof, put the largest containers around the perimeter, where the structure is strongest. No matter how light the containers are themselves — especially plastic and fiberglass types — the potting soil is quite heavy. You can lighten the load in large pots by filling the base with plastic packaging "peanuts"; top with a screen before adding soil.

You need easy access to water and unimpeded drainage for rainwater to run off. Keep drainage in mind when choosing the "ground" surface. Lightweight tiles in a neutral color are good, and decking is attractive and practical.

Provide shelter from the wind and sun with panels of trelliswork or wooden slats, which will preserve the sense of space as well as make a more effective windbreak than a solid fence. A trellis made from

A SHADY BOWER Slabs of stone built into the wall in a curve are canopied by spreading *Cedrus atlantica* 'Pendula' trained over supports. This shady bower is both tempting to sit in and a focal point for the eye to rest on.

UP ON THE ROOF Climbers grown on a light fence screen the roof garden, giving shelter from the wind as well as some privacy. Plentiful watering is needed as containers dry out quickly from the effects of wind and sun.

CANOPY FOR OUTDOOR MEALS

ENSURE THAT YOUR GUESTS and family eat in comfort by providing a canvas canopy for them to dine under. It can make all the difference to the success of a children's birthday party, offering a private pavilion to keep the fair-skinned out of the sun and heat.

Available from garden centers and mail-order companies, canopies are made from rainproof canvas and light-weight galvanized steel tubing. They are simple and fast to set up.

CANOPY OF ROSES Diamond lattice is a strong framework for cascades of roses on this well-proportioned and airy arbor. Choose roses with a tumbling habit rather than upright growers to gain the best effect.

recycled plastic is not only light and low maintenance but also environmentally responsible. Add canvas or bamboo screening on the most exposed side. A sense of security is needed as much as physical shelter; a vast expanse of space without definition can be a little daunting.

Some kind of "ceiling" also helps. A pullout canvas awning is pleasant and cheerful, while a lightweight pergola adds a more formal, structural note to the design. Although a pergola sounds rather grand, it can be a simple design. Set two posts into square metal post anchors to mark the outer corners. Join them at the top with a wooden connector and run another from the top of each post back to a beam secured to the wall. Two or three light crossbeams across this framework complete the job.

PLANTS FOR THE HIGH LIFE

Train wind-tolerant climbers over the beams to create dappled shade; ivies will grow up in time, and honeysuckle and *Clematis montana* add color.

If the roof garden has a wall, cover it with colorful climbers as well. Also choose spiky dryland specimens such as cordylines, phormiums, and yuccas, along with gray-leaved plants that thrive on heat and sun including rock-rose, lavender, rosemary, hebe, lavender cotton, and *Convolvulus cneorum*. In warm climates, you can add such palms as *Trachycarpus fortunei* and *Chamaerops humilis*.

An exuberant atmosphere prevails when every container brims over with a riot of annuals in summer, but if you prefer a more restrained look, plant nothing but evergreen foliage plants.

Whatever your style of garden, create a space to suit your needs and fill it with those plants that give you the most pleasure. Draw inspiration from as many sources as you can — look at books, magazines, and other gardens. Whether you wish to stretch out in the sun or to meditate in the shade, there are sites and seats for all tastes — from the simple and conventional to the wild and whimsical.

BREAKFAST, LUNCH, AND DINNER Eating meals outside with family and friends makes a special event out of an informal occasion. Allow a generous area and border it with plentiful foliage plants for constant interest.

Features To Catch the Eye

EVERY GARDEN BENEFITS from a touch of drama — and it takes so little to transform the well-tended but ordinary into the memorable. There is a wealth of ideas to choose from, some simple and inexpensive, some grander and more costly, but all effective. You can draw the eye with a statue or sundial, or with a striking monkey puzzle tree or purple smoketree. Curiosities will inject whimsy, and plants or mementos that celebrate family occasions and favorite places will keep personal memories vivid.

SPECIAL FEATURES

Gazing down pensively amid a green sea of spotted laurel and lacy ferns,
a weathered statue steals the scene.

FINDING THE FOCUS

◆

Aᴸᴸ ᴛᴏᴏ ᴏꜰᴛᴇɴ you look around the garden and feel vaguely dissatisfied. Despite the time and care lavished, the money spent, something seems to be lacking — but what? One or more decorative features are needed to create interest and pull the design together. An element of drama or wit lifts the garden from the passable to the delectable level, giving a satisfying visual climax that may also be a conversation starter. This focal point can be a statue, an outstanding plant, a curious object that holds memories, or some weathered hunk of wood.

The choice and placement of a centerpiece calls for due consideration. For it is easy to cross the line from dramatic to distracting, original to outrageous, or comical to kitschy.

A focal point should be in harmony with the age and style of the house. Fortunately, objects that are simple or well-designed in themselves tend to fit into any scheme, just as a contemporary sculpture can suit a period house and an antique rug a modern one.

When you choose the location for a main feature, it helps to photograph the garden from strategic points, including from upstairs windows, and have the pictures enlarged. Try out the positioning of focal points on the photographs. Another trick is to cut out pictures of possible ornaments and move them around over the photos of your garden. See if they complement the garden style and give the desired "lift" to a problem area.

DRAWING THE EYE An arch-topped trellis entwined with the evergreen climber *Trachelospermum* breaks up the expanse of brickwork on the high wall and provides a backdrop for the focus of the patio — the cherub statue. Raising the stone figure on a pedestal makes it even more prominent.

FRONT AND SIDE GARDENS

W HEN YOU CONSIDER garden design, you tend to think of the main area for outside relaxation and entertainment — the back garden. But the front garden, particularly the path to the front door, is often the first part that you or your visitors see, so it is worth turning it into an arresting feature. If you have a flower bed in the front or a central ornament to catch the eye, surround it with paving or gravel to accentuate it. Choose features that cannot be easily removed to deter the casual thief.

FRONT GARDENS IN TOWN

How best to make your front garden eye-catching depends partly on where you live. In the city you are likely to have less room than in the countryside. But however little space you have, a plant or ornament can draw the eye.

For a scene-stealing central bed, plant one of the smaller magnolias, such as *Magnolia stellata*, or a camellia, perhaps the elegantly striped 'Contessa Lavinia Maggi.' If you are concerned about security, choose something prickly such as barberry or holly. To set the stage, underplant with bulbs and seasonal bedding plants. An all-white scheme, edged with clipped ivy, is especially pretty: hyacinths and tulips in the spring, followed by impatiens in the summer for a shaded spot or geraniums and silver foliage plants for the sun. In autumn, white chrysanthemums take over.

DUAL-PURPOSE BOUNDARIES

For an even simpler scheme, pave the ground and make a focal point of the boundary. Cut recesses in dark hedging and put a statue inside. Or plant it with a pale shrub, such as a clump of *Cornus alba* 'Elegantissima' or the white standard roses 'Glamis Castle' or 'Iceberg.'

If the boundary is not a hedge, make the most of paving. Choose from pavers, bricks, tiles, or cobblestones. Interplant with low-growing shrubs and perennials. A weeping standard rose, perhaps 'Debutante' or 'Princess Louise,' makes a delightful centerpiece.

In shade, plant a weeping evergreen such as *Cotoneaster salicifolius* 'Pendulus' or *Ilex aquifolium* 'Argentea Marginata Pendula' — or choose the ferny-leaved

Mask and jar catch attention

Dainty flowers set off bold foliage

WINTER CHARM IN THE SIDE GARDEN

With a well-planned design for the narrow strip between the boundary and the house wall, this unpromising spot becomes a corner of delight, even in winter.

WHITE WALLS and a pale gray trellis give the confined space a more open feeling and make an attractive backdrop. The trellis adds structure behind the ivy, whose variegated leaves seem to sparkle.

Rectangular pavers laid across the whole area make the strip seem wider — even when pots and troughs are added, it is the paving that defines the width. Choose the evergreen bergenia for year-round interest, varying the detail with snowdrops and scillas in late winter and spring and petunias or red geraniums with hostas in summer.

The short wall is the most dramatic place for the pièce de résistance, a wall mask hung above a tall terra-cotta jar. Surround the jar with little pots of ivy. A barrel planted with a spiky New Zealand flax draws people from the main garden into the secluded strip.

In summer hanging baskets full of annuals, such as impatiens in a range of warm reds, pinks, and purples, brighten the area further. The mask and jar, too,

come alive — as a wall fountain with a hidden pump that circulates a trickle of water from the mouth of the mask into the jar and back again.

1. *Hedera algeriensis* 'Gloire de Marengo'
2. *Scilla siberica*
3. *Bergenia* 'Silberlicht'
4. Snowdrop (*Galanthus elwesii*)
5. *Hedera helix* 'Glacier'
6. New Zealand flax (*Phormium* 'Dazzler')
7. Hart's-tongue fern (*Asplenium scolopendrium*)

TRAINING A LIVING PYRAMID

TO TRAIN A PLANT in a topiary shape, choose one that grows slowly, has dense form, and tolerates regular clipping. Ideal plants are boxwood, privet, yew, and holly. But you could also use bay laurel, hornbeam, pyracantha, or even rosemary. There is no need to buy a ready-made frame for a simple shape like a pyramid.

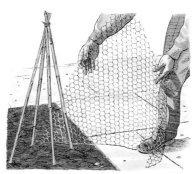

1. Choose four bamboo stakes that measure the desired height of the topiary plus 6 in (15 cm). Tie the stakes together with twine 2 in (5 cm) from the top and spread them to form a pyramid.

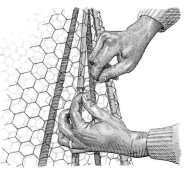

2. Use wire netting with holes larger than the plant's foliage. Wrap it around the frame, leaving 4 in (10 cm) free at the bottom. Tie the netting to each stake with twine at 5 in (12.5 cm) intervals.

3. Place the frame over the young plant in its container. Push the stakes firmly into the soil so the frame will not be dislodged by the occasional knock. The netting should almost touch the soil.

4. As the plant grows, trim back any shoots that come through the wire. Use pruning shears for cutting larger-leaved plants so that individual leaves do not suffer damage and turn brown.

5. Once the plant fills out the frame, gently pull the stakes out of the soil and lift off the frame carefully. The plant will then need regular trimming, usually twice a year, to keep it in shape.

---

rose *Rosa xanthina* 'Canary Bird,' which remains attractive after the small yellow flowers have finished their spring show.

FOCAL POINTS IN A MODERN OR COTTAGE SETTING

The strong lines of modern architecture are set off by ground cover, dramatized by a few specimen plants. Try sweeps of low-growing *Prunus laurocerasus* 'Otto Luyken' around plants of architectural interest. Aralia, fatsia, and bamboos are all excellent in such a situation.

Make a modern sculpture with a grouping of boulders. Or sink five weathered posts of different lengths into the ground together as one pillar; before installation, treat the portion to be sunk underground with a wood preservative. Top the exposed end of each post with a large, smooth stone.

At the other extreme — in a cottage garden — the features that delight are more cozy and familiar. Here is the spot to try your hand at some light-hearted topiary — a teddy bear, teapot, or small, plump bird or two; if the shapes are a little lopsided, it adds to the charm. Instead of foliage plants, use flowering ones, such as hollyhocks, delphiniums, and sweet peas or the long-flowering *Lavatera* 'Barnsley.'

BESIDE THE SEA

Seaside gardens give you the opportunity to use materials that are appropriate nowhere else. In a tiny garden use the surface itself as a center of interest. Lay crushed shells in diamond shapes and outline them with pebbles in different sizes and colors. For a more ambitious design, lay pebbles in a wave pattern and incorporate a gull or fish.

For a living centerpiece in a sea of hard surfacing, plant prickly *Rosa rugosa*. Rugosas tolerate poor, sandy soils, and the flowers are usually followed by large, colorful hips. 'Fru Dagmar Hastrup' grows to about 3 ft (1 m) and has fragrant pink single flowers, huge red hips, and leaves that change color in the autumn.

For a taller, shade-tolerant rugosa, 'Blanc Double de Coubert' is unrivaled. It reaches 6 ft (1.8 m) and has fragrant, semidouble white flowers with golden stamen and good leaf color in fall.

Ship figureheads were once familiar ornaments for seaside houses and gardens. Old ones are hard to come by, but why not carve and paint one yourself? As the originals were often crudely done, a little clumsiness adds an air of authenticity — as does "weathering" the paint work. Rub spots of it away here and there with fine sandpaper to reveal the undercoat or the bare wood.

Failing a figurehead, use an anchor. Paint it black, bolt or cement it to a sunken concrete block, and conceal the block with pebbles or crushed shells. Frame the feature with a blue sea of catmint, then add groups of the silvery-leaved and spiky plants that grow well at seaside — sea holly, globe thistle, artemisia, and the little blue ornamental grass, *Festuca glauca*.

INTEREST IN THE SIDE GARDEN

The side garden is often a difficult area to make attractive. It may be little more than a wind tunnel running beside a garage or wall. Before considering plans for replanting drab, wasted space, look at the paint work. Think of houses in other countries that are painted in striking color combinations — the white and marine blue of the Greek islands, warm terra-cotta and burnt yellows of Italy, turquoise and coral of the Caribbean.

Take photographs of your house and of the facing wall, if there is one. Make tracings from these and color in various schemes until you find one that pleases you. Try pale blue walls and dark blue woodwork, white walls with green woodwork, or dark green or primrose-yellow walls trimmed with sparkling white. A small porch or portico and some shutters make decorative features of doors and windows. Window boxes help, too.

Trellis panels fixed to the wall add points of interest. The paint usually chosen for trellises is white or dark green, but try other colors and consider black for a sophisticated city garden. If the spot is gloomy, set a mirror (with a moisture-resistant film backing) behind the trellis to double what light there is.

For extra color and texture, you can add a few space-saving plant containers, such as hanging baskets, troughs, or wall mangers, or attach a wall plaque.

SEMIDETACHED HOUSES

Many semidetached houses have an L-shaped garden with a narrow leg where two buildings join. Although the garden is often shaded by a wall, it is still valuable

CORNER OF DELIGHTS A lion's-mask fountain and boxwood globes in gaily painted pots transform a dark, narrow side-garden strip.

SAFETY FIRST

KNEEPADS

KNEELING DOWN to tend plants can be hard on the joints, especially where there is a hard paved surface rather than lawn. Kneepads, which are easily attached with Velcro straps, cushion the impact, protecting you from bruises and aches and pains.

CHIMNEY POT CLUSTER To provide variation in height and a splash of color in a narrow, awkward space, fill pots with *Verbena* 'Sissinghurst' or geraniums and slip them inside ornamental chimney pots or other clay pipes. Stand them against a wall or on a step.

TOUCH OF THE EXOTIC The spiky purple-leaved giant dracena always claims the spotlight. *Cordyline australis* is a tender species and can be grown outdoors only in mild areas in the south and west.

space. You can brighten a bare expanse of wall in various ways.

🌢 Use a bit of false topiary. Train a pot-grown small-leaved ivy up a wire spiral or train it on a globe, using a homemade frame of two mesh hanging baskets bound together with strong wire.

🌢 Train a climber up and around an arch or trellis. The larger-leaved ivies (*Hedera colchica* or *H. algeriensis*) thrive in sun or shade. Those with variegated leaves do better in at least partial sunlight. They are all self-clinging and fast growing once established.

🌢 Even simpler, paint an arch on the wall. Try a round-topped or pointed shape, making a template out of cardboard to guide you.

🌢 In front of the real or trompe l'oeil arch, position a statue or urn.

🌢 Plant small beds at the foot of the wall. *Hydrangea anomala petiolaris*, a self-clinging climber, is lovely in shade. It bears lacy white flowers in summer.

MONEY·SAVERS

ON A PEDESTAL

THE SIMPLEST ORNAMENT has more impact when raised. Keep costs down by using a piece of clay drainpipe, about a third taller than it is wide, for a pedestal. Lay a paving stone on a level bed of sand; cement the pipe on it. Fix a slightly smaller slab on top with cement and finish with an ornamental object such as a large seashell.

❧ For flowers in mild areas, the shade-tolerant 'Mermaid' is an excellent, nearly evergreen rose, with large, single creamy-yellow blooms until late fall. Keep the stems tied in close to the wall or use it in wider spaces, as the thorns are vicious.

❧ For fragrance, plant the early and late Dutch honeysuckles *Lonicera periclymenum* 'Belgica' and 'Serotina,' both of which are good in light shade.

At the other end of the narrow leg, where it joins the main garden, plant a couple of graceful shrubs such as *Acer palmatum* 'Bloodgood' or *Olearia virgata* on opposite sides, one a little ahead of the other. They invite you into the secret alley with a promise of delights to come.

SHOW STEALERS OUT OF TOWN

On the outskirts of cities, the gardens generally get roomier. Often there is a garage at or joined onto one side of the house, presenting a large area of blank wall to a narrow side garden. If arches, niches, or patterns of raised brickwork are incorporated at the building stage, they relieve the dullness. But when you inherit the wall, you will have to employ other methods.

A row of evergreens shaped into topiary standards breaks up the base of a blank wall. *Elaeagnus pungens* 'Maculata' or silver-edged *Ilex aquifolium* 'Argentea Marginata' add a light touch, while fast-growing privet is easy to train. At their feet raise half-square or half-circle "pots" of clipped boxwood or privet.

Alternatively, cover the wall with a living "trellis" trained and trimmed into a pattern of diamonds or squares copied from traditional designs. Outline the pattern with strong wires stretched between vine eyes driven into the mortar, then tie in the young stems, clipping to shape as the plants grow. Pyracanthas or small-leaved ivies are suitable.

CLIMBERS FOR COVER

If two walls flank a wider area, train climbers to cover them and to dangle overhead from a loggia or pergola of wooden beams that lead to the main garden. In mild areas, the common kiwi (*Actinidia deliciosa*) is ideal because it is happy in shade and grows in any well-drained soil as long as it is not too dry; it has vigorous, twisting stems and heart-shaped leaves.

Parthenocissus species also do well in shade and can turn a blank space into a living tapestry. They climb by small

HIGHLIGHT ON A HOUSE WALL An espalier pear makes an elegant sentinel spreading its protective arms across the house. Clipped topiary pieces and a handsome bench add to the soothing sense of order.

tendrils with sucker-like pads and have attractive leaves that change color. The Boston ivy varieties *P. tricuspidata* 'Lowii' and *P. t.* 'Veitchii' have small, deeply cut leaves that are purplish when young and scarlet in fall. Silver vein creeper (*P. henryana*) has pink-veined, bronze leaves. For a less vigorous specimen, grow a species clematis such as *Clematis flammula*, *C. chrysocoma*, or the evergreen *C. cirrhosa balearica*.

On a sunny wall, make a central feature of a clematis, but shade its roots by tucking sun-lovers around the base, especially those that release their aroma when touched: lavender, rosemary, sage, artemisia, and *Cistus × hybridus*.

SEASIDE PICTURE Add a breath of sea air to a bare wall by sticking shells and pebbles into wet plaster around a central tile or a fountain mask. A colored glass collage makes an inland substitute for beachcombing finds.

HIGHLIGHTS FOR THE SHADE

MOST GARDENS have areas of shifting shade throughout the day; others are in almost perpetual shadow. Shade is craved and created in a hot climate, but in cooler regions care is needed to prevent it from seeming gloomy.

Painting any walls in warm or sunny colors helps: a pinkish terra-cotta works well, as does a rich burnt cream or an acid yellow. Warm-colored walls provide a pleasant backdrop for luxuriant groups of shade-tolerant plants. A surprising number prefer or even flourish in at least partial shade. Quite a few — aucuba, for instance — put up with very little light if given a soil that is fertile and reasonably moist but well drained.

ADDING VERVE TO A BASEMENT ENTRANCE

Continual shade is most often found in cities, where tall buildings never let the sun reach the ground. One shaded area often encountered is the entrance to a basement apartment, with steps leading down to the front area. A small rectangle of concrete may receive very little light, but it is a pity not to make something of it.

Build a sizable planter in at least one corner of the area, making sure it has drainage holes at the bottom. A shrub will grow comfortably in it for a few years before both soil and plant need replacing. Choose an evergreen to give year-round interest. Suitable plants include *Fatsia japonica*, *Choisya ternata*, *Viburnum tinus*, and *Mahonia* × *media* 'Charity,' which has striking leaves and scented yellow flower spikes. A rhododendron, an azalea, or a camellia needs an acidic soil rich in organic matter. Illuminate the planter at night for extra viewing pleasure.

For a more dashing scheme, paint the steps and the concrete with floor paint, in a strong blue, for example, then paint flowerpots or large tin cans a paler blue or perhaps yellow and place one on each step. Fill the pots with ferns or trailing ivy. For a touch of whimsy, paint the walls sky blue, adding clouds, sun, birds, and silhouettes of palm trees or cacti.

Paint planters, pots, and window boxes to match; continue the green planting theme to soften the boldness with periwinkle, euphorbia, skimmia, and hosta.

Tie the door in with the scheme, painting the frame one color and the panels another. Turn garbage cans into a cheerful feature by painting them, either solid or in bold stripes.

DRAMA IN DEEP SHADE

Many of the ideas for basements can be applied equally well to city backyards. A shady garden allows for adventurous ornaments, and you can draw attention to sculptures and containers by installing lanterns to shine on them. Paving comes into its own. Run a decorative edging around it and add a dramatic central motif. If the area has a smooth concrete base, use floor paint to create stencilled designs or a checkered pattern.

When the garden is enclosed by walls, painting them white or a bright color helps to reflect and make the most of available light. For dramatic greenery, train a vigorous climber on ropes to hang in swags across one wall. More unusual than ivy or *Clematis montana* are

FOX AMONG THE FOLIAGE A surprise element such as a terra-cotta animal lurking in the undergrowth enlivens an area of ground cover. Variegated *Lamium* keeps its silver-white markings even in dense shade.

Schisandra rubriflora and, in mild areas, *Berberidopsis corallina*, both of which have deep red flowers. Within the swags, hang decorations, perhaps medallions of stained glass, ceramic plates, terra-cotta plaques, or stone masks.

When there is not enough light and air to allow even shade-loving plants to flourish, use the hardscape to liven things up. Tiles of black and white marble or terra-cotta, textured concrete, light-colored pavers or brick, or crisp white gravel are all useful in brightening the ground.

Paint the walls white, give them a stenciled frieze, and, as a central feature on each wall, paint a stylized bay laurel, orange, or lemon tree in a tub. At night, hang candle holders of plain or colored glass on hooks around the walls and from an overhead trellis.

Alternatively, fasten a frame of ornamental trelliswork on each wall around the painted tree. Instead of painting on plants, make the "trees" out of twisted

FOCUS ON THE SMALL SCALE Even the tiniest shaded areas can give joy. All you need for the essence of a garden is a few bricks or tiles, a swirl of ivy across white-painted walls, and an old stone trough brimming with alpines.

branches (available at craft and florists' shops), cementing them into pots or directly in the ground. A layer of bricks, pebbles, or sphagnum moss will hide the cement. A spotlight shows off the trees at night, or strings of the small white Christmas-tree lights (rated for outdoor use) add sparkle to the branches.

POTENTIAL OF LIGHT SHADE

In a garden that has intermittent shade or that is covered by the dappled shade of a deciduous tree, reflecting the available light brings the area to life.

Position a weather-resistant mirror so that it bounces any sunlight into the garden. When framed by a shallow arch of brick or wood lattice, this makes an attractive focal point in itself. The effect is doubled by placing something shiny, such

SHRUBS FOR SHADE

Evergreen shrubs make permanent features, and some can be clipped into shapes such as spires and drums.

• Glossy privet (*Ligustrum lucidum* 'Excelsum Superbum'): large with yellow- and cream-variegated leaves.

• California privet (*Ligustrum ovalifolium* 'Aureum'): medium height; gold leaves dotted with green.

• Japanese aucuba (*Aucuba japonica* 'Crotonifolia'): medium height with speckled leaves and scarlet berries.

• *Elaeagnus × ebbingei* 'Gilt Edge': yellow-edged leaves, silvery beneath.

• *Elaeagnus pungens* 'Maculata': large shrub with rich, yellow-centered leaves.

• *Skimmia japonica*: aromatic leaves and white flowers in spring; red fruits on female plants.

• English holly (*Ilex aquifolium* 'Argentea Marginata'): grows to a small tree unless cut back; silver-edged leaves are shrimp-pink when young.

FLICKERS OF LIGHT White heads of *Hydrangea macrophylla* shine like a beacon in a dimly lit garden. Twin pots of the shrub mark the pathway, drawing attention to the low step as well as emphasizing the garden division.

LIGHT AND DARK Get the most from what light there is with pristine white metalwork, the more decorative the better. In the darkness of the corner and set off by the dark ivy, the ornamental arches shine like torches. Matching stone figures frame the centerpiece, leading the eye toward it.

COTTAGE-GARDEN CORNER An old wagon wheel adds to the rustic look of the stone wall, where it doubles as a support for climbers. In front, the herb marjoram (*Origanum vulgare*) offers the twin rewards of flowers and flavor.

as a metal sculpture, or something pale, such as a marble bust, in front of the mirror, where it will be highlighted by the reflected sunshine. Soften the edges of the arch with climbers and feathered clumps of bamboo or a pair of the silvery privets *Ligustrum sinense* 'Variegatum.'

Another trick is to make a focal point of plants whose glossy leaves reflect light or whose flowers and foliage give an impression of light. Plants with gold, silver, or variegated leaves are useful, and white flowers look almost luminous, especially in the evening. Some golden plants, such as *Robinia pseudoacacia* 'Frisia' and the golden hop, tend to lose a degree of their brightness in the shade but, in compensation, take on soft green-yellow tints. Other yellow-leaved plants, such as the fragrant *Philadelphus coronarius* 'Aureus' and Bowles golden sedge (*Carex elata* 'Aurea'), prefer shade for part of the day.

Where space is limited, let one small tree or large shrub with a long season of interest take a starring role. For instance, you could start with the yellow form of common elder, which has lacy white flowers in summer followed by small, dark fruit in the autumn. More elegant is its relative, *Sambucus racemosa* 'Plumosa Aurea.' Underplant this with clumps of a yellow-flowered day lily (*Hemerocallis*) set within a semicircle of a low-growing evergreen such as *Euonymus fortunei* 'Emerald 'n' Gold.'

DEALING WITH SMALL AREAS

In a small garden, a focal point needs to be placed with particular care. Set either against the far boundary or somewhere along one of the sides, it draws the eye over the whole area, giving a feeling of more space rather than halting the gaze in the middle of the garden.

A winding "stream" of gravel and pebbles over sand between clumps of ground cover fits in a tiny corner and creates an element of wit. Outcrops of rocks, cobblestones, small shells, and patches of contrasting pebbles make textural additions to the stream. Alternatively, make a "pool" of a variegated English ivy (*Hedera helix*) among some small boulders and gravel. In a long, narrow garden, two groupings of plants and statuary set on opposite sides, one just in front of the other, act as magnets, inviting you to meander through the garden.

ACCENTS IN GREENERY

There is much to be said for the all-green approach, relieved only by touches of white — with furniture, trellises, statues, and flowers — for the eye to light on. In towns especially, such a plan creates an oasis, cool in summer, charming all winter, and glimmering in twilight.

For a formal garden, you could give pride of place to a camellia, the rich green holly *Ilex* 'Camelliifolia,' or the glossy dark privet *Ligustrum lucidum.* Underplant the privet with *Hedera hibernica,* which has large, mid-green leaves.

If the layout of the garden allows, make everything round. Concentric circles lead the eye to a crowning glory in the middle, made even more dramatic if it is an island of white amid green. Grow *Dicentra spectabilis alba* as the white centerpiece in a circular raised bed. Ring its retaining wall with paving.

White ornaments as well as white-flowered plants give a flicker of light. A white statue against a wall is bound to catch the eye. It attracts even more notice

PONIES ON PARADE High-stepping ponies tucked into a niche clipped in the boundary hedge add an unexpected accent. A pair of figurines or boulders would work equally well, depending on the garden style.

TO THE RESCUE

STEADYING A STATUE

IT IS OFTEN HARD to get an ornament such as a statue to stand straight when it is placed in a flower bed or border rather than set on a pedestal or a hard surface. The problem is usually worse after heavy rain or frost or in boggy soil. If your statue keeps lurching over, give it a level base.

Use a concrete paving slab bedded on sand if the base is hidden by flowers or foliage. A square of bricks is more decorative but needs a stable concrete foundation if the site is soggy.

HIGH AND MIGHTY An imposing pot is raised on an ivy-clad pedestal, and its warm terracotta is enhanced by the fat red buds of *Skimmia japonica* 'Rubella' and the rosy blooms of *Viburnum × bodnantense.*

MAKING COLOR AND FORM STAND OUT The odd light or bright touch catches the eye all the more against a uniform backdrop. Beside the *Argyranthemum frutescens* and *Tulipa* 'Purissima,' an empty jar stands in state — its shape, texture, and color contribute enough without plants.

TOOLBOX

MARKING OUT A CIRCLE

To MARK OUT a circle for paving or planting around a focal point, use a marking line — made by tying and rolling a length of string around two short, sturdy stakes. Push one stake in firmly at the center of the circle, then stretch out the string to the measurement of the circle's radius. Use the second stake to mark the circle in the soil. Show it up even more clearly by sprinkling sand or lime from a bottle around the circle.

---

in younger plants. Remove any shrubs obscuring a plant with compelling character and prune it judiciously so that the dramatic shape emerges. Privet, lilac, euonymus, and magnolia are candidates for this treatment.

Even a tree or shrub past its prime can be transformed. Thread a climbing rose up through aged trees, choosing the shell-pink 'New Dawn' or 'Félicité Perpétue,' whose cream buttonhole blooms are red-flushed in the bud.

PLANTS THAT FLOURISH IN DEEPEST SHADE

The modern climbing rose 'Bantry Bay' thrives in the shade. With a succession of scented pink flowers, it thrives even in a pot and has an open-faced, relaxed look. A pair, planted on either side of the front door and intertwined with blue clematis, make an informal focus.

Honeysuckle evokes the rural past. Try growing one as a small standard, twisting it around a stake that can be removed when the stem is strong enough to support the head. It gains emphasis in a round- or diamond-shaped bed, edged with granite setts and underplanted with primulas, impatiens, and pansies.

For a more quirky rustic feature, plant mint in a battered bucket sunk into the soil beneath an iron pump. Surround it with the tiny, green leaves of baby's-tears (*Soleirolia soleirolii*) trickling between slate stepping-stones. Dot clumps of lily-of-the-valley or Londonpride saxifrage around about.

Awkward areas of deep, dry shade, under the canopy of a greedy-rooted tree for example, present problems. But even here you can make a favorable feature. Grass does not grow here, but paving creates a satisfying feature; if roots protrude above the surface, fill that area with pebbles or cobblestones.

Some plants will grow here, but improve the soil with rotted manure before planting. As feature shrubs, aucuba and the yellow-flowered *Mahonia aquifolium* are happy here. Edge the shrub bed with low-growing ivy, dead nettle (*Lamium*), periwinkle, or × *Fatshedera lizei*.

In spring, snowdrops, purple crocuses, and pink *Cyclamen coum* provide pockets of fresh interest under the bare branches of a deciduous tree. Throughout summer *Oxalis acetosella* offers white blooms on a low mat of gray-green leaves. Follow with clumps of pink and white *Cyclamen hederifolium* in autumn.

---

if set within a frame of dark-green trellis-work or within an arch formed by clipped evergreens such as yew or pyracantha.

Less formally, let the plants flow, seemingly at random, around the edges of a paved garden — here jutting out as a peninsula, there ebbing back to the walls, creating a series of hidden, sheltered areas, each containing a surprise as traditional or as quirky as you like. Place a goddess amid camellias or a bronze toad among lilies-of-the-valley or let a carved snake slither across paving.

IMAGINATIVE WAYS WITH SHADY GARDENS

Shade is usually easier to deal with in the country garden than in the city: it is unlikely to be as dense, and there are probably plants already established.

Never remove mature plants without careful thought, for they have a character that commands attention. With age, many trees and shrubs take on a bold, gnarled form impossible to reproduce

A Place in the Sun

A SUNNY GARDEN is the most desirable. Many plants that do reasonably well in the shade reach their full glory only in the sun, while others barely survive without it. It is far easier to create shade for sun-wary people and plants than it is to let light into a dark garden. The opportunity for focal-point plants is much greater in sun — as it is for accompanying furnishings and ornaments.

PLANTS THAT SPEAK OF WARMTH

Plants enjoy the shelter of a warm, walled garden or terrace as much as people do. Many striking, marginally tender plants can survive cooler climates in a walled south- or west-facing garden — especially in cities, where it is warmer than in the countryside. The walls store heat and give you the chance to grow a show-stopping plant of exotic origins, perhaps from the tropics or desert.

The beautiful, crinkled leaves of the tender evergreen honey-bush (*Melianthus major*) are a subtle color, turning from jade to blue-green. Equally distinctive, the striking palm *Trachycarpus fortunei* has large, fan-shaped leaves and grows well in containers. The sword- and strap-like leaves of agaves, yuccas, cordylines, phormiums, and tender dracaenas also feel at home in sunny, well-drained areas. So do most species of the silver-leaved, spiky *Astelia*, whose rosette of swords makes a dramatic focal point, either on its own or set among plants that have soft, spreading foliage.

COVERING A TERRACE WALL

The terrace, usually in a spot that catches the sun, is where family and friends tend to gather on a summer's day. Plants, furniture, and ornaments can increase the allure. In a small garden, a feature on the wall may be the focal point.

Some wall plants are imposing enough to command attention on their own. In early summer wisteria drips cones of scented white or purple flowers as the leaves are unfurling; in winter the twisted bare branches are sculptural.

The crimson glory vine (*Vitis coignetiae*) — which lives up to its name for autumn color — as well as the green- *(continued on p. 202)*

SUN-SOAKED ELEGANCE Few people nowadays use a sundial to tell the time, but it adds a classical touch to a white border. All-white delphiniums, roses, and *Crambe cordifolia* back up the graceful look of the ornament, and both hard and soft features radiate sun-bleached warmth.

White wedding

Plant the enthusiastic climbing rose 'Wedding Day' to spill like a veil over an old apple tree. Beneath it, grow *Exochorda × macrantha* 'The Bride' behind a stone bench and add groups of delicate *Dicentra spectabilis alba*, whose flowers hang like little heart-shaped lockets.

SOUVENIR GARDENS

It is a pleasure to look back at family anniversaries and happy memories. Why not use the garden as an "album" and record these special times there?

THERE ARE FEW more charming ways to celebrate a birth or a coming of age than to design a part of the garden so that it will always bring the occasion to mind. By the time slow-growing plants reach maturity, the children should be of an age to appreciate them. And if plants are pot grown, they can be moved on when the young adults set up their own home.

Many wedding anniversaries are conveniently color related, providing some rich opportunities for souvenir planting schemes. As well as giving the happy couple enjoyment at the time, the plantings make joyful records as they develop through the years.

Promised pair

For an engagement, make a flower bed in the shape of two entwined rings. Plant it with the cluster rose 'Dearest,' edged with a miniature boxwood hedge of *Buxus sempervirens* 'Suffruticosa.' Clipped lavender cotton (*Santolina chamaecyparissus*) fills the interlocking center.

Welcome arrival

Coming of age

To celebrate a birth, plant the standard rose 'Happy Child' to rise from a soft cloud of *Gypsophila paniculata*. Surround these with lavender — either white (for innocence), or with blue or pink flowers if you prefer.

Instead of laying down a vintage wine for an 18th or 21st birthday present, give something that will mature just as magnificently. *Magnolia grandiflora* 'Galissonière' is a beautiful evergreen that takes about ten years to begin producing its waxy, fragrant flowers. Grow it in a pot for portability, ready for planting out when its owner settles down.

Elegant silver wedding

Underplant a silver birch such as *Betula pendula* 'Youngii' with seasonal bulbs to celebrate 25 years of marriage. For autumn, you could choose drifts of white *Colchicum speciosum* 'Album' and white *Cyclamen hederifolium*. White crocuses and snowdrops would make a spring combination.

Golden days

A golden southern catalpa (*Catalpa bignonioides* 'Aurea') overhangs a sturdy semicircular bench. 'Golden Years' roses, flanked by 'Golden Splendor' lilies, commemorate 50 years of marriage. Carving the couple's names and wedding date on the bench would add a sweet touch.

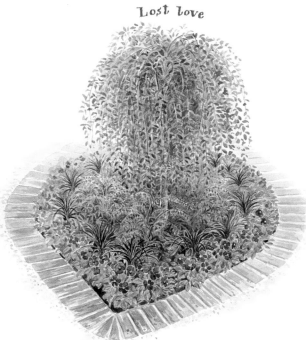

Lost love

Heal a broken heart by planting a heart-shaped bed with a small weeping tree such as *Salix caprea* 'Kilmarnock,' whose catkins hang like fat tears. Surround the tree with bleeding-heart (*Dicentra spectabilis*) and edge the bed with clumps of the black grass *Ophiopogon planiscapus* 'Nigrescens.'

Ruby vintage

Forty years of marriage are aptly marked by trees and shrubs with ruby leaves and flowers. Frame the corner with two specimens of the fragrant rose 'Etoile de Hollande' and underplant with *Artemisia absinthium* 'Lambrook Silver.' Give pride of place to *Hydrangea macrophylla* 'Pia.'

SUNBURST PICTURE UNDERFOOT The ground itself can be a conversation piece, performing double duty with an imaginative use of hard surfacing. A mosaic of cobblestones adds character to the courtyard, and the plain paving stones work in practical, restrained harmony.

of choices. Interesting lanterns, statues, garden furniture, even plants unavailable around home can all be gathered and easily transported. Those traveling by plane or train can bring back a few choice ornaments such as conch shells from the beach, brightly painted pots, or tiles. Group the souvenirs on the terrace as enduring vacation reminders.

COOL IDEAS FOR SUN-DRENCHED BEDS

In a small, sunny garden, a silvery-leaved weeping pear (*Pyrus salicifolia* 'Pendula') makes a deliciously icy-looking cascade of downy leaves. A trailing rose could be used instead. Most roses that ramble and climb flower only once, but 'Awakening' and 'Leverkusen' flower over a long period in summer, as does the climber 'New Dawn.' Clematis or sweet peas are also sun-lovers that would make an arresting feature climbing up an obelisk in a tiny garden.

In a narrow part of the garden, painted or stained arches, cut from marine plywood, act as bold punctuation marks when placed along a central shrub-lined stretch of path, both enticing the viewer on and framing the view into a broader, more open area ahead. Using the same tones for fencing and trellis-work, arches and gates creates a peaceful sense of unity. Where you wish to spice things up, choose hot splashes of pink rock-roses, orange California poppies, or scarlet nasturtiums — all of them ardent sun-worshippers.

PLANTS TO PROVIDE RELIEF FROM SUMMER'S HEAT

The southern catalpa (*Catalpa bignonioides*) has huge heart-shaped leaves for giving the garden some much-needed shade and looks handsome standing in a far corner. Add a circle of clipped boxwood around the trunk for emphasis and winter interest.

If you have enough room, a sunken rose garden below the terrace will win admiration. You could plant it with the most obliging of pink roses, 'Nathalie Nypels,' around a wisteria standard.

In a garden of smooth lawns and undulating borders, focal plants that work well from a distance are varieties of Lawson cypress (*Chamaecyparis lawsoniana*) such as 'Green Pillar,' 'Columnaris' (blue-gray), and 'Lanei' (yellow). At the end of the garden, a classical statue could draw you into the shade of a black locust

leaved *V.* 'Brant' and the purple-leaved *V. vinifera* 'Purpurea' all give a romantic look to a wall. Another dramatic and vigorous climber, *Actinidia kolomikta*, has green leaves splashed with pink and white.

If you can make niches in the terrace walls, they will act as a magnet for the eye, whether they are left bare or furnished with an ornament. You could make a false niche by fixing a framework of brick or wood on the face of the wall.

Many sun-linked features are as useful as they are decorative. Sundials

are always a fascinating conversation piece, even more so with plants climbing up their sides. Traditionally placed at the center of knot and herb gardens, sundials are seen to advantage when raised a little on a pedestal of stone or brickwork. To support the weight of such a heavy feature, put it on a solid base of concrete or on a sturdy flagstone bedded in sand.

Most people collect souvenirs when on vacation yet neglect them once back home. Buying things for the garden will change all that. Car travelers have plenty

(*Robinia pseudoacacia* 'Frisia'), which makes a splash of refreshing lime-yellow, rippling in the breeze.

BOLD AND MODERN TOUCHES

A deck makes a delightful outdoor living area for a modern house. Lay the wood in long diagonals and leave a hole or two in the floor surface for shade-giving plants. Any tall shade tree will do, as long as it does not have particularly messy leaves or fruits or low branches.

Much can be done to give the lawn impact. Inset drifts of ground cover such as the silvery lavender cotton and its green relative, *Santolina virens*.

Islands of stone on the lawn also make a strong statement. Plant them with clumps of *Pennisetum villosum*, *Stipa pennata*, and other ornamental grasses, which come in many sizes and colors and are spectacular when uplit at night.

For a modern centerpiece, choose an abstract sculpture presenting bold shapes in concrete, wood, or metal. Or set a large cogwheel from an abandoned machine on a plinth made from cinder blocks coated with cement.

A NOSTALGIC HAVEN

A sunny cottage garden should be a relaxed miscellany of shapes and color, from a latticed porch smothered with jasmine to a crab apple in a corner, foaming with blossom in the spring and bejeweled with bright fruits well into the winter.

For a raised attraction, make a circle of bricks or stone and top with a painted tub. In spring fill the tub with hyacinths or tulips in a mist of forget-me-nots, followed by geraniums and petunias.

An attractive old-fashioned feature is a millstone, sunk flush with the ground or resting on it. The central hole creates a planter for a small shrub, such as *Hebe albicans* or rosemary. To add height, place a tripod of stakes next to it as a support for annuals such as sweet peas, black-eyed Susan vine (*Thunbergia alata*), or *Convolvulus tricolor* 'Heavenly Blue.'

To make the cottage wall the focus of attention, train a spectacular rose over it, preferably one with an old-fashioned appearance; 'Madame Grégoire Staechelin' is perfect. The large, loosely double, fragrant flowers of deep pink are produced only in early summer, but with unparalleled generosity. Train a clematis — the long-flowering blue 'Mrs Cholmondeley' or sky-blue 'Perle d'Azur' — up through the branches to prolong interest.

WELCOME SHADE-GIVER Pruned to a lollipop, *Pyrus salicifolia* 'Pendula' takes center stage on the lawn and brings a little shade to a south-facing site. The weeping pear arrests the eye wherever you are in the garden.

HEIGHT ON A BUDGET Different levels of interest add dimension, but there is no need to buy costly sculptures. Just a wooden post topped with a stone gives a satisfying mix of rough and smooth, round and hard-edged.

BEST PLANTS

ARCHITECTURAL SHAPE

Plants with a strong outline demand attention. Their shape is often defined by their leaves, which, with some species, last all year.

• *Acanthus mollis*: perennial with glossy spires of leaves topped by mauve or white flower spikes in summer.

• Southern catalpa (*Catalpa bignonioides* 'Aurea'): deciduous tree with large, yellow, heart-shaped leaves, white flowers, and long seedpods.

• *Euphorbia characias*: tall, evergreen perennial with bold leaves and yellow flowers in early summer.

• *Gunnera manicata*: a perennial for damp soil, more than head high, with enormous rhubarb-like leaves.

• *Mahonia × media* 'Charity': large evergreen shrub with long rows of mid-green, holly-like leaflets and scented yellow flowers in late winter.

• Royal fern (*Osmunda regalis*): head-high fern, tinted brownish pink and turning russet as it fades in autumn.

• Staghorn sumac (*Rhus hirta* 'Laciniata'): deciduous shrub with ferny leaves that turn fiery in autumn.

IN SEARCH
OF THE UNIQUE

O NCE YOU HAVE considered the garden's exposure, size, shape, and style, it is time to hunt for the right feature to suit the chosen spot. You may already have a statue that you have been waiting to display, a favorite plant you are longing to include, or an object you want to find a home for. But it is always worth scouting around for new ideas.

Gardens have been adorned with containers and ornaments since ancient times. Many old styles are still popular, helping to create atmosphere by strengthening both the design and the planting.

GARDEN DECOYS Stone partridges squatting on a patch of gravel cut out of the ground cover introduce an element of wit to the garden. As an added advantage, maintenance of this area is cut to a minimum.

ANIMAL MAGIC AMONG THE PLANTS An inspired position exploits the humorous potential of farmyard statuary to the fullest. Peeping inquisitively and unexpectedly out of the flower bed, this pig is likely to cause merriment in anyone strolling around the flowery informal garden.

Antique pieces are still found from time to time, and there are many reproductions around, varying in price and quality. Once weathered, pieces in artificial cast stone make acceptable substitutes for the real thing. Those fashioned from cement are not quite so successful. They lack the texture and take much longer to tone down, although the process can be speeded up by giving them several applications of yogurt or strong brewed tea.

TRADITIONAL ORNAMENTS IN STRIKING SETTINGS

Place classic sculptures and period ornaments on the terrace or at the end of a path, pleached alley, or green tunnel — wherever they will draw the eye. Frame them with recesses, arches, niches, arbors, and pavilions or set them before a semicircle of clipped hedging, at the turn of a path, and between plant groupings of all kinds. Whether a sculpture is of stone, marble, slate, terra-cotta, metal, or wood, there is an appropriate place.

☙ Use wellheads, water cisterns, stone troughs, and old copper kettles both as ornaments and containers. Any one of them makes a fine focal point for the garden, whatever its style.

☙ Wall features include moon windows, masks, plaques, medallions, sundials, and sculptured panels, as well as alcoves, niches, recesses, and wall fountains.

☙ Weather vanes make decorative accents both on rooftops and pedestals.

☙ Nothing creates a picture of rural harmony as readily as an old-fashioned domed straw beehive, called a "skep." No longer used for beekeeping, skeps are now available as garden ornaments.

☙ Ornaments of oriental design — lanterns, Buddhas, dragons — usually look at home in a part of the garden sparsely planted with luxuriant foliage, such as small maples, hostas, and bamboos, among raked gravel.

WHEN TO BREAK THE RULES

While there is something reassuring about the traditional and familiar, an element of surprise spices up the garden. Even a formal scheme may benefit from the unexpected — all rules of style and scale can be broken occasionally. A traditional ornament gains extra attention when used in an unusual way; something bizarre, found where least expected, can make you laugh out loud.

Objects that are out of scale with their surroundings, though usually to be avoid-

INGENIOUS FOCAL POINTS

The ornaments that enhance your garden need not be costly originals — some can be had for a song or even for nothing. Keep an eye open for possibilities around you: auctions and junk shops, yard sales and swap meets may all yield treasures.

ARCHITECTURAL SALVAGE
Many firms specialize in searching out decorative pieces. Demolished buildings may provide fragments of stonework, lanterns, columns, pediments and finials, marble and statuary.

SCRAP IRON
Metal wheels, bits of machinery, gates, knife grinders, saucepan holders, horseshoes, and pieces of cast or wrought iron all make intriguing and offbeat ornaments for the garden.

HOUSEHOLD ITEMS
Choose from mangles, old saucepans, coal scuttles, butter churns, tankards, and more. Either leave them empty or use them as unusual pots, if possible drilling holes in the bottom for drainage.

BESIDE THE SEA
Appropriate items for the seaside garden include a lobster pot, a toy sailboat, lengths of rope (neatly coiled), starfish, and shells. Make smaller pieces into a wall collage or dot them around the garden.

FARM AND GARDEN
Use the wall of a cottage garden to hang or prop up a plough, wagon wheel, beehive, watering can, wheelbarrow, or scythe. Leave them in their weathered state or paint them to inhibit aging.

FROM THE COUNTRYSIDE
Boulders make natural sculptures, and dead trees offer many possibilities. Whittle them into statues, place plant pots and stones on their truncated branches, or carve niches out of them to hold a statue.

SPHERE OF SURPRISE The striking plant mix of ghostly sea holly with fleshy-leaved *Crambe cordifolia* and acid-yellow lady's-mantle is enhanced with the addition of an armillary sphere, originally used to study the stars.

ed, can be very dramatic: one large statue or urn may look magnificent in a small garden. In an L-shaped sunken garden, for example, where a narrow leg of the L ends in a blank wall, place a metal or wooden arch over the top to make an alcove. Paint the inside a warm color and place within it a larger-than-life statue. By all the rules, this is far too big for such a cramped space, but the effect is powerful.

You achieve a similar effect with a showy plant such as datura, cordyline, or one of the large-leaved ivies trained on a metal frame into a cone or spiral. Large plants become even more imposing in a restricted space. In moist, dappled shade, grow a tall bamboo, a tree fern, the big rhubarb-like leaves of *Rheum palmatum*, or the huge ones of *Gunnera manicata*. In a sunny, well-drained site, grow the sword-leaved dragontree (*Dracaena draco*) or the windmill palm (*Trachycarpus fortunei*). Seen against a light, these form dramatic silhouettes.

THE QUIRKY AND UNEXPECTED

A stone urn, whether empty and sculptural or fully planted, is often used on a pedestal, but it has a wistful charm when found lying on its side among ferns and ivy. If a bowl placed on a pedestal is filled with seashells and attractive stones, not with plants, it can have quite a different

BOAT NOVELTY Seaside gardens often boast the oddest objects, such as a dinghy awash with nasturtiums. Set in the front garden, the cheerful, droll greeting brings an instant smile to the lips of startled passersby.

MAKING · IT · EASIER

A SPEEDY BASE

ONE OF THE TASKS that takes up the most time when displaying an ornament is preparing a proper setting for it. Rather than laboriously cutting bricks or slabs to make an outline, set them uncut into the desired shape — be it round, diamond, or square — and fill the gaps with gravel and plants. As the plants grow, they attractively soften the surface, while gravel gives the extra interest of mixed materials.

WATER PUMP AMONG THE FERNS Household aids that no longer fulfill their original role find a new career in the border. A gleaming coat of paint brightens the appearance of metal objects and helps to keep rust at bay.

effect. Enormous stone fruit, scattered over the grass beneath a tree, look plumply beautiful and whimsical. A smile also comes at the sight of a giant foot on a column, a terra-cotta head lying at the foot of a bench, or a stone bunny nestling beneath the berry bushes. Try a classical head among cabbages or a stoneware hot-water bottle at the bare feet of a goddess. Open books in slate or marble look quite at home in the garden lying among greenery, as if just abandoned by a reader.

Hang small trees with medallions of stained glass that twist and gleam as they catch the sun. It would be fun to hang them on the bare, twisted branches of Harry Lauder's walking stick in winter, before the catkins appear. In a similar vein, fat ceramic fruit, say oranges and lemons, give new character to rather formal standards of bay laurel.

A copper "fountain," made from pieces of thin piping and bubbling up from a pool of gravel, is a conversation piece in a modern setting and an amusing feature in a seaside or cottage garden.

Mirrored gazing globes were fashionable in Victorian gardens and are still popular today. You can make an indestructible imitation of one for a children's garden at little cost. Simply place a rubber ball on top of a traffic cone and spray both with a bright metallic paint. For older children, use a larger ball set on a long section of drainpipe — a sturdy pedestal that they can paint in a bright color or decorate with a floral motif.

CUNNING DEVICES TO ATTRACT THE EYE

Use height to enhance effects in the garden, whether in the form of a rustic pergola or simply two or three steps.

🐦 A statue or urn gains instant prominence when raised on some steps.

🐦 Birdhouses, bird feeders, and birdbaths all serve ornamental as well as functional needs.

🐦 Hang fanciful birdcages from walls and trees; let ceramic or stone birds perch inside them.

🐦 A recess in a hollow tree might house a carved figurine, stone owl, coiled snake, or perhaps gnomes.

🐦 In a wilder part of the garden, mossy

TRIUMPH OF TOPIARY You can buy wire frames to train ivy and other plants into specific shapes such as birds. Using different sizes turns a lone feature into a themed corner. The architectural bench is included as a stage for a cast of living sculptures, rather than a convenient seat.

logs catch the eye. Bleached and twisted tree roots, set on a raised circle, become a satisfying piece of sculpture.

🌭 Turn a corner and you may find a green frog in the palm of a giant hand, a bronze butterfly alighting on a mushroom-shaped stone, or a willowy nymph resting among the greenery.

🌭 Figures of people and animals, cut from marine plywood and painted (the more primitive the better), bring instant height and whimsy to a garden. Useful where nothing much will grow, they can be moved around to fill in gaps.

🌭 Hang wind chimes or mobiles of stained glass, ceramic fragments, metal discs, shells, or scraps of driftwood from a prominently placed arch or branch, to throw flecks of light and attractive shadows as the air currents catch them.

🌭 Large shells, fossils, and fragments of carved wood or chiseled stone all have their charms and uses. Tuck them here and there, on steps, at the corner of the terrace, and among the plants.

SHOW-OFFS AMONG PLANTS

Apart from topiary, with its sculptural qualities and humorous potential, many plants are naturally imposing in form and foliage or curious in habit. Position can emphasize their star quality. Dramatize contrasts by placing a pale plant against a somber background, a column of dark green among light foliage, a spreading plant beside an upright one, and sword-like leaves among creeping ground cover.

Where space allows, aim for a succession of plants to take pride of place as the seasons change. The first may be a maple such as *Acer pseudoplatanus* 'Brilliantissimum,' remarkable for its coral spring foliage, heightened by the carpet of *Anemone blanda* at its feet. As it fades, the delectable pink-cream shrub rose 'Penelope' takes center stage. When the rose withers, a previously unnoticed *Fothergilla major* flames with scarlet leaves.

Twisted branches, such as those of *Salix matsudana* 'Tortuosa,' make intricate patterns against the sky in winter. Plants with yellow leaves and autumn color reach a climax of beauty with the sun shining through them. Plants that look spectacular when the sun falls on them include blue conifers, trees with cu-

HISSING GEESE The cord-like stems of willow are particularly pliable and can be twisted and bent into ornaments light enough to move around the garden at whim. Bring them indoors during the winter months.

NOTE OF NOSTALGIA Old gardening implements such as a lawn roller were made to last and are worth keeping to adorn the garden all year, especially when appropriately placed next to the toolshed. The flowering quince against the wall blooms all spring and bears fruit in autumn.

PENSIVE FIGURE A conversation piece arises partly from the feature itself and partly from its position. Seemingly wading through a lake of gray-green hostas, this stone philosopher-poet strikes a pensive pose.

GNARLED WOOD In the countryside, look for twisted roots, branches, and mossy logs that will make a garden feature — at no cost. The little sedums growing in the crevices draw attention to the interesting texture of the bark.

rious or polished trunks — *Prunus serrula*, stewartia, or laceback maple — and those with brightly colored stems, such as red-twig dogwood.

Mistletoe never fails to intrigue but is tricky to establish. Obtain berries from a known tree and use the same species as a host. Wait until the autumn berries are wholly ripe, make a slit in the bark on the underside of the host branch, insert the berry, and seal the cut with clay.

On a bare wall, train climbers up to encircle a round window (real or false), a wall plaque, or a piece of ornamental metalwork such as an iron grill or old fence section. In the shade, use ivy, hop, jasmine, or *Clematis montana*. In the sun, try wisteria, golden hop, passion-flower, *Solanum jasminoides* 'Album,' or *Trachelospermum jasminoides*, with fragrant white flowers.

Make a feature of grass, by setting the mower blades at different heights and cutting it into patterns to surround and highlight a special plant or ornament. In small gardens, a square of lawn does not contribute much to the design, but, if you round off the far end into a horseshoe shape or take a bite out of the edge near the house, it becomes more interesting.

Whatever the size or style of your garden, there is room for at least one feature to stand out, so that the eye has something to focus on before taking in the broad view. As in a painting, a few judiciously placed accents encourage your gaze — and, in a garden, your feet — to meander over its length and breadth. The longer you live with a garden, the more your imagination grows.

CREATIVITY WITH CONTAINERS

WHETHER YOU WANT a vibrant splash of color, year-round pleasure from shapely clipped evergreens, or a bloom-laden camellia when your garden soil won't allow it, plants grown in containers are a boon. Put them where you will, on grass or concrete, to enliven a dull corner, flank an entrance, or stand in groups on a paved terrace. Whatever container you choose — old wheelbarrow, well-used metal bucket, simple wooden trough, weathered terra-cotta pot, or graceful stone urn — an imaginative planting scheme will turn it into a small-scale garden that constantly delights.

Decorative clay pots give added interest to
a lush summer planting of geraniums and verbenas.

THE POTENTIAL OF POTS

GROWING PLANTS in containers is one activity that many gardeners share, whether they own broad country acres, a typical suburban yard, or a tiny postage-stamp plot in town. While container gardening is already popular, most gardens would benefit enormously if it were done even more.

Inspiration is everywhere at hand, both here and abroad. Think of Swiss chalets with their facades draped in geraniums tumbling from window boxes, or of Mediterranean villages where every small courtyard is ablaze with blooms spilling from terra-cotta pots. Also look to public gardens for ideas. Elegant urns lining a pathway or large pots guarding a gate at a historic estate can spark ideas for enhancing the home garden.

Container gardens often begin when there is little or no natural soil, and containers of all types are the only means to accommodate plants. Old pots and bowls from the kitchen, pretty storage tins, baskets, buckets, boxes, troughs, even discarded wheelbarrows and rowboats can be pressed into service. Indeed, it is often the most offbeat container that brings the greatest boost to the garden.

COUNTING THE VIRTUES

Containers offer an instant effect that even the most patient gardener finds hard to resist. A young oak planted in the ground takes years to make an impact. But if your plant is an evergreen shrub in a container, its lush foliage immediately gives the air of a mature garden.

When your containers are light enough to be moved, you can put them wherever they are needed most — to hold a fragrant arrangement beside a favorite summer bench or to give wel-come winter color outside a window. Set a striking container in a prominent position, and it makes a dramatic focal point; or you can use smaller pots to draw the eye to an interesting combination planting. Containers are equally effective in distracting from an eyesore or bare spot or in simply covering up an intractable problem.

Many plants give more return for less investment when you grow them in containers. Half a dozen petunias in a large pot will spill out liberally and — as long as they are well cared for — provide an effect that five times the number would be hard-pressed to achieve in a flower bed. Another benefit: these same few petunias will reveal their subtle scent simply by being lifted closer to you.

If your garden is in alkaline soil, you need no longer do without rhododendrons or camellias. Just plant them in large pots or tubs of acidic soil and bend nature to your will.

POSITIONED TO PERFECTION A wonderfully healthy hosta in a simple terra-cotta pot transforms a shady pathway. Its large leaves with subtle variegations capture any rays of sunlight, intensifying them and making a dazzling focus for the play of light and dark in this cool scheme.

CHOOSING CONTAINERS

W HILE IT IS POSSIBLE to use anything that holds a handful of soil, as long as it has a drainage hole, you achieve the greatest effect by carefully matching a container to its site and the role it has to play. The miscellany of old pots and tin cans that adds whimsy to a sunny southern patio would look dreary in cloudy Seattle.

Over the years most gardeners accumulate sundry containers — some fit to take on star roles in a group, others more utilitarian and better placed in the back row or masked by nearby plants and their own cascades of growth. Hanging baskets, flat-backed pots, and half baskets are invaluable where space is limited.

As far as possible, choose containers whose style, material, and color are in keeping with the overall design of the house and garden. They should not jar. Classical urns outside a simple cottage or a planted dinghy in the middle of a town can look comical rather than pleasing. For prominent display, choose a container that will never bore. It is part of the garden's permanent scene, with the power to transform any green space.

HIGH STYLE AT VARIED COST

Containers, especially large and elaborate ones, often come with a hefty price tag, although it is often worth the cost to add one special piece to the garden. Check with specialty dealers and antique shops for fine terra-cotta, glazed ceramic, stone, or cast-iron pots.

Reproductions of traditional designs help keep the cost down and are often made from sturdy, weather-resistant fiberglass or "cast stone," which is actually a type of concrete. The best pieces will have crisply molded detail.

To help new pots look weathered, spread them with a thin coat of yogurt, which promotes the growth of algae and mosses. The container's location also influences the finish. A pot left in the sun develops gray-white patches of lichen, while one in the shade takes on a green film of moss.

TRADITIONAL AND MODERN

Few shapes have been more successful or more practical than that of the humble flowerpot. Pieces in the traditional terra-

MAKING IT MORE SHAPELY

With their strong architectural shape, urns lend themselves to bold and profuse plantings. Think in terms of shape — height and depth — as well as color when selecting flowers and foliage.

Plantings in urns look meager without height.

URNS ARE among the most stately of all containers and look beautiful even when they are left empty. However, they lend themselves so well to plants that it is a delight to use them. If you have a rather straggly arrangement (as at left), it is easy to improve upon it and create two totally different images. For summer, aim for an exuberant, lively look, with frothy cascades of pretty pastel flowers surrounding a bushy centerpiece.

For spring you can create something bolder. This arrangement of trailing ivy framing the nodding heads of small pansies, which form a ruff around the upright tulips, is ideal. It has plenty of style and makes a balanced shape. The combination of deep green and rich purple-black, offset by white, looks striking without being stark.

Spring contrasts

The tall *Tulipa* 'Diana' and white-flowered forget-me-nots (*Myosotis*) contrast dramatically with the dark pansies (*Viola × wittrockiana* 'Black Beauty'). English ivy (*Hedera helix* 'Eva') cascades around the elegant grouping.

Summer froth

The delicate, trailing stems of *Sphaeralcea munroana* are balanced by the bushy, white, daisy-like flowers of *Argyranthemum foeniculaceum*.

POTS, TUBS, AND BASKETS

Grand or humble, new or antique, elaborate or plain, containers offer more opportunities to stimulate the senses of sight and touch than many other garden features. The pleasure of obtaining a treasure is only the start — creating a striking arrangement in the pot adds the next dimension.

GLAZED CERAMICS
Oriental-style jars can transform a balcony but need to be brought indoors before winter frosts. Choose simple plants that do not compete with the patterns.

STRAWBERRY JARS
Place a tall pot with bulbs or fruit growing out of the sides among a group of plainer containers so it stands out. Put your most precious or hardest-to-grow plant at the top, where growing conditions are kindest. Alternatively, grow several herbs in a strawberry jar by the kitchen door.

CLAY FLOWERPOTS
Every garden needs flowerpots to hold plants at various stages of growth and to set off more elaborate containers. For variation, buy some with colorful glazed rims. A matching saucer helps retain moisture. Plastic pots imitate the mellow tones of clay at a lower price.

CISTERNS
An antique lead cistern, weathered over the centuries, is suited to a planting of bright colors or feathery foliage. Fiberglass planters mimic the real thing and are both cheaper and easier to move.

IMPROVISING, MIXING, AND MATCHING
Part of the fun of container gardening comes from pressing unusual planters into service. Track down an old zinc tub, a brass pan, a galvanized bucket, a wicker basket, a castellated chimney pot, a terra-cotta bowl on a pedestal, some old paint cans, or even a worn-out shoe. Other possibilities include watering cans, teapots, milk jugs, or a wooden wheelbarrow — let your imagination soar.

STYLES IN WOOD
More than any other material, wood can reinforce the style of its setting. A decorative box, planted with an evergreen clipped into shape, enhances a chic city terrace; a half-barrel or bucket brimming with petunias and pinks adds rustic charm to the ordered chaos of a cottage garden. Most wooden tubs are broad and deep. Take advantage of this by planting a shrub — such as a lavatera or hydrangea.

HANGING BASKETS
Invaluable for maximizing growing space, hanging baskets or wall-mounted fixtures raise plants to eye level; some models come with built-in water reservoirs to minimize maintenance. In spring fill them with pansies; in summer let annuals trail and cascade over the edges. For a subtle, sophisticated look, choose foliage plants instead. To conceal the wires, plant with a climber such as morning glory.

TERRA-COTTA ELEGANCE
Some terra-cotta pieces have charm enough even without plants. For a classical look, choose an amphora, a narrow-necked Greek jar, for a prime place — perhaps beside steps or an arch. Pots decorated with swags or other relief designs deserve a formal spot in keeping with their stately grace, while duck shapes are suited to a more relaxed setting.

INSTANT ELEGANCE
Urns in natural or cast stone give a sense of solidity to the garden — in part because they are too heavy to move easily. They may be designed with classically inspired patterns such as dolphin motifs or come in exotic molded shapes. A shallow stone trough is ideal for holding an alpine garden or an array of succulents.

cotta and in plastic are produced by the millions in every size from tiny thimbles to huge two-footers. A group in different sizes, holding a profusion of healthy plants, is a guaranteed eye catcher. Use them to line a patio wall, surround a bench, or march down a flight of stairs, with the heights of the pots and plants descending with the steps.

Today most clay pots are imported, with the higher quality pieces coming from Italy and the less expensive ones from Mexico and Central America. Always check clay pots carefully for flaws and cracks before purchasing.

Besides being attractive and having a shape that makes it easy to turn out a plant and its rootball, clay flowerpots have the advantage of being porous. Water evaporating from them helps to keep plant roots cool during hot weather.

In recent years clay pots have been ousted from favor by plastic. Despite the dire forecasts of gardeners wedded to tradition, plants grow just as well in plastic pots as in clay. Indeed plastic pots do not dry out as quickly, so the plants need watering less often, and the slight flexibility of the plastic withstands frost well.

Brown and dark green plastic pots usually look best in the garden, reflecting the colors of nature; however in shady areas, a light color is often welcome. Decorating pots is easy and can result in remarkable transformations.

VERSATILE WOOD

Whether revealing its natural beauty or painted for elegance, wood enhances its surroundings. Few containers are handsomer than a Versailles box, which was devised in the 17th century for the formal gardens of Louis XIV's palace at Versailles. The orangerie there held several thousand citrus trees in boxes, all of which were carried out every summer to grace the terrace and line the walks.

Scaled down to a size suitable for the typical home garden, this style of box still looks good — basically a cube with feet and finials at the corners. A pair of boxes painted to match the woodwork of the house and holding clipped evergreens adds formality to a doorway or the top of steps leading to a patio.

Less formal is the half-barrel, which is cheap, easily available, and deep, providing attractive opportunities for planting. Check how the wood has been treated before you buy, as some wooden tubs have been coated with chemicals, any

POT GARDEN A cluster of different-sized pots, whether placed on paving stones or gravel, looks superb in a tiny town courtyard or the corner of a larger country garden. For a stunning effect, aim for a variety of leaf shapes and textures and arrange the tallest pots and plants at the back.

traces of which can damage root tips. Keep the barrels moist; if they dry out, the wood shrinks, allowing the metal hoops that hold them together to slip off.

OFFBEAT PLANTERS

Many containers not originally intended for plants work very well. Try to find ones that are nearly as wide as they are high, since the proportions are more pleasing and the pots will be easy to

plant. Most plants appreciate being in a container large enough for their root run. Look for pieces with sturdy handles that make them easier to move.

There are numerous alternatives to grand containers. In fact almost any hollow object can be used — from old copper diaper boilers to discarded boots. After all, it is only a short leap from a valuable stone sarcophagus to a chipped enamel bathtub. If the container is of a

DECORATING POTS

INEXPENSIVE PLASTIC containers are easily transformed with a coat of matt-finish acrylic paint to give splashes of cheery color or to create more formal and elegant plant holders.

If the plant you intend to grow in the container is flowery, decorate the pot discreetly with sponging.

A foliage plant will have added impact in a patterned pot. Six or eight broad stripes in alternate subtle colors always look good, and if you want a little more exuberant detailing, add a stenciled design.

SPONGING Put on the base coat of paint and wait for it to dry completely. Dip a sponge in the second color and dab to give an even, light covering.

STENCILING Cut out a simple repeated motif from cardboard. Tape it in place and dab over the holes. Remove the stencil carefully to avoid smears.

SIMPLE STYLE Tall *Lilium regale* against a backdrop of green foliage look sumptuous even in the plainest pots when set close in a group. The frothy flower heads of *Alchemilla mollis* clustered around their base soften the hard lines of the pots and accentuate the lilies' spiky leaves.

MOVABLE CONTAINER *Argyranthemum frutescens* planted in an old wheelbarrow are displayed in a bare area of gravel to make an informal showpiece. Pink geraniums, brilliant yellow calceolaria, and trails of ivy foliage set off the dazzling white daisy-like flowers.

UNUSUAL POTENTIAL OF TILES Houseleeks (*Sempervivum*) come in a wide range of colors and textures and can grow in very little soil. Their fleshy leaves and curious shapes give them an exotic look suited to such an eccentric container as an upturned roof tile.

material susceptible to frost damage, use it only for annuals and put it in a sheltered spot for the winter.

What makes each pot or curiosity effective in the garden is a combination of placement and associated planting both in and around the container. Old wooden wheelbarrows, stone troughs, decorative chimney pots, laundry tubs, iron cauldrons, and antique galvanized bathtubs can all serve as containers. Even vessels that initially look unappealing soon take on a more attractive appearance when filled with colorful flowers and softened with foliage plants that trail over their sides.

Of course not all unusual containers need be old, as many countries with a long handcraft tradition still produce pots according to time-honored methods. Whether you are using an earthenware jar from the Mediterranean or a crock from China, make sure you provide a drainage hole in the bottom. Also look for handmade wicker or twig baskets and wooden buckets.

🖝 Old chimney pots, which sometimes have attractive patterns around the rim, look wonderful with plants spilling over

MINIATURE LANDSCAPE A stone trough is the perfect spot to experiment with alpines and dwarf plants that would be lost elsewhere in the garden. Set among the fern fronds of *Dryopteris*, the bell-shaped heads of blue *Aquilegia bertolonii* contrast with the narrow leaves of *Iris graminea*.

CHOOSING THE PLANTS

WHEN CHOOSING PLANTS, strike a balance between container size and plant size; a tiny plant looks ridiculous in a vast urn or tub. The container's shape, too, makes a difference in the ratio between plant and pot. A profusion of leaves and flowers tumbling from a narrow, tapered pot is pleasing to the eye, but this abundance will be short-lived when there is not enough soil for the roots to run freely.

Do not skimp when planting; aim instead for luxuriance and extravagance. Compose a harmonious shape, with the taller plants at the back or center and increasingly shorter specimens filling in the rest of the space out to the rim. For a makeshift container, choose plants such as nasturtiums and periwinkle that will quickly tumble out and over its edges to create a dense, concealing curtain.

Every type of plant — bulb, tender annual, sturdy perennial, shapely shrub, or even small tree — offers its own particular benefits, and with a bit of planning you can enjoy container plants in flower year-round. Containers have such eye-catching potential that successes or failures are particularly noticeable, but mistakes are easily rectified.

GETTING THE BEST FROM EVERGREEN SHRUBS

Where containers are a principal part of a garden — in a city courtyard or on a balcony, for example — a permanent framework such as the one that evergreen shrubs can provide is a boon. Fortunately, with proper care and the right size pot, almost any shrub will grow happily.

The "instant garden," every gardener's dream, is attainable with containers and container-grown shrubs; indeed, this is how most plants are sold in nurseries and garden centers. When you want only two or three plants, it is not too extravagant to buy specimens of considerable size and to pick the best available.

Whether left to develop naturally or clipped and trained into topiary shapes, evergreen shrubs are attractive. But make your choice carefully; while topiary shrubs maintain their desirable characteristic — their strong shape — through the year, many flowering shrubs have several undistinguished months. When

the sides and can add valuable height to the back of an arrangement.

❧ Wheelbarrows are best suited to a rustic site in the country and look pretty bursting with simple flowers like the trailing, tumbling blooms of nasturtiums.

❧ Decaying dinghies by the seaside are given new life when planted with unpretentious poppies, such as the yellow horned poppy (*Glaucium flavum*), or tansy (*Tanacetum vulgare*).

❧ Discarded car or even tractor tires look whimsical when ablaze with geranium and salvia blooms.

❧ A shallow trough makes a perfect home for bonsai (miniature trees), tiny alpines, and dwarf bulbs, or plants that need very little soil such as sedums or houseleeks (*Sempervivum*).

❧ Old-fashioned kitchen equipment — stoneware crocks, iron cauldrons, and earthenware pots — make wonderful and unique containers. These are all suitable for accommodating herbs and are especially attractive, and practical, when placed beside a kitchen door.

❧ A beautiful old copper washtub or diaper boiler offers dramatic spring color when planted with bright red tulips.

BEST PLANTS

SUITED FOR TROUGHS

Alpines and other dwarf plants show up best in a shallow stone trough.

• *Androsace sempervivoides*: evergreen rosettes with pink flowers in spring.

• Fairy foxglove (*Erinus alpinus*): perennial with white, pink, or purple flowers in late spring.

• *Campanula waldsteiniana*: saucer-shaped blue flowers in summer.

• Sunrose (*Helianthemum lunulatum*): tiny shrublet with many bright yellow flowers in summer.

• *Achillea × lewisii* 'King Edward': hybrid with lacy, woolly gray leaves and yellow flower heads all summer.

• Spring gentian (*Gentiana verna*): small, deep blue trumpet flowers.

• *Oxalis adenophylla*: gray leaf rosettes with mauve-pink flowers in spring.

• *Phlox caespitosa*: evergreen with white or lilac flowers in summer.

UNDERSTATED SPLENDOR Even the simplest planting looks stylish in such an elegant container as this stone urn. The variegated ivy appears almost golden in the sunshine and will maintain its good looks throughout the year with almost no attention or effort on the part of the gardener.

in summer after a few years' growth.

🌣 Giant dracena (*Cordyline australis*), a tender perennial suited for only the warmest, most protected sites, has statuesque, sword-like leaves.

🌣 Red-hot pokers (*Kniphofia*), with tall spikes of bright tubular flowers, are spectacular. The sword-like leaves of some, such as *K. caulescens*, are evergreen.

🌣 Conifers that are suitable for containers and give year-round interest are the Swiss mountain pine (*Pinus mugo*) and dwarf Siberian pine (*Pinus pumila*).

SMALL DECIDUOUS TREES AND SHRUBS

Even a diminutive garden gains enormously from a beautiful tree that is carefully placed. Many trees thrive in containers, although pot-grown trees cannot be very large or heavy. More important than size is an interesting structure and branching habit. Japanese maples — which make excellent container specimens — develop these virtues naturally, but careful pruning can bring character to other plants.

Look for trees that provide year-round interest. Maples, especially *Acer japonicum* 'Aureum' and the Japanese maple *A. palmatum* 'Rubrum,' are attractively shaped and offer foliage in dramatic shades of red, orange, and gold in autumn. The weeping purple beech (*Fagus sylvatica* 'Purpurea Pendula') also offers vividly colored leaves — the deep purple foliage turns orange and gold before it drops in autumn.

A tree that lights up any corner is the Scotch laburnum (*Laburnum alpinum*). Old plants develop strange, twisted branches and produce cascades of golden-yellow flowers in late spring.

For a mass of frothy blossoms, the genus *Prunus* offers many choices. Among the best dwarf species are the Japanese apricot (*Prunus mume*), which flowers in early spring, and the small ornamental almond shrub *P. tenella* 'Fire Hill,' which has delicate, willowy stems and is smothered in pink flowers in April.

Many deciduous shrubs are quite at home in a container. For spectacular spring blooms nothing surpasses a magnolia. The smallish *Magnolia stellata* is especially suitable for a container as even in open ground it grows to an average height and spread of 10 ft (3 m).

Hydrangeas are popular pot shrubs, and deservedly so, for the full flower heads last for a long time and come in a

placed prominently in a container, they cannot merge into the background as border plants do. Choose shrubs that have more than one brief moment of glory.

🌣 *Rhododendron* × *cilpinense* has a display of pink-and-white flowers in April. A mahogany sheen develops on the bark of old plants, and the hair-fringed leaves are attractive all year.

🌣 *Rhododendron* 'Temple Belle' carries pink bells in loose clusters and, when the bloom is past, still draws the eye with shiny, heart-shaped leaves.

🌣 *Pieris formosa forrestii*, an acid-lover like the rhododendrons, drapes itself in late spring with chains of little white bells. Drama follows with the brilliant scarlet shuttlecocks of the new leaves.

🌣 *Yucca gloriosa* has long, narrow leaves that make a striking architectural statement, especially in the variegated form. A spire of white flowers may be sent up

EASTERN SOPHISTICATION Bonsai trees are a fascinating blend of the minute and the mature. This beautiful Hinoki cypress in a handsome ceramic pot is the product of years of painstaking work, all aimed at making the tree appear ancient — an impression increased by its gnarled trunk.

wide range of colors — from the purest white through brilliant pink to cool blue. Other useful shrubs are forms of bush mallow — *Lavatera* 'Rosea' and the blush pink *L.* 'Barnsley.' Among the many roses that grow well in containers are repeat-flowering hybrids or patio roses such as 'Drummer Boy.'

Some deciduous shrubs provide interest early in the season. Try *Viburnum farreri*, with delicate, pink-budded white flowers that bloom on bare stems, and the dogwood *Cornus alba* 'Westonbirt,' whose clusters of young stems glow red.

THE MATURE CHARMS OF BONSAI

Bonsai take pruning and controlled growth to extremes, with normally full-size trees and shrubs being dwarfed to create beautiful miniatures that suggest great age. A bonsai collection makes a specialized pot garden that needs persistent care as well as a long time span. Some famous specimens are several hundred years old, but there are short cuts to the bonsai effect.

The hardy dwarf conifers used in rock gardens make excellent pseudo-bonsai

and offer solid evergreen foliage in a range of colors — from the dark green upright *Juniperus chinensis* 'Stricta' to the paler shade of the spreading *Picea pungens* 'Montgomery.'

Use a cotoneaster or a pyracantha for quicker growing bonsai. These shrubs allow you to experiment with pruning and training the shoots into the characteristic gnarled shapes.

The choice of container is key, as it should be in keeping with both the shape and the aged appearance of bonsai. The traditional Japanese shallow, glazed containers always look the most elegant and harmonize perfectly with the proportions of the trees. A stone or cast-stone trough also looks suitably ancient and is a perfect depth.

UNTROUBLED BY WINTER

There are really no over-wintering specimens to rival the luxuriant plants of summer, so winter is a good time to bring on the single most valuable evergreen for containers — English ivy (*Hedera helix*). Easy to grow, it can have big or small leaves in various shapes — for instance,

A SPRING PICK-ME-UP Pretty pansies sit perkily in a wall-mounted terra-cotta pot. This takes only minutes to plant and hang, yet it can transform a bare patch of wall into a charming focal point in early spring.

round, heart-shaped, arrowhead, and bird's-foot — and comes in plain green or with gold or cream variegations. Few hardy plants immediately give such an established look to newly planted containers. On top of this, ivy can cope with all but the very worst that winter sends.

Periwinkles (both *Vinca major* and *V. minor*), with their green or variegated (*continued on p. 222*)

A GARDEN CONTAINED

With a half-barrel and a pair of pots you can prepare a floral feast that will brighten the dullest niche. Each recipe can be adjusted to suit the exposure and the season.

As THE EGYPTIANS, the Persians, and the Moors discovered long ago, the answer to a tough climate and a thankless terrain is containers. With their help, a lifeless, neglected corner can be transformed into an ornament of the garden.

Containers, with their height and shape, catch the eye more readily than flower beds and can be filled with plants suited to nearly any growing condition. And just as flower arrangers do, container gardeners can quickly change a display to suit the season, a mood, or an occasion. When planted with a variety of bulbs, perennials, and annuals, pot gardens can provide color and beauty throughout the growing season.

White for Maytime

For late spring bloom in a sheltered site, plant the white tree peony 'Joseph Rock' and give it a daphne with cream-edged leaves for company. Thyme and the blue-flowered 'Severn Sea' rosemary provide a darker contrast. Later, the rose flowers of thyme will complement the mixed colors of love-in-a-mist.

Colour in April shade

Leading a spring display in this shaded site are the white flowers and red leaves of *Pieris* 'Forest Flame' together with blue sprays of *Brunnera macrophylla*. Both *Iris foetidissima* and periwinkles tolerate shade, and their variegated leaves look good against the yellow flowers of *Berberis candidula*. In spring the knotweed (*Polygonum affine*) 'Darjeeling Red' beneath the barberry is no more than a leafy mat, but in summer it will earn its keep with a mass of pink spikes.

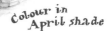

Promise of spring

Sunshine is not always plentiful in late winter, but even in half shade a site can come to life with the catkins of Harry Lauder's walking stick, bright narcissus, the long-lived white blooms of *Arabis caucasica*, the pale green flowers of Corsican hellebore, and the blue of *Chionodoxa luciliae*. The approach of spring is confirmed by the budding dwarf pink *Rhododendron × cilpinense*.

Warm touch in March

In mild climates, the camellia 'J.C. Williams' will still be in flower in early spring and pairs beautifully with *Tulipa kaufmanniana*. Gold narcissus flowers shortly thereafter, and the evergreen *Abutilon* 'Ashford Red' will produce salmon-red flowers from May onward. In summer, the myrtle bears scented white flowers, while the scarlet nasturtium vine scrambles through the camellia.

Ripe September glow

In a partly shaded patch in fall, a large container holds a reddish Japanese maple, with autumn crocuses at its feet. A pair of aucubas flank the bottom step — a female 'Salicifolia' with berries and, across the steps, a berryless male 'Lanceleaf.' In the foreground is *Yucca gloriosa* 'Variegata.'

Midsummer gold

A partly shaded corner suits the blue-leaved *Hosta tokudama*, which flowers in high summer. *Rhododendron concatenans* also has foliage with a blue cast, emphasized by the gray green of Swiss willow and a gold-leaved spirea. Nemesias supply the cream and orange highlights.

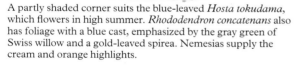

Summer pastels

October fire

Full autumnal sun highlights the color of the spiky *Cordyline australis* 'Purple Tower.' Its richness is accentuated by mauve *Liriope muscari* and some deep red *Sedum* flowers. The few bright *Corokia cotoneaster* fruits will be replaced soon by russet chrysanthemums mixed with silver-leaved *Senecio cineraria*.

June brings full sun to bathe the soaring new leaves of *Aralia elata* 'Variegata' and coax out the first flowers of 'Heavenly Blue' morning glory. The white flowers of the small shrub *Sorbus reducta* are just ending, giving way to white candytuft and the pale pink rock-rose *Cistus* × *skanbergii*.

WARM WINTER SHOW *Pyracantha* 'Orange Glow' is a wall shrub for year-round interest. It comes into its own in winter, when it is covered in orange-red berries, making it an ideal choice for training against a white wall.

SPRING SHOW A mass of delicate pansies tumbling over each other cannot fail to draw the eye. Here the pretty pastel colors of *Viola* 'Antique Lace' look fragile but luxuriant against the somber brown of the rustic basket.

leaves, do not offer the denseness of ivy, but they do share its desirable trailing habit, with the bonus of blue, purple, pink, or white flowers in spring. The double-flowered forms of *Vinca minor* are even more effective in gracing a pot.

In mild areas, invest in some shrubs that will give touches of brighter color to an off-season container display.

🌢 *Daphne odora* 'Aureomarginata' has evergreen leaves with cream edges, and in late winter every twig bears a cluster of fragrant white-and-pink flowers.

🌢 *Skimmia japonica* 'Rubella' has crimson buds among the evergreen leaves on the male plants in winter before the white flower heads open up in spring.

🌢 *Mahonia japonica* is crowned with perfumed sprays of lemon blooms through the winter; its ranks of mid-green holly-like leaflets are striking all year, and some of them take on crimson tints in winter.

🌢 Set some empty pots among your group of container shrubs so that you can plant them with a variety of bulbs that will bloom in succession.

🌢 Put some of the tougher houseplants outdoors. Winter cherries (*Solanum pseudocapsicum*), with marble-like scarlet fruits set amid evergreen leaves, along with chrysanthemums will brighten up a frost-free spot for a couple of weeks.

COLOR IN SPRING

You need relatively few plants to create a feast of color for spring, so buy the best. A typical half-barrel needs only a dozen fine wallflowers, supported with bulbs, to spill over with color and scent.

Pots undoubtedly take center stage when in flower, but they can give pleasure long before, as the swelling buds and

promise of beauty are often as exciting as the real thing. Pots let you cheat nature and celebrate spring a month or so early. Start the plants in a greenhouse, cold frame, or porch to speed their growth.

For your plants to give a good spring display, you must look after them well through the previous summer, never letting them dry out completely, as this is when the flower buds are formed.

Spring bulbs, quietly biding their time just out of sight during the coldest months, provide a wonderful tonic when they eventually burst forth. Plant tulips, hyacinths, and daffodils 8 in (20 cm) deep, with leafy plants above them; the bulbs' pointed shoots have no problem finding their way through.

Deep containers will hold two layers of bulbs. Plant bulbs of the same kind and you will have a spectacular display

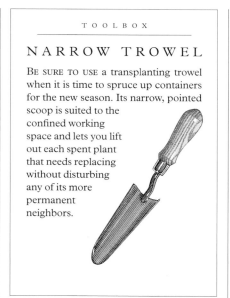

TOOLBOX

NARROW TROWEL

BE SURE TO USE a transplanting trowel when it is time to spruce up containers for the new season. Its narrow, pointed scoop is suited to the confined working space and lets you lift out each spent plant that needs replacing without disturbing any of its more permanent neighbors.

when they all flower together. However, planting layers of different bulbs (such as winter-flowering crocus and fritillaries) will extend the flowering season.

After the bulbs have had their season, non-bulbous plants, if cared for, often continue to flower almost into early summer and certainly until their successors are big enough to make a show. Among the best choices for spring color in containers are wallflowers, forget-me-nots, polyanthuses, and pansies. They respond quickly to spring's increased temperatures and extended daylight but are still hardy enough to withstand the occasional chill.

SUMMER BLOOMING

The ideal plant for a summer container should flower from May to October. Avoid plants that are bred for compact habit, as they do not provide the lushness and profusion you want. Experiment with tender sub-shrubs such as fuchsias, osteospermums, and marguerites (*Argyranthemum frutescens*), which are very fashionable grown as formal standards. They give a suitable height for the center of a pot. Tall summer annuals with a long flowering period — *Salvia coccinea* 'Lady in Red' or blue *S. farinacea* — are also good centerpieces.

For a profusion of flowers with lower growth, few plants are better than the summer classics petunias and nemesias. They come in almost every color of the spectrum — ranging from reds, oranges, and yellows into the purples and blues.

Around the rim of the pot, grow trailing plants, such as begonias, lobelias, nasturtiums, ivy-leafed geraniums, and verbenas, to cascade over the sides.

Try planting a collection of containers with the same type of plant in each one. In the summer, when there is so much mixed color in the flower beds, single-planted containers provide a welcome rest for the eye.

LATE SUMMER INTO AUTUMN

The most striking effects can be obtained from sub-shrubs grown on short stems as low standards — and there is much satisfaction in training them yourself. Fuchsias, geraniums (both the Martha Washington and zonal types), and orange-

COOL COORDINATION Shapely glazed and terra-cotta pots are grouped together in spring for a muted display. Cream tulips pick up the acid yellow of the euphorbia, while white pansies harmonize with variegated ivy.

BARREL OF ROSES With its spreading, tumbling shape, and crowded blooms, the rose 'The Fairy' makes a glorious splash of color; here it is combined with daisy-headed *Erigeron*. The plants are guaranteed to brighten the garden and, with regular deadheading, will flower over a long period.

FIRST-YEAR IMPACT Pots abloom with mauve *Felicia amelloides*, purple *Verbena* 'Loveliness,' white *Argyranthemum foeniculaceum*, and variegated scented geraniums lend immediate height and color to a new garden while a parterre is being established.

flowered *Lantana camara* will all take to this form. You need a season to train a bushy head and clear stem, and the plants must be overwintered in a frost-free spot.

Many gardeners enjoy the mellow, melancholy atmosphere that abounds as summer slips into autumn. This is the time when reds and oranges provide pleasant contrasts to the blues, pinks, yellows, and whites of summer, and there are many plants to bridge the seasons.

The maples come into their own in autumn. Look for *Acer griseum*, with its scarlet leaves and colorful peeling bark, or the coral-barked Japanese maple (*Acer palmatum* 'Senkaki'). Other good shrubs include Chinese witch hazel (*Hamamelis mollis*), which turns golden-leaved in autumn and has red-centered yellow flowers in late winter, and *Caryopteris* × *clandonensis* 'Kew Blue,' which has true blue flowers in late summer.

Hydrangeas, with large mopheads in a wide range of colors, are excellent for autumn. The bonus is the metamorphosis of the colors: the blue of *H. macrophylla* 'Ayesha' or 'Blue Bonnet' fades to pale turquoise and green, while the pinks and reds, such as *H. serrata* 'Preziosa,' deepen to purple and burgundy. The white hydrangeas, such as *H. macrophylla* 'Madame Emile Mouillière,' tend to become pale pink.

Tall, stately flowers always look dramatic in containers and contrast well with bushy plants such as hydrangeas. The crinum, a relative of amaryllis, is elegant and carries as many as 10 large pink-and-white trumpet-shaped blooms

WINTER GLORY The handsome *Viburnum tinus* is evergreen and produces white flowers from winter to spring when so much else in the garden is dull and bare. Its glossy, dark green leaves provide a vigorous contrast to all the bare deciduous shrubs and the fallen autumn foliage.

PLACEMENT AND CARE

Plants in containers are usually easier to care for than plants in the ground. Because they are closer to eye level and often easier to reach, their needs are soon noticed and attended to; deadheading, for example, is promptly done, and any pests are quickly spotted and dealt with. In return for such diligence, the plants fulfill their potential.

The containers themselves require no care at all, except perhaps for an occasional brushing off if they get splattered with mud. They need only be set in the right position for their sculptural beauty to give lasting pleasure, and even unplanted pots can become dramatic features when perfectly placed. Urns work well when raised above eye level. They may not be easily accessible for maintenance in such a position but fortunately look imposing left empty. If they are to be seen close up, they are better planted — with plants that match their elegant form.

COMPOSING GARDENS WITH POTS

While gardeners with only a balcony, courtyard, or roof garden have long known the advantages of "pot gardens," the benefits apply equally to any size space. When the garden comprises nothing but plants in containers, gardening becomes more akin to flower arranging.

Pots let you compose a picture and experiment. There is the further advantage that the components can be moved

on a stem, often all through fall. For light, delicate flowers, choose the African lily (*Agapanthus africanus*). Sitting on thin, erect stems, the rounded flower heads, composed of white or pale to deep blue bells, float above the strap-like leaves and add a graceful touch to the late summer scene. Look for *A. praecox* subsp. *orientalis* and *A.* 'Ben Hope.'

After carefully choosing the containers and appropriate plants, find the best position for them — both for display and growing conditions. Then tend them well and enjoy the best they can give.

A COURTYARD GARDEN

A garden is a place to be used, a room outdoors. Even if you have hardly any space and no flower beds at all, you can still create a wonderful garden with the help of containers.

MOST PEOPLE, it seems, want at least a small garden — even if they live right in the center of a busy city. There are thousands of such little gardens — not much more than courtyards — some enjoying full sun, but others getting only a gleam in high summer. Nevertheless they can all make homes for plants.

In a small space, you cannot afford to waste any corner, so you need plants that tolerate a wide range of conditions.

Owners of little urban courtyards can make good use of the microclimate. Indeed, wherever the courtyard is, it will enjoy the protection provided by the walls and fences.

PAMPERING THE PLANTS

As everything is grown above ground in pots and there is no natural soil, all your plants' needs can be met. For less fussy specimens, there are all-purpose, grow-virtually-anything potting mixes. Of course the plants' roots must be able to cope with the container's restricted area, but controlled feeding works wonders for overall plant health.

Furnish your green room to be inviting and to offer the right balance of relaxation and stimulation. Placing a bench facing south ensures that it will

Evergreen clematis gives the walls year-round colour

choice conifers make a constant green focus

Blue convolvulus softens clipped bays

catch every ray of sunshine. This is just the place to sit, bathed in the fragrance of the rose and the jasmine. The delicate fronds of artemisia in the Chinese jars beside the bench are soft and strokable, releasing a delicious fragrance as you brush against them.

In spring and early summer, floral interest comes from the climbers trained against the walls and from the permanent shrubs. As these shrubs are evergreen, they provide a finished look throughout the year.

The two planting boxes, with their elegant pyramidal bay trees, add a touch of formality that heightens the overall relaxed feel. They can be moved around to frame seasonal color or to hide plants that are at a less attractive stage. The

PICK A SPRIG Pots of herbs such as thyme, rosemary, marjoram, and parsley make an aromatic addition, handy for avid cooks.

pretty group of conifers can also be moved and rearranged as the mood strikes you. Their different shapes provide variety, and, being evergreen, the trees are interesting all year.

ADAPTABLE PLEASURES

In summer the warm nights accentuate the scents of flowering tobacco and mignonettes, while the slightest rain shower brings a sharp aroma from the leaves of rock-rose and ceanothus.

Herbs are another possibility and are versatile plants for those with really small gardens. One large pot of mixed herbs or a selection of small pots looks attractive and is strongly aromatic.

The concept will be particularly useful for all gardeners with no more than a small patch, but the ideas can all be adapted to a larger garden. The glory is that you get instant results — just the thing for impatient gardeners.

Fragrant climbers frame the seat

Nicotiana and mignonette scent the evening air

around to show the plants at their best, with those in decline going to less prominent spots.

Tubs and troughs exploding with impatiens, fibrous-rooted begonias, and brilliant annuals such as petunias, nicotianas, and nemesias are especially valuable, being tolerant of moves in and out of sun and shade.

Put tender plants from a greenhouse or indoor plants in a protected spot for the summer and arrange your especially cherished plants where they can be seen and admired from the house.

BUILDING IN SOME HEIGHT

Any group of containers needs height toward the back. Set your containers on top of inverted empty pots, stacks of bricks or blocks, or pretty pedestals. Another idea is to create a plant "fountain": place a small pot in the center of a slightly larger potted plant, which in turn is set on an even larger potted plant.

A chimney pot also makes an effective stand. Simply slip a potted plant into the top until the container's rim rests securely on the lip of the chimney pot. Or, with a bit more effort, you can

MAKING·IT·EASIER

MOVING POTS

ONCE FILLED with soil and mature plants, even moderate-sized containers become surprisingly heavy, but you can avoid back strain by moving pots on a dolly. You can buy a dolly or make your own model from rigid marine plywood with casters bolted on sturdy wooden struts under it.

Attach ropes through holes on two opposite sides for more pulling power or for a helper to steady the dolly on a slope. When moving the dolly over soft or slightly uneven ground, spread the route with flattened cardboard boxes from the supermarket.

1. *Clematis armandii* 'Apple Blossom'
2. Sweet bay (*Laurus nobilis*)
3. *Convolvulus tricolor* 'Blue Ensign'
4. English ivy (*Hedera helix* 'Goldheart')
5. Japanese cedar (*Cryptomeria japonica* 'Elegans Aurea')
6. Mountain pine (*Pinus mugo* 'Gnom')
7. Cypress (*Chamaecyparis lawsoniana* 'Ellwood's Pillar')
8. Maidenhair tree (*Ginkgo biloba*)
9. Cypress (*Chamaecyparis pisifera* 'Filifera Aurea')
10. Savin juniper (*Juniperus sabina* 'Blue Danube')
11. Common juniper (*Juniperus communis* 'Compressa')
12. *Clematis alpina* 'Frances Rivis' and *Ceanothus impressus*
13. Climbing rose (*Rosa* 'Bloomfield Abundance')
14. Jasmine (*Jasminum × stephanense*)
15. *Viburnum × burkwoodii*
16. *Helichrysum petiolare* and *Petunia* 'Celebrity Ice'
17. *Artemisia absinthium* 'Powis Castle'
18. Rock-rose (*Cistus aguilari*)
19. Flowering tobacco (*Nicotiana* 'Domino' and *N.* 'Sensation')
20. Mignonette (*Reseda odorata*)
21. English ivy (*Hedera helix* 'Glacier')

BUSHY TOP Striking clay pots are well suited to architectural plants, such as this bromeliad, *Fascicularia bicolor*. The vertical foliage of the *Dasylirion* in the foreground contrasts with the soft horizontal ridges of the pot.

BEST PLANTS

BASKETS FILLED WITH COLOR

Choose bushy trailing plants for the rim and base of the basket and taller, upright ones for the central planting.

BUSHY AND TRAILING

• Sweet alyssum (*Lobularia maritima*): grayish leaves and white or pink scented flowers all summer.

• *Lobelia erinus* 'Color Cascade': low masses of lilac, pink, or white flowers in summer and early autumn.

• *Fuchsia*: late summer flowers in white, pink, bright red, or mauve.

• *Pelargonium* 'Mini Cascade': masses of red flowers; evergreen leaves.

• Creeping Jenny (*Lysimachia nummularia*): long stems lined with little evergreen leaves and yellow flowers in midsummer.

• English ivy (*Hedera helix*): evergreen with plain or variegated leaves.

UPRIGHT

• *Pelargonium* 'Dale Queen': pink flowers from summer to autumn.

• Petunias (*Petunia* 'Resisto Series'): strong blue, trumpet-shaped flowers from summer to autumn.

• Impatiens (*Impatiens walleriana* 'Novetter Series'): tender perennial with red flowers from spring to fall.

• Pansy (*Viola × wittrockiana*): range of colors for early spring and fall.

• *Verbena × hybrida* 'Showtime': dark leaves and flowers in white, pinks, reds, and purples through summer into autumn.

plant directly in the chimney pot. First jam crumpled chicken wire into the base to block the open end; this will also reduce the amount of soil required. Then cover the wire with a thick wad of newspaper to keep the soil from trickling out when you water the plants.

A half-barrel is very expensive in terms of potting soil. To cut down on the cost, place crumpled balls of newspaper above the drainage layer of gravel. Besides providing bulk, it prevents the soil from being washed away. And as news-paper is so good at retaining moisture, you will save on watering.

Tall containers are handsome but in vulnerable or exposed positions, as at the top of a flight of steps, should be weighed down with stones in the base or secured with a loop of wire to a handrail or to bricks on the step above to prevent their being knocked or blown over.

Valuable height is also achieved by growing climbers up supports set into the containers. These come in all shapes, sizes, and materials — from the basic bean pole and bamboo tepee to the more sophisticated and elegant wooden or metal obelisk, sometimes topped with a little ball. Some have a disc at the base to ensure they stay upright, others flare out at the bottom so that they press against the side of the pot. Without such built-in stabilizers, supports need to be pushed into deep soil or anchored in crumpled chicken wire. Plants develop an inelegant list if their support is wobbly.

For vibrant color and a mass of foliage, grow sweet peas, passion-flowers

CASCADE OF COLOR Fuchsia and lobelia are well suited to hanging and wall-mounted baskets as they tumble over the sides, completely hiding the utilitarian container with a riot of blooms and foliage.

(*Passiflora*), or runner beans up a tepee made of bamboo stakes. A clematis climbing up an obelisk shows itself to advantage. You can create spectacular effects if you grow two clematis plants with different flowering times in the same container — a half-barrel is an ideal size. There is a profusion of choices for blooms from spring to early autumn. A good early-flowering clematis for a warm climate is *Clematis armandii* — a vigorous evergreen with scented white flowers that first appear in early spring. For later in the year, *C.* 'H.F. Young,' with its violet blooms, is free-flowering.

POTS ON WALLS AND CHAINS

Flat-backed pots, whether freestanding or wall-mounted, as well as semicircular and round hanging baskets are all ideal for framing windows, decorating walls, and dressing up areas that are too awkward for ordinary containers. They are easy to install, needing only rustproof hooks, and look dramatic in a short time.

Hanging baskets and wall-mounted pots are especially useful for balconies and roof gardens, where floor space is limited. In more conventional gardens, set hanging baskets high on the walls of a house or dangle them from an arbor or tree to add color. Change the baskets each season and take advantage of the plants appropriate for that time.

For a winter arrangement in mild climates, line a basket with sphagnum moss and fill it with plants such as Christmas

---

PLANTING A HANGING BASKET

WHERE SPACE for growing plants is limited or when your garden needs a visual boost, hanging baskets are the perfect solution for providing a feast of foliage and color. Do not worry about packing the plants in; they seem to flower better when massed together. A sheet of burlap makes a convenient lining for baskets, but you could also use sphagnum moss, a piece of sod, capillary matting, a plastic sheet, preformed bowls of wood pulp, or coconut fiber.

1. Set the basket on a firm surface, preferably at waist height. Line it with burlap and then with plastic. Jab six or seven drainage holes through the lining at the base, then fill the basket a quarter full with damp potting soil.

2. Make seven or eight slits for the first layer of trailing plants. Cut a corner from a plastic bag and fit a plant's foliage into it. Feed the point into a slit from inside and ease the plant in place; remove the bag. Complete the layer in the same way.

3. Fill the basket to halfway with soil. Make another set of slits and feed in the second layer of trailing plants. Press in soil mixed with slow-release fertilizer granules to 1 in (2.5 cm) below the rim to accommodate the top plants.

4. Plant a circle of bushy plants near the rim of the basket, then put upright plants in the center. Firm the soil well and water the basket thoroughly. Leave it to drain for an hour before hanging it up. Water it every day in hot, dry weather.

---

cactus (*Schlumbergera bridgesii*), flowering stems of heathers, and shoots of variegated eleagnus, pernettya, and holly.

Ferns, with their arching fronds, are unusual in summer hanging baskets, as are strawberries and alchemillas. In spring a basket crammed with small daffodils is an irresistible sight.

THE KNACK IN MOVING

One virtue of containers is that they are movable — but they are very heavy when filled with soil and plants. To avoid a strained back, you can buy a hand truck or use a homemade dolly for repositioning pots. There are also planter boxes available that are already equipped with casters. Another trick is to use containers with handles through which you could slip a couple of broomsticks. These would allow you and a helper to carry the pot like a sedan chair. You can bolt handles onto wooden containers, but they must be sturdy.

As a last resort, thick dowels make very effective rollers, while the problem

COOL ELEGANCE Shapely and stately calla lilies (*Zantedeschia aethiopica*) rise uncluttered from a perfect gray-green foil of trailing *Glechoma hederacea* 'Variegata.' The radiating circle of bricks set in the gravel around the base of the pot adds a subtle emphasis to the placement of the pot.

of steps can be overcome with the aid of a couple of planks and a sturdy rope. Wrap the rope around the container to prevent slipping, then place the planks on the steps and slide the container down them.

DEALING WITH DRAINAGE

Whatever container you choose, remember that handsome looks are not everything. It is crucial for containers to have enough drainage holes in the base. Plants usually recover remarkably well from drying out, but few survive the root rot that accompanies waterlogged soil.

Drainage holes are easy to make; all you need for terra-cotta or ceramic pots is a drill, set at a low speed, and a masonry bit. Make a circle of closely spaced small holes, then knock out the center with a sharp blow. For wooden containers, use a wood bit to drill the hole. The container should be raised off the ground on stones, bricks, or pot feet to make sure water can drain away.

Ceramic pots left outside all winter, especially if they have no drain holes and are full of soil, can crack if the soil freezes. You can help prevent cracking by wrapping wire tightly around the pots; plenty of foliage tumbling over the rim will conceal the wire very effectively. If the pots do break apart due to frost, you can still repair them if you have all the pieces (*see p. 132*).

HOW TO AVOID DAMAGE IN SEVERE WEATHER

Once you put your plants outside, you lose the ability to control their environment. Further, plants in containers do not enjoy the insulating effect of the soil in garden beds, so they are even more at the mercy of capricious elements than other plants are. The top growth is affected by drying winds, and the roots can be nipped by frost penetrating the containers' sides.

The savage effects of wind and cold, which frequently lead to a fatal freezing of the roots, can be countered by grouping containers tightly together in a sheltered spot and insulating them. The

thicker the insulation you can provide, the better for the plants.

The size of the container is also a factor: plants in smaller containers are at greater risk from the elements, as there is less soil volume to insulate the roots. To help protect small pots, you may have to insulate the containers from outside by wrapping them with burlap, plastic bubble wrap, or straw held between pieces of wire or plastic netting. Make sure the pots are raised slightly off the ground to permit drainage.

PROTECTION FOR POTS

If it is not possible to move the container to a garage or enclosed porch, there are other means of protection. Put insulation in before you fill the pot with soil — the soil pressure will keep the insulation in place — or protect pots from the outside.

🌣 Line large planting boxes with expanded polystyrene panels 1 in (2.5 cm) thick and cut to size; make drainage holes to correspond with those of the box. Line half-barrels with the thickest insulating material that will curve to fit.

🌣 Line small containers with a layer or two of bubble wrap.

🌣 Cover the container with a frame made of straw sandwiched between two layers of wire netting.

🌣 To protect tall, delicate shrubs, place a circle of twine-linked stakes around them and wrap with burlap.

🌣 Place small containers in a cold frame and sink them in sand, chopped leaves, or mulch. If the weather is especially cold, cover the frame with pieces of old carpet or bubble wrap, opening it up for ventilation when the temperature rises.

🌣 Place evergreen boughs around the plant and cover with chicken wire secured to the soil with wire loops to stop the fronds from blowing away.

🌣 Protect climbers, which obviously cannot be moved if they are scaling a wall, by draping the upper growth with burlap. Wrap plenty of insulation around the container and base of the plant and mulch well with shredded bark.

It is not only the cold that can wreak havoc with plants. Extreme heat can make them wilt through lack of moisture. To combat this, keep roots cool by covering the potting soil with gravel or sink the pots into gravel to conserve moisture.

The inanimate features in the garden are also in danger from frost and wind. The idea of decorating gardens with elaborate urns and pots developed in

SCULPTURAL SPLENDOR Large ceramic pieces such as this are costly but are worth the expense, as they make outstanding architectural focal points. Even when left unplanted, they catch the eye by rising from the surrounding plants and adding a feeling of weight and solidity.

southern Europe, where winter temperatures are normally a great deal warmer than in much of North America. Yet this has not prevented such garden ornaments from becoming favorite features in gardens throughout this country.

In the past, when garden ornaments were displayed only in estate gardens, there was no lack of staff to do outdoor work, and all the significant artifacts were moved inside from fall to spring.

It still makes sense to protect vulnerable and valuable pieces in the winter. You can move them into a garage or frost-free shed, or you can wrap them with burlap or plastic.

But the garden in winter should still give pleasure, and looking out at plastic-draped containers is no joy. Indeed, when most of the herbaceous plants and deciduous shrubs are in eclipse, the inanimate, architectural features become even more important in decorating the dormant garden.

A far better solution is to make sure that containers with permanent plantings are resistant to weather damage. And there are now pots aplenty that can withstand severe conditions.

Look for containers with frost-proof guarantees, which some now have. Terra-cotta is the most vulnerable material, with the palest clay pots being the weakest, as they are fired at the lowest temperature. So it is best to use terra-cotta solely for warm-weather displays. Fiberglass, stone, cast stone, and plastic are better choices if frost is prevalent in your area.

Containers allow you to be adventurous, take chances, and experiment in a way that is not possible with the more static elements of a garden. They also give the less patient the rare satisfaction of seeing their ideas translated instantly into reality. Containers can provide solutions to the most intractable problems and challenging sites, liven up a gloomy or barren spot, or alternatively provide welcome peace in the midst of abundant color. No garden would be complete without them.

REVIVING FROM DROUGHT

DURING THE SUMMER, containers often need watering daily, or even twice daily in the hottest weather. Unless you have installed an automatic watering system, this is quite a chore — and one that might be shirked if time is short — so it would not be surprising if you occasionally ended up with a dried-out container of drooping plants.

Even if the container cannot be moved, do not despair. Water it well, then heap moist gravel high around it and water the gravel frequently so that the constant evaporation surrounds the plants with moist air. Many wilted plants will revive remarkably quickly, and trimming off any damaged parts will encourage new growth to fill out the plant again.

The gravel looks attractive enough to be a permanent feature of the summer scene if you mound it skillfully. It conserves moisture particularly well when heaped around a cluster of pots, creating a microclimate for them.

ILLUSIONS
AND DISGUISES

Don't lose heart if your garden is marred by a clutter of garbage cans, intrusive utility poles, a propane-gas tank, or even the sight of your neighbor's motor home. Turn each problem into an asset with some ingenious design ideas and well-chosen plants. Sometimes it is more than a localized eyesore that needs disguising; but even if the whole garden is flawed by its awkward shape or ugly proportions, you can create skillful deceptions with dense borders, trellises dressed with trailing plants, and even mirrors. Seize the opportunity to make a path wind out of sight to illusory extra space and transform a gloomy spot into a secret corner that entices with its mystery.

SPECIAL FEATURE

Honeysuckle is fast growing and fragrant, and some varieties are evergreen, making it a beautiful ally in a campaign to conceal unattractive objects.

THE ART OF TRICKERY

P ART OF GARDENING'S enduring fascination, even for those who have made it their lifetime hobby, is that a garden is engaging on so many different levels. There is the joy of creating an attractive display through design and plant selection — a display that satisfies the eyes, ears, and nose. But on another level, there is the pleasure of tweaking the intellect with touches of humor, mystery, and surprise.

Whether individual elements are introduced as part of a more complex overall design or for the sheer fun of playing tricks on the unwary visitor, prolonging the enjoyment of a garden as it unfolds slowly is always worthwhile.

The magnificent landscape garden at Stourhead in Wiltshire is a perfect example of how to keep the visitor guessing. Set around a lake, it looks entirely natural but is in fact very carefully contrived, so that if the correct route is followed — counterclockwise around the lake — new views open up at particular points, some from high vantage points, others from low down at water level.

Though few people have room to create anything so grand, there is no need to reveal everything in a single glimpse. A measure of imaginative trickery benefits most gardens, no matter what their size, if only to disguise an unsightly garbage can.

CREATING AN ILLUSION

P ERHAPS ALL GARDENING is an illusion — the stamping of personal wishes and ideas on a plot of land and thinking that it is transformed. But such achievements are always transient, because it is never long before nature adapts them — and if left alone, restores the plot almost to its original state.

Since many gardens are smaller than their owners would like, any device that gives an illusion of greater space has much to recommend it and is worth incorporating into a garden design.

One of the first steps to take is to lower the surrounding boundaries, thus bringing more of the sky into the garden and making it feel less enclosed. But while open space overhead makes a garden feel bigger, things work differently at ground level.

CREATING GARDEN ROOMS

A garden seen in its entirety at a glance seems smaller than one where some parts are out of immediate view. Many people also like a feeling of intimacy in the garden, and dividing a single space into sections is a way of creating this feeling as well as increasing the apparent size. It allows more opportunities for employing a variety of themes in the garden and for providing areas — or garden "rooms" — for different uses. A number of smaller areas such as this can be defined by hedges, tall shrubs, or fences, perhaps made from decorative trelliswork lightly dressed with climbers.

Rooms can be furnished with seating pieces, which are usually placed against a wall or hedge, as people often prefer to sit with something solid at their backs.

THE PITFALLS OF PERSPECTIVE

The effects of perspective are to make distant objects appear smaller than those in the foreground and to make two parallel lines appear to draw closer together as they recede into the distance.

When considering any illusion that makes use of perspective, bear in mind that these "tricks" have a major disadvantage. They usually work in one direction only and must be planned carefully so that the illusion is seen from the main viewing area. A device that makes the garden appear longer, shorter, or even

TROPICAL OR TEMPERATE? A coat of light-colored paint, *Campsis* 'Madame Galen' clambering over the roof, and pots of geraniums, spiky agaves, and yucca cloak this garage with a sun-drenched character reminiscent of Mediterranean and other warm climates.

CREATING PRIVATE SPACE Outdoor "rooms," such as this one surrounded by a shapely boxwood hedge, are a way of adding a touch of mystery and a feeling of space in a garden. The enclosed room welcomes anyone who enters, through an opening in the hedge, into its calming seclusion.

twice the size from one angle is pointless if the illusion is destroyed when seen from, say, a favorite bench in the center.

When the illusion is good enough, it remains just as convincing after the trick is discovered to be just that. One way to avoid any disappointment is to ensure that the planting and design in the garden are sufficiently varied to hold the interest.

Planting to achieve an illusion may restrict the choice of plants, and particular favorites may not easily fit into the overall plan. But a little discipline in the basic structure is often good for the gardener who is in danger of turning a plot into a collection of plants rather than an area well designed for use and pleasure.

ALTERING PERSPECTIVE WITH LAWN SHAPES

The traditional treatment of a central lawn with beds running the length of the sides is the most practical way of giving the maximum play area for children. The beds are often too narrow to allow satisfying planting, however, and taller plants get buffeted as winds swirl over fences.

You can still keep the arrangement of beds, lawn, and paths so that they all run parallel and accentuate the length of the garden, but the path need not be solid. A series of slabs laid as stepping-stones in the center of the lawn and leading to the far end will draw the eye to the distance and will not interrupt the play area.

You can improve the beds even without widening them. Establish some taller bushes toward the front of the border instead of at the back. This creates more interest and gives shelter to smaller and more delicate plants beneath and behind them. When the children have grown up, the beds can be widened.

Changing the shape of the lawn is another option. Widen the borders but make the lawn narrower at the far end to increase the apparent length. But beware — regular slabs in the lawn, or a regular central path that does not narrow in the same way, spoil the effect.

A combination of stretching the view and creating compartments at the sides makes a long, narrow garden appear wider, while increasing the height of planting and making a path slim make a garden seem narrower.

Not everyone wants to lengthen the appearance of their garden, however. To lose the long, linear shape, divide the garden into distinct sections that have

ESTABLISHING A FOREGROUND

Put unusually large-leaved plants close to the garden's main viewing point to make the space beyond seem larger.

• Angelica tree (*Aralia elata*): huge dissected leaves and palm-like habit.

• Southern catalpa (*Catalpa bignonioides*): a large-leaved tree that is a manageable shrub if pruned hard.

• Giant dracena (*Cordyline australis*): long, spiky leaves on a tall trunk.

• Fig (*Ficus carica*): handsome in summer, and fruits well if pot-grown.

• *Mahonia japonica*: magnificent foliage with scented lemon flowers in winter.

• *Paulownia tomentosa*: large leaves if cut back hard in spring, or pretty blue flowers in spring if left to grow.

• *Yucca gloriosa*: the biggest of hardy yuccas, with spikes of creamy flowers.

• *Acanthus mollis*: huge curved leaves, with purple and white flower spikes.

• *Gunnera manicata*: colossal leaves on prickly stems, some above head height.

• New Zealand flax (*Phormium tenax*): long, sword-like evergreen leaves in a huge tuft and in a variety of colors.

their own identity, making the dividers run across the site. Paved areas with circular and curved shapes, and paths that cross the site diagonally, are also effective.

PLANTING TO ALTER THE SENSE OF SPACE

Some plants are naturally architectural and demand attention, while others fade into the background. Exploit these qualities to shorten or lengthen the garden.

🌢 To arrest the eye, plant cordylines, yuccas, and phormiums either close to the viewer or far away. When they are used in the middle distance, they destroy the impression of length.

🌢 Keep small-leaved plants such as box honeysuckle (*Lonicera nitida*) and privet unclipped when you want them as lesser features in a border; when clipped, their dense habit draws the eye and breaks up the border.

🌢 To emphasize length, place bold and large-leaved plants close to the viewing point, with a progression of smaller-leaved plants used as the borders recede.

🌢 Put exotic evergreens that have large, dramatic leaf shapes on a patio to draw you instantly to a sitting area and to give it a tropical feel. The rest of the garden, noticed more slowly, will seem larger.

🌢 To create a sense of distance, plants at the end of the garden should be airy and ethereal with tiny foliage. The fennels are ideal for this purpose, with diaphanous foliage that appears almost transparent.

🌢 Placing tall trees, and especially a row of dark green conifers, at the far end of the garden brings the garden end forward and seems to shorten the plot.

TOPIARY PERSPECTIVE

A less subtle, simpler use of perspective is to place clipped plants deliberately to punctuate the view. To achieve this, clip privet, boxwood, or yew or other conifers in the borders into symmetrical pyramids or cones. The height and width of the cones should be reduced as they recede into the distance — but reduced gradually, or the effect is curious and gets lost as you walk in the opposite direction.

Even in a small garden, clipped shapes are useful, especially if a plant is chosen that has a smaller "relative" for use in the distance. Boxwood is a good choice for this: plant common boxwood (*Buxus sempervirens*) in the foreground and the dwarf boxwood (*B. s.* 'Suffruticosa'), which has a smaller habit and leaves, in the distance. If you prefer, the boxwood

ALTERING PERSPECTIVE One way of increasing the impression of length in a rectangular plot is to introduce beds that narrow at the far end of the garden. A pathway of paving slabs of decreasing size reinforces the illusion.

SUGGESTING LARGER SIZE Clipped shapes in the border attract and hold the eye, making the viewer take longer to cover the area. Using small-leaved foliage plants at the garden's end makes it seem further away.

DECEPTIVELY EXPANSIVE The luxuriant planting in this generous border along the edge of the lawn suggests that it is a quiet corner in a large, spacious garden. But closer study shows that the boundary wall of the garden lies just behind the tall blue flower heads of *Campanula lactiflora*.

BARK MULCH

REDESIGNING A GARDEN from scratch is a costly undertaking, so it helps to spread the expense over several years.

Until you are ready to lay a permanent path, cheat with bark nuggets, which are easy to lay over a firm base of hard-packed soil. Use different sizes of nugget to create an illusion of distance, with larger nuggets near the house and smaller ones farther away. To enhance the look, narrow the path's far end a bit.

strong shades are sometimes too vivid. Misty gray-blues and pale blues are the ideal choice for the far end of the garden, especially if you are fortunate enough to be able to "borrow" the surrounding countryside as a backdrop, so the colors blend in with the horizon.

AN IMAGINATIVE TREATMENT FOR THE GARDEN'S END

Unless you have a pretty or dramatic view beyond the bottom of the garden, which it would be unthinkable to hide, you can choose how the garden should end. One solution is to pretend that it does not actually end at all, but that there is something beyond just out of sight.

This is most easily achieved by planting a dense, clipped hedge across the garden near the end with an arched opening through the center. In the short gap between this hedge and the actual end of the garden, run a path crossways to give the impression that there is more to come. The archway can frame some eye-catcher, perhaps a statue, a large urn, or a piece of sculpture set against the boundary. Behind the hedge, numerous essential but unsightly features — compost bins, potting shed, wheelbarrow, and the like — can be hidden, provided that they can also be easily reached.

The same deceit works as a divider in the garden at any stage along its length, perhaps to hide a play area or a playhouse. Alternatively, a hedge can frame an attractive fruit tree or vegetable bed, with less attractive beds tucked away to the sides.

Framing a view with an arch or a series of interrupted hedges is theatrical, giving the same impression as a stage set with scenery in the wings, and it has the same effect. The layered appearance convinces the viewer that there is some

can be container-grown and stand in terra-cotta pots in the border or on slabs set into the lawn to create a mini-avenue.

Apart from boxwood, there is a wide variety of plants that can be trained as standards, ranging from restrained evergreens to colorful fuchsias. You could use fuchsias in graduated heights in the summer months, then replace them during the winter with boxwood cones.

A SUBTLER FUNCTION OF COLOR

Every gardener is interested in color, but its effect in a garden landscape is not always appreciated. Any bright color that clamors for attention has the potential to destroy the overall effect, and quieter tones are often preferable throughout most of the garden.

Red is one of the potential problems. It is the color of danger and excitement, and all eyes are drawn to it. Even in vast gardens, red can distract from both a restful atmosphere and the perspective — when brilliantly colored rhododendrons, for example, are in bloom.

Since red seems to leap forward, it always shortens the perspective. Restrict it to the foreground where its warmth can be enjoyed without destroying any illusion. At dusk, red disappears before other colors, so having red flowers close allows them to be appreciated longer.

In complete contrast, white flowers glow at dusk. During the day, however, some gardeners find their pristine whiteness too severe in the garden. Like red, white should not be used at the far end of a view, except to shorten it. The many other flowers in creamy and lavender tints give the effect of whiteness without actually being so stark and icy.

Blue is a valuable color to use for suggesting distance, because it naturally recedes and disappears, although the

feature of interest "offstage," while simultaneously focusing the attention on center stage. In the garden, a statue or sculpture, an exceptional plant, or even a painted scene could be framed by an archway or a break in a hedge.

An Artful Trompe l'oeil

The term "trompe l'oeil" refers to a two-dimensional optical illusion that gives a false sense of depth. For gardeners, however, it often refers to a form of trellis known as treillage, which is made up of adjoining arches to suggest a colonnade or of concentric arches or rectangles that give the illusion of a tunnel. Set onto a wall or a fence, treillage is most effective at giving the impression of depth.

In most gardens, a trompe-l'oeil device works best when at least partially obscured by foliage and framed by a pair of upright matching plants. Formally trained plants such as conifers or bay laurels match the elegant character of trelliswork. Do not paint a newly acquired trellis stark white; the effect is usually better with a slightly understated shade such as sea green or dove gray, especially with ivy or some other climber obscuring the outer edges. Setting the trellis in shade enlists the help of soft lighting to enhance the illusion.

Place a pot of flowers in the window at the center of the trompe l'oeil tunnel or, if you have a talent for art, paint a rural scene. This borrows from the tradition of leaving gaps or windows in walls through which views of the surrounding countryside could be seen. Because these deceits work best at a distance, great skill as a painter is not necessary. Colors should be kept muted so that the view seems to be far in the distance.

In modern gardens, a rural landscape is not necessarily the most appropriate of views; add a touch of fantasy with a glimpse of the Eiffel Tower or the Statue of Liberty.

Tricks with Light and Shade

It is not necessary to incorporate a multitude of elaborate features into a garden to make awkward proportions or shady conditions seem better. Restraint is often a surer route to a successful design. An area of light and an area of shade, for example, can both create intriguing contrasts and bolster an illusion.

In regions without much sun, it is tempting to shun shade and treat it as a problem. But shade can be an effective

THEATRICAL TIPS Theater design has many ideas to offer the imaginative gardener. Here, clipped hedges of boxwood work like wings in a stage set, discreetly screening less attractive parts, such as a play area tucked away at the sides, while leading the eye to a beautiful focal point.

BRINGING LIGHT TO A DARK CORNER

DO NOT DESPAIR of improving a dingy corner of your garden that receives little light. Taking any one or all of these five simple steps can liven up the area, introducing flashes of lighter color that lift the mood and brighten the corner.

If you have an outdoor electrical line, train a spotlight on the holly for a glowing evening display.

Paint the walls a light, summery color — not white, because it is quite cold, but a sunny yellow, ochre, or buff.

Train the variegated ivy *Hedera helix* 'Goldheart' up a trellis fixed on one wall to introduce touches of lightness all year-round.

Add a mid-green circle to the light-colored wall and place a lollipop-shaped variegated holly (*Ilex* 'Silver Queen,' for example) against it.

Lighten the ground surface by flanking soft gray cobblestones or cream gravel with the silver-spotted woodland plant *Pulmonaria officinalis* (left) and evergreen variegated *Arabis ferdinandi-coburgi.*

A ROAD TO NOWHERE An archway is enticing to even the least curious garden stroller, implying sights unseen and further delights. But it can also work effectively as a screen to hide a wheelbarrow and the compost heap.

LUSH CONTRAST If your garden receives a restricted amount of sun, open up the area where it strikes and intensify the effect with a ground cover of light gravel. The plantings around then contribute a welcome lushness.

way to emphasize those areas of the garden that are in sun — the darkness of the one concentrating attention on the brightness of the other.

In many of the best gardens, shady tunnels of ancient yews lead visitors past hidden areas of the garden to another viewpoint, where an unexpectedly sunny scene opens up before them. On a smaller scale, you can grow tall hedges to make quite short corridors linking unrelated areas, with a statue or a blaze of color at the far end to act as a magnet. The ground beneath the hedge need not be wasted; you can plant it with shade-loving, ground-covering cyclamens, colchicums, bergenias, and ivy.

Shady areas are refreshingly cool on a hot day, especially when overhung by the gently moving branches of trees or by a pergola clothed with climbers. A well-planted pergola can be both fragrant and romantic. Some of the loveliest foliage

plants for it are grape vines; a mixture of edible and ornamental varieties gives a plentiful cover of green and purple foliage — and frequently bunches of fruits in just a few years. Twine some honeysuckle and jasmine among the vines for rich fragrance.

Shade allows you to add character and mystery to the garden. A rocky grotto can drip water into an echoing pool, which in the shade never becomes green with algae, and the imagination can run riot with romantic themes. This is the place for fanciful follies or for ancient-looking broken urns and statues half hidden by large foliage plants.

Frothy chervil or spring-flowering bulbs will transform a semi-screened corner into a delightful secret place, reached by a single path. In a spot that is too dark to plant with sun-seeking flowers, create a mass of springtime color with woodland bulbs and primroses. In summer the corner becomes the background for a planting of bright flowers, and a rustic trellis, each side of an arch, will support a lemon-colored climbing rose. The arch creates the illusion of a pathway leading to the secret woodland.

A tunnel designed as a straight line can lead directly into another section of the garden, which you glimpse from the tunnel's entrance. But you can create a private sun space for yourself: make the exit from the tunnel invisible from the entrance and open through its side onto a surprise area, bathed in afternoon sun and sheltered by rose-covered fences.

SKILLFUL USE OF MIRRORS

Mirrors are the adventurous gardener's great ally, but they have to be used with care to be effective. With proper placement a mirror seems to extend the garden in a number of directions, although the view above the mirror and the supporting structure must be masked or the magic is broken.

🌢 Large mirrors are not necessary and are more difficult to mount than smaller ones, which are just as effective.

🌢 Frame the mirror with evergreen climbers such as ivy and *Akebia quinata*.

🌢 Ensure that the mirror is perfectly upright if you wish to reflect a level

---

EXTENDING A SMALL GARDEN VIEW

There is one way to extend a garden without buying an extra plot of land. A carefully placed mirror is the key, drawing the eye to a fresh view that is nothing but illusion.

ONE OF THE MOST ATTRACTIVE aspects of using illusion in the garden is that it can be employed in all manner of subtle ways to give an impression of space, of a larger expanse than is in fact there.

Careful selection and placement of plants helps draw the eye away from the foreground, on toward the undiscovered delights at the garden's end. Pots of bold foliage, in this case the expansive *Trachycarpus fortunei* and slightly taller *Cordyline australis*, serve a double purpose, highlighting the start of a garden path while simultaneously hiding what lies beyond.

The evergreens in the planting scheme will ensure that the intrigue of a curved path such as this is not lost in the off-season. The path still invites the intrepid visitor to investigate, even when there is a crisp layer of frost on the lawn.

BEYOND THE FENCE

In the far corner, a delicate trelliswork arch frames what appears to be the start of yet another path. In the distance is an elegant piece of garden statuary, but the true position of the stone figure is elsewhere, as anyone who tries to reach it quickly finds out.

The statue is behind the evergreen *Photinia* 'Red Robin' on the left side of the garden and is in fact reached by following the mysterious curved path to its end. A closer look at the original glimpse of the statue reveals that it is actually a reflection, caught in a mirror that is artfully framed by the trellis. During the summer months, climbers swath the trellis and disguise the mirror even further.

A small patch of cobblestones at the foot of the mirror appears larger when added to its reflection. It is enough to stop anyone from walking into the glass.

CUSHIONS FOR A MIRROR

IF YOU PLAN to use a mirror in your garden, it is important to mount it securely. Insert rubber grommets into the corner holes of the mirror; then screw it into holes in the wall that have been drilled and fitted with anchors. The grommets cushion the mirror and prevent it from cracking.

Have a glazier drill holes in the corners of the mirror or buy one predrilled. Most drilled mirrors come with rubber grommets and with mirrored screw covers to hide the fasteners.

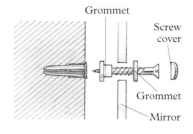

Grommet

Screw cover

Grommet

Mirror

Tall shrubs hide the elusive stone maiden

1. *Sarcococca hookeriana* var. *digyna*
2. *Euphorbia characias*
3. *Skimmia japonica* subsp. *reevesiana*
4. *Camellia* 'Donation'
5. *Photinia* × *fraseri* 'Red Robin'
6. Higan cherry (*Prunus* × *subhirtella* 'Autumnalis')

A mirror arch extends the garden view

A curving path adds tempting mystery

7. *Miscanthus* 'Silver Feather'
8. Japanese cherry (*Prunus* 'Amanogawa')
9. Windmill palm (*Trachycarpus fortunei*)
10. Giant dracena (*Cordyline australis*)
11. Daffodils (*Narcissus*)

12. Peach (*Prunus persica*)
13. *Coronilla valentina* subsp. *glauca*
14. *Rubus idaeus* 'Aureus'
15. *Viburnum × bodnantense* 'Deben'
16. New Zealand flax (*Phormium tenax*)
17. *Heuchera* 'Palace Purple'
18. *Fatsia japonica*

garden; otherwise it gives the impression of a slope up or down.

❧ It is rarely necessary to bring the mirror down to ground level, except when a semicircular pond is set against a mirror to give the illusion of a complete circle of water.

❧ Never position a mirror where you approach it head on. It is best at an angle of 45° so that the illusion holds until you have almost reached the mirror.

❧ Set a mirror at the end of a pergola at an angle and frame it with plants. That way, it reflects a part of the garden to the right or left and makes it appear to be beyond the mirror.

❧ A small mirror fitted in the center of a trompe l'oeil wall feature is very effective when the angle of approach is right. Screen the mirror from view with plants until your path reaches the spot where the mirror shows an open scene, apparently beyond the wall.

❧ Use small mirrors to reflect light from sunny parts of the garden into a shady corner. In a shady part of a patio, bounce shafts of light onto the floor, a pool, or a fountain by mounting mirrors high up on a wall.

❧ Fragments of mirror set into a wall are effective at night when they reflect and so double the light from candles or torches.

It is best to use tempered mirror glass in the garden, rather than just an ordinary mirror intended for indoor use. To extend the life of an outdoor mirror, test a small area of the silvered back with varnish, then varnish the rest. The mirror must be attached to a firm surface, such as a wall or a piece of seasoned wood. Clean the mirror regularly or the effect will be spoiled by rain, plant debris, or soil splashed on the surface.

CREATING SPACE
WITH A CHANGE OF LEVELS

Another way of making a garden seem more spacious than it is in reality is by introducing steps leading to a sunken garden surrounded by hedges. Even a couple of steps up or down clearly separate one area from another and make it easier to give each part a convincingly different character. Having distinct sections increases the feeling of space.

Low retaining walls divide areas even more strongly, and if the walls are double they can hold soil and serve as raised beds. If your garden has existing walls you find unattractive, disguise them with climbers. Rugged alpine plants such as

CONFUSING PATHWAYS This ingenious use of a mirror is barely perceptible, a small arc of frame being the only giveaway that there is not really a long path or a doorway at its end. To create this effect, the mirror starts from ground level and nothing is set in front of it to break the reflection.

THROUGH THE KEYHOLE A small, carefully placed mirror arch introduces a sliver of bright light to this heavily planted corner, engaging the viewer with a false "view" before the illusion is slowly discovered.

aubrietia, arabis, and cerastium dress up loosely constructed dry-stone walls in summer, and low wall shrubs, such as *Cotoneaster horizontalis* and *Chaenomeles japonica*, add winter interest.

Climbers such as everlasting pea (*Lathyrus latifolius*) and the lower-growing clematis — for example, varieties of *Clematis alpina* and *C. macropetala* — provide good cover where it is difficult to plant in the wall. Attach wide-mesh chicken wire or plastic netting over the top of the wall to encourage climbers.

In a garden with a natural slope there is a change of level, but not one that adds apparent space. The slope foreshortens the view and also reveals the whole garden at a glance, which shrinks it. One solution is to make a series of terraced areas and create a hedge or screen along the lower side of one of them. This hides the lower garden, and an opening near

CHANGING LEVELS Introducing a change of level is often a good way of expanding a small garden. No more than a couple of steps are needed to give the feeling of a journey of discovery, and clever planting that hides one section of the garden from another adds to the overall effect.

one end of the screen leads you into a different area. Such a screen also provides an effective backdrop for plants when they are seen from below.

PLANTING ILLUSIONS

Viewed from the upper levels of the garden, an area that has been divided up by changes in level may actually appear smaller. Much depends on the planting, however. The height and spread of the plants, and the size of their foliage, can

have a dramatic effect on how big the garden seems. Tall hedges around its borders make a garden feel claustrophobic, and a small garden with a large specimen tree in the center of its lawn is dominated by the one plant.

To introduce a feeling of space, avoid large-leaved plants and set out several slow-growing bushes or trees of reasonable size at the boundaries. This way, they will not block off too much light from the center of the garden. One good

choice is Mount Etna broom (*Genista aetnensis*) — its green branches are nearly leafless and cast little shade, and its habit is semi-weeping when the plant is young.

Plants with a light and airy appearance also give a sense of space, as do small plants that, when used in groups, do not create a fussy, untidy appearance.

USING PATHS AND OPENINGS FOR A SENSE OF MYSTERY

A curving path around a garden bed always entices, and few people can resist following one, especially if the plants in the bed are tall enough to hide the destination. When the starting point of the path is marked with an arch of foliage or framed with conifers, the journey is all the more irresistible. Having to pass through a simple arch adds to the path's mystery and effectively divides one area of the garden from another.

The arch need not be elaborate and may simply be a group of carefully chosen shrubs. The unusual habit of bamboos, which are narrow at the base and bushy at the top, makes them form natural arches. And their small leaves make them ideal for planting in the distance. If their base needs filling out, aucubas and honeysuckles can tolerate the shade and dry soil that usually exist around bamboo roots.

Although paths are essentially practical, they can contribute to illusions if artfully planned. Paths look longer if their

THE ALLURE OF CURVES A very gently curved path is best for suggesting distant areas of garden that are as yet unseen. A sudden bend, on the other hand, can appear to be nothing more than a disappointing dead end.

COVERING A CLUMSY WALL A change of levels creates space but can be irritating rather than helpful when the structure is unattractive. To cover an unsightly low wall, fill the cracks and crevices with rock plants or disguise its overall shape with distractingly distinctive foliage plants.

PLANTING TO DISGUISE The neat boxwood edges to this curved path seem to propel the visitor along the route, while tall plants in the border obscure what lies around the next corner and so prolong the sense of discovery.

texture is varied — and may slow you down, which makes them feel even longer. Slabs set in gravel or pebbles in concrete, for instance, make the eye travel along the pathway more slowly.

You can use a path to create a visual diversion. A path of stepping-stones set in grass and curving away to the left draws the eye along it and helps an ugly object on the right to go unnoticed, especially if it is partially covered by unobtrusive plants with medium-sized leaves.

ILLUSORY SOUND AND SCENT

If illusion can fool the eyes, other senses, such as hearing, can be misled. A garden is usually regarded as a peaceful sanctuary, a place to relax and entertain. But sound does not travel in straight lines, and even the most solid wall cannot give protection from noisy neighbors.

An impression of serenity is created by introducing peaceful sounds to the garden. The most obvious of these is the sound of running water, although wind-chimes stirred by the breeze, the cooing of doves, or the lilt of birdsong also contribute a mellow touch.

Nothing stirs the emotions like scent. Many strongly fragrant plants have small flowers that are easily worked into elaborate planting plans, while dramatic plants with heavy perfume, especially those that release their scent at night, help to create an air of tropical lushness.

ON TO THE UNKNOWN A canopy of trees and tall flowering shrubs enclose this path, giving it an appealing air of mystery. The unswept nature of the path, and the way the plants billow over its edges, add to the feeling that you are discovering the way to a rarely visited secret garden.

CAMOUFLAGING DRAINAGE

Drains are necessary, but are rarely as attractive as they are practical. Help is at hand, however, with a number of ingenious aids to hide unsightly fixtures.

DRAIN COVERS
Shaped troughs that hold several pots — here, of aubrietia and pansies — can be used to soften the junction of a downspout with the drain. They are available from garden centers, or a metal fabricator can make one to order.

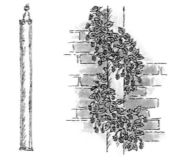

PLANT BAGS
Long, narrow soil-filled growing bags are easily made from black plastic sheets. Once the bags are wound around the pipe, they can be planted through slits in the sides with specimens of your choice, in this case wild strawberries.

TRELLIS SCREEN
Make a cover for a drainpipe with two lengths of trellis 9 in (23 cm) wide. Use wire to join them at the front and behind the pipe. Train *Tropaeolum speciosum*, ivy, or some other climber up the screen.

DOWNSPOUT POT HOLDERS
Adjustable metal or plastic pot holders that clip onto drainpipes of any size are often available at garden centers or can be assembled from pipe clamps. Plant the pots with trailing evergreen ivy for shape and basket-of-gold for color.

INVISIBLE UTILITY BOX COVERS
Utility box covers are hard to disguise, but it is possible to buy shaped fiberglass covers to hold either paving stones — if they are to be inserted in driveways — or sections of sod. The covers are hard to spot and can be removed whenever necessary.

DISGUISES FOR EYESORES

GREAT GARDEN PLANNERS of the past "borrowed" the surrounding landscape, incorporating it into their designs so that the owner's land seemed to extend to the horizon. This was achieved by inserting gaps in surrounding woodland, by building unobtrusive boundaries such as sunken barriers, and with major earth-moving projects that opened new vistas.

As today's gardens are generally small, it is more common now to attempt to block out the surrounding views and next-door neighbors. Even so, a garden that is completely surrounded by tall fences can make you feel barricaded into your yard.

SCREENING UNWELCOME VIEWS OUTSIDE THE GARDEN

When screening an unpleasant outside view, or trying to gain privacy from prying eyes, many people erect a board fence — and then try to cover up its bare expanses. This is not always easy, since many fences are not strong enough to support the weight of heavy climbing plants. The fact that the climbers are growing on only one side of the fence makes a weak fence even more unstable.

One alternative is to erect a tall, strong fence of steel posts with chain-link mesh between them. It looks uninspiring in the early stages, but provides real support for plants and allows light and air to reach them on all sides.

Hardy and reliable year-round cover is vital in such a situation, so choose a mixture of evergreens — including some with flowers and berries to add color. Ivy, evergreen honeysuckle, and clematis can be mixed with roses, summer or winter jasmine, everlasting pea (*Lathyrus latifolius*), and the self-supporting pyracantha. The cranesbill geranium *Geranium procurrens* is not usually a climber, but it will thread its way through other plants whenever it gets the opportunity.

VANISHING UTILITY POLES

A utility pole is a common eyesore, and the usual solution to dealing with one is to plant a tall conifer in front of it. Often, however, this simply emphasizes that there is something tall behind, especially if the top of the pole is visible above the plant. It is more effective to ignore the

SOFTENING SOLID SHAPES Oil tanks can be hard to disguise, but are more easily "lost" if painted a neutral color. Striking foliage plants may soften the contours more effectively than will shape-hugging climbers.

pole and place something eye-catching nearby to draw attention away from the previously dominant feature.

With careful design, similar unsightly objects at the edge of a view are upstaged by something attractive and become less obvious. Elegant pieces of topiary, or an obelisk or arbor swathed with climbers, are permanent distractions.

Another possibility is to make a negative feature into a positive one by planting an ivy or other fast-growing climber up a pole. This is not a possibility with utility poles, because they require regular inspection and maintenance. But this is the sort of trick that could be used with a similarly shaped eyesore.

HIDING CANS AND TANKS

An eyesore that nearly everybody has to deal with is the garbage can. Gardeners usually have compost bins too, but these pose less of a problem; they are usually set at the far end of the garden where

CAPTURING THE INTEREST A successful way of pulling the attention away from unsightly garbage cans is to place a bold plant nearby. Here, a light-colored ground cover of gravel and the ribbed, blue-green leaves of *Hosta sieboldiana* var. *elegans* deter the eye from straying behind.

MASKING A GREENHOUSE A trellis facade breaks up the substantial outline of a greenhouse. In winter, when it is not covered in foliage, the trellis allows a significant amount of light to reach the plants in the greenhouse. In the summer, when the sun is brighter, it supports climbing annuals.

MOVABLE HEDGE

IF YOU HAVE garbage cans on a hard surface, plant a movable hedge. A wooden trough at least 15 in (38 cm) wide and deep and filled with heavy potting soil is suitable for a conifer or beech hedge.

Beech hedges that mix green and copper colors are particularly pretty. Clip the sides once a year, in late summer, to promote bushiness. Once the hedge reaches about 4 ft (1.2 m) or the desired height, clip the top as well.

follow the contours of a solid object. An unattractive shape that you cover with climbers is still an unlovely shape if that's all you do. But add shrubs clipped into blocks around it, and together they make a sort of Cubist sculpture.

Many an unaesthetic object is in a prominent place because it needs to be accessible. Screen the thing with decorative trelliswork, with a climber as cover. If you decide to grow climbers over the object itself, an undercovering of netting is essential. When access is needed, or the object needs maintenance, such as painting, the netting can be pulled back easily, leaving the plants undamaged.

Once in place, netting provides good support for most climbers. But make sure you consider the ultimate heights of the plants. They can quickly become a nuisance if they roam too vigorously over the top of the supporting structure.

UTILITY BOX COVERS

The art of disguise is a difficult one. Great restraint is needed, or the disguise itself becomes so artful that it attracts the eye, actually drawing attention to the object you want to hide. This is sometimes a drawback of devices that are sold to hide eyesores. The standard utility box cover found in many yards and lawns is

they can be screened from view with fencing or plants. You could build an enclosure around the cans, but a structure may call even more attention to them. Take a leaf from nature's book instead. The stripes of a zebra break up its outline, making it difficult to recognize, especially in shifting grass. It is not actually hidden, but it is hard to see.

The same principle works in the garden: plants and screens can break up the outline of an unsightly object. Evergreens are the best choice for screening

material, because their foliage is effective camouflage throughout the year.

A screen of open-textured evergreens of various heights works well. Ferns and hebes are discreet, and the grass *Miscanthus sinensis* keeps its shape in winter and quickly puts up new growth after being cut back in spring. *Brachyglottis* 'Sunshine' has loose growth and loves the sun, while *Mahonia japonica* is upright in its growth and tolerant of shade and wind.

Climbers can be great disguisers, but they will give the game away if they

TO THE RESCUE

COVERING UP A TREE STUMP

IF IT IS TOO DESTRUCTIVE to remove the stump of a dead tree — perhaps because favorite plants are growing around it — smother it with fast-growing annuals such as nasturtiums or dwarf sweet peas.

Another solution is to leave a knee-high stump, drill out the center, and plant it. But keep in mind that plants grown in such a "container" will be less vigorous than those in the ground.

hardly a thing of beauty, yet it has to be lived with. It does not look too unpleasant in the back corner of a yard, but in a front lawn, it spoils the view. A common solution is to place plants on the cover, making a feature in itself. But does such treatment really disguise the cover?

The answer must often be no, because the tub of flowers is awkwardly placed, thanks to the position of the utility cover. One solution that works quite well, though, is to pave the surrounding surface with gravel or slabs; thus it becomes an island — a deliberate feature.

Where the cover is not too far from the edge of a lawn, extend a flower bed to engulf the offending object. Plant periwinkles for ground cover, along with prostrate *Cotoneaster dammeri* and an ornamental bramble such as the nonfruiting pink-flowered *Rubus ulmifolius* 'Bellidiflorus,' both of which will send out long shoots. When the time comes to open the cover, peg back the plants or, if necessary, cut them back. They will soon recover.

BLOCKING SIGHT, NOT LIGHT

One of the most difficult garden features to screen effectively is a greenhouse, because it is essential that light reach it at all times, especially in the winter when the

SUMMER SCREENING Make the best use of plants that overwinter in the greenhouse by bringing them outside in late spring and arranging them to hide an unattractive structure. As the sun sinks lower in the sky toward summer's end, return them to their place of warmth and let in more light.

sun is low in the sky. The problem does not arise, of course, if you choose a greenhouse that is attractive in itself, with shapely windows and an elegant frame, rather than one held together with a web of utilitarian struts and metal frames.

Even when you take over a garden with an unattractive greenhouse, there are ways to lessen its impact.

❧ A tall summer screen of herbaceous plants in a flower bed will cover the sides but rarely the roof. *Rudbeckia laciniata*, *Macleaya microcarpa*, *Helenium autumnale*, and perennial sunflower (*Helianthus decapetalus*) are all suitable.

❧ Tall plants in pots, such as standard fuchsias, which winter inside, earn their keep by covering the sides in summer.

❧ In summer, cover a trellis barrier with annual climbers such as sweet peas and morning glory to give a complete screen. Ornamental, painted trelliswork fitted to the greenhouse itself provides effective shading in summer.

❧ A temporary screen of stakes covered

with runner beans is especially effective when combined with a few flowers, such as climbing nasturtiums, morning glory, or black-eyed Susan vine.

❧ An informal planting of trees and shrubs such as fatsia, broom, lilac, and mock orange (*Philadelphus*) provides an effective screen. You can incorporate your favorite plants.

MAKING FANCIFUL FEATURES FROM SHEDS

Disguise need not always be a low-key operation. Putting up a bold front sometimes creates the most convincing appearance of genuine beauty, so that few observers ever notice the plainness of the features beneath.

A lean-to greenhouse, for example, is a workaday, practical place to grow plants, enjoy winter sunshine, and trap precious warmth. But why not make it a visual asset as well? When a lean-to greenhouse is elaborately framed and equipped with graceful wheeled carts to

IMPROVING DARK CORNERS Overhanging trees can create a dark, dank corner in the garden that is hard to plant. To counter this, construct an archway to trick the viewer into thinking it leads somewhere, and plant light, bright colors in the foreground. The dark corner fades away.

serve as plant stands, it becomes a conservatory and is then proudly displayed to the world.

If you have a positive approach, you can turn a utilitarian shed into almost anything you want. All you need to transform it are a little wood, some effort, and a liberal amount of imagination.

❦ With pierced, wavy eaves and shutters, and some pots of geraniums, it becomes a chalet.

❦ A turret on the roof and pointed arches at the windows and door make it a Gothic lodge.

❦ Create a grotto with a crenellated roofline, slit windows peering through ivy, a deep porch housing a trickling water feature, a grotesque wall mask, and moss-covered rocks flanked by ferns.

❦ Painted classical columns and a portico around the door make it a temple. Add bay laurel standards or conifer cones for greenery of equal formality.

❦ Give the shed a Chinese look, with a pagoda-style gable and a coat of bright red paint.

❦ Paint the shed white and install black beams on the outside to give it the look of a Tudor-style cottage.

❦ If there are young children in the family, paint the shed in candy colors and add wooden "gingerbread" trim to make it a fairy-tale cottage.

❦ Face the sides of the shed with split poles, and grow dwarf pines around it, for a log-cabin look.

GUILE WITH PAINT

Color is an essential element of disguise, and paint in the garden is a great asset, though it may take some experimenting to get just the right effect. Because paint has to be renewed regularly, and can be painted over almost immediately if a mistake is made, any indiscretions or unsuccessful experiments are not permanent.

Objects in the garden are often painted brown, as though that makes them more attractive or more natural and therefore less obvious. But, in fact, very few items in the garden are brown; even the soil and tree trunks have tints of gray or red.

The other temptation is to paint them green, but there are innumerable shades to choose from when it comes to green. Caution is also in order when choosing the tone you will use for painting a solid shape, since little natural greenery has such a rigid shape.

While green can be suitable in some cases, it is always better to avoid bright green and choose a dull, mossy shade, a blue-green, or a subtle, dark gray-green. Place plants around it that have interesting foliage texture so that the immutable object acts as a foil for the plants.

COLOR DISGUISE IN SHADE

When the object to be hidden is in a dim corner of the garden, perhaps set against a somber background and overhung by trees, a dark paint color makes it disappear; black or deep green work best.

The surrounding plantings must be able to tolerate low light levels without becoming sparse or leggy. Look for such bold-leaved shade-lovers as fatsia, ferns, and bergenias, along with the more delicate privet and skimmia.

The evergreen species of euonymus are available in bright variegated forms. If the front of the bed is a bit sunnier, euonymus will mix well with primulas, yellow-flowered St.-John's-wort (*Hypericum calycinum*), lilies, and white-flowered *Trillium grandiflorum.*

Avoid the temptation to position a tall variegated or white-flowered plant against any object you want to hide,

To disguise a large object in a shady part of the garden, paint it black or a deep green to make it disappear, then use it as a backdrop for colorful plants placed well forward in the light.

BEST PLANTS

LEAFY DISGUISERS

Whatever the season, there are plants whose eager growth covers an eyesore.

• *Euonymus fortunei* 'Emerald 'n' Gold': yellow and green leaves form excellent wall or ground cover all year.

• *Cotoneaster horizontalis*: small-leaved with pink flowers, copious red berries, and a herringbone growth pattern.

• Winter jasmine (*Jasminum nudiflorum*): good climber with yellow flowers emerging before the leaves.

• Boston ivy (*Parthenocissus tricuspidata*): a vigorous plant that provides excellent extensive leaf cover.

• *Akebia quinata*: a small-leaved twining evergreen with small, deep-purple, scented flowers in spring.

• Tree poppy (*Romneya coulteri*): fast-spreading, bluish-leaved, with large, white, poppy-like summer flowers.

• *Humulus japonicus* 'Variegatus': fast-growing annual with white markings.

• Plume poppy (*Macleaya cordata*): tall, herbaceous plant with large leaves.

• Persian ivy (*Hedera colchica*): huge-leaved, glossy evergreen that will swarm anywhere.

---

because the result is to draw attention to it and make it more obvious. White flowers are beautiful in any garden, but pure white is too much of a contrast against dark green when the idea is to blend an object into the shadows. Employ subtlety, and avoid clashes and contrasts of color that demand notice.

COLOR DISGUISE IN LIGHT PLACES

Matching the colors of a planting scheme to the color of an object that needs to be disguised is a very effective way of making the two work as a harmonious whole in a bright area.

To achieve this sense of harmony, first choose the type of plants to go around the object as a key for the color theme. This theme suggests what color to paint the object in full sun. Black is rarely the answer, as it is the most difficult color to hide in bright light.

One effective scheme is to plant a collection of conifers around the object, choosing mainly golden-leaved varieties. Painting the object a shade of earthy ochre or a neutral yellow that is duller than the conifers helps it to recede gently into the background. It is the brightly colored conifers that hold the eye.

Similarly, a steely blue color for the object would be effective when paired with gray-leaved lavender, gray conifers, and bluish *Hosta sieboldiana* 'Elegans.'

Light colors, especially misty blues and lavenders, make objects fade into the distance. These colors are especially effective in winter, when the cold, thin light matches their pale tone.

If the object to be hidden is large — a shed, for example — make it work as scenery. Bands of bronze and gold shades painted around the base of the object, with blue above, make a background for the sun-loving, silver-leaved *Santolina chamaecyparissus*, *Brachyglottis* 'Sunshine,' *Artemisia schmidtiana*, and *Stachys byzantina*. Frame the sides of the shed with *Yucca gloriosa* and tall grasses set in silver-gray gravel.

With imaginative use of paint, screening, plants, and layout, you can improve the most unpromising scene, concealing its bad points, enhancing its virtues, and increasing your pleasure in the garden.

REFLECTING SUNLIGHT Use variegated and yellow ivies to give a sunny covering to an inexpensive wire-netting fence. Behind it you can discreetly hide a garbage can, compost bin, or any other unattractive objects.

BEAUTY WITH A PRACTICAL PURPOSE

GARDENS CAN BE BOUNTIFUL as well as beautiful. Ornamental fruits and vegetables will look handsome in the borders and be delicious to eat, while herbs that flavor your food brighten the garden as they grow. Make some space in the garden for flowers and foliage that not only look beautiful out-of-doors but add equally to arrangements indoors, whether fresh or dried. And remember that your perfumed plants can be blended into a potpourri to bring the garden's freshness into the house. With a little planning and know-how you can double the pleasure from your garden.

SPECIAL FEATURE

*Adaptable pansies mirror the deep purple foliage of beets,
making a pretty edging for a vegetable plot.*

LETTUCE AND LAVENDER In this garden, patterned brick paths run between neat boxwood-edged beds that combine vegetables, flowers, fruits, and herbs in a subtle blend of colors .

COMBINING
USE AND BEAUTY

◆

WITH SOME FRESH IDEAS, the right plant varieties, and careful planning, it is easy to combine a beautiful garden with a productive one, and all without wedding yourself to the hard labor of the traditional type of vegetable garden. There are no rules about the shapes of the beds or about plant combinations to curb your imagination. In fact the only restraints are physical — what the fruits, flowers, and vegetables require in terms of light, space, and soil.

The key to such gardening satisfaction is to abandon the utilitarian idea of sowing a crop in a square plot, watching it mature, and then harvesting it. There is no reason why food crops cannot be grown alongside flowers, although in the flower bed they must, like flowers, perform attractively for an extended period to justify their prominent position.

There is plenty of decorative potential in food crops if you look at them with a fresh eye. What could be more effective than an edging of frilled lettuce to set off a colorful flower bed? Or perhaps a towering silvery-gray globe artichoke plant as a central feature?

You can grow fruits, vegetables, and herbs in containers or train them into interesting shapes to make a feature out of them. Espalier pears on a wall for a bumper crop from a small area, or train apples as "living fences" for a space-saving display.

FLOWERS FOR THE HOUSE

Flower arranging is a passion with many people — sometimes to such a degree that the garden's main role is as a resource for arrangements. The passion can be an expensive one if all the materials have to be bought, but fortunately an average garden can provide most of what is needed. A little prudent planning ensures that raiding the beds for flowers to arrange indoors does not spoil the garden's appearance. You can grow a varied supply of desirable foliage in place of a hedge and find plenty of choice items for display in an informal bed of mingled flowers, shrubs, and vegetables.

The garden is not just a source of fresh materials. You can preserve flowers and leaves for winter arrangements or capture their essence in potpourri.

FRUITS AND VEGETABLES

I N PLANNING a useful garden, concentrate on crops that are luxury items, either difficult to buy or of poor quality in stores. It is best to avoid such staples as common potatoes; these are easy to buy, and they are greedy for garden space.

The current fashion for combining food plants and ornamental ones owes something to the old cottage-garden miscellany of vegetables and flowers, and a good deal more to the French tradition of a formal ornamental vegetable garden. Indeed, it is the French word *potager*, meaning "kitchen garden," that is generally used now for such vegetable gardens.

Place your potager in full sun, as most vegetables cannot tolerate shade. Prepare the soil well, incorporating compost or rotted manure, and keep the beds liberally mulched. Ensure a steady supply of vegetables, and avoid having to harvest

ORDERLY ABUNDANCE Vegetables, flowers, and fruit trees flourish within this precise, symmetrical design. Its beauty stems from the lush profusion of the plants and the clipped neatness of the harmonious layout.

all the crops at once, by planting in succession. For example, you can sow leaf lettuces every two to three weeks, from as soon as the soil can be worked until the weather turns warm; one crop will be germinating just as another is emerging and another is ready for harvesting.

DESIGNS FOR POTAGERS

A potager usually consists of a number of beds arranged in a geometric pattern — most often rectangular, although it can

take the form of a diamond or even have triangular beds radiating from a central point. The beds are edged with wood, brick, or stone and are frequently raised, with narrow paths of stone, brick, grass, or even stepping-stones in gravel between them.

The simplest design is a square divided into quarters, with a cross-shaped path. In large gardens there is room for a more elaborate plan, with more beds and an attractive though space-consuming edging

LOOKING GOOD ENOUGH TO EAT The visual pleasure of mingled vegetables, flowers, and herbs is apparent here, where mauve chive flowers are fronted by lettuce seedlings interspersed with feathery fennel foliage — and all these are in turn bordered by colorful pansies and frilly rue.

ORNAMENTAL CABBAGES With their frilly leaves veined or splotched with pink, red, purple, or white, ornamental cabbages and kales add richness to a planting scheme. Harvest through autumn and winter.

DECORATIVE CROPS A well-composed planting with varied leaf tone, shape, and height makes rows of strawberries, parsley, onions, lettuces, and cabbages a pleasure to look at — even before the bonus of food for the table.

of clipped dwarf boxwood, lavender, or santolina. In a small garden define the beds with a narrow hedge of ivy trained over a push-in plastic-coated-wire fence.

Try to arrange the beds so that none is more than 5 ft (1.5 m) wide. This allows you to work from the edge of the bed without stepping on the soil and compacting it. All the soil remains usable, and a surprisingly large amount of food is harvested from a small area.

The juxtaposition of colors, textures, and shapes — such as tall, fluffy fennel, low, broad-leaved lettuce, and silvery cabbage — contributes to the beauty of the potager, yet a great deal of its attractiveness lies in the overall design.

MAKING THE RIGHT CHOICES

The choice of vegetables is a matter of personal taste, but where space is short, stick to good producers with ornamental value. Runner beans are high performers that look as good as they taste, and red cabbages are certainly not out of place in the flower bed. Chives and thyme make a pretty edging to a garden path and are equally decorative for planting under rose standards in the border.

Groups of vivid ruby chard and beets, whose green tops are crisscrossed with strong red veins, make striking focal points. Even the brussels sprout has an ornamental version — 'Rubin,' which besides glowing with crimson-red leaves has a delicious nutty flavor.

It is best to exclude such a mainstay as peas — except for the edible-podded types, which are easy to grow, produce over a long period, and are delicious cooked or raw. If you want to grow potatoes, raise a few new potatoes early, under row covers, or grow the unusual knobby salad potato 'Pink Fir Apple,' which is rarely found in stores.

WAYS TO ADD HEIGHT

Potagers look somewhat flat unless you include plants that provide vertical points of interest. Add height and decorative value with a tepee smothered in runner

TRAIN A RED CURRANT STANDARD

WHEN IT IS LADEN with its glistening red chains of ripe fruits, a red currant bush is the ideal combination of beauty and utility. It is often grown as a low bush or as one of a row of cordons, but it is shown off to perfection when trained as a standard in either a potager or a flower bed so that its head is held above the surrounding plants. It needs no more care than other styles of bush.

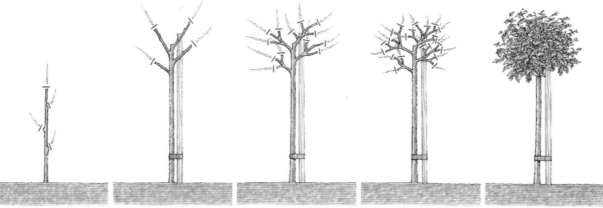

I. Plant a vigorous one-year-old rooted cutting and remove all its sideshoots. The main stem will reach about 3 ft (1 m) during the season — about the right height for a standard. In fall cut the tip off the main stem and remove any further sideshoots.

2. The following year three or four sideshoots will arise near the top. Leave them to develop as leaders, but cut out all other shoots. When the growing season is over, prune back each leader by half to two thirds, cutting just above an outward-facing bud.

3. Early in the third spring, keep about seven of the shoots at the top to form a framework of main leaders, well spaced to admit light and air. Cut half to two thirds off the length of these leaders, and cut out entirely any other shoots that have developed on the trunk.

4. By the fourth spring, each cut-back leader will have produced two new leaders and some laterals (sideshoots). Keep one or two laterals on each branch to create an even shape; remove the others, then trim all shoots by one third, cutting above outward-facing buds.

5. In subsequent years, cut back the leaders by half in late winter, and cut laterals back to two or three buds to produce fruiting subsidiary shoots. Every June trim back the subsidiary shoots to about six leaves to open up the head and encourage the fruit to ripen.

---

beans or sweet peas as a centerpiece in each bed, a rose arch at the entrance to each path, fruit bushes at all the corners, or small topiary shapes spaced out along the paths.

As a single tall feature in a small potager, make an arbor at the center where two paths cross. Keep the structure simple — four wooden posts with crossbeams over the top. Plant it with peas, beans, ornamental gourds, runner beans, cucumbers, or the purple-podded climbing beans, which change to green when cooked.

Do not separate your flowers from these climbing vegetables. Plant morning glory (*Ipomoea*), *Mina lobata*, canary creeper, or sweet peas to grow through them. The flowers attract pollinating insects, ensuring good crops, although a little extra feeding and room are necessary because the different plants are competing for the same nutrients.

For a spectacular entrance to the garden, grow a pair of rose standards to serve as ornamental gateposts, or be more original with a pair of red currant standards. The lobed leaves are decorative on their own, but the main glory comes with the chains of glistening ruby fruits in June. From a practical viewpoint, the compact head at shoulder height is easy to net if birds are a problem, and the formal shape makes a focal point all year.

Globe artichokes can do the same job for a single season. These imposing gray-green plants are like giant thistles, with huge flower heads to pick at bud stage for a table delicacy.

HEIGHT WITH SCREENS AND EDGINGS

A screen of vegetables or fruits is useful and ornamental for separating the potager from the rest of the garden. It is even more useful in blocking an ugly view or hiding one particular eyesore, such as your valuable but unsightly compost heap. As a temporary screen, staple netting to a row of sturdy stakes, and let runner beans or a vigorous variety of pea scramble up it. Runner beans come with flowers in a range of shades from white to red, or both in the case of the ancient but incomparably flavored 'Painted Lady.'

As a denser screen, erect a double row of 6 ft (1.8 m) poles and cover them with a thick mixed planting of runner beans, peas, and climbing flowers such as black-eyed Susan vine (*Thunbergia alata*) — or even cranesbill geraniums and Peruvian lilies, which reach up remarkably when they are given support.

A lacy screen for summer is created by a well-nourished permanent bed of asparagus. Young asparagus shoots are a culinary treat in early summer, and later the ferny foliage grows more than head high, providing a pretty background for flowers and looking dainty in arrangements, especially with sweet peas.

Jerusalem artichokes, a relative of the sunflower, are very easy to grow. Their tall stems, clothed in rough green leaves, make an effective windbreak and are so tough that even after they are dead the strongest serve as temporary stakes for small plants. The knobby tubers of this artichoke are delicious boiled or made into soup. Sunflowers have similarly tough stems, and a row of these large-flowered hardy annuals makes an attractive hedge in summer — especially if you choose one of the multistemmed varieties with smaller blooms in shades of white, gold, or even deep red.

Corn, another tall, large-leaved crop, makes a thick screen in a sunny spot. It is usually planted in blocks for the best pollination of the ears, but a double row planted as a screen also works well. Look for unusual varieties with variegated foliage or ears with colorful kernels.

As a more permanent woody screen along the garden's boundary, set out apples, pears, gooseberries, or currants as cordons. Or train loganberries, blackberries, or raspberries on horizontal wires. Such screens are best for the northern side of the plot, where they cast no shade.

Gooseberries are a productive edging for paths. Train them as slim, low cordons so that their scratchy branches do not encroach. The knobbly shapes make a strong outline through the winter.

Colorful summer edgings for the beds are purple-podded peas and beans with yellow and purple pods.

CROPS IN CONTAINERS

For gardeners with a space problem who long to grow vegetables, there is an easy solution. Many types of vegetable do well in containers. Besides growing new potatoes in tubs, try putting leeks, carrots, and even the luxurious asparagus in big plastic buckets that are pierced with several drainage holes at intervals around the base.

There is no need to confine yourself to ground-level containers. Raised or hanging ones will give some rewarding results — and at a convenient height.

☙ Mix zucchinis and nasturtiums in a hanging box for display as well as food.

☙ Suspend miniature tomatoes and bush basil or New Zealand spinach in deep hanging baskets.

☙ Raise herbs in a handy window box outside the kitchen to provide instantly accessible seasonings when cooking.

A cheap and easy container for bringing vegetables, fruits, and flowers into growth in unpromising spots is the soil-filled, plastic grow bag, which is planted by cutting slits in the top. Anywhere you can reach with water becomes a potential growing site. Tomatoes, peppers,

STANDING TALL A fruit bush trained as a standard adds height to a flat planting scheme and utilizes space well. This gooseberry standard is set off by pink alliums that are easy to grow from bulbs planted in autumn.

eggplants, zucchinis, lettuces, and beans all thrive in these bags — in fact the only limit to your success is the amount of water and fertilizer you supply. Brighten up a bag by putting a few extra plants along its edges as decoration. Lobelias and petunias will flourish and will soon attract pollinating insects as well.

TRY SOMETHING DIFFERENT

Experiment with unusual vegetables for the sheer sparkle they bring. Ruby chard, a plant related to beets, gives double value, with long thick stalks and midribs that can be served like asparagus, and leaves to be eaten like spinach. The plant is easy to grow, and the stalks can be pulled throughout summer and into autumn. Rainbow chard is white and yellow as well as red.

Endive and chicory are both very decorative, endive with frilly, lacy leaves and chicory with red-tinged leaves. Just as striking is the burgundy-and-white chicory known as radicchio.

Chinese vegetables include a variety of greens besides the white-veined cabbage called bok choy. Some greens run to

PRETTY AND PRODUCTIVE Even a trough of flowers has potential for food crops. You can grow a few cabbages, among the brightly colored nasturtiums, to harvest for foliage that is decorative as well as edible.

seed if sown too early, but since the young flowering shoots of all are tasty both raw and cooked, none need go to waste. They are fast growing, with most ready to harvest in 8–10 weeks, but some varieties can be picked after 3 weeks and are ideal for filling gaps between other crops or in flower beds. Look for mizuna greens and komatsuna.

Peppers and chilies are both easy-to-grow plants, and though the flowers are not large, the glossy green fruits — changing to red, yellow, or purple — are long lasting. They crave sun, so tuck them in the warmest spot.

Tomatoes, both the "indeterminate" slicing types and "determinate" sauce

BE YOUR OWN SEEDSMAN

SAVE MONEY not only by growing your own crops but also by saving their seeds for the next season's production.

Runner-bean and tomato seeds are good candidates, as the characteristics bred into the parent reappear consistently in the offspring. Do not save seeds from F_1 hybrids, however, because they do not come true.

Let a few runner beans hang on one of the best plants until frost is likely, then take the seeds from the pods and keep the unblemished ones.

Choose a large, fully ripe tomato, cut it open, and scoop the seeds into a fine-meshed strainer. Hold it under running water while you gently clean every bit of pulp from the seeds. Spread out the seeds on newspaper until they are dry.

Put each kind of seed in its own clearly labeled paper bag, and store in an airtight canister in a cool place until you are ready to sow them in spring.

types, do well in sheltered, sunny spots, and their homegrown fruits have the best flavor. Grow some novelties along with the old favorites, for example the tiny, sweet cherry and pear types, yellow and orange varieties, and striped "zebra" tomatoes.

OLD-FASHIONED FRUITS

Although most gardeners who grow fruit choose apples and pears, raspberries and strawberries, there are other fruits that are particularly worth growing because they are difficult to buy.

One such fruit is the old-fashioned medlar, which is rarely eaten nowadays, mainly because it is inedible until bletted (nearly rotten). The strong, winy flavor was appreciated with a glass of port at the end of elaborate Victorian dinners. The fruits also make a tangy jelly that is excellent for serving with rich, gamy meats. They are borne on a small tree, whose large white spring flowers are beautiful, and whose leaves turn yellow, purple, and scarlet in autumn.

The edible quince (*Cydonia oblonga*) is neglected, too, due to frequent planting

GROWING UP Purple sage and broccoli front the long narrow leaves of corn. These, along with the round-leaved, clambering squash plants, add vertical interest to the beds of a densely planted kitchen garden.

DUAL-PURPOSE PLANTING Brilliantly colored ruby chard and red *Nicotiana* growing together show how attractive vegetable and flower combinations can be. They are also handy — you can pick blooms for displaying in the house while gathering food for the kitchen.

the pH range of 4.5–5.0. Lowbush blueberries, surface huggers that make a good ground cover, are the best choice for cold, northern gardens. Highbush blueberries, which make handsome bushes 6–12 ft (1.8–3.6 m) tall, bear larger but still flavorful berries. From Tennessee southward, the choice blueberry is the rabbiteye; it can grow to 18 ft (5.5 m) or be contained at 5 or 6 ft (1.5 or 1.8 m) with pruning. Rabbiteye blueberries need mild winters, with some chilling, and do not thrive in the warmest areas. They bear large crops in drier soils, but they need irrigation in summer droughts.

Plant blueberries with other acid-lovers such as heathers, azaleas, or rhododendrons. They are especially attractive in autumn, when the leaves turn brilliant scarlet and crimson before falling.

GET THE BEST FROM BERRIES AND CURRANTS

If you do not want to grow red or white currants as showpiece standards, buy bushes with several stems coming from the root system. Prune these as open-centered bushes for a mixed bed, or plant them against a wall or screen and train them into fan espaliers. Look for fine-flavored 'Rovada' and 'Stanza' red currants and 'White Versailles' white currants.

Black currants are easy to train as hedging to frame a potager's beds. They are long-lived plants that thrive in heavy soil. The tough 'Ben Sarek' is particularly suitable, but new varieties of soft fruit are introduced each year.

The key to success is to cut the stems back to buds within 2 in (5 cm) of the ground as soon as you plant them. Most of the fruits are produced on the previous year's growth, so as soon as the leaves fall each year cut out a third of the stems, choosing the oldest ones. New fruiting shoots spring from just below the cuts.

Blackberries and raspberries are naturals to train as a hedge or screen, but there are also more decorative things to do with them. Blackberries are attractive grown over a pergola or arch, especially if you choose the ferny-leaved 'Oregon Thornless,' which will not scratch you as you pass beneath it.

Make a stunning centerpiece to your garden by planting four or five raspberries together and training them up poles. They display the startling white undersides of the leaves whenever breezes stir

of the ornamental quince (*Chaenomeles*), which is a shame as the large white flowers look so attractive among the dark, white-backed leaves. In autumn the golden round or pear-shaped fruits hang heavy on the slender twigs until frost strikes. They have a powerful aroma that makes them doubly delightful to display in the house. Do not store the fruits touching other foods though, or they will pass on their taste.

A small tree to grow in a patch of grass is the crab apple. Resist the most showy flowering cultivars and plant the old 'John Downie,' whose scarlet and yellow fruits make delicious jelly to spread on muffins or to use as the base for a range of mint jellies, adding your own chopped apple mint, orange mint, or other kind of mint.

A TRIO OF FRUITFUL SHRUBS

Blueberries are admirably adapted to garden conditions found throughout the Eastern half of the United States, and with some extra care they perform satisfactorily wherever soils are acidic — in

PREPARE A COLORFUL HARVEST

Plant fruits and vegetables that please the eye as well as the palate.
You can choose an ornamental variety of a favorite and familiar crop, such as striped tomatoes, or grow exotic plants whose brilliance of color or unusual form adds interest to the garden and at the table.

CAPE GOOSEBERRIES
These golden yellow fruits from Peru are the size of cherries and are enclosed in papery outer cases, which look like Chinese lanterns and make decorative clusters on the plant.

KOHLRABI
Some varieties of this quick-growing root vegetable have purple skin and flushed leaves; others are all green. It takes only 10 or 12 weeks to mature and produces crops late into autumn.

ORNAMENTAL CORN
Grow this corn, *Zea mays japonica* 'Multicolor,' for its mixed kernel colors. It is not served as a vegetable but makes a vivid garnish, is dried for arrangements, and may be dried for cornmeal.

ASPARAGUS PEAS
A low-growing plant with cinnamon-scarlet flowers and gray-green leaves, this pea is pretty enough to grow in a flower bed. The edible pods, which have four wavy flanges, should be eaten when they are very small.

RED BRUSSELS SPROUTS
The late-maturing 'Rubin' variety, with dark purplish-red leaves, bears flavorful sprouts for gathering from early winter. Plant a row for a welcome addition of color at a bleak and bare time of year.

HIGHBUSH BLUEBERRIES
This bushy plant, native to North America, has abundant crops of sharp-flavored slate-blue fruit in summer. In autumn the foliage takes on vivid colors that contribute to its ornamental value.

STRIPED TOMATOES
Tomatoes always look decorative growing on stakes, and the 'Tigerella' variety has the added interest of ripening to red with golden stripes. The plant grows tall and has fruits ready for picking in August.

PATTY PAN SQUASHES
Yellow patty pan squashes, with their curious flying-saucer shape and frilled edges, look rather like huge creamy flowers. They are best eaten young while the flesh is tender.

them. Extend the season for enjoying fresh raspberries from the garden by growing some autumn-fruiting varieties: 'Fallgold' and 'Zeva,' for example, are excellent. Cut all the varieties down to ground level once they finish fruiting.

STRAWBERRY NOVELTIES

Few plants can outdo the strawberry in combining productivity with prettiness. But take note: unless you remove stray runners regularly, the plants are apt to take over huge areas with leafy growth and not be particularly productive.

To make them even more suitable for the flower bed, breeders have crossed the strawberry with the marsh cinquefoil. A recently developed variety is 'Serenata,' which has pink blooms and gives a good crop of fruit.

Alpine strawberries make a decorative and fruitful edging. These are easily raised from seed, give reasonable crops of small fruits, and are now bred to form clumps without producing runners. The fruits are produced over a long period and, although rather laborious to pick, have fragrance and full flavor that are lacking in many of the larger kinds. One of the best varieties of alpine to grow is 'Baron Solemacher.'

Lovers of two-colored leaves sometimes choose a variegated strawberry, but this is best treated as an ornamental plant, since it rarely sets much fruit. It does make wonderful ground cover for semi-shade with lamium and periwinkle.

Strawberries are far more adaptable to different situations than was once thought, so use every stratagem to extend both the space and the season for this most eagerly anticipated summer fruit.

🍓 Grow strawberries in stacking towers, traditional strawberry jars, and even hanging baskets.

🍓 Extend the season until the first frost by planting one of the new varieties that fruit throughout the summer — 'Aromel' or 'Pegasus,' for example.

🍓 Propagate new plants by rooting the plantlets in pots while still attached by the runner to the parent plant.

🍓 Use your home-raised plantlets for experiments to see how they grow in a variety of containers and soils.

🍓 Look for the yellow-fruited 'Alpine Yellow,' said to taste of pineapple. Birds have trouble finding the fruits.

🍓 Search for delicious old varieties such as 'Late Pine' and 'Royal Sovereign.'

🍓 For ground cover, make a mixture of

APPLE EDGINGS Training apple trees into living fences uses space well and makes for easy picking. The neat linear pattern formed by the branches is in harmony with the formalized layout of a potager.

alpine strawberries, violets, and London-pride saxifrage (*Saxifraga* × *urbium*).

🍓 Plant alpine strawberries around rose beds for dainty, productive edgings.

🍓 Place straw or grass clippings around each strawberry plant, as soon as the fruits start to form, to keep them clean.

🍓 Surround strawberries with a little sawdust to deter slugs and snails, which cannot stand its texture and stay away.

SPACE-SAVING TREES

The small gardens of most modern homes have put many people off growing the old-style fruit trees. Now, however,

FRUITFUL RUFF A generous edging of strawberries is spangled with creamy-white flowers in early summer and follows them with luscious fruit. Put the plants in a sunny, sheltered spot for the most successful crops.

SHEARS THAT CUT IN STAGES

A STRAINED FOREARM and bruised ball of the thumb all too often follow an afternoon's pruning. It is the prolonged squeezing on the handles of pruning shears that does the damage.

Ratchet shears take much of the hard work out of cutting. You can apply pressure on the handles in short bursts, and handles and blades will lock in place after each squeeze.

This allows you to let go, relax your grip, then grasp again when you are ready. Tough, woody growths yield bit by bit to the blades.

STRAWBERRY PINK Pink-flowered strawberries are pretty enough to grow in a container set among ornamental plants. Developed from crossing strawberries with cinquefoil, some varieties are more decorative than fruitful.

you can have a mini orchard without vast acreage. New dwarf and semi-dwarf fruit trees need little ground space; consequently, they are being grown in many suburban and small country gardens. These compact plants suffer badly when starved or too dry, though, so you must plant them in rich soil and keep them well fed and watered.

A FRUIT-TREE FENCE

Apples are ideal for training as living fences along the edges of beds in the potager. Cut back the leading shoot of the dwarf tree at about 8 in (20 cm) high and train the two main sideshoots in opposite directions along wires. Remove any other sideshoots from the main stem. This controls the growth and ensures that short, fruit-bearing spurs develop evenly along the two sideshoots. Further pruning is not usually needed because there is very little growth of leafy shoots. Another method is to let two shoots grow upright, then carefully lower them to the horizontal and tie them to the wires.

Though called a living fence, such apple trees are suitable for edging only where they are not likely to be brushed against. Knocking them may damage the buds or developing fruits. These are easy to reach for picking (and spraying), and the trees look good all year round, presenting rows of delicate blossom, then of developing fruits. Even in winter the trees make an interesting pattern.

CORDONS AND ESPALIERS

More productive than living fences, though needing no more ground area, are cordons — single-stemmed dwarf trees grown at a 45° angle and tied to four horizontal wires with about 2 ft (60 cm) between tiers. Because many trees fit into a small space, you can easily mix suitable pollinators. A long succession of apples will be produced by 'Discovery,' 'George Cave,' 'Golden Delicious,' 'Crispin,' and 'Tydeman's Late Orange.'

Be just a little bolder, and you can train your apples or pears as espaliers to make a striking formal screen across one end of your garden — or, indeed, anywhere in the yard. Espaliers are trained as a series of horizontal layers coming out from a vertical stem, in much the same way as pleached trees (*see p. 49*). They can line a bed or path or be grown against a wall to give them more shelter.

In the early stages, make sure there is no serious competition for nutrients and

FRUITING ARCHES TO WALK UNDER Apple trees can be trained over strong metal supports to form a beautiful tunnel. As well as bearing generous crops of delicious fruit, the tunnel provides a focal point in the garden from spring blossom through leaf drop in fall.

light. Later on, a few annuals around their feet—some knee-high sweet peas, for example — do no harm.

An arch formed by two trees of restricted growth fits in a surprisingly small space, and a short tunnel with perhaps three trees on each side takes no more space than one full-size tree.

COLONNADE TREES

Alternatives to carefully pruned apple trees are colonnades. These have all been bred from a single shoot on one tree that showed a desire to grow strong and tall but produced few sideshoots.

The resulting trees make columns of foliage, flowers, and fruits that serve as accents where you need a tall specimen that casts little shade. However, only a limited number of cultivars have been bred in this form so far, and these do not include many favorite apples.

A similar effect can be achieved through careful training. The usual apple varieties are grown on dwarfing rootstocks and trained as a column. Unlike genetically programmed colonnades, the trained trees have the potential to grow into normal bushes and need regular pruning to keep them in shape. Both types of trees do well in containers as well as in flower beds.

LUXURIES AND CURIOSITIES

Figs have a luscious sweetness when ripe and fresh. Grow 'Marseilles' or 'Negro Largo' as a compact bush or a full standard. The leaves, which resemble large

hands, are striking, and because the fruits do not need pollination, there are no fertilization problems. Figs produce best when their roots are restricted and make perfect pot plants for a sheltered patio. This is the best way to grow figs north of zone 8, as potted plants can be overwintered in a cool, frost-free place.

If you grow a fig in the ground, put it by a warm wall and restrict the roots by digging a planting pit 2–3 ft (60–90 cm) square. Line the pit with bricks or paving slabs before filling it with soil.

Grapes make attractive ornamental plants as well as good fruit producers, but they do not need to be grown in the traditional way — on walls or horizontal wires. All varieties climb up and over pergolas and arbors. Once the leading shoot has reached the desired height, pinch out the tip to encourage branching. In winter reduce each sideshoot to just one or two buds; when these grow in spring and a

flower cluster opens, nip off the shoot one or two leaves beyond the cluster.

You can grow dessert grapes as standards in pots, pruning to develop a small round head that will bear up to a dozen bunches of grapes. 'Black Hamburgh' and 'Bacchus' are suitable cultivars.

Look for locally adapted grape types: French–American hybrids or Concord in the Northeast and Upper Midwest, muscadines in the South, and *Vitis vinifera* grapes on the West Coast.

Some fruits are so unusual in America they are curiosities. The most impressive is the banana. True bananas (*Musa*) are not often seen, but with a 'Dwarf Cavendish,' you stand a real chance of getting some fruit in a sunny indoor space. Once a stem has produced fruit, it slowly dies, but by then new stems have grown.

Occasionally the most unexpected plants yield crops of fruit. This can

HERB GARDENS

FEW PLANTS OUTDO herbs for the number of uses to which they can be put. Herbs have been popular since Roman times for flavoring food and preparing cosmetics and medicines; some also repel insects, or are used in dyes. And if all that were not enough to guarantee them a place in the garden, they look good and release invigorating scents when you brush against them.

Almost everyone tries a few chives or some mint in a corner of the garden at some point. But the recent enthusiasm for growing herbs reflects a general trend toward using more natural ingredients, and an eagerness to sample new cuisines that use exotic herbs. Many herbs are easy to grow, being very undemanding plants that thrive when they are ne-glected. They actually prefer poor soil, and their only requirements are good drainage and plenty of heat and sun.

DESIGNS FOR HERB GARDENS

Herbs thrive in containers, and a selection in pots outside the kitchen door is the simplest and most convenient type of herb garden. You can also plant them in a box hanging on a kitchen window.

However, there are many other possibilities. To grow herbs together as a collection, create a "ladder": alternate paving stones and blocks of herbs along the sunny side of a fence or even the driveway. There is a satisfying formality in this "checkered" layout, with the herbs as dark squares and paving as the light ones. Work out your own design to give more space to the herbs you use most.

A wheel design has a beautiful symmetry. A real wagonwheel is not big enough for most people's herbs, but it is easy to mark out a wheel with bricks or

happen with the passion-flower (*Passi-flora caerulea*), whose lovely blooms may be followed in hot summers by pale orange, egg-shaped fruits. They add color to fruit salads or can be halved when ripe and wrinkled, sprinkled with sherry, and eaten.

Cape gooseberries (*Physalis peruviana*) are half-hardy annuals. Start them out on a windowsill, then plant them outside in summertime, in a sheltered place. Gooseberries resemble the invasive perennial Chinese lantern (*Physalis alkekengi*) but are taller and furry. The lanterns turn a straw color when the berry is ripe. Make an edible garnish by turning back the cases and dipping the fruits in chocolate or sugar.

For sheer novelty, grow strawberry spinach — a true spinach with fleshy red berries among the leaves. The fruit is bland, but the plant is so strange that it is worth growing at least once.

BLEND OF COLOR, AROMA, AND TASTE *Contrasting foliage spills out onto brick paving in a profuse herb bed. Chives and purple-leaved sage add height and color variation behind golden-leaved marjoram and thyme, while a spider plant in a pot brought out for summer adds height.*

A Patchwork
of Herbs

*Herbs look attractive, taste delicious,
and have invigorating aromas — and,
as if that were not enough, almost all of
them are easy to grow.*

HERB GARDENS require only a sunny
position to flourish, so this southwest-
facing garden is ideal. Shown here at the
height of summer, it is bursting with
colors and scents that stimulate and
satisfy the senses.

Most herbs are quite tough, thriving
in conditions that would kill off more
demanding plants. They love poor soil
and heat — many are native to the
Mediterranean region — so growing
them in small beds among paving stones
is easy. Besides looking lovely, the paving
stones hold the warmth, make it easier to
separate and contain the different types
of herbs, and contribute to the pretty
patchwork of colors.

PRACTICAL PLACEMENT

Keeping the beds small allows easy
access to all the plants, while placing the
most commonly used herbs along the
edges of the beds ensures they are
convenient for picking.

Putting different mints together in
one bed looks attractive and provides
you with a variety of garnishes and
flavorings. The paving restrains the
invasive stems, which run rampant just
below the surface if left unchecked. You
can push barriers down between the
different varieties if you want to prevent
them from mingling and save the less
vigorous ones from being swamped.

Lemon-scented verbena is not hardy,
so is grown in a pot that is moved
indoors in winter. A pot of basil, a tender
annual, is started early in a sunny spot
indoors, then put outside once all danger
of frost is past.

As in every other part of the garden,
colors are important. Having a few small
beds makes it easy to separate clashing
colors. The main colors are purple and
pink, but the orange marigolds and
yellow lemon balm in the front corner
provide a cheerful contrast. Similarly

the blue and white of the borage and
coriander stand out against the pink
of the roses.

The bay laurel is grown in a pot so
that the bold vertical accent it provides
can be moved around. Bay laurel is
hardy to zone 7, but in a pot it is
especially vulnerable to cold. Move it to
a warm corner for the winter or, better,
take it into a sunny, frost-free porch.

The dill and fennel beside the bench
also add height, while the thyme and
prostrate rosemary beneath are placed
where they are frequently stepped on
and so release their glorious aromas.

Tender bay stands outside in summer

Paving restrains rampant mints

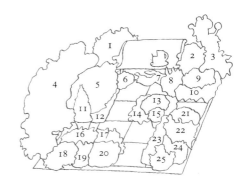

Crushed thyme smells sweet underfoot

Cheerful colours brighten the corner

1. Bronze fennel (*Foeniculum vulgare* 'Purpureum')
2. Dill (*Anethum graveolens*)
3. Angelica (*Angelica archangelica*)
4. Rose (*Rosa* 'Ispahan')
5. Borage (*Borago officinalis*) and coriander (*Coriandrum sativum*)
6. Prostrate rosemary (*Rosmarinus officinalis* Prostratus Group)
7. Creeping thyme (*Thymus serpyllum*)
8. Lemon-scented verbena (*Aloysia triphylla*)
9. Purple sage (*Salvia officinalis* 'Purpurascens')
10. Chives (*Allium schoenoprasum*)
11. Bay laurel (*Laurus nobilis*)
12. Golden marjoram (*Origanum vulgare* 'Aureum')
13. Sage (*Salvia officinalis*)
14. Parsley (*Petroselinum crispum*)
15. Basil (*Ocimum basilicum*) and purple basil (*O. b.* 'Purpureum')
16. Peppermint (*Mentha × piperita*)
17. Pineapple mint (*Mentha suaveolens* 'Variegata')
18. Apple mint (*Mentha suaveolens*)
19. Curly spearmint (*Mentha spicata* var. *crispii*)
20. Spearmint (*Mentha spicata*)
21. Golden-leaved lemon balm (*Melissa officinalis* 'Aurea')
22. Pot marigold (*Calendula officinalis*)
23. Common (or garden) thyme (*Thymus vulgaris*)
24. Hyssop (*Hyssopus officinalis*)
25. French tarragon (*Artemesia dracunculus*)

little hedges of boxwood, dwarf lavender, or santolina as the spokes. In between, plant beds of parsley, thyme, basil, sage, chives, marjoram, tarragon, mint, fennel, coriander, lemon balm, and rosemary. Set a sundial or a pot of bay laurel in the center. In a more informal setting, use a whirligig or favorite piece of folk sculpture as the centerpiece.

One way of giving different amounts of space to the herbs without disturbing the pattern is to make a spiral that widens the farther it is from the center.

The ultimate in herb garden designs is a knot with the loops marked in clipped boxwood or germander and herbs growing in the spaces between. Use string and pegs to mark out the shapes, adjusting them until you are satisfied they are right, then define them by pouring a line of sand from a bottle before planting.

Herbs among the Flowers

Many herbs are easily integrated into the flower border — convenient in a small garden — although mints need to have their spreading underground stems contained by bottomless buckets or plastic pots sunk into the ground.

Mix curly spearmint with variegated pineapple mint in a bed planted in a patio, where you can harvest them and enjoy their aroma from a deck chair.

Grow creeping herbs — chamomile, Corsican mint, pennyroyal (*Mentha pulegium*), and lemon-scented thyme — in the cracks between paving stones. They look pretty and release a delicious fragrance when stepped on.

Sow seeds of coriander, fennel, dill, sweet cicely, and angelica among other tall flowers, and encourage borage, too. It will self seed, and though the flowers are not big, they are of such a bright blue that errant seedlings can be forgiven.

Herbs provide some of the best silver and gold foliage in the garden. Among silver-grays are the curry plant (*Helichrysum angustifolium*), thymes, sages, and rosemary, which also smothers itself in blue flowers in spring. The yellow-leaved plants include golden marjoram and golden thyme, both of which make bright edging plants. Yellow lemon balm makes a bushy plant in summer and has an intense, fresh scent. Cut off the flowers before seed is set, or you will end up with a forest of seedlings. Rosemary adds a touch of gold in its gilded form, and both the 'Icterina' and 'Kew Gold' forms of sage stand out in summer.

PLANTS FOR FLOWER ARRANGERS

C UT FLOWERS bring the scent, color, and freshness of the garden into your home. But before you rush to plant your favorite flowers for cutting, remember that foliage also makes a valuable contribution to arrangements. Every bloom will have more impact, and fewer blooms will be needed when they are partnered with plenty of foliage.

You can grow foliage in the hedge, in screens within the garden, and as shrubs scattered in the borders. Do not restrict yourself to green foliage; other colors — especially silver and blue-gray — are just as valuable. Make careful plans for a range of leaf sizes, from tiny conifers to bold fatsias and hostas. Vegetables, too, provide useful leaves, and this is one of the best reasons to grow asparagus: even when yields are sparse, the feathery, fern-like foliage, in a soft green, is perfect with cut flowers.

ESSENTIAL GREENERY

Among the most common kinds of foliage at the florist are eucalyptus and pittosporum, both of which are evergreen and grow well in most West Coast gardens. The easiest eucalyptus is gray *Eucalyptus gunnii*. Clipped back to ankle height each spring once the danger of frost is past, it forms a low bush, producing wands of round leaves, the youngest flushed with pink. *Pittosporum tenuifolium* has black stems with small and glossy green, variegated, or purple wavy-edged leaves, depending on the cultivar. In spring there is the bonus of sweetly scented chocolate-brown blooms.

One quick-growing Leyland cypress (× *Cupressocyparis leylandii*) supplies all you need by way of mid-green foliage. For small gardens the slower-growing *Chamaecyparis* 'Green Hedger' is better.

Other shrubs that fit comfortably into borders and are tolerant of cutting are the evergreens Mexican orange blossom (*Choisya ternata*), *Coronilla glauca*, and *Elaeagnus*. *Choisya*, with its shiny deep green leaves in sets of three, makes a

STRIKING SPECIMENS Gain the double benefit of height and drama in the garden with outstanding foliage for flower arrangements. Gray-green, toothed *Melianthus major* grows behind sword-shaped *Phormium* leaves.

strong foil for all flowers, while *Coronilla glauca* provides blue-gray leaves that complement blue, mauve, and pink flowers. *Elaeagnus pungens* 'Maculata' has generous splashes of yellow in the leaves. *E. × ebbingei* is faster growing, but is plain green; the form 'Limelight' is splotched with yellow and has scented, silvery autumn flowers, sometimes followed by orange berries.

DOUBLE-VALUE FOLIAGE PLANTS

When your garden needs a hedge, make sure you plant one that has foliage attractive enough for flower arrangements. For a low hedge, consider *Euonymus fortunei* and *E. japonicus*. Both are evergreen and best known with yellow or white variegations. Euonymus does well in shade as long as it is well fed and watered.

Another low-growing evergreen is *Viburnum davidii*, whose handsome large leaves have three deep grooves from stem to tip. With both male and female plants mingled in a hedge, you get a bonus of unusual turquoise berries after the flat heads of white midsummer flowers.

A loose, open screen is formed by the evergreen fatsia, whose large leaves are prized by flower arrangers. The stems are rather sparse and the leaves need to be removed individually. An underplanting of periwinkles fills out the bare base and gives extra evergreen foliage.

Garrya elliptica is quick-growing and bushy, with crinkled evergreen leaves and long gray catkins in winter. Plant the scented, winter-flowering *Viburnum × bodnantense* 'Dawn' beside it — and use the two together in arrangements as well.

Rather similar to garrya is *Itea ilicifolia*, which produces its long, scented, greenish catkins in midsummer. It needs a sunny wall, while garrya will tolerate one facing north or northwest.

COLORFUL SPECIMEN PLANTS

Just because privet (*Ligustrum*) is widely grown, do not overlook its virtues. Golden privet (*L. ovalifolium* 'Aureo-marginatum') is a bright spark in a border or vase to accompany fiery *Crocosmia* 'Lucifer,' *Dahlia* 'Bishop of Llandaff,' or *Lilium* 'Enchantment'; alternatively, aim for a contrast with cool blue delphiniums, lupines, or anchusa.

The English holly *Ilex aquifolium* and the bolder *Ilex × altaclerensis* are valued for their shapely, glossy leaves, which, with the addition of white or gold variegations and brilliant scarlet berries, look

BOLD BACKDROP Evergreen *Fatsia japonica* grows as an open shrub with large, glossy leaves. Picked individually and brought indoors, the leaves make a stunning backdrop to choice flowers.

WARM TINTS *Cotinus coggygria* 'Royal Purple' adds depth and contrast to pink *Alstroemeria* flowers in the garden or in a vase.

SHADES OF RED The young leaves of *Photinia × fraseri* 'Red Robin' are shiny red and make an interesting variation in foliage color.

WINTER STYLE The white-veined, arrow-shaped leaves of *Arum italicum* 'Pictum' are prized for winter arrangements — as are the green flowers and toothed foliage of *Helleborus argutifolius*.

PALE BEAUTIES Honesty (*Lunaria annua* 'Alba Variegata') may have the background role while the tulip 'White Triumphator' blooms in spring. But honesty's handsome leaves persist after the tulips fade — and it has papery silver seed disks for fall arrangements.

superb when they are mixed with luminous white flowers. Do not clip the bushes into small dumplings. Instead, cut out long stems as you need them; this keeps a more open bush and provides more stems suitable for arrangements.

New Zealand flax (*Phormium*) has sword-like leaves up to 6 ft (1.8 m) long — and even taller flower spikes. The common forms have green or bronze leaves, but there are cultivars striped in yellow, pink, red, and orange. The leaves last for weeks in water. In a border they go well with hebes and prostrate conifers.

Senecio cineraria (formerly known as *Cineraria maritima*) is a silvery-leaved, ferny plant popular in summer bedding schemes. In milder regions, however, it survives the winter and is excellent for winter picking. *Brachyglottis* 'Sunshine' makes long stems of oval gray leaves that fit into any scheme.

DECIDUOUS BEAUTY

Shoots of many deciduous shrubs wilt quickly, and thus are rarely seen at florists. You must use them quickly after cutting or condition them before use by standing them in deep cold water overnight. The European red elder (*Sambucus racemosa*) in the yellow-leaved variety 'Plumosa Aurea' has divided leaves of a rich butter-yellow with a purplish flush. The elder family includes some desirable garden plants that do well in the poorest soil and almost any conditions. The best is *Sambucus nigra*, especially 'Guincho,' which is purple when grown in the sun. It has the added bonus of pretty, pale pink flower heads in early summer.

The purple forms of the smoketree (*Cotinus coggygria*) have become more popular than the green. When pruned hard every second year, the bushes make compact growth with long stems for cutting; the green forms have vivid scarlet autumn color. Grape vines offer rich purple leaves with extra autumn fire. For the biggest leaves on the biggest plant, try *Vitis coignetiae* or in small gardens grow *V. vinifera* 'Purpurea.'

The most admired herbaceous leaves must be the hostas. Leaves vary from just a few inches long to broad plates in green, gray, or yellow; in autumn and

winter the hardiest ones take on a golden translucence and last for weeks before hard frosts fell them. More substantial for winter arrangements are the leathery, round, evergreen bergenia leaves, which are tinged red at the rim.

FERNS, GRASSES, AND ANNUALS FOR DISPLAY

Ferns, especially the hardy *Dryopteris filix-mas* and *Athyrium filix-femina*, are excellent for cutting. Common Solomon's seal (*Polygonatum × hybridum*) grows well with ferns, and its arching stems, holding up rows of paired leaves like wings, add grace to arrangements.

Though annuals are usually grown for their flowers, some, such as *Euphorbia marginata*, are valued for their foliage. The leaves are rimmed and veined with white. *Kochia scoparia*, a mass of feathery growth, is a perfect foil for sculptured blooms. Cosmos and larkspur also produce dainty, finely cut leaves.

Allow your imagination to spread to the unorthodox. Ornamental grasses, especially those with colorful blades, are easy to incorporate in arrangements.

Cabbages, kales, and ruby chard are among the many vegetables that have striking foliage worthy of display.

CUT BLOOMS FROM THE BORDER

Establishing a long succession of flowers for cutting is quick, easy, and not costly. Grow quantities of perennials from seed, such as yarrows, delphiniums, campanulas, lupines, and lobelias, and you have flowers from their second season, increasing in number each year.

Before the perennials mature and spread, fill the spaces between with hardy annuals such as larkspurs, pot marigolds, and Italian white sunflowers — all fast growers with numerous flowers. Half-hardy annuals add to the choice with, for example, orange and bronze French and African marigolds, red salvias, and blue ageratums. All last well in water. Once you have planted your range of quick-to-establish flowers, fine-tune with particular colors and improve the succession.

FLOWERS TO CUT IN SPRING

Tulips and daffodils are always available at florists' in spring, but the varieties tend to be rather limited. Grow a few of the newer shades and forms, in particular the split-corona or "orchid-flowered" daffodils such as *Narcissus* 'Cassata' or the miniature *N*. 'Tête à Tête,' which puts up several stems from each bulb.

Double, parrot, and lily-flowered tulips such as white 'Schoonord,' rosy 'China Pink,' and brilliant 'Orange Parrot' are superb in arrangements. Prick the stem below the flower before use so that it does not droop over.

Plant out potted hyacinth bulbs in the garden after they flower. They usually make a cluster of small stems that are perfect for picking. Choose the salmon-pink 'Gipsy Queen' and deep purple 'Distinction' as well as the commoner pastels. 'Gipsy Queen' goes particularly well in both garden and vase with the blues of scilla and chionodoxa.

COOL OR WARM FOR SUMMER

Summer blues make subtle arrangements used with foliage alone. Mixed with white, they are cool and elegant; with lemons they are fresh; they also temper exuberant reds and pinks.

In early summer the dainty blooms of Siberian iris (*Iris sibirica*) are excellent for cutting. The leaves are easy to use too, being long and grassy. To follow, grow the striking blue African lily (*Agapanthus*) in a warm, sheltered spot. The narrow-leaved Headbourne hybrids are the hardiest and produce many slender flower spikes. A more homely source of blue is the tall *Campanula persicifolia*, with large, pale blue flowers.

Delphiniums often have main stems that are too big for cutting. However, if you remove them, you bring on a forest of more useful sideshoots. 'Belladonna' types with sparse flowers on branched stems are best for arrangements.

If you prefer warmer colors, the Peruvian lily (*Alstroemeria*) is among the

SECURING A CANE TEPEE

TYING BAMBOO into a tepee for runner beans or sweet peas can be tricky — and the result is often unstable, as the canes can shift within the twine.

Making the framework stable is easy with a specially designed clip. Each cane is held in its own slot on an unobtrusive disk or ring; there are similar versions made in plastic or metal.

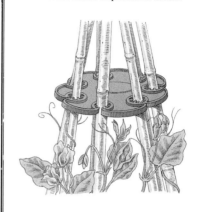

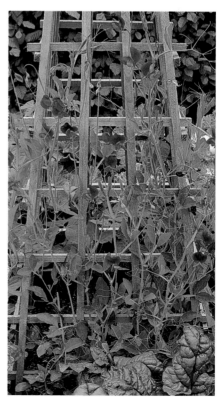

TRIPLE CROP Fast-growing, fragrant sweet peas are trained on a trellis pyramid with ruby chard at the base. The beautiful blend provides spinach-type leaves for harvesting and abundant flowers for cutting.

PINK TRUMPET FLOWERS A tempting group to gather for the house is composed of pink-flushed creamy-white *Lilium regale*, clusters of pink alstroemeria, and clouds of starry gypsophila. All are easy to grow in the garden and last well in water once they have been cut.

very best cut flowers — long-lasting and long-stemmed, light in form, and full of interesting detail for close scrutiny. The tall spires of foxgloves rival it for close-up interest, with intricate freckling inside the sculpted flower tubes. Both plants are so easily grown from seed that you can plant plenty. Select the smallest for cutting and leave a few main spikes to set seed.

Another self-seeder that no gardener or flower arranger should be without is *Alchemilla mollis*. Its rounded leaves are pretty in themselves, and the froth of tiny yellow flowers makes it doubly valuable.

SUMMER SPECIALS

For pure luxury, grow silky-petaled, fragrant peonies. The later-flowering Chinese peonies have three or four buds on each stem, and once the crown bud has opened, you can cut the smaller buds for arrangements. The pale pink, double 'Sarah Bernhardt' and the rosy 'Bowl of Beauty' filled with golden stamens are both exquisite.

A few lilies can transform arrangements, especially the heavily scented trumpet types such as 'Pink Perfection,' 'African Queen,' and *Lilium regale*. The bulbs are not expensive, so plant double quantities — half for cutting. For variety try bright yellow 'Connecticut King,' an upward-facing hybrid, and dramatic 'Casablanca,' with its huge white blooms.

Once, roses were set apart in their own formal bed, but it is common now to use them anywhere, and there are roses for mixed borders, patios, rockeries, slopes, and tubs. The choice of colors is vast, but white is the most useful. Though it is old, 'Iceberg' is hard to beat for vigor; in milder regions, it is still bearing flowers at Christmas.

Try some of the more unusual shades, particularly when you are mingling roses with other flowers. The greenish-tinged 'Peppermint Ice' emphasizes the purity of white flowers.

The "blue" roses, actually lilac and mauve shades, should be used more often in pink, silver, and gray schemes. Most of them have an intense perfume. Try the gray and brown roses, too, such as 'Edith Holden' and 'Nimbus.' In the flower bed they tend to fade from view,

but in an arrangement they are moody and subtle used with gray leaves and show up well against glossy, dark foliage.

FROM SUMMER INTO WINTER

Dahlias are the most eye-catching border flowers as summer fades and are indispensable for cutting. Those with bronze foliage and copper or red blooms, such as 'David Howard' and 'Bishop of Llandaff,' make a superb hot-color arrangement with cotinus and rudbeckias.

For more delicate schemes, *Anemone hupehensis* var. *japonica* has tall stems whose buds open to wide disks of pink or white. Masterwort (*Astrantia major*) has a cottage-garden charm, with white flower bracts, sometimes flushed pink, around green flowers on long, strong

AN UNASSUMING ASSET In a partly shaded spot grow *Astrantia major* and *Campanula lactiflora*. The simple beauty of the flowers shows to advantage in a vase.

PRETTY AS A PICTURE Summer flowers cut to bring color and scent inside the house are best picked early in the morning or in the evening and placed immediately into a deep bucket of cold water for several hours before they are trimmed again and arranged.

stalks. One of the best forms is 'Shaggy.' *A. maxima* has brighter pink shades.

Among the best of the asters are the Italian aster (*Aster amellus*) in pink, mauve, and violet, and *A.* × *frikartii* 'Mönch.' Sedum's flat heads of pink flowers make perfect companions for asters. As they age, sedums turn crimson then russet. The most spectacular forms have purple leaves and deep pink flowers.

Foliage and berries take pride of place in winter, but flowers add sparkle. The Christmas rose (*Helleborus niger*) and the green-flowered hellebore species excel, and if you work in miniature, grow snowdrops, winter aconites, crocuses, and the honey-scented *Iris danfordiae*.

MAKE CUT FLOWERS LAST

Pick flowers and foliage early in the morning or, failing this, in the evening. Cut newly opened flowers, using sharp pruning shears or scissors, and put them in water immediately. Cut most stems again once indoors, cutting under water and at a slant. This gives more stem cells access to water and keeps them from being blocked by resting flat on the bottom of the vase. Put the trimmed flowers in deep cold water in a cool place for several hours.

Narcissus, poppies, bluebells, and other flowers that exude a slimy or milky sap when cut need different treatment. Hold the stem ends in a flame for 30 seconds or protect the flower heads with a paper bag and plunge the stem ends into boiling water for 20 seconds. Immediately after treatment, put the flowers into deep water for two or three hours.

Add a couple of drops of bleach or florist's flower food to the vase water to help the flowers stay fresh. Remove any leaves that would be below water, or they rot and foul the water. Every other day change the water, trim the stems, and remove any wilting flowers. Put the display in a cool, but not drafty, place.

PRESERVING FLOWERS

PLAN AHEAD for winter flower arrangements and preserve blooms and leaf shoots. Some require very little effort; simply put the flowers and foliage of late summer and early autumn, such as sedums, in buckets or bowls with about 2 in (5 cm) of water in the bottom, then allow that to dry out naturally. This method preserves their color well.

Hydrangeas are even easier to preserve. Many mop-head Hortensia types (*Hydrangea macrophylla*) take on burnished copper and green tones if left to age on the plant and then hung to dry. The tiny 'Pia' and the neat, deep-red 'Prezioza' age to rich colors. But for something different, try the hardier *H. paniculata*, whose pyramidal white heads will age to pink. Leave some hydrangea flowers even longer to skeletonize into pale, delicate globes.

Other means are needed to preserve spring and summer flowers. The key to drying them successfully is speed, which helps retain the shape and color. Pick the plants when there is no moisture on them. Look for well-colored flowers that are just opening and for grasses that have not started to drop their seeds.

Prepare flowers immediately after picking them. Strip the leaves off the stems. Wire plants with large heads and thin stems or the heads will be too heavy for the dried stems. To do this, cut off the stem 1 in (2.5 cm) below the bloom. Make a hook on a piece of florist's wire and push the wire through the center of the flower until the hook grips the head.

The easiest drying medium is simply air. Tie the prepared flowers into small bunches, using a slipknot that you can tighten with minimum disturbance as the stems shrink. Hang the bunches upside down in a cool, dark, well-ventilated place until the flowers are crisp.

Instead of drying the plants in air, you can use sand, borax, or silica-gel powder or crystals (sold at craft shops). Sprinkle a thin layer of drying agent in an airtight tin or plastic box, place the flowers on top, then sprinkle more drying agent over the flowers and between the petals. Close the box, seal it with tape,

RANUNCULUS Brilliantly colored and long lasting when cut, ranunculus flowers dry well using the silica gel method.

HELICHRYSUM Pick the papery flowers before the bracts are fully open and hang them in bunches in an airy spot out of bright sunshine.

STATICE Delicate sprays of papery statice (*Limonium* spp.) in assorted colors look good in the garden and are dried by hanging.

FOR WINTER COLOR A late summer gathering of flowers from the border for drying includes blue sea hollies (*Eryngium*) with feathery ruffs, and globe thistles (*Echinops*) with their steely-blue spherical heads. Both are tall plants adding height and interest to a bed and an indoor display.

then put it in a warm spot like an attic until the flowers are crisp — usually 2 to 3 days in silica, 3 to 4 days in sand, and 3 to 4 weeks in borax. Do not leave them too long, or the flowers will become brittle. Lift them out carefully. You can use the drying agent again and again, letting it dry between uses.

There is a huge selection of plants and flowers that are easy to preserve. Larkspur, delphinium, foxglove, yarrow, thistle, and white daisy-like helipterum are all easy to dry. For a spectacular display, choose the opium poppy *Papaver somniferum* and *Allium giganteum*, both of which have huge dramatic seed heads. Among roses, choose red and orange ones for drying, because they maintain their color especially well.

For preserving sprays of foliage, stand the stems in a mixture of two parts hot water to one part glycerine. Beech, eleagnus, and eucalyptus are reliable. The leaf color often changes as the glycerine is absorbed into the stems and leaves.

Try drying anything you like; nothing is lost if you fail, and there is always a chance of some subtle color giving a new character to a familiar flower.

Be bold in arranging preserved material. For example, an unusual winter decoration is made by combining beech leaves with the papery orange seedpods of Chinese lantern. There is no rule against mixing dried and fresh flowers. Whether dried ones have their own stems or wires, protect any parts that will be in water with a coating of varnish or dip them in melted candle wax.

CAPTURE SUMMER'S ESSENCE

Potpourri preserves the unique perfumes of summer for you to enjoy in the house during winter. It is simple to make from a mixture of petals and aromatic leaves; they are preserved with a fixative oil or essence, both available from garden centers and some craft shops.

Adjust the ingredients to make the scent that pleases you. Be ready to experiment with whatever flowers you have available. Among the leaves you can use are lemon balm, hyssop, mint, thyme, santolina, marjoram, cranesbill geranium, angelica, artemisia, and bee-balm.

As a basic recipe, try using 10 dried pot marigold heads, 6 dried geranium leaves, the dried petals of 5 roses, 2 teaspoons of dried lavender, and 2 drops of rose fixative. Mix all the ingredients well in a large bowl. Seal the potpourri in a

---

BEST PLANTS

FLOWERS FOR DRYING

Grow a selection of flowers for drying that will give you a varied palette of colors and an assortment of textures and shapes.

• Yarrow (*Achillea filipendulina* 'Coronation Gold'): large flat heads of deep yellow flowers. Air dry by hanging or standing.

• Strawflower (*Helichrysum bracteatum*): large daisy-like flowers in a range of red, orange, pink, white, and yellow. It is among the easiest flowers for air drying.

• Hare's-tail grass (*Lagurus ovatus*): grows in tufts with slender stems bearing soft, fluffy, white flower spikes; hang to dry.

• Globe thistle (*Echinops*): globular, spiky flower heads with a steely-blue metallic sheen; easily air dried.

• Honesty (*Lunaria annua*): purple flowers followed by flat and silvery moon-shaped seedpods that are easily dried by hanging.

• Bells-of-Ireland (*Moluccella laevis*): erect spikes of small fragrant flowers, surrounded by bell-shaped pale green papery calycles. Dry with silica gel.

• Love-in-a-mist (*Nigella damascena*): many-petaled flowers, generally blue, with feathery foliage; hang dry for their balloon-shaped seedpods.

• Sunflower (*Helianthus annuus*): the dramatic large heads of dark seeds, set in concentric circles, look spectacular when dried for flower arrangements. Use silica gel.

---

dry, airtight jar for two weeks before putting it out in bowls.

For a more bracing perfume, follow the method above but combine 16 tablespoons of snipped balsam needles, about 20 miniature pine cones, 8 tablespoons of rose hips, and 2 drops of pine-scented fixative. If any potpourri's scent fades, add a drop more fixative.

Lavender makes a particularly fresh-scented potpourri. Mix 4 cups of dried lavender, 6 drops of lavender essential oil, and 1 tablespoon each of ground cinnamon, allspice, and mace. Mix all the ingredients, then put in paper bags and fold over loosely. Keep in a dark, cool place to cure for about 7 weeks before putting the potpourri out in bowls.

TEASEL Dry the prickly heads of teasels (*Dipsacus*) and keep them their natural color or spray them a festive silver or gold.

LAVENDER As well as adding color to dried flower arrangements, lavender brings a fresh fragrance to potpourri and scented sachets.

WATER IN THE GARDEN

WATER GENTLY TRICKLING into a pond, or a fountain's droplets sparkling in the sun, give a garden movement and music that never pall. No matter what size or shape garden you have, there is a water feature that can enhance it — whether your choice is a wall fountain, an overflowing pitcher, a jet bubbling over pebbles, or a more formal pool, tranquil and shimmering, reflecting the graceful goblets of water lilies. Keep the feature simple or install a pumped, circulating arrangement — and if you like, take the opportunity to add at the same time an automatic watering system for the rest of the garden, to end forever the need to carry cans or rely on leaky hoses.

Clear water spills over weathered rocks, studded with ferns, flowers, and grasses, onto intricately coiled and textured fossils.

The Allure of Water

THE SENSUAL QUALITY of water is a pleasure that never fades, and there is seldom a garden, no matter what size, that is not the better for its inclusion. Even where the concept, construction, color, and scent of a garden appear to give all that could be asked, water introduces a play of light and movement for what can be an immediate and sometimes dramatic change.

The soothing effect of still water's steady reflections, the refreshing sound as it flows, and the crystal sparkle of a fountain plume all contribute to making water a constant center of attraction, irresistible both to people and wildlife. Even a public pool is visited by birds, butterflies, frogs, and newts; and since such creatures are increasingly under threat in the wild, any kind of water feature in the garden provides a valuable haven for them, no matter what its size.

Some people are fortunate enough to have some form of natural water in or around their garden. An overgrown pond, a unused well, a bubbling spring, a small stream, or even the banks of a canal or river are a delight to the gardener, all providing an opportunity to develop a natural water garden or a bog garden and extend the garden's range of plants. Others may take over a garden where a water feature has already been installed — a formal pool, perhaps, or a cascade or graceful fountain.

Making the Most of the Extra Element

Those who have such luck can use judicious planning and planting to integrate the water source into a design of their own making or even rework the existing feature. A pond might be enlarged as part of a new overall scheme, perhaps; more ambitiously, a stream could be diverted to form a new feature altogether. This might take the form of an island, with a pool large enough to provide a home for fish.

If you are adding a water feature to the garden for the first time, you will find that the size and style of the house and garden largely determine the feature you choose. Where there is limited space, small prefabricated pools, birdbaths, freestanding or wall fountains, and wall masks may be the best way to introduce water to the garden, and ready-made, simple-to-install examples are on sale in many garden centers.

These are among the easiest of water features to maintain. People who are less mobile, very busy, or away frequently might also consider installing a watering system for the garden. With water conservation and costs now a concern for gardeners, it makes sense to use water prudently and avoid wasting it.

TIME FOR REFLECTION Water lilies form the centerpiece of this tranquil pool, its perfect circle interrupted by *Primula florindae*, bogbean, iris, and water forget-me-not. The pool lends serenity to this corner of a country garden, where a bench beneath a tree promises secluded leisure.

SIMPLE
WATER FEATURES

◆

I T IS PERHAPS in the smallest gardens that water is most appreciated. In a restricted space, every inch counts, and the shallowest saucer pool or trickling wall fountain makes an impact quite disproportionate to its size. Even a balcony or the tiniest roof garden is enlivened by a water-filled tub planted with a miniature water lily, or by the soft murmuring of a bubble fountain in a ceramic bowl.

CREATING AN INSTANT POOL

Birds love to perch on the edge of a dish and dip their beaks in water or plunge in for an energetic splash. Birdbaths and saucer pools are the simplest way to bring water into the garden. Any shallow container serves the purpose, even an upturned garbage-can lid with its edges hidden by plants and pebbles.

Simple pools that you can empty and scrub clean are the most practical, because such containers, in the sunshine, quickly become green with algae. Partly fill a dish with pebbles if it is a little too deep, to raise the water level and give the birds' feet a firmer grip.

The bowl of a garden urn makes a charming mossy pool if the drainage hole is plugged, and you can create an unusual bath out of large, coiled fossils, giant clamshells, sculpted hands, ceramic leaves, or leaden water-lily pads.

Try a variety of containers in different positions to see what looks the best. Arrange a collection of low bowls or shallow dishes as a collage to catch and reflect the light, or scatter flowers on the water to imitate miniature water lilies. Alternatively, sink a plain, saucer-shaped birdbath into the lawn to serve as a pool. Set it just below the surface of the ground, so the mower can skim over the rim without making contact.

UNLIKELY CONTAINER POOLS

Practically anything that holds water or will support a liner can be used as a trough or a small, sunken pool. Ceramic sinks, half-barrels, plastic tubs and barrels, galvanized water tanks, dishpans,

MINIATURE POOLS Even the smallest gardens benefit from a mini pool. The lilies and hostas around this pool disguise how tiny it really is, but even so it has room for water-loving sweet galingale (*Cyperus longus*) to flourish.

PROTECTING TODDLERS

IF YOU MOVE to a house with a pond in the garden and you have small children, make the pond safe at once. Turn a shallow pool into a sandbox, but make sure it has a well-fitted cover. Fill larger pools with sand or bark mulch to use as a play area.

If you want to keep the pool, cover it with a strong, ornamental metal grill or a homemade cover of wooden decking. Leave the odd small hole for taller water plants to grow through. A temporary frame of extra-strong lattice covered with mesh netting is useful for placing over the pool when you have occasional young visitors. The frame can be secured in place quickly with wooden pegs or metal tent stakes.

Larger pools and natural streams must be fenced off, and any gates padlocked. Well-made fencing screened by cornus, golden elder, rhododendrons, or bamboos is unobtrusive and easy to live with while the children are small.

Older children should be safe with a shallow pool with sloping sides.

SIMPLE POOL Water in a shallow stone bowl resting on cobblestones reflects sunlight and foliage, bringing a different quality to a garden. It will also be appreciated by birds.

and even the foam packaging that protects newly bought appliances such as microwave ovens can be fitted with a liner or sealed.

Some metals are poisonous to plants, and it is important that metal containers be coated inside with a nontoxic paint or a sealant such as asphalt.

The humble origins of more mundane containers are easily disguised with paint to imitate lead, marble, terra-cotta, or verdigris-coated copper. You can also mask them with an outer shell of loose

RURAL TOUCH A stone trough nestling among golden lemon balm and a crowd of geraniums looks at home in cottage gardens and is large enough to grow irises, mimulus, and glyceria.

bricks, tongue-and-groove lumber, or stones. Do not stifle your imagination — one gardener used a small, ancient convertible car as a pool. Its interior was lined and filled with water and became home to a number of goldfish, water lilies, and irises.

POSITIONING MINI POOLS TO ADVANTAGE

Mini pools look their best when their shape and materials are sympathetic to the style of the garden — a Chinese jar standing among bamboo, for example. Pots and bowls make excellent mini pools, suitable both for outdoors and for a small sun room. Pots with drainage holes can be sealed with silicone caulk.

If frequent refills are necessary in hot weather, make certain there is always water available that has stood for a few days in a watering can. This ensures that the water is not too cold and allows some of the chemicals in tap water to evaporate.

Half-barrels or tubs look good in most gardens, even on a formal terrace. They can be used singly in a very small garden.

Where there is a little more space, put them in a group with each one holding a different variety of the same plant — a miniature water lily, for example.

TUMBLING MOVEMENT IN A CASCADE

Where water runs from an old iron tap or pump into a container below, it can also be made to spill over the edge of the first container and into another.

A pretty development of this idea is a sunken cluster of overlapping wooden tubs set into the ground at various depths or perhaps into a slope. The water spills from one tub into the next to form an attractive cascade and then down into a concealed reservoir, from where it is pumped back up to the tap to start its fall again.

Surround the sunken tubs with stones, pebbles, and shells and edge them with ferns and hostas, bright blue *Brunnera*, creeping Jenny (*Lysimachia nummularia*), and a clump of *Iris sibirica*.

Grow suitable water plants in the tubs. Water lilies should be in the sun for at least half the day to flourish. Varieties that do well in a small space include the two smallest: *Nymphaea × helvola*, which grows in 4–9 in (10–23 cm) of water and has tiny yellow flowers, and the similar *N. tetragona*.

PLANT A CONTAINER POOL

SUCCESSFUL PLANTING of a container pool depends in part on filling it without disturbing the soil and gravel on the base. Spread a 6 in (15 cm) layer of garden loam in the empty container and cover it with 2 in (5 cm) of lime-free gravel or pebbles.

Cover the gravel with a wad of newspaper and add the water in a gentle trickle from a hose or watering can. Remove the paper carefully, and let the pool settle for a day or two before planting.

To plant, carefully press the roots of small water lilies, marginal plants, floaters, and oxygenators through the gravel and into the soil, then firm them in. In a slightly deeper pool, plant marginals in plastic containers and place them on up-ended bricks to keep them at the right level, as they like to have their roots in shallow water.

Each tub or similar-sized container will hold one miniature water lily, a couple of marginal plants, and two or three underwater oxygenators.

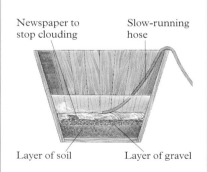

Newspaper to stop clouding

Slow-running hose

Layer of soil

Layer of gravel

MULTIPLYING THE IMPACT Grouping similar containers of differing sizes is an easy way to create striking effects. Fill them with irises and dwarf water lilies for a water garden display that costs less than building a pond.

CIRCULATING WATER

MANY WATER FEATURES, such as fountains, cascades, and artificial streams, require a pump to circulate the water. A submersible pump hidden in the trough below a fountain or under a cascade is the most practical and is surprisingly easy to install.

Choose the right pump for the feature you want to build. A small, low-voltage pump with a transformer is all that is needed for a soft bubble fountain, for example, while a taller jet requires a more powerful pump.

GENTLE TRICKLE A fish seems to leap from pool to pool, a trickle of water escaping from its mouth onto the *Houttuynia cordata*.

RING OF BOXWOOD Gleaming, colored stones surround this simple spray fountain, encircled by a boxwood hedge. The tank and the pump mechanism are hidden underground.

White-flowered *N. candida*, scented *N.* 'Odorata Minor,' pink *N.* 'Pygmaea Rubra,' and wine-red *N.* 'Laydekeri Purpurata' are also suitable.

Among the prettiest floating plants are frogbit, *Hydrocharis morsus-ranae*, which is similar to a tiny white water lily, and the ivy-leaved duckweed, *Lemna trisulca*, with its delicate green fronds.

Oxygenators are sometimes invasive, but are easily controlled in small pools by removing surplus growth when necessary. The water buttercup (*Ranunculus aquatilis*) is one of the less invasive oxygenators, whereas *Elodea canadensis* and *Lagarosiphon major* should only be introduced in pools where it is possible to thin them out in autumn, because they can get invasive if left to grow unchecked.

EASY-TO-FIT MOVING WATER

Simple wall fountains are especially suited to shady corners, where few water plants flourish. They are also among the

CLASSICAL FORMALITY Clipped boxwood topiary and banks of lavender, with *Rosa rugosa* behind, combine to create a feeling of timelessness in this quiet corner. A cherub fountain stands in a small formal pool, with a brick edge softened by the elegant flowers and foliage of *Iris laevigata* 'Alba.'

safest features to install if your garden is used or visited by young children, for whom water is an irresistible magnet.

Traditional designs for wall fountains include the heads of lions, gods and goddesses, or cherubs, as well as dolphins and seashells. Such a feature is all the more effective when it is surrounded by an arch, an alcove, or an "illusion" trellis suggesting an alcove.

Some striking contemporary garden features have water running over a series of chutes of brick, slate, timber, metal, glass, or even glass bottles.

A simpler variation on this idea is made by setting a row of outlets along a wall with the water flowing from them into a long, narrow trough, with a concealed pump returning it to flow continuously from the outlets. The choice of outlets includes masks, spouts, short pipes of clay or metal, or V-shaped chutes of stone, tiles, or slate. Such a feature has great visual impact in gardens of all sizes, and yet the sound is gentle.

In a small garden, set a freestanding fountain in a flower bed, on a raised circle of brickwork, or on a low plinth in one corner. In a slightly bigger garden, a freestanding fountain makes an attractive centerpiece for a larger pool.

REGULATE THE FLOW

In general, the larger the pool, the better a fountain looks, so allow a reasonable surface both for the play of falling water and for plants beyond. Water plants, especially lilies, dislike being splashed.

The height and spread of any fountain spray needs to be appropriate. If the spray is too wide, it wastes water and leaves surrounding surfaces wet and perhaps slippery. As a rough guide, you should have a pool that is at least twice as wide as the height of the water jet.

With a narrow-mouthed container such as a Mediterranean oil jar, on the other hand, you can let the water brim over to trickle down the sides. This looks cool and soothing, whereas a bubble or spray jet is busier and more contrived.

Small fountains and wall cisterns have to be turned off and drained in winter, unless they are in a spot guaranteed frost free; the water trickle can freeze if left on and damage the fitting. And always bear in mind that, while the sound of water might be soothing to you, neighbors may not share your enthusiasm for an uncontrollable noise close by; so choose and site a fountain carefully.

FOUNTAIN DESIGNS

There is a remarkable range of fountain designs available in garden centers. Most of them come with their own pump and electrical fixtures. Installing them is generally straightforward and certainly rewards the small effort with ample pleasure.

FORMAL WALL FOUNTAINS
Wall fountains can be placed almost anywhere, from roof gardens to sunken patios. Most spout water from a pipe or an ornamental feature, such as a mask or the mouth of a fish, into a container below.

WATER CISTERNS
Cisterns are similar to wall fountains but have a tap in place of the waterspout. Like wall fountains, they are made in a variety of materials, and many designs are safe if young children use the garden.

TIERED FOUNTAINS
Although they can be installed as freestanding features, tiered fountains look best when placed in the center of a larger pool with the overflow spilling out of the bowl and into the surrounding water.

BUBBLE FOUNTAIN
The safe, low jet of water runs over pebbles held in a container. Bubble fountains are sold with their own pumps and reservoirs, both of which are hidden.

SMALL FOUNTAINS
Freestanding fountains sitting in their own bowl are useful in a limited space and look good set in flower beds. They range in style from traditional bowls, with or without pedestals, to tall terra-cotta jars.

TRADITIONAL FOUNTAINS
Fountains come in many designs, from the classical to the quirky. For a formal garden, look for traditional motifs such as dolphins and gods; in a relaxed setting, a whimsical frog adds wit.

INFORMAL
PONDS

A NATURAL-LOOKING POND is a still sheet of reflective water, its only movement a gentle rippling as fish rise or wind ruffles the surface. Perhaps soft eddies mark the spots where a small stream flows in and out.

Most man-made pools and ponds can be divided loosely into formal features and informal ones, which are generally more naturalistic. A large garden could employ both, with perhaps a classical wall fountain or formal pool near the house, and an irregular pool or a small stream in a wilder corner. But in smaller gardens, you generally have to decide on one or the other.

Though apparently artless, informal streams and ponds need meticulous care in design and placement. The pond in particular should be as large as possible — the more generous its proportions, the more convincing it will be — and curves must look natural from all viewpoints.

GETTING THE SHAPE RIGHT

In the wild, most ponds are roughly circular or elliptical, with a few indentations here and there; while streams, in the wild, meander between sloping banks or gush through rocky, fern-lined gorges. In a garden, such ponds or a simulated

BRIDGE WITH A PURPOSE Bridges always look best where they are really needed, not simply decorative. Here the bridge leads across the banks of a small stream planted with water irises, rhododendrons, and *Hosta undulata*.

IN THE SHALLOWS

Marginal plants, found in the shallows of ponds, are good for softening the edges of an artificial pool. Put the plants in plastic boxes of ordinary loam and place them so the box rim is just below the surface.

• Bog arum (*Calla palustris*): glossy leaves and arum-like sheathed flowers in late summer, followed by red berries.

• Bowles golden sedge (*Carex elata* 'Aurea'): foliage plant that grows to 16 in (40 cm) in very shallow water.

• Loosestrife (*Lythrum virgatum* 'Rose Queen'): bears purple spires from June to September; grows in water or mud.

• Bogbean (*Menyanthes trifoliata*): broad leaves, pink buds, and fringed white flowers in May.

• Golden club (*Orontium aquaticum*): waxy leaves and yellow and white sheathed flowers in May.

• Japanese flag (*Acorus gramineus* 'Variegatus'): small, invasive semi-evergreen with grass-like leaves.

• Dwarf cattail (*Typha minima*): a dainty bulrush with round, velvety heads from midsummer.

• *Iris laevigata* 'Variegata': hardy iris that flowers in June and July.

RED BLAZE Flowering evergreen azaleas add glowing color to the dense green foliage that leans down to the water. Rough stone boulders circle the pool, giving a natural edging that blends with the plants.

stream work best some way from the house and in the sort of spot where a natural feature might occur — coiling around the land's contours, for example, or settling in dips and hollows.

To help a stream look more natural, make it seem to rise as a spring bubbling up among stones and plants. On fairly flat ground, the flow of a stream can be altered by placing rocks on the stream bed, while on a sloping site, the water might run briskly down over a ledge or a series of falls and pools.

A small pond or short stream appears larger when its edges are in part concealed by carefully placed plants, so the water seems to disappear around a corner. A similar effect is achieved by placing a low bridge at one end so that the water appears to flow out from under it and then disappear into a group of plants at the other end, suggesting further reaches on either side.

PLANTING AN INFORMAL POND

A little cheating is allowed at the planting stage, for a truly natural pond contains only native water plants. Most gardeners want some variety, however — a few cultivated and more showy plants, perhaps, or at least some goldfish.

It is tempting to combine water and trees, which are so beautiful when reflected in still water. But trees often cast too much shade, and their dead leaves require a lot of cleaning up in autumn. Rotting leaves give off gases that will kill fish if they are trapped when the water freezes over, so you should either cover the pond with mesh to catch the leaves as they fall or scoop them out daily.

If you are intent on planting a tree nearby, try the neat little weeping willow *Salix caprea* 'Kilmarnock' for tiny ponds and the graceful *S. purpurea* 'Pendula' for a medium-sized pond. These have all the grace of the more common ones but are half the size or less. Another willow, *Salix exigua*, is not a weeper, but its elegant habit and silver leaves make it an excellent centerpiece for a group of gray, white, and blue plants.

The many varieties of Japanese maple have an affinity with water. Their lobed foliage, reddish flowers, brilliant autumn

CONVINCING STREAM Astilbes and hostas adorn one bank and a birch surrounded by forget-me-nots the other beside this artificial stream. Its authentic appearance comes from following what seem to be natural curves.

HIGH NOTES AND LOW In a small garden, a pond may be the major feature. Give it splashes of color as in this planting, where bright flowers are set among contrasting foliage — ribbed hostas, sword-shaped leaves, and the graceful plumes of pampas grass (*Cortaderia richardii*).

SAFETY FIRST

LOG BARRIER

TO MAKE a pleasing psychological barrier and protect the pond margins from impetuous children and heavy-footed adults, drive a number of logs or short lengths of wood into the ground about 8–10 in (20–25 cm) apart, a short way from the edge of the pond. Stagger the height a little if you prefer. Using them around roughly a third of the pond's circumference looks best, with taller plants guarding the rest.

You can prevent children from walking along the top of the logs by rounding off the sawn wood. To deter herons, use a staple gun to attach fishing line along the posts, about 8 in (20 cm) high. The line will not hurt the long-legged birds, but it will keep them away from any fish.

stance, or the bronze leaves and red flowers of *Lobelia cardinalis*. In a garden where there is much shade and muted color, the pond may be the main feature, and one you want to draw attention to.

CHOOSING MARGINALS

Attractive plants for the margins include the flowering rush, *Butomus umbellatus*, and marsh marigolds, surely the essence of spring. *Caltha palustris*, the familiar marsh marigold, has bright buttercup flowers, while the double form, *C. p.* 'Plena,' is smothered with yellow pompons.

Iris ensata, mimulus, primulas, and the twisted corkscrew rushes, *Juncus effusus* 'Spiralis' and *J. inflexus* 'Afro,' are also good for pond edges.

Where there is room, grow the invasive sweet galingale *Cyperus longus* or the less rampant *C. eragrostis*. Most people want a water lily or two, and goldfish appreciate their shady leaves. Excellent lilies for a small to medium pond are the red-flowered *Nymphaea* 'Froebelii,'

color, and intriguing winter outlines make them attractive trees to have in the garden no matter what the season.

With the choice and placement of shrubs and other plants in or near water, much the same considerations apply as for the rest of the garden. Climate and soil, contrasts of size, shape, and tones of foliage, and the subtle groupings of

colors with occasional "hot spots" all need to be taken into account when working out the plantings around a pond.

Plants are the most natural adornments to use in an informal water garden, and muted colors blend more easily. Foliage plants are ideal, with a few splashes of color — the blues and yellows of irises and marsh marigolds, for in-

N. 'James Brydon' (which is pinkish-red and scented and will stand a little shade), the pink *N.* 'Firecrest' and *N.* 'Rose Arey,' white *N.* 'Marliacea Albida,' and yellow *N.* 'Marliacea Chromatella.'

When planting directly into soil, use smooth stones to hold new plants in position. If the plants are in containers, mulch the soil with smooth pebbles and if necessary use larger stones to weight the roots down.

POND SURROUNDS AND FINISHING TOUCHES

Informal ponds and streams, edged in part with shrubs and marginal plants, are set off best by a surround of pebbles and cobblestones. Grass laid right up to the water's edge can become muddy.

If you wish to transform a formal pool into an informal one, a good way is to establish a shallow, irregularly shaped bog garden around the straight edges of the pool and fill it with moisture-loving plants. Such a garden would quickly disguise the earlier formality.

Bridges, stepping-stones, benches, and buildings all give character to a garden. Bridges especially are best placed where really necessary — not in an arbitrary and unconvincing fashion over a tiny stream you could easily step across.

- A stone slab, a pair of landscape ties, or a couple of thick, weathered planks make a strong, attractive bridge.
- A staggered run of roughly hewn stones or slices of tree trunk used as stepping-stones looks natural. Make sure they are level, stable, and moss-free.
- Keep seating simple. Benches by an informal pond or stream should have a casual, weathered look, with nothing so new that it spoils the effect.
- A deck chair or an old bench, a swing or a string hammock under an apple branch, some mossy logs, a plank or a slab of stone supported on bricks — all provide seating that does not jar.
- Buildings must be unpretentious — a rustic arbor of logs, for example, with a roof of brushwood.

Any number of ideas can be used to give a water garden its own character. A garden shed next to the pond could turn into a "boathouse" if given a veranda and a coat of bright paint and surrounded with exuberant plants. And sculpture, "found" objects — driftwood, stones, and shells — and figurines such as a stone frog or a pair of stately cranes add interest to ponds of all sizes.

CREATING A WATERFALL To seem convincing, waterfalls need a considerable drop over a wall or an outcrop of rock; here, maples frame the tumbling water and stand out against the stone around it.

RELAXING THE FORMALITY To soften the regular outline of a formal pool, replace some of the paving with cobblestones. Thick plantings of evergreens, yellow irises, and corydalis also help.

OVER THE WATER If you have a large body of water, create a quiet jetty from which to enjoy it. Wooden decking can provide a seating area among bamboos, gunnera, and cattails.

FORMAL POOLS AND FEATURES

A FORMAL POOL may lie bare and still as a dark mirror, be enlivened by water spurting up from the surface, or brim with water plants beneath which fish silently glide.

The pool might be at the center of a terrace or small garden. Where there is a little more space, it might divide one area of the garden from another and be crossed by a bridge or stepping-stones.

Whatever their size and shape, formal pools and other formal features look best near the house, in paved areas, or in any part of the garden that is laid out with a geometric design.

In many gardens, one component of a formal water design is often linked to another — a pool is fed from a cascade or wall fountain, for example, or is set at the far end of a narrow canal. The pool may be in virtually any geometric shape — oval, round, semicircular, rectangular, square, hexagonal, octagonal, and even, occasionally, triangular.

BEING INVENTIVE WITH SHAPE

Where space is at a premium, an L-shaped pool at the boundary or at the corner of a paved area is very useful, leaving the center of the garden free as a seating area. A pool of this shape is composed of two adjoining or overlapping rectangular shapes.

Other devices that serve to make a layout interesting include turning the whole design of the garden at an angle to the plot. A square pool becomes diamond-shaped, for example, or an area of paving becomes diagonal and runs between the long sides of two triangular pools. As the plantings around the garden boundary and the pool are thus swung into the garden, they too become diagonal and create hidden areas that give a feeling of extra space. A set of interlocking circles, one containing water, can be swung to create similar effects.

Circular or semicircular pools have a less rigid feel to them than other geometric designs and work in both formal and informal settings. A semicircular pool is

MODERN LINES Contemporary materials, designs, or sculptures often look stunning in a formal garden. Here, low jets in the mini pool and the sprays falling from it add gentle ripples to the strong, still, angular forms.

SPLASH OF COLOR A fountain adds movement to this pool, the height of the spray kept low so as not to disturb the water lilies. Softening the formal pool shape and paved terrace are scatterings of cranesbill geranium, rose campion, blue-eyed grass, lady's-mantle, campanula, and sunrose.

ROPES TO HELP PLANT A POOL

A SIMPLE METHOD for placing a large container of water plants in a large, filled pool is to thread two lengths of rope or clothesline through the holes in the container. With one person on each side of the pool, use the ropes to suspend the plant over the water.

When it is correctly positioned, lower the container into the water. Once the container is firmly on the bottom of the pool, pull the ropes through the holes and out of the water.

slightly less formal), or grass. Grass looks very attractive laid up to the water, but its edge will sink under foot traffic unless it is laid over a firm rim of some kind, such as chamfered concrete.

HOW TO CREATE ATMOSPHERE

Whatever pool shape and type of edging you choose, the planting radically alters the feel of any stretch of water in the garden. A rectangular pool, edged with flagstones and unadorned on a terrace or a fine, level lawn, for example, is an austere but handsome sight.

Purists insist that no plants should rise above the rim of such a pool to detract from its symmetry, but you can add a fountain so that its plume gives movement. Framing the pool with pleached hornbeams heightens the formality and gives a hint of mystery, while a planting box at each corner holding strap-leaved, blue-flowered agapanthus makes it less severe. Replace the agapanthus with generously planted urns and a few pots at each corner for an atmosphere altogether warmer and more welcoming.

In a tiled courtyard garden, an unplanted pool — quite shallow, lined with matching tiles, and boasting a central fountain — adds a Mediterranean look. Grow plenty of plants such as figs, cape

often used against a garden wall as the basin of a fountain. If the garden is fenced, build a freestanding wall to back the pool and support a wall fountain. Give the wall an arched or stepped top, and frame the edges with foliage to complete a pleasing and self-contained feature.

WISE CHOICES FOR POOL SURROUNDS

The materials that surround a formal pool, whether level, raised, or at the center of a sunken garden, should complement the materials used to build the house and employed elsewhere in the garden. Local stone, slate, and brickwork

are all possible edging materials, and where they tie in with the house walls, the paths, and any terracing, the whole gives a restful and unifying impression.

Concrete, engineering bricks, substantial timbers, and decking all go well with contemporary architecture, while frost-proof quarry and terra-cotta tiles complement most types and periods of brick houses. An added advantage to terra-cotta tiles is that they can be laid both inside and outside the house, thereby providing a link between the garden and house interior.

The surround for a level pool might be made of paving, gravel (which is

CHANGING THE MOOD OF A POOL

ELEGANT SIMPLICITY A low hedge of clipped boxwood surrounds the pool, level with the stone coping, and is surrounded by a formal area of gravel. Magnificent water lilies take pride of place.

SOFTER CHARM The pool frame is almost hidden by profuse plantings spilling over its edges. White petunias flank the large-leaved *Bergenia cordifolia*, while alchemillas foam along the sides.

TO THE RESCUE

REPAIRING A CONCRETE POOL

A CONCRETE POOL that is leaking can usually be repaired with a flexible liner. As the damage was probably caused by settling or a weak mix of concrete, fresh cracks are likely to appear if you simply fill existing ones.

Drain the pool. Any cracks should be filled with mortar and then left to dry before the pool is relined.

It is possible to order a preformed or flexible liner direct from the manufacturers in the correct size for your pool. This is slightly more expensive than fitting one yourself, but does save time and ensures a neat finish.

---

plumbago, jasmine, and star-jasmine as wall cover, with lilies, daturas, geraniums, palms, oleanders, and yuccas in containers to create a lush, southern mood. Put the foliage plants in the shade and the bloomers in the sun. Mosaic, marble, slate, pavers, granite setts, or terra-cotta tiles all work well as lining materials for the pool, especially with matching or similar materials alongside.

THE BEST SHAPES FOR RAISED POOLS

Most raised pools belong near the house or in formal parts of the garden, since natural ponds — with the exception of some rock pools — are seldom above the surrounding grade level.

Stone troughs and specially designed fiberglass tanks make handsome raised pools and are perhaps the simplest way to introduce a sculptural element into the garden. They are particularly suited to small spaces, tucked away in a corner.

If a trough or similar container is not available, you can build a raised pool of any size quickly and inexpensively. Most raised pools are about 18 in (45 cm) high, but if you want a deeper pool — to accommodate fish, perhaps — sink it partly into the ground, or the rim becomes inconveniently high. Any excavated soil can be used in raised beds.

Reclaimed stone, old bricks, stuccoed and painted concrete blocks, or landscape ties are all suitable materials for such a pool, which is then lined with a preformed or flexible liner. A raised pool is safer than a ground-level one for very small children and people with impaired sight and is easy to care for.

For a central pool in a restricted space, choose a round, hexagonal, or octagonal shape. These take up less room, have no sharp corners, and combine well with raised, triangular beds in each corner. Alternatively, use a space-saving triangular pool across one corner of a small garden or sunken area, adding a wall fountain above or a bubble fountain within the pool. Surround the pool with large containers of fatsia, choisya, and bamboo, underplanted with ferns and some trailing ivy. And if you long for blossoms, add summer pots of white impatiens frothing around tall flowering tobacco.

Fish thrive in a raised pool as long as you provide them with water that is deep enough and some shade. Short pieces of clay drainpipe lying on the base, or slates supported on bricks, make good havens, while lily pads and floating aquatics also provide cover.

MORE UNUSUAL FORMAL FEATURES

The term "rill" or "canal" sounds a bit grand but refers to a long, narrow pool or channel, usually with straight edges. The most elaborate ones link a series of small, formal pools or lead into a larger pool, adorned by two or more fountains, perhaps. Two rills, one set on each side of a path, lead the eye most effectively to a view, a garden bench, or an ornamental building of some kind.

Rills, whether plain or planted, alter a garden considerably, giving an impression of different proportions. In a long, narrow garden, for example, a rill cutting across from one side to the other, with a

Water gently trickles from an elegant urn

Fish dart beneath delicate scented lilies

A border of bricks circles the pool

A PLACE FOR REFLECTION

Broad slabs of stone offer a tempting place to sit, trail a hand through the water of this raised hexagonal pool, and enjoy the gentle sound and motion in a few minutes of contemplation.

A FLASH OF GOLD darting out of sight under the broad, gleaming leaves of a water lily, a splash of purple from a cluster of irises, the sound of trickling water — all draw the young and old to the edges of this pool. Scent, sight, and sound merge to form a harmonious whole, with the plants and edgings around the pool creating a flattering frame for the water-loving plants inside it. As water trickles from the mouth of the urn into the pool, a few lazy ripples shiver on the surface.

PLANTS FOR THE POOL

The open gravel setting allows for an approach to the pool from any of its six sides. Small ferns, lady's-mantle, and grasses soften the juncture of the low brick walls with the ground, while a circle of matching brick edging defines the pool area and keeps the lush foliage of hostas, irises, and bergenias at bay.

Within the pool, a small scented water lily (*Nymphaea* 'Rose Arey') takes pride of place while an elegant *Zantedeschia aethiopica* 'Crowborough' rises serenely above the pool's broad stone coping, each small yellow flower spike wrapped protectively in a sculptured white sheath.

No matter what the shape or size of a garden, the reflective quality and movement of water add an extra dimension to the design, and its depths provide a home for water-loving plants.

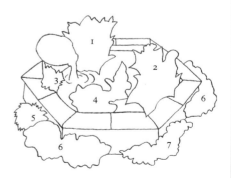

1. *Iris × robusta* 'Gerald Darby'
2. *Zantedeschia aethiopica* 'Crowborough'
3. Blue lobelia (*Lobelia siphilitica*)
4. Water lily (*Nymphaea* 'Rose Arey')
5. Sedge (*Carex oshimensis* 'Evergold')
6. Lady's-mantle (*Alchemilla mollis*)
7. *Blechnum penna-marina*

DISCREET RAISED POOL Wooden decking flanks this unusual pool, adding a change of level to the small garden. A trickle of water falls from the fish's mouth, while a pot of pink *Nerium oleander* softens an awkward corner.

SIMPLE AND PRACTICAL Slabs of paving stone placed at regular intervals serve as attractive bridges across an extended rill. The lush *Lysichiton*, hostas, and *Ligularia* on either bank obscure the hard lines of the rill's edges.

TO THE RESCUE

CONTROLLING POND INVADERS

ALGAE AND PONDWEED are rarely a problem in a pond properly planted with floating and oxygenating plants and stocked with fish.

If algae should multiply out of control, try tying a bundle of straw to a brick or other weight and sinking it in the water. Leave it in until the water has cleared. For best results, treat the pond every spring and autumn — and keep it free of dead leaves and decaying vegetation.

To remove blanket weed algae (an aptly named green slime), use a forked branch or rake. Simply twirl the branch or rake in the weed, which will wrap itself around it and be easily lifted out.

The floating common duckweed (*Lemna minor*) can be removed from a large pond by two people holding a long rope. Skim the rope across the pond's surface and lift out the weed.

---

stone slab laid across here and there to bridge it, effectively shortens and widens the garden. The impression is reinforced if each end is blurred by bamboos and evergreen plants, and the water seems to flow out of sight beneath an arch in each of the side walls.

Circular or semicircular rills can be used to create most unusual designs. They might be used to border a seating area, enclose a flower bed, or simply to surround a statue on a circular pedestal. As long as the water is still and at least 18 in (45 cm) deep, the rill can be stocked with fish.

Where a bridge is needed to cross a formal pond or canal, match the bridge's design to the period of the house or the style of the garden. Stepping-stones are another alternative; they should stand slightly above the water's surface and be laid securely on their supports of brick or concrete. Again, they work best when they match the style of the pool and its surround, but above all they should always be absolutely level so that they appear to be floating on the water.

RUNNING WATER ON A SLOPE

One formal design feature that is often combined with a pool is a cascade or a series of cascades. Although these are most often associated with the gardens of great estates, a small garden — where the sound of falling water has a tremendous impact — will easily accommodate a miniature version.

The water might fall from a chute, flow over a straight lip, or run down a ramp or two or three steps into a pool or trough below. It is then returned to the top of the cascade by a submersible pump hidden in the pool or trough.

Where a garden is on two levels, set a short, wide flight of steps into a sloping bank and edge the steps with a cascade on either side. More ambitiously, construct a ramp or fall of steps to carry a rush of water from a pool in the upper level into another below.

Although it appears complicated to construct, the building of a cascade is a relatively simple affair — its construction is similar to that of a recessed flight of garden steps. It may well be set into a sloping site and lead into a pool below, faced with materials as diverse as bricks, salvaged curbstones, slabs of stone or slate, or landscape ties. The steps of the cascade can be edged with either a hard surface or a green one of lawn or plants.

A cascade is one of the few formal features that also works successfully in an informal setting, looking at home, for example, in an unmown grassy slope planted with a few bulbs.

MAKING A POND MORE FORMAL

If you inherit an irregular, informal pool from previous owners of the garden and would like to give it a more geometric, formal look, there are a number of ways in which you can achieve this without removing the feature totally.

Wooden decking is particularly attractive when used with water features. Decking can be laid over the existing curves of a pool, leaving a rectangular or L-shaped opening that harmonizes with the rectangular lines of a terrace or patio made of more decking, of gravel, or of bricks, stone, or concrete slabs. Small changes of level add interest, while the raised and overhanging edges of the decking work to make a pool feel larger because the water seems to continue underneath it farther than it really does.

Where you are adapting a larger pool, treat the part nearest the house in this way or create a straight line along the near side with slabs, planks, or landscape ties. Blur the edges at the pool's far end with bold, shapely plants; clumps of bamboo and the enormous leaves of *Gunnera manicata* are good for this, as is the giant rhubarb, *Rheum palmatum*, especially *R. p.* 'Bowles Crimson' and red-leaved *R. p.* 'Atrosanguineum.' *Rodgersia aesculifolia* also has impressively large, sculptural leaves.

Closer to the house, and particularly where there are awkward angles as the curves join the straightened edges, the rather formal and upright *Iris ensata* and *I. sibirica* work well. The sweet flag *Acorus calamus* — especially the attractive *A. c.* 'Variegatus,' and the stately *Zantedeschia aethiopica* 'Crowborough' — are striking. You can also obscure any abrupt angles with a large, elegant container or two, planted with an architectural fatsia or a strap-leaved, white- or blue-flowered agapanthus.

TESTING BEFORE DIGGING

Before spending anything on a water feature for the garden, draw a plan of the garden's current layout on graph paper. Make a tracing of the layout and then use cut-outs from a catalog to try out various sites, sizes, and shapes for the water feature, remembering that all pools

UNDISTURBED CORNER Water lilies love still water and sun, and a scattering of *Cistus* petals at the margin indicates how undisturbed the water is in this brick-edged pool. *Cistus*, too, is a sun-lover and makes the perfect full-flowering companion to set off the sculptural character of water lilies.

should be sited out of the wind, away from frost pockets, and in the sunlight for at least half the day, especially if they are going to contain fish. If you live in an area of very heavy rainfall or frequent flooding, site a pond where there is no danger of excessive runoff fouling it. If you have no choice about where the pond is to be placed, avoid this risk by building a raised pool.

Next, try out your design in the garden by marking out possible shapes, using straight boards for the straight lines and right angles cut from plywood for the corners. Circles and semicircles can be drawn with a string-and-peg compass.

MOCK-UP PLANTING

Place containers of plants and pots of houseplants in and around the outlined pool for a rough idea of planting possibilities. Also try out an assortment of objects to represent rocks, boulders, or cobblestones.

Push in bamboo stakes to indicate reeds and clumps of irises, while opened umbrellas of various sizes, tied to stakes, can represent weeping trees and shrubs. All this preparation is well worthwhile; mistakes made when the feature is built either irritate forever or are costly and time-consuming to correct.

ELECTRICITY AND WATER SUPPLIES

Lights transform any garden at night. But when set underwater, beneath pools, fountains, and cascades, or playing over the surface of a pond and nearby plants, lighting makes a garden seem magical, and the dark gleam of water adds a certain mystery.

Outdoor lighting and recirculating pumps both require an outdoor electrical line. This must conform to local codes and should be installed by a licensed electrician, with cable laid in conduits to guard against damage by garden tools. A circuit breaker is essential.

A few lights and a standard fountain or small waterfall can run off a low-voltage transformer (12 volt), which can be connected to an outlet inside the house. Again, both protected cable and a circuit breaker are needed.

A water supply near a pool is useful for filling and later refilling it. In dry climates, this may be a regular task in summertime. Keep in mind that too much tap water added at one time can upset the ecological balance of the pool.

PRACTICAL WATER USE

SAVING WATER becomes more urgent every year as prices rise and supplies cannot meet the growing demand. It makes sense to reduce non-essential water consumption in the garden.

Install water barrels to catch rainwater from the roofs. You can buy specially designed plastic rain barrels — complete with lid, downspout connector, overflow pipe, and spigot — from garden centers and catalogs. Or you can make your own from a clean steel, wooden, or plastic barrel. Make sure you use a lid, or even a piece of fine mesh, to block out insects and debris; you also want to install a tap at a convenient height so you can draw off water into a bucket or watering can. Surround the barrel with gravel or a layer of bricks so that any splashing will not disturb the soil.

Most well-established plants can survive long periods of drought without sustaining much harm. However, if you live in a low-rainfall area and are choosing new plants, consider those that tolerate dry soil and baking sun. These include artemisia, broom, ivy, buddleia, cactus, ceanothus, rock-rose, genista, cotoneaster, *Convolvulus cneorum*, eleagnus, euphorbia, *Geranium macrorrhizum*, lavender, lilac, oriental poppy, periwinkle, pinks, *Rosa rugosa*, rosemary, salvia, santolina, tamarisk, and yucca, among many others.

Even these drought-tolerant species need water until their root systems become established, however. Rig up temporary shade in sunny weather and mulch the soil with gravel.

MINIMUM CARE FOR MOISTURE-LOVERS

Save moisture-lovers for naturally damp or shady places, digging in plenty of organic matter before planting.
- Water in new plants and apply a 2 in (5 cm) mulch of compost.
- Use black plastic or newspaper as a mulch and cover it with grass clippings, pebbles, or shredded bark.
- Plant thick ground cover to help the

CUTTING BACK ON WASTE Install a water barrel, or more than one, to collect rainwater from the roof rather than letting this valuable resource go to waste. Rainwater is slightly acid, so reserve it for your acid-loving plants.

ECONOMICAL LUSHNESS This tiered fountain, recessed into an alcove, uses the minimum of water. A mere trickle is needed by the tenacious mosses and liverworts, flanked by maidenhair ferns, clinging to the stone and giving it a velvet texture. A pot of *Zantedeschia* completes the scene.

PERFORATED HOSE SYSTEM

INSTALLING a watering system need not be expensive and can save both water and money by directing water only where it is needed. Use a soaker hose fitted to an outside faucet and laid along the surface of flower beds or a lawn, to be turned on and off as required. The similar seep hose leaks water from a seam to soak an area 18 in (45 cm) wide along its length.

plants together in a shady spot or put them, in their pots, in a larger container filled up with damp soil or gravel.

🍂 Line hanging baskets with black plastic and push a small plastic bottle pierced with holes into the soil to fill with water for slow release.

🍂 Provide constant moisture for plants in pots by mixing water-absorbing polymer with the soil.

You need to water a lawn only in long periods of very hot, dry weather. In dry spells, simply let the lawn grow tall to 3 in (7.5 cm) or more and leave the cuttings on the ground. When absolutely necessary, give the lawn a good soaking once a week at the most and, if possible, leave some areas unmown and unwatered.

WHICH HOSE TO USE WHEN?

A watering can gives you the best control for watering, but if you are using a hose, always check faucets, hose connections, and the hose itself for drips and leaks. Use a hose fitted with a screw nozzle, trigger nozzle, or adjustable watering wand to prevent waste.

It is good safety practice to fit any type of hose to a tap with an anti-siphon valve. This cuts out all risk of polluted water siphoning back into the household supply.

Tangled hoses are likely to split and leak. In a small garden, keep the hose coiled away in a tub or terra-cotta pot that has been drilled to allow one end of the hose through to the faucet connection. Or install a wall-mounted hose reel, which is a tidy way to store a hose.

Small accessories that are also helpful are hose guides — small plastic spools with a zinc spike that sticks into the ground. These are also sold as cable guides and allow the hose to swivel freely as it is used, thus preventing both kinks in the hose and damage to plants.

soil stay moist. Keep down weeds, which compete for moisture, by hoeing or hand weeding. Hoeing also loosens the soil so that moisture penetrates more easily.

🍂 Do not water unnecessarily or too often. Give water to plants that really need it. Most prefer an occasional deep soaking to a daily sprinkling.

🍂 Any especially thirsty or fragile plants can have their own watering system. Cut

off the end of a plastic bottle, stick it neck downward into the soil just above the roots, then fill the bottle with water.

🍂 The same direct watering works for trees and shrubs. Use a short piece of 4 in (10 cm) plastic pipe instead of a bottle and drill holes along the length. Fill it with gravel so that it does not become blocked by soil and insert it above the plant roots.

🍂 During a very hot spell, group potted

IN TUNE
WITH NATURE

RESPECT FOR NATURE'S PROCESSES is strong in gardeners, and many feel a growing reluctance to risk causing long-term damage with unnecessary applications of chemicals. Cooperating with nature, rather than conquering it, is the spirit of the times. Whether you want to improve soil fertility, banish weeds, or control pests, there are plenty of "green" methods that work — and that let you be more environmentally responsible.

Poppies, feverfew, and sage flourish in an informal bed. Growing a wide variety of plants together makes them less susceptible to attack by a particular pest.

TAKING A GREENER LINE

RATHER THAN WORRY that chemicals are harming plants and creatures in your garden, why not use "greener" methods? Even without converting to strictly organic techniques — though you may want to do so — you can take a few easy steps toward plant care that does not harm the environment.

In the long term, chemical-free or almost-chemical-free gardening leads to stronger and more self-sufficient plants.

Most pesticides do not distinguish between friend and foe, killing both the pests and the beneficial creatures that feed on them, so chemicals may even increase the number of garden pests. Some weed-killers may leave poisonous residues and weaken the plants they are intended to protect. Storage and use of such toxic chemicals also involve risk, especially to children and pets.

STEPS TO GREENER GARDENING

Fortunately, there are ways to maintain the quality of your plants without using chemical products. Use home-grown "green manures" and compost made from garden and household waste to improve soil structure, retain moisture, and replenish vital nutrients.

Help reduce the number of pests by growing plants that attract their natural predators — such as frogs and birds — or by changing to more varied planting schemes. As a last resort, use biological pest controls, which are more narrowly targeted and much less harmful to the environment than chemical ones.

Assure your plants the best chance of success by giving them a little attention every year and by acting in harmony with the natural balance among plants, soil, bacteria, insects, and animals.

TOP-LEVEL DISPLAY Adopting simple green techniques, such as growing ground cover rather than using weed-killers, is not just kind to the environment. It also cuts down on garden maintenance and leads to a lovely garden packed with healthy plants, such as these roses and pinks.

Taking Care of the Soil

THE BEST WAY to keep plants strong and healthy, and produce a fine display of flowers and healthy crops of fruits and vegetables, is to improve the soil. Because gardening tends to involve growing many plants in a confined space, it is inevitable that they take more out of the soil than they give back. Adding bulky organic matter and natural fertilizers replaces the lost nutrients and keeps the soil in good condition.

To manage your soil to the best advantage, you need to know whether it is light or heavy. Sand is lightest and coarsest in texture. It feels harsh and gritty, and the particles scarcely hold together at all, even when moist. Clay is heaviest and finest in texture. It feels sticky like putty when wet and dries out into rock-like clods. In between the two extremes are the silty soils that feel smooth, soft, and floury.

What Your Soil Needs

Light and sandy soils are quick-draining and need organic matter such as garden compost or rotted manure incorporated to improve their capacity to hold water and nutrients.

Heavy soils such as clay and silt need to be opened up, as in their natural state they are slow-draining and hard to work. Adding organic matter, again, helps improve the soil. With very heavy soil, it is also worth digging in a conditioner such as gypsum (calcium sulfate).

Use the weather to your advantage. Do heavy work such as breaking new ground or turning over a plot in autumn. Don't bother to break up the large clods; the frost will get to them and help break them down to a crumbly texture.

Garden compost is one of the most effective materials both for feeding the soil and improving its structure. Others are rotted manure, leaf mold, and materials available at a garden center such as composted bark.

Turn Waste into Compost

You can make compost at home easily. Kitchen and garden waste are immensely valuable sources of nutrients and soil conditioners, so it is worth making use of them rather than throwing them away. To make the best compost, you need the

Compost Bins for Convenience

Inside a bin, garden debris heats up rapidly, the rotting process is faster, the amount of moisture in the pile can be controlled, and everything stays neatly in one place. You need more than one container to make enough compost, unless your garden is small.

SECTION BOX
Cheap and easy to make, each square is made from four straight pieces of board nailed to four battens. You can add sections as the pile builds up, then take them away to mix or remove compost or move the pile.

DOUBLE ACTION
Some bins are divided into two sections for the most convenient use of space. The compost on one side can "cook" while the other side is being filled.

INSULATED PANELS
Plastic bins with insulated panels help debris to heat up and rot rapidly. These bins are raised off the ground with bricks and mesh to improve air circulation and are easy to take apart for emptying.

OPEN-FRONT BOX
With a slotted front for easy access, this type of box is solid and long-lasting. Either buy one or make one from 3 ft (1 m) planks. If you make two bins, arrange them side by side so they share one wall and save on wood and heat.

CHICKEN WIRE AND BURLAP
Make your own cheap compost bin by stapling wire mesh around four posts. Line the inside with burlap or a tarp. An unlined container is best for making leaf mold.

COMPOST TUMBLER
Made of plastic on a metal frame, a tumbler saves the job of emptying, mixing, and reloading the pile. The compost rots quickly because you can aerate it frequently by turning the bin.

MAKE THE BEST COMPOST

THE RICHEST COMPOST comes from a mixture of moist debris, such as lawn clippings and kitchen waste, with drier materials such as fallen leaves or prunings. Adding animal manure speeds up decay, but all organic material rots eventually. After about six months most piles are brown, crumbly, and ready to use.

1. Spread a thick layer of coarse, woody prunings in the base. Push it into the corners but do not press down. This layer raises the pile slightly off the ground, allowing air to circulate so that the compost rots more quickly.

2. Place a layer of weeds (but not the roots of perennial types), ornamental-plant trimmings, and spent bedding plants onto the pile. If you are using an open-front container, put another slat in place to keep compost from spilling out.

3. To speed the decomposition process, mix the weeds with grass clippings or manure as you fill the bin. Combining coarse, dry materials with fine, moist ones aerates the pile and keeps it from turning slimy and smelly.

4. If the pile seems dry, sprinkle it with water. It is better to water as you go along rather than at the end, to achieve an even consistency. The material needs to be damp enough to encourage the bacteria that make it rot, but not soaking wet.

5. Cover the pile so that you can prevent moisture loss but keep out rainwater. A lid also helps the compost heat up more quickly. A piece of old carpet does the job well; cover it loosely with a sheet of plastic to keep the rain out.

6. Once the bin is full, leave it for a month or two. If you have enough space, turn the compost to mix it. Empty the material out and fork it back in. Turn the pile sides into the middle as it goes back in; the center is hotter and rots faster.

right balance of air, water, and debris. The tidiest way to combine the three elements is in a container, although you can simply make a pile on the ground and cover it with a thick sheet of black plastic or a tarp while it slowly decomposes into usable compost.

Virtually any vegetal waste can be added to the pile except diseased plant material and perennial-weed roots, which will continue to grow unless the mixture becomes very hot.

Collect kitchen scraps, such as vegetable and fruit peelings, coffee grounds, and tea bags, for the pile, but avoid dairy products, fats, and meats, which turn rancid and attract rodents. Eggshells, nutshells, and seafood shells can also go on the pile, but they will take a long time to decay.

Cardboard boxes, wastepaper, and old newspapers can be torn up or shredded and mixed into the pile.

Ideally, add a nitrogen-rich material at about every 1 ft (30 cm) of depth as the pile builds up to increase fertility and speed decomposition. This could be fresh manure, fresh grass clippings, or comfrey leaves. There are also organic compost activators available.

Worms burrow in and out, breaking down the material. Bacteria also work on the compost. To increase their activity and improve drainage, stand the bin on soil rather than paving. If possible, place the compost pile where you are going to grow vegetables in the future. Then you make the most of nutrients that may seep out from the bottom of the pile. This natural feeder makes the soil very fertile.

Make sure your bin is easily accessible with a wheelbarrow. You may be adding heavy material such as manure and large quantities of debris too awkward to carry.

SETTING UP A WORM BIN

A worm bin is a container for kitchen and garden waste inhabited by a colony of worms that break down organic material into extremely fertile compost. It takes up less room than a compost pile, and debris in it rots more quickly.

You can buy a worm bin, but it is very easy to make your own from a plastic garbage can with holes drilled through the bottom. Raise the bin just off the ground and slide a drip tray under it because liquid will drain out. To start the colony, put into the bin about 100 red worms bought from a bait shop. Add the waste slowly at first so that the worm

A HOMEMADE WORM BIN

MAKING YOUR OWN WORM BIN is a dual money saver — garden compost is free, and you save on the price of a store-bought bin.

Make a few holes in the bottom of a plastic garbage can or old barrel big enough to hold at least a month's waste. Prop it up on bricks at each side, with a drip tray underneath. Put a layer of gravel in the bottom to improve drainage, then a layer of well-rotted compost or manure about 3 in (7.5 cm) deep. Add the worms and cover them with a thinner layer of compost or manure. When the colony has become established, after a couple of weeks, start adding kitchen scraps.

Lid secured with brick

Fresh kitchen waste

Processed material

Layer of gravel

Bin raised on bricks

Drip tray to catch liquid

population has time to build up. Do not add fresh waste until the last batch is almost digested and starts to resemble ready-to-use compost. The worms will work their way up, processing the waste. As the drip tray beneath fills up, collect the liquid, which is rich in nutrients; dilute it with ten times as much water and use it as plant food.

Once the bin is full, take out the processed material to use in the garden. The worms will be in the top layer. Skim the layer off and set it aside while you empty out the rest of the compost, then put it back in the bottom of the bin. Alternatively, push the compost through a garden sieve to sift out the worms.

As winter sets in, move the bin into the basement, garage, or tool shed where

THE PRIDE OF THE BORDER The bark of a flowering cherry (*Prunus serrula*) glistens with health above the perennials. The cherry's leaves are used for leaf mold and the spent border plants for compost, both returned to the border to sustain its fertility.

LEAVES TO IMPROVE SOIL

AUTUMN HARVEST Collect deciduous leaves in autumn to make leaf mold — one of the best soil conditioners. To see its effect, go for a walk in the woods and, as your feet rustle through the leaves, look at the rich, crumbly soil under the trees, the result of decades of decayed foliage.

MAKING LEAF MOLD Some gardeners prefer to compost tree and shrub foliage separately from other wastes, because leaves are fibrous and will decompose more slowly than grass clippings, spent flowers, and kitchen scraps.

READY TWO YEARS LATER When the leaves have crumbled to a flaky, soil-like consistency, spread the leaf mold onto bare ground as a mulch or fork it into the top layer of soil, where it greatly improves the structure.

RENTING A SHREDDER

IT IS OFTEN BETTER to rent a shredder than buy one. A shredder is expensive, especially the large models that allow you to chip large branches. The smaller models can be laborious to use, as you can feed in only a couple of twigs at a time. Shredders are also noisy, and a large one does the job more quickly. Check costs with a tool rental shop, and see if neighbors are interested in sharing one for a weekend. Wear gloves, safety goggles, and ear plugs when you use a shredder.

the temperature is at least 59° F (15° C), as the worms do not function as efficiently at lower temperatures.

HOW TO MAKE LEAF MOLD

A container to hold leaf mold (composted leaves) is cheap and quick to build. Hammer four posts, 4 ft (1.2 m) tall, into the ground to make a square about 3 ft (1 m) across and run wire netting around them, securing it with galvanized metal staples. Make sure that the netting can be removed easily from one side of the square for emptying out the leaf mold.

Use smaller containers if you are not likely to have a large number of leaves. Make a compact version by hammering just one post into the ground and fixing both ends of the netting to it, forming a cylinder. Alternatively, store the leaves in plastic garbage bags with a few holes pierced in them.

In autumn, gather up the leaves every few days, because they soon form a solid layer that smothers and kills any grass or other plants underneath. Put the leaves in the container and pile them loosely; if packed tightly they rot more slowly. Water them if they are dry. Check the pile from time to time to make sure it is damp enough, as rotting slows down if there is not enough moisture. Patches of a white, thread-like fungus are a typical symptom of dryness.

Leaves take a year or two years to rot down, so it is best to keep each year's batch separate. For a labor-saving alternative to gathering and storing leaves, take a tip from nature and let them rot where they fall — but only leave them to rot if they are on bare soil. Rake the leaves off any plants or the lawn, and put them on the ground under shrubs or trees and between herbaceous plants, where worms and other insects will take them into the soil during winter.

Choose a way to collect the leaves that you find easiest according to the amount.

🍂 Use a spring rake with plastic or metal tines for small areas.

🍂 If you have large areas to clear, consider a hand-pushed leaf sweeper.

🍂 Leaf vacuums suck up the leaves into a large bag. Blowers quickly blow the leaves into piles and corners where they can be picked up.

🍂 You can wait for a strong autumn wind to blow leaves into piles, provided they are not left for very long.

USES FOR WASTE WOOD

Use a shredder to cut your unwanted tree prunings and branches to a manageable size. Then add them to the compost pile or save them to spread as mulch. Shredding makes use of valuable material and keeps debris out of landfills.

Safety is a prime concern when using a shredder. If the machine is electrically powered, always use a properly grounded cord that cuts off the power supply immediately if any electrical fault occurs. Keep children and animals at a safe distance and always turn off and unplug the machine when it is unattended.

Never put fresh wood chips directly onto the soil as a mulch, because they draw nitrogen from the soil as they rot. Instead, stack them in a pile, cover it, and leave for at least six months.

ANIMAL MANURES AS SOIL AMENDMENTS

Manures are useful for building fertility and tilth in both new garden beds and established ones. The only caveat is: never use fresh manure around plants, as the rapid release of nitrogen as it decom-

poses can burn the roots and stems, especially of tender young seedlings. Let it rot for six months to a year by stacking it in a pile and covering it with a plastic sheet, so that the nutrients will not be leached out by rainwater. Turn it occasionally to speed decay and add wood chips or dead leaves to minimize any odors in summer. You can use fresh manure, however, in the compost pile — it is a potent activator.

Obtain manure from farms, stables, and feedlots. City gardeners can contact zoos. You can also ask animal handlers for manure when the circus passes through town. Always make sure that the manure from any source has not been treated with pesticides, and the animals have not been given medicines. Processed manure is available in bags at garden centers.

Bird and bat guano are the "hottest" manures, with the highest nitrogen content. Of the commonly available farm manures, those from sheep, rabbits, and poultry are the hottest, while manures from cows, pigs, and horses are relatively cold. Never use droppings from household pets, not even as additions to the compost pile.

Dig rotted manure into the top six inches of soil or into the planting hole when preparing new ground or spread it over the beds as a mulch, making sure to leave space around the plant stems.

READY-MADE SOIL CONDITIONERS

Mushroom compost, which is the spent soil from growing mushrooms, is good for opening up the dense structure of clay soil, although it contains few nutrients. It also makes an attractive, deep brown mulch. You can sometimes buy it in bags from garden centers or obtain it in bulk directly from mushroom farms, who may deliver for a fee. Check in your telephone book for local growers.

Prepackaged soil conditioners, such as bales of peat moss and bags of processed sludge, are on sale at garden centers and nurseries but can be expensive. These products not only improve structure but also contain nutrients to enrich the soil.

Tree- and shrub-planting mixes are also available. They contain fertilizer and are specially blended to get new plants off to a good start.

Planting mixes and soil conditioners may be sold alongside potting soils, but

SOIL-IMPROVING PLANTS So-called "green manure" is provided by plants such as mustard that grow quickly and are then dug into the soil, where they decompose to release nutrients and open up the soil structure.

BREAKING HEAVY GROUND Annual rye grass has deep roots that break down heavy soils and improve sandy ones. While still standing, it prevents weed growth and holds nutrients that are otherwise washed out of bare soil.

SOURCE OF NITROGEN In fall, sow clover seed in rows or broadcast it over an empty bed and rake it in lightly. In addition to preventing erosion on bare ground, it helps fix nitrogen in the soil once the crop is turned under.

GROWN FOR GREEN MANURE

Some of the most popular choices for green manures — crops that put nutrients back into the soil — are common plants that are extremely easy to grow:

- White clover (*Trifolium repens*): perennial legume that provides an excellent source of nitrogen; prefers clay soil and tolerates shade. Grows well throughout the country, but thrives in cool, moist climates.

- Mustard (*Brassica nigra, B. rapa,* and *Sinapis alba*): quick-growing plants that mature in 3–6 weeks. Do not grow where club root is a problem, as it is susceptible to the disease.

- Oats (*Avena sativa*): annual grass that tolerates acid soil but dislikes heavy clay. Especially good for the South, where it overwinters.

- Winter rye (*Secale cereale*): annual grass; well-suited to cold climates. Prefers well-drained loam and tolerates acid soil. Needs ample moisture for best growth.

- Winter vetch (*Vicia villosa*): annual legume that will tolerate any type of soil as long as it is well-drained. Withstands drought and cold.

- White lupine (*Lupinus albus*): annual legume that is best for the South, Northeast, and Central Plains. Prefers light, sandy, acidic soils, but also a good conditioner for heavy clay.

PRACTICAL BUT PRETTY Comfrey hybrids, for example *Symphytum* 'Hidcote Pink,' make vigorous ground covers. Though the common comfrey is most beneficial for making compost, the hybrids have showier flowers.

note that potting soils have a totally different function, being prepared for growing plants in containers.

GROWING GREEN MANURES

Do not allow patches of soil to remain bare for any great length of time. You risk weed infestation as well as soil erosion. Plant "green manure" instead to improve soil structure and fertility and protect bare ground.

Simply sow seed in the fall and turn the crop under before it flowers. The decaying matter adds nutrients, opens dense soil, and retains moisture. Wait a week or two after tilling before you plant the soil.

The most common crops used as green manures are legumes and grains. Trouble-free choices include clover, fava beans, barley, oats, wheat, and rye.

Related to traditional green manures, but used in a different way, is comfrey (*Symphytum officinale*), a perennial with large leaves that are rich in potassium. You can harvest and use the leaves in several different ways.

For the compost pile, add comfrey leaves in a layer every 1 ft (30 cm) or so as an activator. Alternatively, shear the plants and leave the foliage directly on the soil as a nutrient-rich mulch. This is especially good for vegetables, soft-fruit bushes, and flowering plants, which all have a high potassium requirement.

You can also make a liquid fertilizer from comfrey. Drill a couple of holes in the bottom of a large bucket, pack it full of comfrey leaves, and place a cover over the leaves; weight down with a brick. Stand the container on a couple of bricks with a tray underneath. Dilute the liquid that seeps out with ten parts water; apply to plants.

OTHER WAYS TO DISPOSE OF GARDEN DEBRIS

Sometimes, despite compost piles, worm bins, and shredders, you still have too much garden debris to handle at home. Trash haulers may not take large woody prunings, grass clippings, and leaves, but the material can be of use elsewhere.

Many communities are now composting garden debris, so take garden waste that you cannot recycle yourself to municipal disposal sites or call your local government or trash collector about pickup days. In some communities, residents can also take home without cost wood chips or finished compost.

Aside from leaves, the biggest single source of organic waste is Christmas trees. Use the boughs to spread over dormant perennials as a protective winter blanket; the remaining trunk is easily disposed of. Some municipalities also collect trees for use in stabilizing sand dunes or for shredding into mulch.

PRECAUTIONS TO OBSERVE WITH BONFIRES

Bonfires are illegal in many parts of the country but are still permitted in some rural areas. Where they are permitted, they offer an easy way to dispose of bulky, rot-resistant garden wastes such as brush or tree trimmings.

To avoid getting on bad terms with the neighbors, bear a few points in mind before lighting a fire.

🖝 Check with your municipality to see if bonfires are allowed. Many areas have been designated as "clean air" zones, and burning may be permitted only in certain seasons, if at all.

🖝 Site the bonfire well away from any buildings, fences, or plants.

🖝 Stack and cover the bonfire material until it is completely dry. It will burn much faster and give off less smoke than green, damp waste.

🖝 Choose a still day, as strong winds could easily blow the fire out of control. Keep a spade and a couple of buckets of water or a hose close by, in case the fire gets out of hand.

🖝 Light the fire late in the evening, not during the day on a fine weekend when neighbors are outside in the fresh air enjoying their gardens.

🖝 Do not leave a fire unattended or leave it smoldering when you go to bed.

🖝 It is courteous to tell your neighbors before you light a fire, so that they can close their windows or take in any laundry if they wish.

🖝 Check that there are no creatures such as rabbits or toads hiding in your bonfire pile, especially in autumn, when they tuck themselves away for the winter.

🖝 Scatter the ash from the fire on the soil or in the compost pile — it contains potassium and other useful minerals.

Fallen leaves are gathered for leaf mould

Stored logs make mulch when shredded.

Comfrey is used for nutritious plant feed

RECYCLING IN A WILDLIFE CORNER

With a little ingenuity, most plants can be recycled for the garden's next generation. A sheltered spot in the dappled shade of a deciduous tree is a perfect site.

TURN ONE CORNER of your garden into a hardworking "recycling" center. Everything in the site serves more than one purpose and can be reused — either by you or other garden occupants.

The most valuable material is foliage. In fall, after the flowers have provided a season of beauty, as well as food and shelter for wild creatures, their spent top growth can be collected and added to the compost pile. The deciduous linden leaves can also be turned into leaf mold or shredded for mulch. The comfrey leaves are a rich natural source of potassium that can be used to brew a liquid fertilizer or applied directly on the soil as a nutritious mulch.

The log pile can provide shelter for a variety of helpful garden denizens — toads, for instance, that eat insect pests, and worms that "recycle" debris into castings. The log bark can be shredded,

and the wood chipped, for mulch.

Even the bird-seed hulls beneath the feeder can be added to the compost pile.

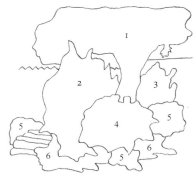

1. Littleleaf linden (*Tilia cordata*)
2. Foxglove (*Digitalis purpurea*)
3. English ivy (*Hedera helix*)
4. Comfrey (*Symphytum officinale*)
5. Herb Robert (*Geranium robertianum*)
6. Forget-me-not (*Myosotis sylvatica*)

BEATING THE WEEDS

T HE TREND TOWARD informal and densely planted mixed borders is a great help in combating weeds. The weeds are crowded out by ornamental plants, and there is less bare soil where they could otherwise flourish.

One of the most pleasant aspects of gardening today is the more relaxed "live and let live" attitude toward weeds in the lawn. A more informal style calls for a new outlook on many so-called weeds, as long as they are not too invasive.

Many gardeners no longer take pains to rid the lawn of daisies, clover, violets, and other wild plants, preferring to allow a flower-studded carpet. Similarly, some people simply leave moss in the lawn. It provides a smooth green carpet, which is the chief point of having a lawn. However, moss can gradually eliminate grass and cannot take hard wear.

PREVENTING WEEDS

If you do not want weeds in the lawn or border, be ruthless. Even if you prefer the "natural" look, aggressive perennials such as wild garlic or ground ivy can become a plague. Such weeds are hard to get rid of once they have taken hold, so make conditions as unfriendly for them as possible and act immediately when you spot a seedling.

There is a clear line between a well-groomed lawn dotted with wildflowers and a scraggly patch of grass overrun with weeds. Make sure you stay on the right side of the line by following a few good practices.

LAWN KNOW-HOW

For a new lawn, prepare the ground well. The soil needs the same attention whether you are starting a lawn from sod or seed. The best times to begin are autumn and spring, when seed germinates and establishes quickly, and the soil is not likely to dry out. Remove all perennial weeds and dig or rototill the soil. Firm and level the area thoroughly, or you will end up with a lumpy lawn.

Dig up weeds by hand, taking care to remove all the roots of deep-rooted weeds such as dandelions. Use a fork for this or an asparagus knife that lets you penetrate deep down to pry out the weed roots. If you have to use a chemical, use

TOOLBOX

AERATING A TIRED LAWN

IF THE SOIL is especially heavy and the lawn is too large to spike with a garden fork, buy or rent an aerator — a tool that pulls out plugs of soil. For a small lawn, a foot-powered aerator is adequate, although it is hard work — rather like jumping on a pogo stick. For a large lawn, rent a gas-powered model. After aerating, simply leave the small plugs on the lawn to decompose.

the least toxic available and dab it on the foliage with a paintbrush rather than spraying the whole area indiscriminately.

MAINTAINING THE LAWN

Having a weed-free "green" lawn is not difficult — it simply requires a bit more elbow grease instead of synthetic chemicals. Start with good drainage to ensure dense turf: even in well-drained ground, foot traffic compacts the soil. In fall, when the soil is slightly moist, spike the lawn with a garden fork, pressing it into the ground to the depth of its tines and rocking it back and forth to create holes.

You can also improve soil condition and drainage by giving your lawn a compost treat each spring and fall. Pass the compost through a screen, and spread a half-inch layer over the entire lawn. For grass in heavy clay soil, apply gypsum each spring as well, either with a mechanical spreader or by hand. It helps grass roots penetrate more deeply and aids drainage.

In early spring, scarify the lawn by going over the whole surface with a spring rake or a mechanical scarifier to remove thatch and moss, which impede drainage and air circulation. Scarifying also lifts up the spreading stems of weeds

such as buttercup, which can then be cut off by the mower. But watch out for earthworms, which are highly beneficial — they aerate soil and pull decaying organic matter into the ground.

🌢 Scatter compost on any bare patches and reseed; otherwise, weeds will overtake the exposed soil.

🌢 Promote lush turf by feeding the lawn with a slow-release chemical or organic fertilizer. Feed just twice a year with a fertilizer formulated for blade growth in spring and root growth in fall.

🌢 Do not cut the grass too short: longer blades stimulate deeper roots, creating a dense turf in which weeds cannot take hold. Long blades also shade out weed seedlings. The recommended height for a lawn varies from less than 1 in (2.5 cm)

PRETTY BUT INVASIVE The creeping buttercup lives up to its name, building up a network of plants once it takes hold in the soil. Despite the prettiness of its flowers, it is best to pull it out before it puts out runners or sheds seeds.

PERENNIAL PERIL Greater bindweed can get the better of garden plants. In autumn or spring, dig up clumps of weed-infested decorative perennials. Divide them, remove and destroy all the weed roots, then replant.

VIBRANT BORDER Dense plant growth is the best weed suppressor. A layer of gravel mulch between plants provides extra ground cover to help marigolds, gazania hybrids, and *Portulaca grandiflora* crowd out weeds.

to 4 in (10 cm), depending on the type of grass, the season, and the climate.

- Mow as often as needed, but never remove more than the top third of the grass blades.
- Keep mower blades sharp and properly adjusted for a clean, even cut. Frayed grass blades will weaken the grass; and if there are scalped patches, they can be overrun by weeds.
- Use a mulching mower so that the fine clippings will fall between the blades and serve as a nutritious, weed-suppressing mulch.

How To Deal with Weeds

There are several ways to tackle weeds, in a lawn or border, depending on whether they are annual or perennial. Deal with perennial weeds as soon as they appear among established plants in your borders, or very quickly they will get out of control. Hand weeding is simplest. Use a fork to dig out every last bit of root, otherwise any remaining pieces will regrow. The stems can be composted, but leave them in the sun for several weeks to dry out first. Do not put the roots on the compost pile, as they will probably survive the composting process to reinfect the garden. Throw them away or burn them instead.

Annuals are straightforward to control, because they grow fresh from seed every year, and the whole plant dies once the top growth is hoed off or pulled up. But perennial weeds, such as ground elder and bindweed, are more persistent. They continue to grow from year to year from tough root systems, and they spread by means of underground shoots that go beneath paths and fences into your borders, where both roots and stems exert a stranglehold on plants.

Renting a tiller to cultivate overgrown ground is a good plan as long as the weeds are annuals. Do not till if there are any perennial weeds, because the spinning blades will chop the roots into dozens of pieces, and each piece will produce a new plant.

Modern Methods of Controlling Weeds

Where you cannot dig out weed roots, perhaps because they are entwined in established shrubs, you may be forced to

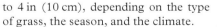

DECORATIVE MULCHES

LEAVES UNDER POTENTILLA Spread an organic mulch around newly planted and established shrubs to moderate temperature extremes and suppress weeds. Apply when the soil is damp and do not let it touch the stems.

WOOD CHIPS AROUND CRANESBILLS Wood chips suit a rustic-style garden. Mulches derived from wood range from fine shredded bark to rough nuggets. Either shred the wood yourself or buy prepared bark mulch.

COMPOST AROUND GAILLARDIAS Most annuals produce their best display in fertile, compost-rich soil. It is easiest to mulch when you are sowing seed or planting out potted seedlings in the garden. Use only fully rotted compost.

PEA GRAVEL WITH SAXIFRAGE Gravel of all sizes makes a suitable mulch for alpines, which thrive in shallow, stony soil that is reminiscent of mountain shale. Gravel drains freely but does not provide nutrients.

MAKING·IT·EASIER

CARPET CONTROL

DEPRIVING WEEDS of light will kill an infestation within a year, without your having to lift a finger. Just put down an opaque covering. Old pieces of carpet, sheets of cardboard or black plastic, or thick layers of newspaper all do the job admirably. Ensure that the edges are buried in the soil and that separate pieces overlap completely, so that not a scrap of light gets through.

use a weed-killer. Always start with the least toxic product available. There are organic herbicidal soaps containing fatty acids, which destroy by dissolving the coating on foliage. But "organic" does not mean harmless — these must be handled carefully and can easily harm ornamentals.

When possible, use a selective herbicide, which kills only certain weeds but leaves other plants unaffected. A systemic weed-killer is absorbed through the foliage and circulates throughout the plant without leaving a residue in the soil. Spray or brush it only on the weeds you want to destroy, as it can also kill desirable ornamentals if it gets on their leaves. Long-established pests may need several applications to kill them.

Apply herbicides on a mild, calm day so that a breeze will not cause the chemicals to drift; wear protective clothing just in case. Also, do not apply weed-killers when rain is expected.

Bindweed is a particularly intractable pest to deal with. One trick is to put bamboo canes near its base so the weed climbs up them. When there is plenty of growth, slip the bindweed off the canes, lay it on a plastic sheet, and treat it with a systemic herbicide.

HOW TO REPEL INVADERS

Perennial weeds do not recognize boundaries such as garden fences. Weeds invading your garden from outside first need to be killed, then prevented from

repeating the attack. Ideally, you should tackle the weeds at their source — even if the source is a neighbor's yard.

If you prefer not to approach your neighbor, tackle the weeds from your side, either by digging out as much of the roots as possible or by treating the top growth with systemic herbicide. Once the ground is clear on your side of the boundary, prevent another invasion by sinking metal or plastic barriers into the ground to a depth of 12–18 in (30–46 cm). If that is not possible, run a 6–12 in (15–30 cm) wide strip of black plastic sheeting along the lower rim of the fence, stapling it securely and burying the bottom edge in your border soil.

SMOTHERING WEEDS

Taking on a weed-infested plot does not have to mean using herbicides. Blotting out the light kills even the toughest weeds and requires nothing from you except patience. Provided you want to kill all the plant growth in an area, cover the ground with a sheet of black plastic that excludes all light. Leave it in place for six months to a year.

Deprived of all daylight, even the strongest weeds eventually succumb. Once they are dead, remove the covering material. The ground underneath should be reasonably dry and in an ideal state to be dug up, ready for cultivating the plants of your choice.

MULTIPURPOSE MULCHES

Mulching — spreading a layer of material on the ground to prevent weeds from growing — offers many other benefits. It reduces water loss from the soil through evaporation and insulates the plant's roots to prevent damage from rapid changes in temperature. Some mulches also add vital nutrients and conditioning to the soil.

Mulches can be organic — consisting of plant or animal material — or manufactured, such as a plastic or geotextile sheet. Spread an organic mulch on bare soil in a layer about 2 in (5 cm) deep but keep it away from plant stems, or they might rot. Lay a manufactured mulch on a bed before planting, then cut slits or holes in it to set in plants or sow seed.

CHOICES FOR ORGANIC MULCHES

There are numerous organic materials useful as mulch, from compost to corncobs. For year-round use in borders, most gardeners prefer an ornamental mulch, such as shredded bark, bark nuggets, or cocoa shells. It is left in place and replenished as needed to maintain the desired depth. For seasonal use, as in a vegetable patch, you can spread straw, hay, chopped leaves, or shredded newspaper (as long as it does not contain colored inks). Simply turn it into the soil at season's end.

Never use any organic matter that mats down, such as coffee grounds or peat moss, as a sole mulch. Mix it with chopped leaves or another "airy" material before applying. Take note that some mulches, including fresh sawdust and wood chips, deplete nitrogen from the soil as they decay. Compost them for six months before use and dig some extra nutrients, perhaps bloodmeal or rotted manure, into the soil before spreading them.

Match your mulch to the plants. For acid-lovers, including azaleas and camellias, use a material that is acid forming: pine needles, oak-leaf mold, or composted sawdust from cypress or oak. Boxwood likes the extra potash that cocoa shells provide. Buckwheat hulls, chopped corncobs, and straw are neutral and can be used on plants that do not need acid.

Many organic mulches are available from garden centers in bags or in bulk. You can also hunt up your own sources — ask a local brewery for their spent hops,

PROTECTION UNDER PLANTS A mulch of well-rotted, straw-flecked manure under roses adds nutrients to the soil, retains moisture, and smothers weeds. The naturally abundant flowers and robust growth of *Rosa* 'Iceberg' are a tribute to the fertility and balanced structure of the soil.

which make an excellent mulch, or contact arborists and utility companies that trim trees around power lines to see if they have surplus wood chips. Some communities also have leaf-composting or brush-chipping sites and offer free mulch. Make your own mulch by chopping fall leaves or newspaper in a shredder or with a lawn mower. Or feed brush through a chipper.

GETTING THE BEST FROM ARTIFICIAL MULCHES

Plastic mulches, though not attractive, are the vegetable garden's best friend. They warm the soil to allow earlier planting and prevent mud from splashing on plants and ripening fruits. Plastic sheets with a reflective surface also help repel some insect pests. One drawback is that plastic mulches are not permeable, so water and nutrients must be provided under the sheets.

The latest in manufactured mulches is geotextiles, or landscape fabrics, which are permeable woven or bonded materials. They are safe to use in permanent plantings, such as shrub borders, as they allow water and air to penetrate. Because they degrade when exposed to light and are unattractive, you need to cover them with a layer of ornamental mulch such as shredded bark or pea gravel.

KEEPING PLANTS HEALTHY

O NE OF THE KEYS to ensuring healthy plants is to choose robust ones in the first place. Nurseries, garden centers, and mail-order firms vary considerably in the quality of the plants offered, so it is best to know what to look for.

Reputable plant purveyors stand behind their goods. Although details may differ, they will generally guarantee to replace hardy plants that die within a certain period, unless the plants have suffered from obvious neglect. Inquire about warranties before you buy.

SELECT NEW PLANTS WITH CARE

Choose plants that look vigorous and are free from pests, diseases, and weeds. All plants should be clearly labeled, but avoid those with faded labels that have clearly been on sale for a long time. Reject any plants that are pot-bound — with their roots bulging out of their pots — as their growth will have been impeded and they may not recover fully when planted out. The exception is herbaceous perennials, which can often be rejuvenated by division. During the growing season, do not buy any plants obviously suffering from lack of water.

The ideal time to buy roses, trees, and shrubs is spring, when the new season's stock comes on sale, although it is possible to buy container-grown plants year-round. You can often buy woody and herbaceous plants more cheaply as bare-root specimens when they are dormant. Never buy bare-root evergreens, however, as their roots need constant moisture, which a soil ball can provide, to replace the water lost through the leaves.

Buy disease-resistant varieties whenever possible, particularly of roses. Some cultivars, especially the newer ones, are selected for resistance to common diseases such as black spot, mildew, and rust. If you are buying fruit bushes, check that the stock is certified virus-free.

THE BEST PLANT FOR THE SITUATION

Rather than trying to force plants to do what you want, be guided by their needs. Putting plants in suitable conditions and soil — be it sun or shade, acid or alkaline — ensures that they will flourish. It also

LEAFY SPLENDOR The leaves of a variegated hosta and the reddish tints of a Japanese maple provide as much beauty with their shapes and colors as a bed of flowers would. As a bonus, hostas form dense, spreading ground cover, so they keep down weeds and prevent erosion.

saves you money, because a plant may fail if the conditions are wrong. Although there are some tolerant, unfussy plants that grow well almost anywhere, most have particular preferences. For instance, rhododendrons must have acid soil and part shade, while abutilon needs a warm, sheltered location.

Select plants suited to the site where you want to put them. Gather as much information as practical before you buy — look in books, talk to fellow gardeners, and ask growers at reliable nurseries and garden centers. Going armed with as much detail as possible on the site and type of soil in your garden will help you pinpoint the ideal plants.

THE RIGHT MOVES TO PREVENT DISEASE

Vigorous plants are unlikely to succumb to disease. A plant under stress from lack of food or water, or just from poor grow-

ing conditions, is much more liable to fall prey to sickness. If you practice good garden hygiene, disease is less likely to take hold. Diseases are spread by spores that may continue to breed on dead material, so pick off or gather up any diseased leaves, flowers, or fruits and dispose of them off site — do not put them on the compost pile. A little tidying saves you time and money in having to replace weakened plants.

When a plant keeps suffering from the same disease year after year, get rid of it. The plant could be old or may not like the conditions in your garden.

When you are replacing a dead plant, choose a different species. Diseases specific to the former plant can remain in the soil to attack the new arrival. "Rose sickness" is a prime example — new roses may not thrive in soil that has previously grown roses at any point over the past 10 or even 15 years. The reason is unclear,

BENEFICIAL PREDATORS Hoverflies prey on aphids, so try to encourage as many of these wasp-like insects as possible. Hoverflies are drawn to the garden by open blooms rich in pollen and nectar such as single-flowered roses. You can also set out French marigolds to attract them.

SLUG DAMAGE There are several measures you can take to reduce the slug population. One is to sink small bowls or cartons into the ground and fill them with beer. The liquid is irresistible to slugs, which fall in and drown.

LACEWING HOTEL Lacewing larvae feed on aphids, so encourage the adults to lay eggs by hanging a "hotel" in a tree in winter. Cut the bottom off a plastic bottle and line the inside with corrugated paper, secured with wire.

NATURAL PEST CONTROL Ladybugs are the most efficient aphid predator. The aphids suck the sap from young growth and flower buds, disfiguring and weakening the plant and sometimes spreading viral diseases.

COMMON DISEASE Roses may be afflicted by black spot, except in industrial areas where air pollution works to your advantage, keeping the disease at bay. Look for rose cultivars bred to resist black spot if it is rife in your region.

but it seems that the roots of new roses are more vulnerable than the older, more robust roots of long-established roses.

MAKE FRIENDS OF PREDATORS

The best way to control pests is to let nature do the work for you. Many birds, frogs, and toads eat pests. There are also insect predators: ladybugs, hoverflies, lacewings, spiders, parasitic wasps, and praying mantises are your friends.

Encourage these creatures to live and flourish in your garden by providing a friendly habitat for them. Beetles and other ground-living insects like long grass, so it is worth having a meadow area, however small. Leave some stones and pieces of wood on the ground for a daytime hiding place.

Ladybugs hibernate in dry crevices or on the leaves and stems of dead herbaceous perennials, so do not cut these down until early spring. If you have to burn garden prunings and debris, shake the stems out first to dislodge any ladybugs. You can even buy "lures" that are

CARE WITH CHEMICALS

SPRAY ONLY on a windless day, so that there is no danger of the chemicals drifting on the breeze. Spray insecticides in the evening, when fewer beneficial insects, such as bees, ladybugs, and hoverflies, are around.

Use as little of the chemicals as possible by treating only the plants that are directly infected, rather than spraying indiscriminately. Keep chemicals away from ponds and other water bodies. Label them and keep them locked up.

HERB AS REPELLENT The strong smell of chives is said to repel pests that are attracted by scent, so try growing the herb near susceptible plants. The flowers appear in the summer and are edible along with the stems.

treated with a pheromone that attracts ladybugs and other aphid-eaters.

Hoverflies are drawn to flowers full of nectar. They also love carrot and parsley flowers, so leave a few of these plants when you harvest; usually the flowers bloom in the second season of growth.

COMPANION PLANTING

Planting nectar-rich flowers to attract pest-controlling insects is just one form of companion planting, which is the use of plants to benefit each other. Some plants are said to prevent pests and diseases in the first place. Strong-smelling ones such as onions and garlic deter pests. Interplanting rows of carrots with onions masks the carrot smell that attracts carrot root fly.

Planting marigolds is believed to help prevent pests, thanks to the strong, pungent smell of the flowers and foliage.

Bee-attracting plants are especially useful with runner beans, fruit trees, and tomatoes, which need to be pollinated to set fruit. Bees home in on blue- and purple-flowering plants in particular, such as bugloss, phacelia, globe thistle, hyssop, lavender, and rosemary. They are drawn to the fragrant flowers of sweet peas, so plant them to grow up stakes alongside poles of runner beans.

DISADVANTAGES OF CHEMICALS

If you use chemical pesticides, you may also kill the pests' natural predators, so the next infestation will have a better chance to flourish. Spraying roses with a general insecticide, for instance, may kill the ladybugs and hoverflies that feed on destructive greenfly.

The effect of killing such beneficial garden creatures can make the problem worse in the long run. Widespread chemical use has also made some pests more resistant, and as a result new or stronger chemicals have to be formulated to combat them.

Gardening without chemicals saves you money and time, and it prevents potential damage to your health and harm to the health of the garden's natural pest controllers. Most horticultural problems can be efficiently tackled using safe, alternative methods.

GUIDELINES FOR THE USE OF CHEMICALS

If there is no choice but to use a chemical, there are guidelines you can follow for maximum safety and minimum impact on your garden.
- Choose pesticides that are derived from natural sources, such as neem and pyrethrum. But remember that some products may still kill beneficial insects, including bees, as well as pests.
- Always follow the manufacturer's instructions and wear protective clothing if recommended.
- Store chemicals in a locked cabinet, away from children and animals.
- Spray only infected plants or parts of plants. Blanket spraying, apart from the expense, can harm wildlife in the garden.
- Keep pets away from the treated area for a couple of days.

SCIENCE FOR THE GARDENER

Introducing a natural predator that will attack one type of pest without harming another is called biological control. Many large-scale commercial food and plant producers are using biological controls instead of chemicals, with such success that gardeners are taking up the idea, too. Such controls are mostly available by mail-order. One of the commonest is the nematode, a tiny parasitic roundworm used against beetle grubs.

Most biological controls are especially effective when used in an enclosed environment such as a greenhouse. Do not use chemical sprays as well, or you will kill the introduced predator.

Biological controls are safe to use and extremely effective, provided that you follow a few rules. The environment needs to be reasonably warm — but the minimum temperature requirement varies according to the type of predator. As soon as you notice a growing pest population, introduce the predator. Once all the pests have been consumed, the predator will die out, and you will have to reintroduce it for any future infestations.

Make sure that you use the correct predator for each pest.
- The tiny but effective parasitic wasp called *Encarsia formosa* for whitefly.

(continued on p. 314)

Hoverfly grubs devour aphids on roses and broad beans

Hoverflies gather on fennel flowers in midsummer

Blue phacelia and poached-egg plant feed hoverflies all summer

A BORDER OF COMPANION PLANTS

In a border of mixed species, each plant attracts a different predator to its pests and draws on different nutrients. Companion planting takes this natural scheme a step further.

TO MAKE MIXED PLANTING effective, place species that are susceptible to a particular pest close to plants that attract the natural predators of that pest.

Aphids infest many garden plants. Blackflies have a special fondness for broad beans, lettuce have their own lettuce aphid, and roses are often smothered in greenfly. Lupines also attract aphids, but, like broad beans, they put nutrients back into the soil.

ATTRACTING THE DEFENSE

Aphid eaters such as hoverflies and ladybugs follow supplies of their food but may not gather until pest numbers have built up. Speed up the process with judicious planting.

The best way to attract hoverflies is with nectar-rich flowers. Among their favorites is poached-egg plant (*Limnanthes douglasii*), an easily grown hardy annual that makes a lovely path or border edging. It self-seeds easily, so if you plant it once, you will have it for years to come. Its delicately scented flowers appear from June to August.

Phacelia, another annual good for edging, and the tall fennel, which bears flat heads of flowers, also attract predators. The bronze-leaved variety of fennel is especially beautiful.

A cottage border is the perfect site for a well-balanced, informal planting of ornamental plants, herbs, and vegetables handsome enough to deserve a place in full view. Choose a sunny, sheltered, well-drained site and watch the beneficial insects come and do the job of pest control for you.

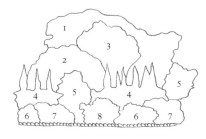

1. Hall's honeysuckle (*Lonicera japonica* 'Halliana')
2. *Rosa* Alexandra Rose
3. Bronze fennel (*Foeniculum vulgare* 'Purpureum')
4. Lupine (*Lupinus* Russell 'Blue Jacket')
5. Broad bean (*Vicia faba*)
6. Poached-egg plant (*Limnanthes douglasii*)
7. Lettuce 'Salad Bowl,' green and bronze
8. Tansy phacelia (*Phacelia tanacetifolia*)

CODLING MOTH TRAP

THE EASIEST WAY to trap the common apple-tree pest called a codling moth is with a pheromone trap. It contains a piece of sticky cardboard and the pheromone given off by female moths. This attracts males, which are trapped and so cannot mate with the females.

One trap is enough for up to five trees within a radius of about 50 ft (15 m). Hang it in the branches at about head height in mid-May, or earlier if the weather is warm.

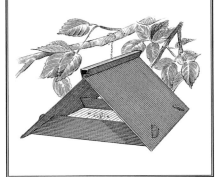

GRUB SOLUTION

A BIOLOGICAL CONTROL against Japanese and other destructive beetle grubs is provided by a parastic nematode, or roundworm. The nematode culture can be ordered from mail-order suppliers. It is mixed with water in a watering can or sprayer and applied to the soil for effective control for up to 12 weeks.

for red spider mites, a nuisance especially in conservatories.
- The ladybug *Cryptolaemus montrouzieri* for mealybugs.
- The predatory midge *Aphidoletes aphidimyza* for aphids.
- The predatory wasp *Metaphycus helvolus* for scale insects.
- The miniature mite *Amblyseius cucumeris* for thrips.
- The bacterium *Bacillus thuringiensis* for caterpillars.

TRAPPING SLUGS AND SNAILS

Slugs and snails are a nuisance in most gardens, but you can combat them without resorting to slug pellets, which are harmful to birds, toads, and other creatures that will eat the poisoned slugs. Cats and dogs are also at risk, because the damp pellets can get into the cracks between the pads on their paws, and they will swallow the poison while grooming. They should not be used around young children, either.

Certain plants are delicacies for slugs and snails, especially runner beans, delphiniums, hostas, and lilies, all of which often need protection throughout the season. In dry weather, try surrounding the plant with a deep layer of gravel or

HOMEMADE PLANT PROTECTORS As soon as you put in young plants, protect them from slugs and snails with covers made from clear plastic bottles. Leave the lid of the bottle off so that air can circulate around the plant.

wood ashes to deter the pests. But avoid mulching plants with organic materials, which only give slugs a hiding place.

Lay old carpet, paving stones, or planks on the ground overnight. Slugs and snails gather in such cool, dark places during the day. Turn the "trap" over in the morning to provide a feast for the birds.

You can catch slugs and snails by hand if you are not squeamish. Go hunting with a flashlight in the evening after sundown, preferably in damp weather when slugs and snails are most active. You can prevent slugs, snails, and other common garden pests from attacking your crops with simple traps or by putting up barriers.

KEEPING PESTS OFF CROPS

Birds often peck at young plants and seedlings in spring, at ripe fruits in summer, and at vegetable crops in fall. The best way to deter them from stripping seedbeds and ripening vegetables is to cover the crop with fabric row covers or fine-mesh netting. But make sure the edges are securely anchored to the ground with pegs or stones so that the birds cannot reach in underneath the material or get entangled in it. For fruit trees and bushes, drape fine-mesh netting over the plants. You can also try to scare the birds away by tying strips of tin foil or the tape from old cassettes onto stakes to flutter in the breeze.

Control codling-moth larvae, which burrow into apple cores, with a sticky pheromone trap.

Hang sticky light-green balls in fruit trees to trap plum curculios — beetles whose larvae tunnel into young fruits, causing them to drop prematurely.

When beetles appear in traps, spread plastic sheets under the trees in early morning and shake the beetles off the branches. Roll up the sheets and remove and destroy the beetles.

DETERRING PETS AND WILD ANIMALS

Not all creatures are welcome in the garden; much depends on your own view. While some people enjoy watching bunnies browse in the woods, for example, others consider the animals to be destructive pests. However, a bit of strategic planning usually keeps unwelcome visitors at bay.

Cats visit most gardens, so locate bird feeders and birdbaths away from poten-

tial hiding places from which cats can pounce. Put any birdhouses at least 10 ft (3 m) off the ground.

Fit your own cat with a collar and bell that warns birds of its approach. If you have an outdoor cat, installing a pet door can also pay dividends — most cats will prefer snoozing indoors and thereby spend much less time outside stalking birds. There are other ways to deter cats; see which works best.
- A cat or dog of your own often keeps away the neighbors' cats.
- Scatter prickly prunings of trees and shrubs such as hollies, roses, and barberries where cats enter the garden.
- Chemical deterrents in powder and liquid form are available. But be sure to buy a brand that states on the label that it is safe for use around children and animals. Apply it frequently, especially after a rain.
- Some cats detest citrus fruits, so try leaving out a few lemon halves or some orange peels.

PROTECTING PLANTS FROM DEER AND SQUIRRELS

Rural and even suburban gardens are often visited by deer. A wire or plastic mesh fence at least 8 ft (2.4 m) high or a three-stranded electrified fence are the only sure defenses against deer. Surround new plants with wire netting for a couple of years or until they are well established. An active dog will also help protect the yard.

Gray squirrels consume bird food and can damage young shrubs and trees. Wire netting makes a good shield for the plants, but keeping bird food away from the squirrels is more difficult.

Place bird feeders several yards away from trees and roofs, from which squirrels can make a flying leap. Use baffles on feeder poles or cages around the feeders themselves. You can also make a feeder harder to reach by suspending it from a clothesline run between two trees or posts. Or you can attach a pie plate toward each end of the line, with the feeder in the middle. The squirrels will eventually find a way around the plates, but their antics will keep you entertained in the meantime.

FOR THE BIRDS

Birds can be friend or foe: while some are delightful to watch and useful in attacking insects, others are a bother around plants, ponds, and even other birds.

Herons can remove all the fish in a garden pool unless the water is covered with a net. A more attractive alternative to netting is to run a thin wire around the pool about 1 ft (30 cm) high and the same distance from the water's edge. The wire will catch the bird's legs and scare it off. Create hiding places for the fish, such as large stones raised on bricks and large-leaved aquatics such as water lilies.

Small birds are sometimes attacked and killed by larger birds of prey, such as hawks, falcons, and owls. Give the little birds a better chance of survival by providing dense plantings of prickly shrubs around feeders or birdbaths so that they will have somewhere to hide. Or you can leave a shed or garage window open for the same purpose.

A bird feeder provides rich pickings for predators so, if their attacks are frequent, surround your feeder with 3 in (7.5 cm) wire mesh. This will allow only small birds to slip through.

Whatever your views on environmental matters, taking a greener approach can often offer shortcuts to keeping the garden in top condition. The rewards for using green ideas instead of chemicals are peace of mind on health and safety, natural beauty, and the satisfaction and low cost of recycling.

BIRD FEEDERS

Bring beauty and pleasure to the garden with a bird feeder during the bleak winter months. Place it away from predators such as cats and within view from indoors. A bonus: birds will remain in spring to eat insect pests.

NUT TOWER
Peanut feeders must have mesh fine enough to keep birds from pulling out whole nuts. Models with perches let several birds feed at once. Look for feeders made of strong, rustproof stainless steel.

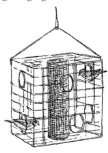

SQUIRREL RESISTANCE
A caged feeder keeps out larger birds as well as squirrels, allowing chickadees, titmice, and other small birds to feed at leisure. For a feeder as sturdy as this, use a strong hanging bracket to secure it.

POST-MOUNTED BOX
A flat-backed feeder is easy to screw or tie to a post, fence, wall, or tree. The overhanging lid prevents rain from falling on the seeds inside, and a ledge at the base gives birds a place to perch.

FINCH FEEDER
Entry holes in the outer cage allow only finches and smaller birds to reach the food; models are available with holes in varied sizes for different species. The feeder tube has fine mesh for seeds rather than nuts.

HOMEMADE MODEL
Make your own bird feeder from an old cup or mug suspended by a length of wire. Put scraps of bread, seeds, and suet in it, but not peanuts, unless chopped, as whole ones can choke small birds.

WINDOW FIXTURE
Supple but strong suction cups hold the feeder against the window. The birds soon get used to people moving around indoors, and you can watch their feeding from the comfort of an armchair.

USING THE TEMPERATURE ZONE MAP

Plants vary in their tolerance for cold; some are remarkably resilient, others are tender and die with the first hard frost. Thus, when choosing plants for your garden, it is important to determine how cold the winters are in your area. To do this, refer to the color-coded temperature zone map shown at right. The map is based on the 11 temperature zones identified by the US Department of Agriculture. Each zone represents a range of average minimum temperatures, indicating the severity of winter in the region.

When identifying a plant's hardiness, or its ability to withstand cold, most nurseries and gardening experts refer to these zones. When a plant is described as "hardy to zone 6," for example, it means that the plant will generally withstand temperatures between 0°F and -10°F (-18°C and -23°C).

The alphabetized plant chart on pages 318–328 includes USDA zone information, but when choosing plants you should also note that the microclimate in your garden may differ from the average by several degrees. The altitude of the land, its exposure to wind and sun, and its proximity to water can affect the temperature there.

TEMPERATURE ZONE
KEY

Zone 1   Below -50°F (-46°C)

Zone 2   -50°F to -40°F (-46°C to -40°C)

Zone 3   -40°F to -30°F (-40°C to -34°C)

Zone 4   -30°F to -20°F (-34°C to -29°C)

Zone 5   -20°F to -10°F (-29°C to -23°C)

Zone 6   -10°F to -0°F (-23°C to -18°C)

Zone 7   0°F to 10°F (-18°C to -12°C)

Zone 8   10°F to 20°F (-12°C to -7°C)

Zone 9   20°F to 30°F (-7°C to -1°C)

Zone 10   30°F to 40°F (-1°C to 4°C)

Zone 11   Above 40°F (4°C)

THIS CHART SUMMARIZES the characteristics and growing conditions of the garden plants recommended in the body of the book. Plants are listed in alphabetical order under their botanical name. The number(s) immediately after a name refers to the page where the plant is mentioned. Several botanical names have changed recently as plants have been reclassified: for example, the genus for wallflower is now *Erysimum*, not *Cheiranthus*. The former name is listed and directs you to the current name.

Sometimes plants are referred to in the text by common name only; their botanical names are listed on p.329 so that you can find them in the chart. Vegetables, fruits, cover crops (green manures), and wildflowers or wild plants are not included, but the general index (pp.329–336) shows where they are mentioned in the text.

The abbreviations used in the chart are explained in the key below. In the column for plant type, the designation refers to how the plant should be treated rather than its official botanical type; some plants that are tender or short-lived perennials, for example, are often grown as annuals. The column for soil requirements shows an entry only when a plant has particular needs; many plants are adaptable and will grow in most soils.

A

	PLANT TYPE	SOIL	SITUATION	TEMPERATURE ZONE	HEIGHT
Abies pinsapo 150	E Tr	-	☼	6	20ft (6m)
Abutilon 'Ashford Red' 221	E Sh	-	☽	8	10ft (3m)
vitifolium 'Veronica Tennant' 111	Sh	-	☽	8	12ft (3.7m)
Acacia dealbata 40	E Tr	-	☼	8	25ft (7.5m)
Acanthus mollis 39, 111, 203, 235,	P	-	☽	6	3ft (90cm)
spinosus 109	P	-	☼	6	3ft (90cm)
Acer griseum 151, 209, 224	Tr	-	☼	5	10ft (3m)
japonicum 'Aureum' 218	Tr	-	☼	5	30ft (9m)
negundo 'Auratum' 175	Tr	-	☼	2	30ft (9m)
'Flamingo' 175, 178	Tr	-	☼	2	30ft (9m)
palmatum 92, 150	Tr	-	☽	5	20ft (6m)
'Bloodgood' 193	Tr	A	☽S	5	10ft (3m)
'Rubrum' 218	Tr	-	☼	5	20ft (6m)
'Senkaki' 224	Tr	-	☼	5	20ft (6m)
pseudoplatanus 82	Tr	-	☽	5	20ft (6m)
'Brilliantissimum' 208	Tr	A	☽W	5	20ft (6m)
rubrum 'October Glory' 137	Tr	A	☽S	3	20ft (6m)
Achillea filipendulina 'Coronation Gold' 275	P	-	☼	3	4ft (1.2m)
× *lewisii* 'King Edward' 217	Rc	-	☼	5	4in (10cm)
'Moonshine' 29, 71	P	-	☼	3	4ft (1.2m)
'Schwefelblüte' ('Flowers of Sulphur') 144	P	-	☼	3	2ft (60cm)
taygetea 144	P	-	☼	5	18in (45cm)
Acidanthera murieliae (now *Gladiolus callianthus* 'Murieliae')					
Aconitum carmichaelii 162	P	-	☽	3	4ft (1.2m)
Acorus calamus 293	P	M	☼	3	3ft (90cm)
'Variegatus' 293	P	M	☼	3	2½ft (76cm)
gramineus 285	P	M	☼	5	10in (25cm)
Actinidia chinensis (now *A. deliciosa*)					
deliciosa 124, 193	Cl	-	☽	7	30ft (9m)
kolomikta 14, 175, 182, 202	Cl	-	☽S	4	20ft (6m)

	PLANT TYPE	SOIL	SITUATION	TEMPERATURE ZONE	HEIGHT
Adiantum venustum 87	P	-	☽	5	9in (23cm)
Aethionema 'Warley Rose' 40	Rc	-	☼	5	6in (15cm)
Agapanthus africanus 225	P	-	☼	9	4ft (1.2m)
'Ben Hope' 225	P	-	☼	9	3ft (90cm)
Headbourne hybrids 111, 271	P	-	☼	7	3ft (90cm)
praecox subsp. *orientalis* 225	P	-	☼	9	12in (30cm)
Ajuga reptans 68, 109	E P	-	☽/●	6	9in (23cm)
Akebia quinata 240, 251	Cl	-	☼	5	30ft (9m)
Alcea rosea 16, 25, 87, 88, 141, 190	P	-	☼	2	6ft (1.8m)
Alchemilla mollis 26, 103, 121, 135, 161, 175, 206, 216, 229, 272, 289, 290, 291	P	-	☽	3	18in (45cm)
Allium giganteum 275	Bu	-	☼	7	6ft (1.8m)
schoenoprasum 71, 89, 156, 180, 255, 256, 265, 267, 312	Bu	-	☼	5	12in (30cm)
Aloysia triphylla 175, 266, 267	Sh	-	☼	8	4ft (1.2m)
Alstroemeria ligtu hybrids 145, 146	P	-	☼	9	3ft (90cm)
psittacina 143	P	-	☼	8	2ft (60cm)
Althaea rosea (now *Alcea rosea*)					
Alyssum montanum 40	Rc	-	☼	6	6in (15cm)
saxatile (now *Aurinia saxatilis*)					
Amaranthus caudatus 109, 110, 150	An	-	☼	-	3ft (90cm)
Amelanchier lamarckii 51, 88, 127	Sh	-	☽	4	20ft (6m)
Androsace sempervivoides 217	Rc	-	☼	5	3in (7.5cm)
Anemone blanda 208	Bu	-	☽	5	4in (10cm)
'Radar' 125	Bu	-	☽	5	4in (10cm)
hupehensis var. *japonica* 162, 272	P	-	☽	6	4ft (1.2m)
nemorosa 62	P	-	●	5	6in (15cm)
pulsatilla 150	P	LM	☽	5	12in (30cm)
sylvestris 144	P	M	☽	4	18in (45cm)
Anethum graveolens 266, 267	P	-	☼	8	3ft (90cm)

PLANT TYPE An annual; Aq aquatic; Bam bamboo; Bi biennial; Bu bulb, corm, rhizome, tuber; Cl climber; E evergreen; P perennial; Rc rock plant; Ro rose; Sh shrub; Tr tree.

SOIL A needs acid soil; L needs alkaline soil; M needs moist to wet soil; D needs dry soil.

SITUATION ☼ does best in full sun; ☽ thrives in full sun or light shade; ● does best in full shade; ☽/● grows well in full sun, light shade or full shade; ●/☽ does best in full shade or light shade; S needs shelter; W tolerates wind.

TEMPERATURE ZONE numbers refer to the hardiness zones on the map on pp.316–317.

HEIGHT represents height at maturity (or 20 years for trees and shrubs).

	PLANT TYPE	SOIL	SITUATION	TEMPERATURE ZONE	HEIGHT
Angelica archangelica 267, 275	P	-	◑	4	6ft(1.8m)
Anthemis cretica 148	P	-	☼	6	12in(30cm)
cupaniana (now *A. punctata* subsp. cupaniana)					
nobilis (now *Chamaemelum nobile*)					
punctata subsp. *cupaniana* 144	An	-	☼	-	9in(23cm)
Anthriscus cerefolium 239	An	M	◑	-	2ft(60cm)
sylvestris 'Ravenswing' 161	P	-	◑	7	4ft(1.2m)
Antirrhinum 22, 137, 150	An	-	☼	-	18in(45cm)
Aquilegia bertolonii 217	Rc	-	☼	5	12in(30cm)
canadensis 146, 162	P	-	☼	3	2ft(60cm)
formosa 162	P	-	☼	3	2ft(60cm)
viridiflora 143	P	-	☼	3	2ft(60cm)
Arabis caucasica 220	Rc	-	☼	4	6in(15cm)
ferdinandi-coburgi 'Variegata' 21, 239	Rc	-	☼	6	3in(7.5cm)
Aralia elata 92, 235	Tr	-	◑	4	20ft(6m)
'Variegata' 221	Tr	-	◑	4	20ft(6m)
Araucaria araucana 90	ETr	-	☼	8	20ft(6m)
Arbutus menziesii 151	ETr	-	☼	7	20ft(6m)
unedo 178	ETr	-	☼	7	15ft(4.5m)
Argyranthemum foeniculaceum 213, 224	EP	-	☼S	9	3ft(90cm)
frutescens 17, 198, 216, 223	EP	-	☼S	9	3ft(90cm)
Armeria maritima 64, 65, 100	Rc	-	☼	4	9in(23cm)
Artemisia abrotanum 155	P	-	☼	4	4ft(1.2m)
absinthium 155	P	-	☼	4	3ft(90cm)
'Lambrook Silver' 111, 182, 201	P	D	☼	4	2½ft(76cm)
'Powis Castle' 227	EP	-	☼	6	3ft(90cm)
dracunculus 80, 155, 180, 267	P	D	☼S	3	18in(45cm)
schmidtiana 251	P	-	☼	4	12in(30cm)
'Nana' 150	Rc	-	☼	4	6in(15cm)
Arum italicum 'Pictum' 269	Bu	M	◑	6	12in(30cm)
Asarum europaeum 81	EP	M	●/◑	5	8in(20cm)
Aspidistra elatior 35	EP	-	◑	7	12in(30cm)
Asplenium nidus 177	EP	M	●	10	2ft(60cm)
scolopendrium 19, 129, 161, 189	EP	M	◑/●	5	2ft(60cm)
Astelia 199	EP	-	◑	9	2ft(60cm)
Aster amellus 273	P	-	☼	5	2ft(60cm)
× *frikartii* 'Mönch' 273	P	-	☼	4	2½ft(76cm)
novae-angliae 'Andenken an Alma Pötschke' 128	P	-	☼	2	2½ft(76cm)
'Harrington's Pink' 128	P	-	☼	2	4ft(1.2m)
Astrantia major 272	P	-	◑	6	2ft(60cm)
'Shaggy' 273	P	-	◑	6	2ft(60cm)
maxima 273	P	-	◑	6	2ft(60cm)
Athyrium filix-femina 270	P	M	◑/●	4	4ft(1.2m)
Aubrieta deltoidea 21, 29, 40, 45, 65, 80, 98, 103, 111, 130, 137, 162, 243, 246	Rc	-	☼	6	3in(7.5cm)
Aucuba japonica 86, 152, 198, 244	ESh	-	◑	7	10ft(3m)
'Crotonifolia' 195	ESh	-	◑	7	8ft(2.4m)
'Lanceleaf' 221	ESh	-	◑	7	8ft(2.4m)
'Salicifolia' 221	ESh	-	◑	7	8ft(2.4m)
Aurinia saxatilis 14, 246	Rc	-	☼	3	9in(23cm)
var. *citrina* 111	Rc	-	☼	3	9in(23cm)

B

	PLANT TYPE	SOIL	SITUATION	TEMPERATURE ZONE	HEIGHT
Ballota pseudodictamnus 142	EP	-	☼	8	6in(15cm)
Bassia scoparia 270	An	-	☼	-	3ft(90cm)
Berberidopsis corallina 34, 35, 194	ECl	A	◑S	8	12ft(3.7m)

	PLANT TYPE	SOIL	SITUATION	TEMPERATURE ZONE	HEIGHT
Berberis candidula 220	ESh	-	◑	5	6ft(1.8m)
× *stenophylla* 48, 49	ESh	-	◑	5	8ft(2.4m)
thunbergii 36	Sh	-	◑	4	4ft(1.2m)
Bergenia cordifolia 88, 135, 181, 239 250, 270, 290, 291	EP	-	◑	3	18in(45cm)
'Silberlicht' 111, 189	EP	L	◑	3	15in(38cm)
Betula pendula 71	Tr	-	◑	2	30ft(9m)
'Youngii' 201	Tr	-	◑	2	10ft(3m)
utilis var. *jacquemontii* 150, 151	Tr	-	◑	7	20ft(6m)
Blechnum penna-marina 291	EP	-	◑/●	8	6in(15cm)
Borago officinalis 266, 267	An	-	☼	-	2½ft(76cm)
Brachyglottis 'Sunshine' 14, 52, 71, 105, 248, 251, 270	ESh	-	☼	7	4ft(1.2m)
Briza maxima 157	An	-	☼	-	18in(45cm)
Brugmansia candida 'Knightii' 180	ESh	-	◑	9	12ft(3.7m)
Brunnera macrophylla 144, 220	P	M	◑	3	18in(45cm)
Buddleia alternifolia 175	Sh	-	☼	5	12ft(3.7m)
fallowiana var. *alba* 111	Sh	-	☼	8	6ft(1.8m)
Butomus umbellatus 286	PAq	-	☼	5	3ft(90cm)
Buxus sempervirens 236	ESh	-	◑	5	10ft(3m)
'Elegantissima' 14	ESh	-	◑	5	6ft(1.8m)
'Handsworthensis' 183	ESh	-	◑	5	10ft(3m)
'Suffruticosa' 43, 200, 236	ESh	-	◑	5	3ft(90cm)

C

	PLANT TYPE	SOIL	SITUATION	TEMPERATURE ZONE	HEIGHT
Calendula officinalis 137, 151, 154, 267, 271, 275	An	-	☼	-	2ft(60cm)
'Art Shades' 109	An	-	☼	-	12in(30cm)
Calla palustris 285	P	M	☼	4	12in(30cm)
Calluna vulgaris 'Cramond' 83	ESh	A	☼	4	18in(45cm)
'Darkness' 83	ESh	A	☼	4	12in(30cm)
'H.E. Beale' 83	ESh	A	☼	4	18in(45cm)
'Serlei' 83	ESh	A	☼	4	2ft(60cm)
Caltha palustris 82, 286	P	M	☼/◑	3	12in(30cm)
'Plena' 286	P	M	☼/◑	3	12in(30cm)
Camellia 'Contessa Lavinia Maggi' (now *C. japonica* 'Lavinia Maggi')					
'Freedom Bell' 125	ESh	A	◑S	8	10ft(3m)
japonica 'Lavinia Maggi' 189	ESh	A	◑S	8	15ft(4.5m)
× *williamsii* 'Donation' 240	ESh	A	◑S	8	10ft(3m)
'J.C. Williams' 221	ESh	A	◑S	8	12ft(3.7m)
Campanula lactiflora 237, 272	P	-	◑	5	4ft(1.2m)
'Alba' 88	P	-	◑	5	4ft(1.2m)
persicifolia 88, 271	P	-	◑	3	3ft(90cm)
poscharskyana 40, 72	Rc	-	◑	3	6in(15cm)
waldsteiniana 217	Rc	-	☼	6	6in(15cm)
Campsis 'Madame Galen' 234	Cl	-	☼	4	30ft(9m)
Carex elata 'Aurea' 196, 285	P	M	◑	7	2ft(60cm)
flagellifera 150, 159	EP	-	☼	7	12in(30cm)
oshimensis 'Evergold' 291	EP	-	☼	7	12in(30cm)
Carpinus betulus 43, 45, 49, 66, 88, 190	Tr	-	☼/◑	5	20ft(6m)
'Fastigiata' 67	Tr	-	☼/◑	5	20ft(6m)
Caryopteris × *clandonensis* 'Kew Blue' 67, 107, 224	Sh	-	☼S	6	4ft(1.2m)
Cassia didymobotrya (now *Senna didymobotrya*)					

	PLANT TYPE	SOIL	SITUATION	TEMPERATURE ZONE	HEIGHT
Catalpa bignonioides 175, 202, 235	Tr	-	☼	5	20ft(6m)
'Aurea' 201, 203	Tr	-	☼	5	12ft(3.7m)
Ceanothus arboreus 'Trewithen Blue' 175	ESh	-	☼S	8	15ft(4.5m)
× *delileanus* 'Gloire de Versailles' 111	Sh	-	☼	7	5ft(1.5m)
impressus 62, 227	ESh	-	☼	7	10ft(3m)
thyrsiflorus 'Repens' 14	ESh	-	☼	8	5ft(1.5m)
Cedrus atlantica 'Pendula' 184	ETr	-	☼	6	15ft(4.5m)
Centaurea cyanus 109, 110, 146	An	-	☼	-	18in(45cm)
montana 109	P	-	☼	3	18in(45cm)
Cercis siliquastrum 62, 88, 127, 137	Tr	LD	☼	6	20ft(6m)
Chaenomeles 'Geisha Girl' 12	Sh	-	☼	5	4ft(1.2m)
japonica 41, 243	Sh	-	☼	5	3ft(90cm)
'Pink Lady' 12	Sh	-	☼	5	4ft(1.2m)
'Rowallane' 12	Sh	-	☼	5	5ft(1.5m)
speciosa 12, 158, 209	Sh	-	☼	5	15ft(4.5m)
Chamaecyparis lawsoniana 43, 44, 45	ETr	-	◑	6	40ft(12m)
'Columnaris' 202	ETr	-	◑	6	15ft(4.5m)
'Ellwood's Pillar' 227	ETr	-	◑	6	10ft(3m)
'Fletcheri' 50	ETr	-	◑	6	25ft(7.5m)
'Gimbornii' 17	ETr	-	◑	6	3ft(90cm)
'Green Hedger' 268	ETr	-	◑	6	20ft(6m)
'Green Pillar' 202	ETr	-	◑	6	20ft(6m)
'Lanei' 202	ETr	-	◑	6	30ft(9m)
'Pembury Blue' 71	ETr	-	◑	6	25ft(7.5m)
obtusa 219	ETr	-	◑	5	40ft(12m)
'Nana Gracilis' 22	ETr	-	◑	6	6ft(1.8m)
pisifera 92	ETr	-	◑	6	30ft(9m)
'Filifera Aurea' 227	ETr	-	◑	6	15ft(4.5m)
Chamaemelum nobile 84, 85, 100, 112, 151, 155, 173, 267	EP	-	☼	4	4in(10cm)
'Treneague' 84, 100	EP	-	☼	4	4in(10cm)
Chamaerops humilis 185	ETr	-	☼	9	5ft(1.5m)
Cheiranthus (now *Erysimum*)					
Chimonanthus praecox 40, 153, 154, 156	Sh	-	☼	7	10ft(3m)
Chionodoxa luciliae 132, 220, 271	Bu	-	◑	4	6in(15cm)
Choisya ternata 17, 27, 51, 71, 175, 184, 194, 268	ESh	-	☼S	7	8ft(2.4m)
'Sundance' 145	ESh	-	☼S	7	3ft(90cm)
Chrysalidocarpus lutescens 177	Tr	-	◑	10	15ft(4.5m)
Chrysanthemum (now *Argyranthemum, Dendranthema*)					
Cimicifuga racemosa 109, 162	P	-	◑	4	5ft(1.5m)
Cineraria maritima (now *Senecio cineraria*)					
Cistus × *aguilari* 227	ESh	-	☼	8	5ft(1.5m)
× *corbariensis* (now *C.* × *hybridus*)					
× *hybridus* 13, 193	ESh	LD	☼	7	4ft(1.2m)
skanbergii 221	ESh	-	☼	8	5ft(1.5m)
Citrus limon 'Meyer' 133	ESh	-	☼S	9	6ft(1.8m)

	PLANT TYPE	SOIL	SITUATION	TEMPERATURE ZONE	HEIGHT
Clarkia unguiculata 109	An	-	☼	-	18in(45cm)
Clematis alpina 181, 243	Cl	L	◑	5	6ft(1.8m)
'Frances Rivis' 227	Cl	L	◑	5	6ft(1.8m)
armandii 12, 16, 229	ECl	-	☼	5	15ft(4.5m)
'Apple Blossom' 227	ECl	-	☼	5	15ft(4.5m)
chrysocoma 193	Cl	-	◑	7	10ft(3m)
cirrhosa var. *balearica* 193	ECl	-	◑	7	10ft(3m)
'Ernest Markham' 41, 108	Cl	-	◑	7	12ft(3.7m)
flammula 193	Cl	-	◑	6	10ft(3m)
florida 'Sieboldii' 133, 158	Cl	A	◑	7	10ft(3m)
heracleifolia 60, 153	P	-	☼	3	3ft(90cm)
'H.F. Young' 229	Cl	-	◑	3	12ft(3.7m)
'Huldine' 124	Cl	A	◑	3	13ft(4m)
× *jackmanii* 36, 128	Cl	-	◑	5	12ft(3.7m)
'Superba' 12	Cl	-	◑	5	15ft(4.5m)
macropetala 130, 181, 243	Cl	-	◑	5	8ft(2.4m)
'Markham's Pink' 127	Cl	A	◑	5	12ft(3.7m)
'Madame Julia Correvon' 128	Cl	-	◑	5	6ft(1.8m)
montana 158, 185, 194, 209	Cl	L	◑	6	20ft(6m)
'Elizabeth' 124	Cl	-	◑	6	30ft(9m)
'Mrs Cholmondeley' 203	Cl	L	◑	6	12ft(3.7m)
'Nelly Moser' 34, 35	Cl	L	◑	6	12ft(3.7m)
'Perle d'Azur' 203	Cl	L	◑	6	12ft(3.7m)
tangutica 33, 150	Cl	L	◑	5	20ft(6m)
texensis hybrids 38	Cl	A	◑	5	10ft(3m)
viticella 38	Cl	L	◑	6	12ft(3.7m)
'Alba Luxurians' 127	Cl	L	◑	6	12ft(3.7m)
'Minuet' 50	Cl	-	◑	6	8ft(2.4m)
Cobaea scandens 51, 182	Cl	-	☼S	9	12ft(3.7m)
Colchicum 'Lilac Wonder' 134	Bu	-	◑	5	10in(25cm)
speciosum 132	Bu	-	◑	6	10in(25cm)
'Album' 83, 134, 201	Bu	-	◑	6	10in(25cm)
'Rosy Dawn' 83	Bu	-	◑	6	8in(20cm)
Convallaria majalis 28, 127, 129, 198	Bu	L	●	3	8in(20cm)
Convolvulus althaeoides 179	P	-	☼	8	trailing
cneorum 14, 91, 160, 185, 294	ESh	-	☼S	8	2ft(60cm)
tricolor 'Blue Ensign' 227	An	-	☼	-	12in(30cm)
'Blue Flash' 12, 147	An	-	☼	-	12in(30cm)
'Heavenly Blue' 203	An	-	☼	-	12in(30cm)
'Royal Ensign' 109	An	-	☼	-	12in(30cm)
Cordyline australis 192, 218, 235, 240, 241	ETr	-	☼	10	15ft(4.5m)
'Purple Tower' 221	ETr	-	☼	10	10ft(3m)
'Purpurea' 24	ETr	-	☼	10	10ft(3m)
Coriandrum sativum 151, 155, 156, 266, 267	An	-	☼		2ft(60cm)
Cornus alba 71	Sh	-	◑	3	10ft(3m)
'Aurea' 124	Sh	-	◑	3	8ft(2.4m)
'Elegantissima' 53, 178, 189	Sh	-	◑	3	8ft(2.4m)
'Spaethii' 22	Sh	-	◑	3	8ft(2.4m)
'Westonbirt' 53, 219	Sh	-	◑	3	8ft(2.4m)
controversa 'Variegata' 137	Tr	-	◑	3	15ft(4.5m)
Corokia cotoneaster 221	ESh	-	☼S	8	10ft(3m)
Coronilla glauca (now *C. valentina* subsp. *glauca*)					

PLANT TYPE **An** annual; **Aq** aquatic; **Bam** bamboo; **Bi** biennial; **Bu** bulb, corm, rhizome, tuber; **Cl** climber; **E** evergreen; **P** perennial; **Rc** rock plant; **Ro** rose; **Sh** shrub; **Tr** tree.

SOIL **A** needs acid soil; **L** needs alkaline soil; **M** needs moist to wet soil; **D** needs dry soil.

SITUATION ☼ does best in full sun; ◑ thrives in full sun or light shade; ● does best in full shade; ◑/● grows well in full sun, light shade or full shade; ●/◑ does best in full shade or light shade; **S** needs shelter; **W** tolerates wind.

TEMPERATURE ZONE numbers refer to the hardiness zones on the map on pp.316–317.

HEIGHT represents height at maturity (or 20 years for trees and shrubs).

	PLANT TYPE	SOIL	SITUATION	TEMPERATURE ZONE	HEIGHT
valentina subsp. *glauca* 241, 268, 269	ESh	-	☼	9	5ft(1.5m)
Cortaderia richardii 286	P	-	☼	8	8ft(2.4m)
Corylus avellana 'Contorta' 142, 150, 207, 220	Sh	-	◑	4	15ft(4.5m)
Cosmos atrosanguineus 153	P	-	☼	8	2½ft(76cm)
Cotinus coggygria 270, 272	Sh	-	☼	5	10ft(3m)
'Purpureus' 137, 145	Sh	-	☼	5	10ft(3m)
'Royal Purple' 109, 111, 269	Sh	-	☼	5	10ft(3m)
Cotoneaster dammeri 60, 72, 249	ESh	-	☼	5	12in(30cm)
horizontalis 86, 126, 162, 243, 251	Sh	-	☼	4	2ft(60cm)
salicifolius 'Pendulus' 189	ESh	-	◑	6	10ft(3m)
simonsii 115	Sh	-	☼	5	10ft(3m)
× *watereri* 'Cornubia' 178	Sh	-	☼	6	15ft(4.5m)
Crambe cordifolia 179, 199, 206	P	D	◑	6	6ft(1.8m)
Crataegus monogyna 49, 87	Tr	-	☼	5	15ft(4.5m)
Crocosmia 'Lucifer' 269	Bu	-	☼	5	3ft(90cm)
Crocus ancyrensis 124	Bu	-	☼	6	4in(10cm)
'Pickwick' 136	Bu	-	☼	4	4in(10cm)
speciosus 83	Bu	-	☼	4	4in(10cm)
Cryptomeria japonica 'Elegans Aurea' 227	ETr	-	☼	6	6ft(1.8m)
× *Cupressocyparis leylandii* 44, 66, 86, 112, 268	ETr	-	☼	7	50ft(15m)
Cyclamen coum 124, 125, 198	Bu	LD	●S	6	3in(7.5cm)
hederifolium 50, 62, 83, 125, 144, 198, 201	Bu	LD	●	6	4in(10cm)
Cyperus eragrostis 286	EP	M	☼	8	2ft(60cm)
longus 279, 286	EP	M	☼	7	3ft(90cm)
Cytisus battandieri 40, 175	Sh	D	☼	7	15ft(4.5m)
× *kewensis* 111, 130	Rc	D	☼	6	2ft(60cm)
× *praecox* 108	Sh	D	☼	5	5ft(1.5m)

D

	PLANT TYPE	SOIL	SITUATION	TEMPERATURE ZONE	HEIGHT
Daboecia cantabrica 83	ESh	A	☼	6	18in(45cm)
Dahlia 'Bishop of Llandaff' 145, 269, 272	P	-	☼	9	3ft(90cm)
'David Howard' 272	P	-	☼	9	3ft(90cm)
'Ellen Houston' 147	P	-	☼	9	3ft(90cm)
Daphne laureola 153	ESh	L	◑/●	7	4ft(1.2m)
cneorum 'Alba' 12	ESh	L	◑	5	12in(30cm)
mezereum 154	ESh	L	◑	4	5ft(1.5m)
odora 'Aureomarginata' 222	ESh	-	◑	7	5ft(1.5m)
retusa 21, 131	ESh	-	◑S	6	2ft(60cm)
Datura inoxia 133	An	-	☼	-	3ft(90cm)
Delphinium elatum hybrids 71, 88	P	-	☼	3	6ft(1.8m)
'Belladonna' 271	P	-	☼	3	3ft(90cm)
Dendranthema 'Mei-kyo' 161	P	-	☼	6	18in(45cm)
Dianthus × *allwoodii* 'Doris' 14, 148, 153	P	L	☼	3	10in(25cm)
'Show Pearl' 14	P	L	☼	3	12in(30cm)
barbatus 87, 135, 148	Bi	-	◑	4	16in(40cm)
'Dad's Favorite' 148, 153	P	L	◑	4	10in(25cm)
deltoides 40, 62, 103	Rc	LD	☼	3	9in(23cm)
'Houndspool Ruby' 183	P	L	☼	3	12in(30cm)
'Sops in Wine' 153, 155	P	L	☼	3	6in(15cm)
Dicentra spectabilis 201	P	M	◑	6	2½ft(76cm)
alba 197, 200	P	M	◑	6	2ft(60cm)
Digitalis purpurea 163, 305	Bi	-	◑	-	5ft(1.5m)

	PLANT TYPE	SOIL	SITUATION	TEMPERATURE ZONE	HEIGHT
'Sutton's Apricot' 161	P	-	◑	5	3ft(90cm)
Dorotheanthus bellidiformis 14	An	-	☼	-	3in(7.5cm)
Dracaena draco 206	ETr	-	◑	9	10ft(3m)
Dryas octopetala 124	ERc	LD	☼	2	3in(7.5cm)
Dryopteris filix-mas 270	P	M	◑/●	2	4ft(1.2m)

E

	PLANT TYPE	SOIL	SITUATION	TEMPERATURE ZONE	HEIGHT
Eccremocarpus scaber 51	Cl	D	☼S	9	10ft(3m)
Echinops 191, 274, 275, 312	P	-	☼	3	4ft(1.2m)
Echium pininana 81	Bi	-	☼		3ft(90cm)
Elaeagnus × *ebbingei* 48, 269	ESh	-	◑	6	15ft(4.5m)
'Gilt Edge' 195	ESh	-	◐	6	15ft(4.5m)
'Limelight' 67, 269	ESh	-	◐	6	10ft(3m)
pungens 'Maculata' 193, 195, 269	ESh	-	◑	7	12ft(3.7m)
Elodea canadensis 282	Aq	M	☼	3	-
Embothrium coccineum 135	ETr	AM	◑S	8	12ft(3.7m)
Epimedium alpinum 124	P	-	◑	5	18in(45cm)
perralderianum 88	P	-	◑	6	12in(30cm)
× *youngianum* 'Niveum' 129	P	-	◑	5	9in(23cm)
Eranthis hyemalis 68, 124, 161, 273	P	-	◑/●	5	4in(10cm)
Erica arborea 83	ESh	-	☼S	7	12ft(3.7m)
× *darleyensis* 83	ESh	-	☼	6	18in(45cm)
Erigeron karvinskianus 103	P	-	☼	7	4in(10cm)
Erinus alpinus 40, 217	Rc	D	☼	6	3in(7.5cm)
Erysimum 'Bowles' Mauve' 162	P	-	☼	7	2ft(60cm)
cheiri 'Harpur Crewe' 109, 155	P	-	☼	7	18in(45cm)
'Tom Thumb Mixed' 14	Bi	-	☼	7	9in(23cm)
Escallonia 'Iveyi' 179	ESh	-	◑S	8	10ft(3m)
'Red Hedger' 48	ESh	-	◑	8	8ft(2.4m)
rubra var. *macrantha* 179	ESh	-	◑	8	10ft(3m)
Eschscholzia californica 109, 110, 141, 145, 147, 202	An	-	☼	-	12in(30cm)
Eucalyptus gunnii 22, 268	ETr	-	☼	8	40ft(12m)
pauciflora subsp. *niphophila* 111	ETr	-	☼	7	20ft(6m)
Eucryphia × *nymansensis* 'Nymansay' 134	ETr	-	●S	7	15ft(4.5m)
Euonymus fortunei 269	ESh	-	◑	5	15ft(4.5m)
'Emerald 'n' Gold' 196, 251	ESh	-	◑	5	2ft(60cm)
'Silver Pillar' 93	ESh	-	◑	5	5ft(1.5m)
'Silver Queen' 21	ESh	-	◑	5	3ft(90cm)
japonicus 179, 269	ESh	-	◑	7	12ft(3.7m)
Euphorbia amygdaloides var. *robbiae* 135, 158	P	L	◑	7	18in(45cm)
characias 13, 29, 32, 203, 240	EP	L	☼	8	4ft(1.2m)
dulcis 'Chameleon' 161	P	-	☼	6	12in(30cm)
griffithii 162	P	-	☼	5	3ft(90cm)
'Dixter' 146	P	-	☼	5	3ft(90cm)
'Fireglow' 146	P	-	☼	5	3ft(90cm)
marginata 270	An	-	☼	-	2ft(60cm)
polychroma 146	P	-	☼	6	18in(45cm)
Exochorda × *macrantha* 'The Bride' 200	Sh	-	☼	5	10ft(3m)

F

	PLANT TYPE	SOIL	SITUATION	TEMPERATURE ZONE	HEIGHT
Fagus sylvatica 43, 59	Tr	LD	☼	5	30ft(9m)
'Purpurea Pendula' 183, 218	Tr	-	☼	5	10ft(3m)
Fargesia murieliae 159	Bam	-	◑	6	13ft(4m)

	PLANT TYPE	SOIL	SITUATION	TEMPERATURE ZONE	HEIGHT
Fascicularia bicolor 228	EP	-	☼S	8	18in(45cm)
× *Fatshedera lizei* 24, 198	ESh	-	☼/☽	7	6ft(1.8m)
Fatsia japonica 35, 92, 194, 241, 269	ESh	D	●/☽	8	10ft(3m)
Felicia amelloides 224	P	-	☼S	9	12in(30cm)
Festuca glauca 60, 191	P	-	☼	5	9in(23cm)
Ficus benjamina 121	Tr	-	☼	9	50ft(15m)
carica 235	Sh	-	☼S	7	12ft(3.7m)
Filipendula ulmaria 'Aurea' 161	P	M	☼	2	2½ft(76cm)
Foeniculum vulgare 180, 255, 256, 266, 267	An	D	☼	-	6ft(1.8m)
'Purpureum' 150, 156, 267, 313	An	D	☼	-	6ft(1.8m)
Fothergilla major 208	Sh	A	☼	5	6ft(1.8m)
Fritillaria imperialis 162	Bu	-	☽	4	3ft(90cm)
Fuchsia magellanica 51, 137	Sh	D	☽	7	6ft(1.8m)
var. *molinae* 51	Sh	-	☽	7	6ft(1.8m)

G

	PLANT TYPE	SOIL	SITUATION	TEMPERATURE ZONE	HEIGHT
Galanthus elwesii 136, 189	Bu	-	☽	6	10in(25cm)
nivalis 68	Bu	-	☽	4	6in(15cm)
Galium odoratum 181	P	-	☽	5	6in(15cm)
Galtonia candicans 111	Bu	-	☼	5	4ft(1.2m)
Garrya elliptica 38, 40, 135, 269	ESh	-	☽S	8	9ft(2.7m)
Gaultheria procumbens 100	ESh	A	☽	4	6in(15cm)
Genista aetnensis 244	Tr	-	☼	8	15ft(4.5m)
Gentiana septemfida 144	Rc	-	☼	3	6in(15cm)
verna 217	Rc	-	☼	5	3in(7.5cm)
Geranium pratense 63, 70, 71	P	-	☼	5	2½ft(76cm)
macrorrhizum 294	P	-	☽	5	18in(45cm)
× *magnificum* 145	P	-	☽	3	18in(45cm)
× *oxonianum* 'Claridge Druce' 35	P	-	☼	5	18in(45cm)
procurrens 246	P	-	☼	7	12in(30cm)
robertianum 305	P	L	☼	6	9in(23cm)
sanguineum 60, 142	P	L	☼	5	12in(30cm)
'Album' 60	P	L	☼	5	12in(30cm)
Geum 'Lionel Cox' 124	P	-	☼	3	18in(45cm)
Ginkgo biloba 227	Tr	-	☽	4	20ft(6m)
Gladiolus callianthus 'Murieliae' 137, 154	Bu	-	☼	9	3ft(90cm)
Glaucium flavum 217	Bi	-	☼	7	12in(30cm)
Glechoma hederacea 'Variegata' 230	EP	-	☼	4	trailing
Griselinia littoralis 49, 179	ETr	-	☽S	7	10ft(3m)
Gunnera manicata 104, 132, 141, 203, 206, 235, 293	P	M	☽S	8	8ft(2.4m)
Gypsophila paniculata 200	P	-	☼	4	3ft(90cm)
repens 98	Rc	-	☼	4	6in(15cm)

H

	PLANT TYPE	SOIL	SITUATION	TEMPERATURE ZONE	HEIGHT
Hakonechloa macra 'Aureola' 149, 158, 159	P	-	☽	5	12in(30cm)

	PLANT TYPE	SOIL	SITUATION	TEMPERATURE ZONE	HEIGHT
Hamamelis mollis 152, 154, 155, 224	Sh	-	☽	6	12ft(3.7m)
Hebe albicans 203	ESh	-	☼	7	2ft(60cm)
'Autumn Glory' 88, 111	ESh	-	☼	8	5ft(1.5m)
brachysiphon 115	ESh	-	☼	7	6ft(1.8m)
buxifolia 'Nana' 21	ESh	-	☼	7	6in(15cm)
× *franciscana* 'Blue Gem' 115	ESh	-	☼S	7	3ft(90cm)
'La Seduisante' 51	ESh	-	☼S	7	3ft(90cm)
'Midsummer Beauty' 51, 67	ESh	-	☼	8	6ft(1.8m)
pinguifolia 'Pagei' 100	ESh	-	☼	6	6in(15cm)
salicifolia 51, 115	ESh	-	☼S	7	6ft(1.8m)
Hedera algeriensis 192	ECl	-	☽	8	30ft(9m)
'Gloire de Marengo' 182, 189	ECl	-	☽	8	30ft(9m)
colchica 192, 251	ECl	-	☽	6	20ft(6m)
'Dentata Variegata' 67, 182	ECl	-	☽	6	15ft(4.5m)
'Sulphur Heart' 182	ECl	-	☽	6	15ft(4.5m)
helix 50, 52, 182, 196, 219, 228, 305	ECl	-	☽	5	30ft(9m)
'Eva' 213	ECl	-	☽	5	4ft(1.2m)
'Glacier' 71, 183, 189, 227	ECl	-	☽	5	6ft(1.8m)
'Goldheart' 182, 227, 239	ECl	-	☽	5	20ft(6m)
var. *hibernica* (now *H. hibernica*)					
'Pedata' 124	ECl	-	☽	7	12ft(3.7m)
'Tricolor' 14	ECl	-	☽	7	6ft(1.8m)
hibernica 182, 197	ECl	-	☽	7	20ft(6m)
Helenium autumnale 249	P	-	☼	3	5ft(1.5m)
Helianthemum lunulatum 100, 103, 217, 289	Rc	-	☼	7	9in(23cm)
'Mrs Earle' 124	Rc	-	☼	6	12in(30cm)
'Wisley Primrose' 124	Rc	-	☼	6	12in(30cm)
Helianthus annuus 109, 275	An	-	☼	-	6ft(1.8m)
decapetalus 249	P	-	☼	5	6ft(1.8m)
Helichrysum angustifolium (now *H. italicum*)					
bracteatum 131, 275	An	-	☼	-	2½ft(76cm)
italicum 151, 267	ESh	-	☼	8	2ft(60cm)
petiolare 227	ESh	-	☼S	10	12in(30cm)
Helictotrichon sempervirens 107, 149	EP	-	☼	5	3ft(90cm)
Helleborus argutifolius 111, 269	EP	M	●/☽	7	2ft(60cm)
foetidus 36	EP	M	●/☽	6	2ft(60cm)
lividus 28, 220	P	M	●/☽	8	2ft(60cm)
niger 132, 273	P	M	●/☽	3	12in(30cm)
orientalis 125, 130, 136, 144	P	M	●/☽	6	18in(45cm)
Hemerocallis citrina 174	P	-	☼	4	2½ft(76cm)
Hepatica transsilvanica 124, 125	Rc	-	☽	5	6in(15cm)
Hesperis matronalis 155, 176	P	-	☽	3	3ft(90cm)
Heuchera micrantha 'Palace Purple' 241	P	-	☽	5	12in(30cm)
Hippophae rhamnoides 179	Sh	-	☼	3	12ft(3.7m)
Hordeum jubatum 150	P	-	☼	5	2ft(60cm)
Hosta fortunei var. *albopicta* 144	P	-	☽	3	18in(45cm)
sieboldiana 71, 132, 144	P	-	☽	3	2ft(60cm)
var. *elegans* 247, 251	P	-	☽	3	2½ft(76cm)
'Snowden' 156	P	-	☽	3	4ft(1.2m)

PLANT TYPE An annual; Aq aquatic; Bam bamboo; Bi biennial; Bu bulb, corm, rhizome, tuber; Cl climber; E evergreen; P perennial; Rc rock plant; Ro rose; Sh shrub; Tr tree.

SOIL A needs acid soil; L needs alkaline soil; M needs moist to wet soil; D needs dry soil.

SITUATION ☼ does best in full sun; ☽ thrives in full sun or light shade; ● does best in full shade; ☽/● grows well in full sun, light shade or full shade; ●/☽ does best in full shade or light shade; S needs shelter; W tolerates wind.

TEMPERATURE ZONE numbers refer to the hardiness zones on the map on pp.316–317.

HEIGHT represents height at maturity (or 20 years for trees and shrubs).

	PLANT TYPE	SOIL	SITUATION	TEMPERATURE ZONE	HEIGHT
'Sum and Substance' 156	P	-	◑	3	18in(45cm)
'Thomas Hogg' 144	P	-	◑/●	3	2½ft(76cm)
tokudama 221	P	M	◑	3	18in(45cm)
undulata 284	P	M	◑	3	2ft(60cm)
Houttuynia cordata 282	P	M	☀	5	9in(23cm)
Howeia forsteriana 177	E Tr	-	◑/●	10	15ft(4.5m)
Humulus japonicus 'Variegatus' 51, 251	Cl An	-	☀	-	20ft(6m)
lupulus 'Aureus' 36, 39, 196, 209	Cl P	-	☀	5	20ft(6m)
Hyacinthoides non-scripta 81, 101, 144, 273	Bu	-	◑/●	5	12in(30cm)
Hyacinthus 'Distinction' 271	Bu	-	☀	3	9in(23cm)
'Gipsy Queen' 136, 271	Bu	-	☀	3	9in(23cm)
'Myosotis' 136	Bu	-	☀	3	9in(23cm)
orientalis 154	Bu	-	☀	3	9in(23cm)
'Ostara' 125	Bu	-	☀	3	9in(23cm)
Hydrangea anomala petiolaris 12, 17, 36, 40, 42, 71, 72,192	Cl	-	◑	5	30ft(9m)
arborescens 'Annabelle' 71	Sh	M	◑	3	3ft(90cm)
'Grandiflora' 67	Sh	M	◑	3	3ft(90cm)
macrophylla 195	Sh	M	◑	5	6ft(1.8m)
'Ayesha' 224	Sh	M	◑	5	5ft(1.5m)
'Blue Bonnet' 224	Sh	M	◑	5	5ft(1.5m)
Hortensia Group 274	Sh	M	◑	5	5ft(1.5m)
'Madame Emile Mouilliere' 224	Sh	M	◑	5	6ft(1.8m)
'Pia' 201, 274	Sh	M	◑	5	4ft(1.2m)
paniculata 274	Sh	M	◑	3	10ft(3m)
serrata 'Preziosa' 224, 274	Sh	M	◑	5	4ft(1.2m)
Hydrocharis morsus-ranae 282	Aq	M	☀	4	3in(7.5cm)
Hypericum calycinum 60, 112, 250	E Sh	-	☀	6	18in(45cm)
perforatum 63	P	-	☀	3	2ft(60cm)
Hyssopus officinalis 52, 81, 84, 267, 275, 312	E P	-	☀	3	12in(30cm)

I

	PLANT TYPE	SOIL	SITUATION	TEMPERATURE ZONE	HEIGHT
Iberis sempervirens 40, 124, 142, 221	E Rc	-	☀	4	9in(23cm)
Ilex × altaclerensis 269	E Tr	-	◑	6	15ft(4.5m)
'Camelliifolia' 197	E Tr	-	◑	6	20ft(6m)
'Golden King' 162	E Tr	-	◑	6	15ft(4.5m)
'Lawsoniana' 93	E Tr	-	◑	6	15ft(4.5m)
aquifolium 269	E Tr	-	◑	6	15ft(4.5m)
'Argentea Marginata' 193, 195	E Tr	-	◑	6	15ft(4.5m)
'Argentea Marginata Pendula' 189	E Tr	-	◑	6	12ft(3.7m)
'Handsworth New Silver' 134	E Tr	-	◑	6	15ft(4.5m)
'J.C. van Tol' 134	E Tr	-	◑	6	20ft(6m)
'Madame Briot' 129	E Tr	-	◑	6	20ft(6m)
'Silver Queen' 239	E Tr	-	◑	6	15ft(4.5m)
Impatiens walleriana 'Novetter Series' 228	An	-	☀	-	6in(15cm)
Inula magnifica 146	P	-	☀	6	8ft(2.4m)
Ionopsidium acaule 103	An	-	◑	-	3in(7.5cm)
Ipomoea 'Heavenly Blue' 221	An	-	☀	-	10ft(3m)
hederacea 182	An	-	☀	-	10ft(3m)
Iris danfordiae 125, 273	Bu	-	◑	5	4in(10cm)
ensata 73, 286, 293	P	M	◑	4	2½ft(76cm)
foetidissima 220	E P	D	◑	6	2ft(60cm)
graminea 217	P	-	◑	5	18in(45cm)
kaempferi (now I. ensata)					
laevigata 'Alba' 282	P	M	◑	5	2½ft(76cm)
'Variegata' 285	P	M	◑	5	2ft(60cm)

	PLANT TYPE	SOIL	SITUATION	TEMPERATURE ZONE	HEIGHT
pseudacorus 'Variegata' 161	P	M	◑	5	4ft(1.2m)
pumila 14	P	-	☀	3	6in(15cm)
× robusta 'Gerald Darby' 291	P	-	◑	6	3ft(90cm)
sibirica 71, 124, 271, 281, 293	P	M	◑	4	3ft(90cm)
variegata 62	P	-	☀	4	18in(45cm)
Itea ilicifolia 133, 269	E Sh	-	◑ S	7	10ft(3m)

J, K

	PLANT TYPE	SOIL	SITUATION	TEMPERATURE ZONE	HEIGHT
Jasminum grandiflorum 'De Grasse' 177	E Cl	-	☀	7	6ft(1.8m)
nudiflorum 40, 251	Cl	D	◑	6	10ft(3m)
odoratissimum 176	E Sh	-	◑	9	6ft(1.8m)
officinale 40, 108, 133, 155	Cl	D	◑	7	10ft(3m)
sambac 'Maid of Orleans' 176	E Cl	-	◑	9	10ft(3m)
× stephanense 227	Cl	-	☀	7	12ft(3.7m)
Juncus effusus 'Spiralis' 286	E P	M	☀	4	12in(30cm)
inflexus 'Afro' 286	E P	M	☀	4	12in(30cm)
Juniperus chinensis 'Stricta' 219	E Tr	-	☀	4	15ft(4.5m)
'Pfitzeriana' (now Juniperus × media 'Pfitzeriana')					
communis 'Compressa' 227	E Sh	-	☀	4	2½ft(76cm)
× media 'Pfitzeriana' 21, 93	E Sh	-	☀	3	10ft(3m)
'Pfitzeriana Aurea' 62	E Sh	-	◑	3	3ft(90cm)
sabina 'Blue Danube' 227	E Sh	-	☀	3	12ft(3.7m)
'Tamariscifolia' 21, 72	E Sh	-	☀	3	2½ft(76cm)
scopulorum 'Skyrocket' 93	E Tr	-	☀	4	12ft(3.7m)
Kerria japonica 'Pleniflora' 41	Sh	-	☀	4	6ft(1.8m)
'Variegata' 35	Sh	-	☀	4	4ft(1.2m)
Knautia macedonica 142	P	LD	☀	6	2½ft(76cm)
Kniphofia caulescens 24, 108, 146, 161, 218	E P	-	☀	7	4ft(1.2m)
Kochia scoparia (now Bassia scoparia)					

L

	PLANT TYPE	SOIL	SITUATION	TEMPERATURE ZONE	HEIGHT
Laburnum alpinum 218	Tr	-	☀	5	15ft(4.5m)
Lagarosiphon major 282	Aq	-	☀	4	-
Lagurus ovatus 150, 275	An	-	☀	-	15in(38cm)
Lamiastrum galeobdolon (now Lamium galeobdolon)					
Lamium galeobdolon 112	P	-	◑	6	12in(30cm)
maculatum 163	P	-	◑	4	6in(15cm)
'Album' 28	P	-	◑	4	6in(15cm)
'Beacon Silver' 60	P	-	◑	4	6in(15cm)
Lantana camara 224	E Sh	-	☀ S	10	6ft(1.8m)
Lathyrus latifolius 12, 33, 36, 50, 243, 246	Cl P	-	☀	5	8ft(2.4m)
odoratus 33, 179	Cl An	-	☀	-	10ft(3m)
'Painted Lady' 156	Cl An	-	☀	-	6ft(1.8m)
Laurus nobilis 14, 15, 16, 18, 23, 24, 90, 184, 190, 207, 226, 227, 250, 266, 267	E Tr	-	◑ S	8	15ft(4.5m)
Lavandula angustifolia 'Hidcote' 52, 107	E Sh	-	☀	5	2ft(60cm)
'Hidcote Pink' 155	E Sh	-	☀	5	2ft(60cm)
'Munstead' 52, 111, 183	E Sh	-	☀	5	3ft(90cm)
Lavatera 'Barnsley' 178, 190, 219	P	-	☀	8	5ft(1.5m)
'Rosea' 178, 219	P	-	☀ S	8	6ft(1.8m)
thuringiaca 'Barnsley' (now L.					

	PLANT TYPE	SOIL	SITUATION	TEMPERATURE ZONE	HEIGHT
'Barnsley')					
'Rosea' (now *L.* 'Rosea')					
trimestris 109	An	-	☼	-	2ft(60cm)
'Silver Cup' 62	An	-	☼	-	2ft(60cm)
Lemna minor 292	Aq	-	☼	4	-
trisulca 282	Aq	-	☼	4	-
Leucojum vernum 125, 132	Bu	-	◑	5	9in(23cm)
Liatris spicata 39	P	-	☼	3	2½ft(76cm)
Ligularia przewalskii 181	P	M	◑	4	6ft(1.8m)
Ligustrum lucidum 197	ETr	-	◑S	7	15ft(4.5m)
'Excelsum Superbum' 175, 195	ETr	-	☼	7	20ft(6m)
ovalifolium 'Aureo-marginatum' (now *L. o.* 'Aureum')					
'Aureum' 195, 269	ESh	-	◑	5	12ft(3.7m)
sinense 'Variegatum' 196	ESh	-	◑	7	12ft(3.7m)
Lilium 'African Queen' 272	Bu	-	◑	6	5ft(1.5m)
auratum 155, 162	Bu	A	◑	6	5ft(1.5m)
candidum 153, 154, 155	Bu	L	◑	6	4ft(1.2m)
'Casablanca' 272	Bu	-	◑	6	4ft(1.2m)
'Connecticut King' 272	Bu	-	◑	6	2½ft(76cm)
'Enchantment' 269	Bu	-	◑	6	2½ft(76cm)
'Golden Splendor' 201	Bu	-	◑	5	5ft(1.5m)
hansonii 71	Bu	-	◑	5	5ft(1.5m)
lancifolium 146	Bu	-	◑	4	4ft(1.2m)
longiflorum 183	Bu	-	◑	5	12in(30cm)
monadelphum 71	Bu	-	◑	5	3ft(90cm)
'Pink Perfection' 175, 272	Bu	-	◑	6	4ft(1.2m)
regale 152, 154, 216, 272	Bu	-	◑	5	4ft(1.2m)
speciosum 154	Bu	-	◑	8	4ft(1.2m)
Limnanthes douglasii 137, 313	An	D	☼	-	6in(15cm)
Liriodendron tulipifera 127	Tr	-	☼	4	20ft(6m)
Liriope muscari 221	EP	-	☼	6	12in(30cm)
Lobelia cardinalis 286	P	M	◑	3	2½ft(76cm)
erinus 'Color Cascade' 228	An	-	☼	-	6in(15cm)
siphilitica 291	P	M	☼	5	2½ft(76cm)
Lobularia maritima 228	An	-	☼	-	6in(15cm)
Lonicera × *americana* 154	Cl	-	◑	6	20ft(6m)
fragrantissima 153	Sh	-	◑	5	6ft(1.8m)
japonica 'Aureoreticulata' 35	Cl	-	◑	4	20ft(6m)
'Halliana' 38, 136, 154, 182, 313	Cl	-	◑	4	30ft(9m)
nitida 43, 45, 47, 49, 173, 183, 236	ESh	-	◑	7	6ft(1.8m)
'Baggesen's Gold' 49	ESh	-	☼	7	6ft(1.8m)
periclymenum 174	Cl	-	◑	4	20ft(6m)
'Belgica' 85, 155, 193	Cl	-	◑	4	20ft(6m)
'Early Dutch' (now *L. p.* 'Belgica')					
'Graham Thomas' 124, 155	Cl	-	◑	4	20ft(6m)
'Serotina' 85, 183, 193	Cl	-	◑	4	20ft(6m)
Lotus berthelotii 133	EP	-	☼S	8	6in(15cm)
Lunaria annua 26, 135, 162, 275	Bi	-	◑	-	2½ft(76cm)
'Alba Variegata' 28, 144, 270	Bi	-	◑	-	2½ft(76cm)
Lupinus Russell 'Blue Jacket' 313	P	-	◑	4	3ft(90cm)

	PLANT TYPE	SOIL	SITUATION	TEMPERATURE ZONE	HEIGHT
Lysimachia nummularia 228, 281	P	-	◑	4	3in(7.5cm)
'Aurea' 109	P	-	◑	4	3in(7.5cm)
Lythrum virgatum 'Rose Queen' 285	P	M	☼	3	2ft(60cm)

M

	PLANT TYPE	SOIL	SITUATION	TEMPERATURE ZONE	HEIGHT
Macleaya cordata 251	P	-	☼	3	6ft(1.8m)
microcarpa 249	P	-	☼	5	6ft(1.8m)
Magnolia grandiflora 'Galissonière' 200	ETr	A	◑S	6	20ft(6m)
stellata 189, 218	Sh	-	◑S	4	10ft(3m)
Mahonia aquifolium 51, 71, 108, 198,	ESh	-	◑	5	5ft(1.5m)
japonica 24, 154, 222, 235, 248	ESh	-	◑	6	6ft(1.8m)
lomariifolia 93	ESh	-	◑S	7	8ft(2.4m)
× *media* 'Charity' 27, 135, 184, 194, 203	ESh	-	◑S	7	10ft(3m)
'Lionel Fortescue' 34, 35	ESh	-	◑	7	10ft(3m)
Malus 'John Downie' 260	Tr	-	☼	5	20ft(6m)
× *moerlandsii* 'Profusion' 175	Tr	-	☼	5	20ft(6m)
'Red Sentinel' 162	Tr	-	☼	3	20ft(6m)
sargentii 62	Tr	-	☼	4	8ft(2.4m)
Matteuccia struthiopteris 161	P	-	●/◑	2	3ft(90cm)
Matthiola bicornis 174, 176	An	-	☼	-	18in(45cm)
incana 109, 154, 155	Bi	-	◑	-	18in(45cm)
Meconopsis betonicifolia 144	Bi/P	A	◑	7	3ft(90cm)
cambrica 129, 162, 163	P	A	☼	6	18in(45cm)
× *sheldonii* 107	P	A	●	6	5ft(1.5m)
Melianthus major 199, 268	ESh	-	☼	9	10ft(3m)
Melissa officinalis 267, 275	P	-	☼	4	2½ft(76cm)
'Aurea' 267, 280	P	-	☼	4	2½ft(76cm)
Mentha piperita 267	P	-	☼	3	2ft(60cm)
× *piperita citrata* 153	P	-	☼	3	2ft(60cm)
pulegium 267	P	-	☼	7	9in(23cm)
requienii 103, 267	Rc	M	◑	6	½in(1.3cm)
spicata 156, 267	P	-	◑	3	2ft(60cm)
var. *crispii* 267	P	-	◑	3	12in(30cm)
suaveolens 151, 260, 267	P	-	☼	6	18in(45cm)
'Variegata' 267	P	-	☼	6	18in(45cm)
Menyanthes trifoliata 278, 285	Aq	-	☼	3	9in(23cm)
Mesembryanthemum criniflorum (now *Dorotheanthus bellidiformis*)					
Milium effusum 'Aureum' 161	P	-	◑	6	12in(30cm)
Mina lobata 51, 257	Cl	-	☼	8	15ft(4.5m)
Miscanthus giganteus 179	P	-	☼W	5	10ft(3m)
sacchariflorus 51	P	-	☼W	8	10ft(3m)
'Silberfeder' ('Silver Feather') 241	P	-	◑	4	6ft(1.8m)
sinensis 158, 248	P	-	☼W	4	6ft(1.8m)
Moluccella laevis 143, 275	An	-	☼	-	2ft(60cm)
Montia sibirica 141	An	-	●/◑	-	6in(15cm)
Muehlenbeckia complexa 124	ECl	-	◑	8	2ft(60cm)
Muscari armeniacum 144	Bu	D	◑	4	9in(23cm)

PLANT TYPE An annual; Aq aquatic; Bam bamboo; Bi biennial; Bu bulb, corm, rhizome, tuber; Cl climber; E evergreen; P perennial; Rc rock plant; Ro rose; Sh shrub; Tr tree.

SOIL A needs acid soil; L needs alkaline soil; M needs moist to wet soil; D needs dry soil.

SITUATION ☼ does best in full sun; ◑ thrives in full sun or light shade; ● does best in full shade; ◑/● grows well in full sun, light shade or full shade; ●/◑ does best in full shade or light shade; S needs shelter; W tolerates wind.

TEMPERATURE ZONE numbers refer to the hardiness zones on the map on pp.316–317.

HEIGHT represents height at maturity (or 20 years for trees and shrubs).

	PLANT TYPE	SOIL	SITUATION	TEMPERATURE ZONE	HEIGHT
Pittosporum tenuifolium 115, 268	ETr	-	☼	9	20ft(6m)
Plectranthus coleoides 'Variegatus' 133	EP	-	☼S	10	2ft(60cm)
Pleioblastus auricomus 142, 161	Bam	-	◐	7	6ft(1.8m)
variegatus 159, 161	Bam	-	◐	7	4ft(1.2m)
Plumbago auriculata 91, 176, 289	ESh	-	☼S	9	10ft(3m)
Polygonatum × *hybridum* 270	P	-	◐	6	4ft(1.2m)
Polygonum affine 61	P	M	◐	3	18in(45cm)
'Darjeeling Red' 220	P	M	◐	3	18in(45cm)
Polystichum setiferum 19, 161	EP	L	●/◐	7	3ft(90cm)
'Acutilobum' 129	EP	L	●/◐	7	2ft(60cm)
Portulaca grandiflora 307	An	D	☼	-	9in(23cm)
Potentilla recta pallida 126, 144	P	-	☼	4	2ft(60cm)
recta 'Citrina' (now *P. r. pallida*)					
Pratia angulata 103	P	M	◐	7	½in(1.3cm)
Primula bulleyana 162	P	M	☼	6	2ft(60cm)
elatior 129	P	-	◐	5	9in(23cm)
florindae 61, 162, 278	P	M	☼	6	3ft(90cm)
juliana 'Wanda' 161	P	-	☼	6	6in(15cm)
sikkimensis 162	P	-	☼	6	2ft(60cm)
vulgaris 163	P	-	☼	6	6in(15cm)
Prunus 'Amanogawa' 241	Tr	-	☼	5	15ft(4.5m)
avium 'Plena' 88	Tr	-	☼	3	20ft(6m)
cerasifera 'Pissardii' 45	Tr	-	◐	4	20ft(6m)
laurocerasus 44, 152, 158, 183	ESh	-	◐	7	15ft(4.5m)
'Otto Luyken' 190	ESh	-	◐	7	20ft(6m)
lusitanica 34, 35, 67, 142	ESh	-	◐	7	15ft(4.5m)
mume 156, 218	Tr	-	☼	6	10ft(3m)
persica 92, 241	Tr	-	☼	5	12ft(3.7m)
sargentii 134, 137	Tr	-	◐	4	15ft(4.5m)
serrula 71, 134, 150, 151, 209, 301	Tr	-	☼	5	15ft(4.5m)
spinosa 49	Sh	-	☼	4	15ft(4.5m)
× *subhirtella* 'Autumnalis' 125, 240	Tr	-	◐	5	15ft(4.5m)
'Tai Haku' 10	Tr	-	◐	5	20ft(6m)
tenella 'Fire Hill' 218	Sh	-	☼	2	5ft(1.5m)
Pulmonaria officinalis 60, 239	P	-	●/◐	6	12in(30cm)
saccharata 125	P	-	●/◐	3	12in(30cm)
'Cambridge Blue' 144	P	-	●/◐	3	12in(30cm)
Pyracantha atalantioides 71	ESh	-	◐	7	10ft(3m)
'Aurea' 67	ESh	-	◐	7	10ft(3m)
'Orange Glow' 222	ESh	-	◐S	6	15ft(4.5m)
Pyrus salicifolia 'Pendula' 183, 202, 203	Tr	-	☼	4	15ft(4.5m)

R

	PLANT TYPE	SOIL	SITUATION	TEMPERATURE ZONE	HEIGHT
Ramonda myconi 40	Rc	-	●/◐	6	6in(15cm)
Ranunculus aquatilis 282	Aq	-	☼	5	-
Reseda odorata 122, 155, 162, 226, 227	An	-	☼	-	2ft(60cm)
Rhamnus alaternus 'Argenteovariegatus' 178	ESh	-	◐	7	6ft(1.8m)
Rheum palmatum 122, 132, 141, 156, 158, 206, 293	P	-	◐	6	6ft(1.8m)
'Atrosanguineum' 159, 181, 293	P	-	◐	6	6ft(1.8m)

	PLANT TYPE	SOIL	SITUATION	TEMPERATURE ZONE	HEIGHT
'Bowles Crimson' 293	P	-	◐	6	6ft(1.8m)
Rhododendron bureavii 83	ESh	A	◐	6	10ft(3m)
calophytum 83	ESh	A	◐S	6	20ft(6m)
× *cilpinense* 218, 220	ESh	A	◐	5	5ft(1.5m)
concatenans 221	ESh	A	◐	6	8ft(2.4m)
'Lemonora' 83	Sh	A	◐	6	5ft(1.5m)
luteum 108, 175	ESh	A	◐	5	8ft(2.4m)
'Mars' 108	ESh	A	◐	6	10ft(3m)
obtusum 83	ESh	A	◐	6	3ft(90cm)
'Temple Belle' 218	ESh	A	◐	6	8ft(2.4m)
Rhus hirta 150	Tr	D	◐	3	15ft(4.5m)
'Laciniata' 203	Tr	D	◐	3	15ft(4.5m)
typhina (now *R. hirta*)					
Ribes sanguineum 'Brocklebankii' 124	Sh	D	◐	6	8ft(2.4m)
Ricinus communis 147	An	-	☼	-	6ft(1.8m)
'Impala' 147	An	-	☼	-	6ft(1.8m)
Robinia hispida 40	Sh	D	☼S	5	10ft(3m)
pseudoacacia 'Frisia' 66, 67, 86, 90, 196, 203	Tr	D	☼	3	15ft(4.5m)
Rodgersia aesculifolia 293	P	M	◐	5	3ft(90cm)
pinnata 'Superba' 142	P	M	◐	6	4ft(1.2m)
tabularis 141	P	M	◐	7	3ft(90cm)
Romneya coulteri 108, 111, 251	P	-	☼S	7	6ft(1.8m)
Rosa 'Alba Semiplena' 85	Ro	-	☼	4	8ft(2.4m)
'Albéric Barbier' 124	Ro	-	☼	6	15ft(4.5m)
'Albertine' 16, 39, 128	Ro	-	☼	6	15ft(4.5m)
Alexandra Rose 313	Ro	-	☼	5	6ft(1.8m)
'Allgold' 67	Ro	-	☼	4	2½ft(76cm)
'Aloha' 183	Ro	-	☼	5	10ft(3m)
'Awakening' 202	Ro	-	◐	5	10ft(3m)
banksiae 'Lutea' 40, 65	Ro	-	☼	5	20ft(6m)
'Bantry Bay' 198	Ro	-	☼	6	12ft(3.7m)
'Blanc Double de Coubert' 190	Ro	-	☼	3	5ft(1.5m)
'Bloomfield Abundance' 227	Ro	-	☼	6	6ft(1.8m)
'Buff Beauty' 161	Ro	-	◐	5	7ft(2m)
centifolia 85	Ro	-	☼	5	4ft(1.2m)
'Chinatown' 34	Ro	-	☼	6	5ft(1.5m)
'Complicata' 53	Ro	-	☼	6	10ft(3m)
'Dearest' 200	Ro	-	☼	6	2½ft(76cm)
'Debutante' (weeping standard) 189	Ro	-	☼	6	5ft(1.5m)
'Drummer Boy' 219	Ro	-	☼	6	3ft(90cm)
'Edith Holden' 272	Ro	-	☼	6	2½ft(76cm)
eglanteria 152, 158, 175	Ro	-	☼	6	6ft(1.8m)
'Emily Gray' 128	Ro	-	☼	6	15ft(4.5m)
'Etoile de Hollande' 201	Ro	-	☼	5	12ft(3.7m)
'Felicia' 34	Ro	-	☼	6	4ft(1.2m)
'Félicité Perpétue' 198	Ro	-	☼	7	15ft(4.5m)
'Fragrant Cloud' 153	Ro	-	☼	6	5ft(1.5m)
foetida 'Persiana' 92	Ro	-	☼	4	6ft(1.8m)
'Fru Dagmar Hastrup' 190	Ro	-	☼	2	3ft(90cm)
gallica 'Versicolor' 148	Ro	-	☼	5	2½ft(76cm)
'Glamis Castle' 189	Ro	-	☼	6	3ft(90cm)
glauca 109	Ro	-	☼	2	6ft(1.8m)
'Golden Showers' 13, 34	Ro	-	☼	5	10ft(3m)
'Golden Years' 201	Ro	-	☼	6	2½ft(76cm)
'Happy Child' 200	Ro	-	☼	6	3ft(90cm)
'Iceberg' 145, 189, 272, 309	Ro	-	☼	5	4ft(1.2m)
'Ispahan' 267	Ro	-	☼	6	5ft(1.5m)

PLANT TYPE **An** annual; **Aq** aquatic; **Bam** bamboo; **Bi** biennial; **Bu** bulb, corm, rhizome, tuber; **Cl** climber; **E** evergreen; **P** perennial; **Rc** rock plant; **Ro** rose; **Sh** shrub; **Tr** tree.

SOIL **A** needs acid soil; **L** needs alkaline soil; **M** needs moist to wet soil; **D** needs dry soil.

SITUATION ☼ does best in full sun; ◐ thrives in full sun or light shade; ● does best in full shade; ◐/● grows well in full sun, light shade or full shade; ●/◐ does best in full shade or light shade; **S** needs shelter; **W** tolerates wind.

TEMPERATURE ZONE numbers refer to the hardiness zones on the map on pp.316–317.

HEIGHT represents height at maturity (or 20 years for trees and shrubs).

	PLANT TYPE	SOIL	SITUATION	TEMPERATURE ZONE	HEIGHT
'Königin von Dänemark' 148	Ro	-	◑	4	4ft(1.2m)
'Lady Hillingdon, Climbing' 153	Ro	-	☼	7	18ft(5.5m)
'La Reine Victoria' 155	Ro	-	☼	5	4ft(1.2m)
'Laura Ford' 36	Ro	-	☼	6	7ft(2m)
'Leverkusen' 202	Ro	-	☼	6	10ft(3m)
'Madame Alfred Carrière' 134, 174	Ro	-	☼	5	20ft(6m)
'Madame Grégoire Staechelin' 203	Ro	-	☼	6	20ft(6m)
'Maiden's Blush' 148	Ro	-	◑	5	6ft(1.8m)
'Maigold' 17	Ro	-	☼	6	15ft(4.5m)
'Masquerade, Climbing' 38	Ro	-	☼	6	18ft(5.5m)
'Meg' 11	Ro	-	☼	6	12ft(3.7m)
'Mermaid' 193	Ro	-	◑S	7	30ft(9m)
moyesii 137	Ro	-	☼	5	10ft(3m)
'Mundi' (now R. gallica 'Versicolor')					
'Nathalie Nypels' 202	Ro	-	☼	4	3ft(90cm)
'Nevada' 167	Ro	-	☼	5	8ft(2.4m)
'New Dawn' 154, 155, 198, 202	Ro	-	☼	6	10ft(3m)
'Nimbus' 272	Ro	-	☼	6	3ft(90cm)
× odorata 156	Ro	-	☼	7	15ft(4.5m)
'Mutabilis' 34	Ro	-	☼	7	5ft(1.5m)
'Viridiflora' 143	Ro	-	☼	7	3ft(90cm)
'Parade' 183	Ro	-	☼	6	10ft(3m)
'Paulii' 60	Ro	-	◑	4	3ft(90cm)
'Penelope' 34, 208	Ro	-	☼	6	6ft(1.8m)
'Peppermint Ice' 272	Ro	-	☼	6	3ft(90cm)
'Pink Perpétué' 183	Ro	-	☼	6	12ft(3.7m)
'Pompon de Paris, Climbing' 41	Ro	-	☼	6	12ft(3.7m)
'Princesse Louise' (weeping standard) 189	Ro	-	☼	7	6ft(1.8m)
'Prosperity' 145	Ro	-	☼	6	6ft(1.8m)
'Queen Elizabeth' 34	Ro	-	☼	5	6ft(1.8m)
'Queen of Denmark' (see Königin von Dänemark)					
'Rambling Rector' 34	Ro	-	☼	5	20ft(6m)
'Roseraie de l'Haÿ' 153, 155	Ro	-	☼	3	7ft(2m)
rubiginosa (now R. eglanteria)					
rugosa 36, 62, 63, 190, 282, 294	Ro	-	☼	2	7ft(2m)
'Seagull' 34	Ro	-	☼	5	15ft(4.5m)
'The Fairy' 224	Ro	-	☼	4	2ft(60cm)
'Wedding Day' 200	Ro	-	☼	5	30ft(9m)
xanthina 'Canary Bird' 190	Ro	-	☼	5	8ft(2.4m)
'Zéphirine Drouhin' 13, 136, 150, 155	Ro	-	☼	6	9ft(2.7m)
Rosmarinus officinalis 70, 71, 79, 81, 87, 153, 155, 175, 180, 185, 190, 193, 203, 226, 266, 267, 294, 312	ESh	-	☼	7	6ft(1.8m)
Prostratus Group 267	ESh	-	☼	7	18in(45cm)
'Severn Sea' 220	ESh	-	☼	7	3ft(90cm)
Rubus idaeus 'Aureus' 241	Sh	-	◑	3	2½ft(76cm)
ulmifolius 'Bellidiflorus' 249	Sh	-	◑	7	8ft(2.4m)
Rudbeckia laciniata 109, 249, 272	P	-	☼	3	7ft(2m)
Ruta graveolens 149, 255	ESh	-	☼	5	2ft(60cm)

S

	PLANT TYPE	SOIL	SITUATION	TEMPERATURE ZONE	HEIGHT
Sagina subulata 85, 100, 103	Rc	-	☼	4	2in(5cm)
Salix acutifolia 'Blue Streak' 124	Sh	M	☼	5	15ft(4.5m)
alba 'Chermesina' 49	Tr	M	☼	2	20ft(6m)
caprea 125	Sh	-	☼	5	15ft(4.5m)
'Kilmarnock' 150, 201, 285	Sh	-	☼	5	6ft(1.8m)
chaenomeloides 150	Sh	-	☼	5	25ft(7.5m)
daphnoides 49	Sh	-	☼	5	25ft(7.5m)
exigua 285	Sh	-	☼	4	12ft(3.7m)
fargesii 150	Sh	-	☼	4	10ft(3m)
gracilistyla 'Melanostachys' 143	Sh	-	☼	5	10ft(3m)
hastata 'Wehrhahnii' 150	Sh	-	☼	5	6ft(1.8m)
matsudana 'Tortuosa' 208	Tr	-	☼	5	20ft(6m)
purpurea 'Pendula' 285	Sh	-	☼	4	8ft(2.4m)
Salvia coccinea 'Lady in Red' 223	An	-	☼	-	2ft(60cm)

	PLANT TYPE	SOIL	SITUATION	TEMPERATURE ZONE	HEIGHT
elegans 152, 156	Sh	-	☼	9	3ft(90cm)
farinacea 223	An	-	☼	-	2ft(60cm)
officinalis 52, 71, 79, 155, 175, 180, 182, 193, 265, 267	ESh	-	☼	5	3ft(90cm)
'Icterina' 267	ESh	-	☼	5	2ft(60cm)
'Kew Gold' 267	ESh	-	☼	5	2ft(60cm)
'Purpurascens' 111, 267	ESh	-	☼	5	2ft(60cm)
'Tricolor' 183	ESh	-	☼	5	2ft(60cm)
patens 133	P	-	☼	8	2ft(60cm)
sclarea 88	Bi	-	☼	-	3ft(90cm)
Sambucus nigra 49, 270	Tr	-	◑	5	15ft(4.5m)
'Guincho' 270	Tr	-	◑	5	15ft(4.5m)
racemosa 'Plumosa Aurea' 22, 196, 270	Sh	-	◑	4	10ft(3m)
Santolina chamaecyparissus 71, 200, 251	ESh	-	☼	6	2ft(60cm)
'Nana' 14	ESh	-	☼	6	9in(23cm)
rosmarinifolia 26	ESh	-	☼	7	18in(45cm)
virens 203	ESh	-	☼	7	2ft(60cm)
Sarcococca confusa 21, 131	ESh	-	◑	6	5ft(1.5m)
hookeriana var. digyna 240	ESh	-	◑	6	5ft(1.5m)
var. humilis 154	ESh	-	◑	6	18in(45cm)
humilis (now S. h. var. humilis)					
Satureja montana 81	P	-	☼	5	6in(15cm)
Saxifraga cotyledon 40	ERc	-	◑	6	2ft(60cm)
× urbium 13, 175, 198, 262	EP	-	●/◑	7	12in(30cm)
Scabiosa caucasica 'Clive Greaves' 62	P	-	☼	4	2ft(60cm)
'Mount Cook' 126	P	-	☼	4	2ft(60cm)
Schisandra rubriflora 194	Cl	-	◑S	9	20ft(6m)
Schizophragma hydrangeoides 42	Cl	-	◑	5	30ft(9m)
Schlumbergera bridgesii 229	P	-	◑	9	12in(30cm)
Scilla siberica 107, 110, 132, 189, 271	Bu	L	◑	5	6in(15cm)
Scrophularia aquatica 'Variegata' 142	P	-	◑	5	3ft(90cm)
Sedum 'Ruby Glow' 14	P	-	☼	5	12in(30cm)
spectabile 142	P	-	☼	5	18in(45cm)
Sempervivum montanum 40	ERc	-	☼	5	6in(15cm)
Senecio cineraria 142, 221, 270	ESh	-	☼	8	2ft(60cm)
'Sunshine' (now Brachyglottis 'Sunshine')					
Senna didymobotrya 152	ESh	-	☼	10	10ft(3m)
Shibataea kumasasa 17	Bam	-	◑	6	2ft(60cm)
Skimmia japonica 195	ESh	-	◑	7	5ft(1.5m)
subsp. reevesiana 240	ESh	-	◑	7	2ft(60cm)
'Rubella' 197, 222	ESh	-	◑	7	5ft(1.5m)
Smilacina racemosa 129	P	-	●/◑	4	3ft(90cm)
Solanum crispum 38, 107	Cl	-	☼S	8	20ft(6m)
'Glasnevin' 40, 124	Cl	-	☼S	8	20ft(6m)
jasminoides 'Album' 209	Cl	-	☼S	9	20ft(6m)
pseudocapsicum 222	ESh	-	☼	9	2ft(60cm)
Soleirolia soleirolii 102, 198	ERc	-	◑	9	1in(2.5cm)
Sollya heterophylla 176	ECl	-	◑S	9	10ft(3m)
Sorbus aria 82	Tr	-	☼	5	20ft(6m)
aucuparia 83	Tr	-	◑	2	20ft(6m)
cashmiriana 175	Tr	-	☼	5	10ft(3m)
hupehensis 28, 175	Tr	-	☼	6	20ft(6m)
reducta 221	Sh	-	☼	6	12in(30cm)
vilmorinii 175	Tr	-	☼	6	10ft(3m)
Spartium junceum 108	ESh	-	☼	8	10ft(3m)

	PLANT TYPE	SOIL	SITUATION	TEMPERATURE ZONE	HEIGHT
Sphaeralcea munroana 213	P	-	☼	4	18in (45cm)
Spiraea japonica 'Goldflame' 39, 221	Sh	-	☼	5	5ft (1.5m)
Stachys byzantina 29, 80, 81, 102, 111, 145, 148, 150, 251	EP	-	☼	5	6in (15cm)
'Silver Carpet' 100	EP	-	☼	5	6in (15cm)
macrantha 142	P	-	☼	5	2ft (60cm)
Sternbergia lutea 132	Bu	-	☼	7	6in (15cm)
Stipa pennata 149, 203	P	D	☼	7	2½ft (76cm)
Symphytum 'Hidcote Pink' 304	P	-	◗	5	2ft (60cm)
officinale 300, 304, 305	P	M	◗	5	4ft (1.2m)
Syringa vulgaris 108, 175, 198, 249, 294	Sh	-	☼	5	15ft (4.5m)

T

	PLANT TYPE	SOIL	SITUATION	TEMPERATURE ZONE	HEIGHT
Tagetes erecta 145, 271	An	-	☼	-	2½ft (76cm)
patula 102, 145, 311	An	-	☼	-	12in (30cm)
Tamarix pentandra 49	Sh	-	☼	5	12ft (3.7m)
Tanacetum parthenium 151	P	-	☼	6	12in (30cm)
'Aureum' 161	P	-	☼	6	12in (30cm)
vulgare 217	P	-	☼	3	3ft (90cm)
Taxus baccata 14, 43, 44, 45, 47, 49, 88, 183, 190, 198, 236, 239	ETr	L	◗	6	15ft (4.5m)
Teucrium chamaedrys 98, 267	EP	-	☼	5	9in (23cm)
Thunbergia alata 13, 181, 203, 249, 257	An	-	☼ S	-	10ft (3m)
Thymus × *citriodorus* 151, 267	ESh	-	☼	7	6in (15cm)
serpyllum 100, 102, 103, 173, 183, 267	ERc	-	☼	5	2in (5cm)
vulgaris 267	ESh	-	☼	7	12in (30cm)
Tiarella cordifolia 28	EP	-	●/◗	3	12in (30cm)
Tilia cordata 47, 305	Tr	-	◗	3	25ft (7.5m)
Trachelospermum jasminoides 124, 154, 175, 181, 209, 290	ECl	A	☼ S	8	12ft (3.7m)
Trachycarpus fortunei 90, 92, 128, 185, 199, 206, 240, 241	ETr	-	☼	8	6ft (1.8m)
Tradescantia 'Isis' 14	P	-	◗	7	2ft (60cm)
Trillium grandiflorum 250	P	A	◗		12in (30cm)
Triteleia laxa 62	Bu	-	☼	6	9in (23cm)
Tropaeolum majus 50, 51, 65, 87, 89, 110, 147, 156, 202, 206, 217, 221, 223, 249, 258	An	-	☼	-	8ft (2.4m)
peregrinum 16, 33, 50, 257	ClAn	-	◗ S	-	12ft (3.7m)
speciosum 246	ClAn	-	◗ S	-	15ft (4.5m)
Tulipa 'Apricot Beauty' 109, 161	Bu	-	☼	5	15in (38cm)
'Black Parrot' 109	Bu	-	☼	5	2ft (60cm)
'China Pink' 271	Bu	-	☼	5	2ft (60cm)
'Clara Butt' 148	Bu	-	☼	5	2½ft (76cm)
'Couleur Cardinal' 146	Bu	-	☼	5	15in (38cm)
'Diana' 213	Bu	-	☼	5	15in (38cm)
'Greenland' 148	Bu	-	☼	5	2½ft (76cm)
kaufmanniana 221	Bu	-	☼	5	10in (25cm)
'Negrita' 161	Bu	-	☼	5	18in (45cm)
'Orange Parrot' 271	Bu	-	☼	5	2ft (60cm)
'Purissima' 10, 198	Bu	-	☼	5	18in (45cm)
'Queen of the Night' 143	Bu	-	☼	5	2½ft (76cm)
'Red Riding Hood' 12	Bu	-	☼	5	6in (15cm)
'Schoonord' 271	Bu	-	☼	5	15in (38cm)
'Spring Green' 144	Bu	-	☼	5	3ft (90cm)
'Springtime' 161	Bu	-	☼	5	2ft (60cm)
'White Triumphator' 270	Bu	-	☼	5	2½ft (76cm)
Typha minima 285	P	M	☼	6	2½ft (76cm)

U, V

	PLANT TYPE	SOIL	SITUATION	TEMPERATURE ZONE	HEIGHT
Ursinia anethoides 147	An	-	☼	-	18in (45cm)
Veratrum nigrum 137	P	-	◗	6	6ft (1.8m)
Verbascum bombycifermum 137, 141, 150, 160	Bi	L	☼	6	6ft (1.8m)
Verbena × *hybrida* 'Showtime' 228	An	-	◗ S	-	3ft (90cm)
'Loveliness' 224	An	-	☼	-	6in (15cm)
'Sissinghurst' 192	An	-	☼ S	-	9in (23cm)
Viburnum × *bodnantense* 153, 197	Sh	-	◗	7	12ft (3.7m)
'Dawn' 35, 269	Sh	-	◗	7	12ft (3.7m)
'Deben' 241	Sh	-	◗	7	12ft (3.7m)
× *burkwoodii* 26, 227	ESh	-	◗	5	8ft (2.4m)
carlesii 140	Sh	-	◗	4	7ft (2m)
davidii 17, 21, 269	ESh	-	◗	7	4ft (1.2m)
farreri 125, 153, 154, 219	Sh	-	◗ S	6	8ft (2.4m)
rhytidophyllum 71, 127	ESh	-	◗	5	15ft (4.5m)
tinus 51, 88, 194, 225	ESh	-	◗	7	12ft (3.7m)
Vinca major 219	EP	-	◗/●	7	18in (45cm)
'Variegata' 21, 183	EP	-	◗/●	7	18in (45cm)
minor 219, 222	EP	-	◗/●	4	6in (15cm)
'Aureovariegata' 60	EP	-	◗/●	4	6in (15cm)
Viola 'Antique Lace' 222	An	-	☼	-	6in (15cm)
'Mollie Sanderson' 143	P	-	◗	7	6in (15cm)
odorata 'Coeur d'Alsace' 153, 154	P	-	◗ S	8	9in (23cm)
'Admiral Avellan' 153	P	-	◗ S	8	9in (23cm)
'Quatre Saisons' 154	P	-	◗	8	9in (23cm)
tricolor 'Bowles' Black' 143	An	-	◗	-	6in (15cm)
× *wittrockiana* 228	An	-	☼	-	6in (15cm)
'Black Beauty' 213	An	-	◗	-	6in (15cm)
Vitis 'Brandt' 202	Cl	-	◗	6	20ft (6m)
coignetiae 199, 270	Cl	-	◗	5	30ft (9m)
vinifera 264	Cl	-	☼	6	20ft (6m)
'Purpurea' 39, 183, 202, 270	Cl	-	◗	6	20ft (6m)

W, Y, Z

	PLANT TYPE	SOIL	SITUATION	TEMPERATURE ZONE	HEIGHT
Weigela florida 'Aureovariegata' 88	Sh	-	◗	5	6ft (1.8m)
'Foliis Purpureis' 39	Sh	-	◗	5	6ft (1.8m)
'Variegata' 142	Sh	-	◗	5	6ft (1.8m)
Yucca filamentosa 80, 109	ESh	-	☼	7	5ft (1.5m)
flaccida 17	ESh	-	☼	7	5ft (1.5m)
gloriosa 218, 235, 251	ESh	-	☼	7	8ft (2.4m)
'Variegata' 221	ESh	-	☼	7	8ft (2.4m)
Zantedeschia aethiopica 230	EP	-	◗	8	3ft (90cm)
'Crowborough' 291, 293	EP	-	◗	8	3ft (90cm)

PLANT TYPE An annual; Aq aquatic; Bam bamboo; Bi biennial; Bu bulb, corm, rhizome, tuber; Cl climber; E evergreen; P perennial; Rc rock plant; Ro rose; Sh shrub; Tr tree.

SOIL A needs acid soil; L needs alkaline soil; M needs moist to wet soil; D needs dry soil.

SITUATION ☼ does best in full sun; ◗ thrives in full sun or light shade; ● does best in full shade; ◗/● grows well in full sun, light shade or full shade; ●/◗ does best in full shade or light shade; S needs shelter; W tolerates wind.

TEMPERATURE ZONE numbers refer to the hardiness zones on the map on pp.316–317.

HEIGHT represents height at maturity (or 20 years for trees and shrubs).

COMMON AND BOTANICAL NAMES

The chart on pp.318–328 lists plants by their botanical names; below are the botanical names of plants mentioned in the text by common name only, so that you can look them up in the chart.

African marigold *Tagetes erecta*
aubrietia *Aubrieta deltoidea*
autumn crocus *Colchicum*
azalea *Rhododendron*
bamboo *Fargesia, Nandina, Phyllostachys, Pleioblastus, Shibataea*
barberry *Berberis*
basil *Ocimum basilicum*
basket-of-gold *Aurinia saxatilis*
bay laurel *Laurus nobilis*
beech *Fagus sylvatica*
birch *Betula*
black-eyed Susan vine *Thunbergia alata*
black locust *Robinia pseudoacacia*
blackthorn *Prunus spinosa*
bluebell *Hyacinthoides non-scripta*
bogbean *Menyanthes trifoliata*
borage *Borago officinalis*
Boston ivy *Parthenocissus tricuspidata*
boxwood *Buxus*
broom *Cytisus, Genista*
California poppy *Eschscholzia californica*
calla lily *Zantedeschia*
canary creeper *Tropaeolum peregrinum*
candytuft *Iberis empervirens*
cape plumbago *Plumbago auriculata*
catmint *Nepeta racemosa*
cattail *Typha*
chamomile *Chamaemelum nobile*
cherry *Prunus*
cherry laurel *Prunus laurocerasus*
chervil *Anthriscus*
Chinese lantern *Physalis alkekengi*
chives *Allium schoenoprasum*
chrysanthemum *Argyranthemum, Dendranthema*
columbine *Aquilegia*
comfrey *Symphytum*
coral plant *Berberidopsis corallina*
coriander *Coriandrum sativum*
cornflower *Centaurea cyanus*
cowslip *Primula florindae*
crab apple *Malus*
cranesbill geranium *Geranium*
curry plant *Helichrysum italicum*
cypress *Chamaecyparis, × Cupressocyparis, Cupressus*
daffodil *Narcissus*
dill *Anethum graveolens*
dogwood *Cornus*
dracena *Cordyline australis*
elder *Sambucus*
evening primrose *Oenothera biennis*
false Solomon's seal *Smilacina racemosa*
fennel *Foeniculum vulgare*
fern *Asplenium, Athyrium, Dryopteris, Matteuccia, Onoclea, Osmunda, Polystichum*

feverfew *Tanacetum parthenium*
fig *Ficus*
flag *Acorus, Iris*
flowering quince *Chaenomeles speciosa*
flowering tobacco *Nicotiana*
forget-me-not *Myosotis*
foxglove *Digitalis*
French marigold *Tagetes patula*
fritillary (crown imperial) *Fritillaria*
gentian *Gentiana*
geranium *Pelargonium*
germander *Teucrium chamaedrys*
globe thistle *Echinops*
grape hyacinth *Muscari*
grapevine *Vitis*
hawthorn *Crataegus*
Harry Lauder's walking stick *Corylus avellana* 'Contorta'
heath *Daboecia, Erica*
heather *Calluna vulgaris*
heliotrope *Heliotropium*
hellebore *Helleborus*
holly *Ilex*
hollyhock *Alcea rosea*
honesty *Lunaria annua*
honeysuckle *Lonicera*
hop *Humulus*
hornbeam *Carpinus betulus*
hyacinth *Hyacinthus*
hyssop *Hyssopus officinalis*
ivy *Hedera*
jasmine *Jasminum*
juniper *Juniperus*
lady's-mantle *Alchemilla mollis*
lamb's-ears *Stachys byzantina*
lavender *Lavendula*
lavender cotton *Santolina*
lemon *Citrus limon*
lemon balm *Melissa officinalis*
lemon verbena *Aloysia triphylla*
Lenten rose *Helleborus orientalis*
lilac *Syringa vulgaris*
lily *Lilium*
lily-of-the-valley *Convallaria majalis*
love-in-a-mist *Nigella damascena*
love-lies-bleeding *Amaranthus caudatus*
lupine *Lupinus*
mallow *Lavatera*
maple *Acer*
marguerite *Argyranthemum frutescens*
marjoram *Origanum*
marsh marigold *Caltha palustris*
meadow geranium *Geranium pratense*
Mexican orange blossom *Choisya ternata*
mignonette *Reseda odorata*
mint *Mentha*
mock orange *Philadelphus*
morning glory *Ipomoea*
mountain ash *Sorbus*
mullein *Verbascum*
nasturtium *Tropaeolum majus*

New Zealand flax *Phormium tenax*
oleander *Nerium oleander*
oxlip *Primula elatior*
pansy *Viola*
parsley *Petroselinum crispum*
passion-flower *Passiflora caerulea*
peach *Prunus persica*
pearlwort *Sagina*
peony *Paeonia*
periwinkle *Vinca*
Peruvian lily *Alstroemeria*
pine *Pinus*
pink *Dianthus*
poppy *Papaver*
Portugal laurel *Prunus lusitanica*
pot marigold *Calendula officinalis*
primrose *Primula*
privet *Ligustrum*
red-hot poker *Kniphofia caulescens*
reed *Juncus*
rock-rose *Cistus*
rose *Rosa*
rosemary *Rosmarinus officinalis*
rowan *Sorbus aucuparia*
rue *Ruta graveolens*
sage *Salvia officinalis*
savory *Satureja montana*
saxifrage *Saxifraga*
scarlet runner bean *Phaseolus coccineus*
sedge *Carex*
serviceberry *Amelanchier*
silver vein creeper *Parthenocissus henryana*
snapdragon *Antirrhinum*
snowdrop *Galanthus*
Solomon's seal *Polygonatum*
spirea *Spiraea*
star-jasmine *Trachelospermum jasminoides*
stock *Matthiola*
strawflower *Helichrysum bracteatum*
sunflower *Helianthus*
sunrose *Helianthemum*
sweet briar *Rosa eglanteria*
sweet cicely *Myrrhis odorata*
sweet pea *Lathyrus*
sweet William *Dianthus barbatus*
sycamore *Acer pseudoplatanus*
tarragon *Artemisia dracunculus*
thrift *Armeria maritima*
thyme *Thymus*
tulip *Tulipa*
violet *Viola*
Virginia creeper *Parthenocissus quinquefolia*
wallflower *Erysimum*
water lily *Nymphaea*
Welsh poppy *Meconopsis cambrica*
wild ginger *Asarum europaeum*
willow *Salix*
winter aconite *Eranthis hyemalis*
witch hazel *Hamamelis mollis*
yarrow *Achillea*
yew *Taxus baccata*

INDEX

A number in *italics* indicates that the reference is to a caption only.

A

Acid soil, 59, 60-61, 63, 82, 96, 260
  rainwater for, *294*
  testing for, 58
Aconite, winter, *68*
Adirondack chairs, 169
African lilies, 271
Alkaline soil, 58-61, 62-63, 96
Alpines, 24, 40, 63, 242-243, *308*
  in troughs, 217
Amphorae, 91, 214
Animals:
  control of pests by, 311-312
  deterring of, 314-315
  as manure source, 303
  See also Wildlife in garden.
Annuals, 110, 271
  bright-colored, 145, 146-147
  first-year border show, 109
  for island beds, 90
  scented, 154
  sowing seeds from, 79
Antique garden ornaments, 205
Apples, apple trees, 254, 258, 259
  as colonnades, 264
  crab, 260
  espaliered, 263
  as living fences, *262, 263*
Arbors, 85, 166, 181-182, 257, 264
Arches, *90, 114, 115*, 181
  concealing eyesores with, 122, *239*
  creating illusions with, *237, 239*, 240, 244, *250*
  as focal points, 192, 205
  framing entrances with, 19
  fruiting, 264
  living, 47-48
Architectural plants, 80, *130*, 141, 184, 203
Aromatic plants, 152-156
  herbs as, *149*, 155, 156, 312
  See also Fragrant plants; Scented plants.
Arranging flowers. *See* Flower arranging.
Artichokes:
  globe, 254, 257
  Jerusalem, 257-258
Asparagus, 257, 258, 268
Asparagus peas, 261
Avenues, 85, 141
Awnings, 170, 175, 185

B

Back gardens, 10
  deeply shaded, 194-195
  path to back door through, 18
Balconies, 119, 120, 121, 131-133, 229
  pool on, 279

Bamboo:
  for fencing, 37
  for screens, 184, 185
  for tepees, 228-229, 271
Banana, *78*, 264
Barbecues, 179-180
Bark, chipped or composted, 100, 237, 299, 303, *308*, 309
Barrier, sunken (ha-ha), 32, 246
Basement gardening, 128-131, 194
  climbers in, 130
  window view onto, 119, 120, 121, 128-131
  in winter, 121
Beans, 258
  broad, 81, 151
  runner, 13, 256, 257, 259, *271*
Bedding plants, 87, 120, 127
Beds, flower:
  color schemes, 108-109, 189
  cool ideas for sunny, 202
  edgings, 98-99, 255
  island, 90, 106-107
  planning of, 106-111
  raised, 59, 80-81, 93
  See also Borders.
Bees, beehives, 305, 312
  plants attracting, 312
Beetles, 311
Beets, 256, 258
Below-grade gardens. *See* Basement gardening.
Benches, 167-169, *207*
  cast-iron, *171*
  farmhouse, 169
  metal, *168*
  rustic "twig," 170
  securing of, 167
  stone, 166, 167
  storage, 169
  turf, 173
  wooden, *167, 169*
  See also Chairs; Seats, seating.
Best plants:
  for alkaline soil, 62
  alpines for wall crevices, 40
  architectural, 203
  climbers for tall frames, 124
  cover for slopes, 60
  to create illusion of space, 235
  for crevices, 103
  for drying, 275
  first-year show, 109
  for green manure, 304, 305
  for hanging baskets, 228
  leafy disguisers, 251
  for long-lasting interest, 137
  low-allergen, 88
  for reliable formal hedge, 43
  scented, 175
  for shade, 195
  in the shallows (marginals), 285
  for summer fragrance, 155
  to touch, 150